THE LIPPINCOTT CURRICULUM AND INSTRUCTION SERIES
Under the Editorship of
Alexander Frazier, Ohio State University

Critical Reading

Critical Reading

Edited by

Martha L. King, Bernice D. Ellinger, Willavene Wolf

OHIO STATE UNIVERSITY

J. B. LIPPINCOTT COMPANY

Philadelphia and New York

Copyright © 1967 by J. B. Lippincott Company
Library of Congress Catalog Card Number: 67-15516
Printed in the United States of America

Preface

THE TOPIC OF critical reading has received more exposition than consensus in the professional literature. Interpretations of critical reading have ranged from a narrow definition, such as the identification of propaganda techniques, to an all-inclusive description, which includes skills usually classified as comprehension and study skills. The editors of this book define critical reading as an analytical and evaluative process which requires the reader to make rational judgments about both the content and style of writing based upon valid criteria. According to their view, critical reading is dependent upon accurate word perception and skillful interpretation of language. However, it goes beyond these processes to include thoughtful reaction to what is read. Critical reading is applicable to all kinds of materials, but the reader varies the criteria he uses for analysis and evaluation according to the type of material and his purpose for reading. When reading *informational materials,* for example, he may be primarily concerned about accuracy, clarity, and authority. In reading *persuasive writing* he will probably search for validity and reliability. In reading *literature* he will be sensitive to the relationships between form and content; the development of character, theme, and symbol; and the multiplicity of meanings in selections. The criterion of worth of content permeates all of his reading. Critical reading may be considered as a sub-set of comprehension skills within the total framework of reading. These are dependent upon and contribute to the other comprehension skills; however, they are unique in the emphasis placed on *analysis* and *evaluation* according to established *criteria.*

It is obvious from the number of articles about critical reading in the literature that educators consider it an important goal in reading instruction. The fact that they continue to write about it, however, indicates that this goal has not been fulfilled. For example, in a speech to the International Reading Conference, Nila Banton Smith stated that she considers the need so grave that critical reading should be considered a national obligation.

The limited accomplishments in teaching critical reading might reasonably be attributed to several causes: inadequate treatment of this aspect of reading in college reading methods courses, the tendency of many school systems to avoid study of topics of a controversial nature, the paucity of materials and practical teaching techniques available to teachers, the general neglect of the area by reading researchers, and the considerable confusion that surrounds the concept. In this day of specialization and rapidly accumulating knowledge located in a myriad of sources, the retrieval and organization of information on a given subject becomes a highly important factor in its use. The purpose of this book is to make a significant portion of the literature pertaining to the above-stated problems of critical reading readily available to those who are teaching, researching, or studying in the area.

Articles included in this collection were selected from more than one hundred and fifty titles that were considered relevant to the topic of critical reading. It was the aim of the editors to include the best and most representative articles while avoiding extensive repetition. Related sources are listed in the footnotes of the various articles and in the annotated bibliography.

The text is organized in four parts which provide some answers to the following questions: (1) Why is critical reading considered important? What is the nature of critical reading? (2) What is the relationship between critical reading and critical thinking; critical reading and creative reading; critical reading and comprehensive or interpretive reading? (3) What are the effective methods and materials for teaching critical reading? and finally, (4) What aspects of critical reading have been the subject of research? The literature for this volume has been organized around these topics. Introducing each section of the text is a brief statement by one of the editors which provides a structure for the articles in that section, identifies salient features of the separate selections, cites divergent points of view represented in the material, and relates that section to the rest of the volume.

The editors believe that pupils in the elementary and secondary schools can learn the skills of critical reading if their teachers value it and have the knowledge necessary to teach the skills. They trust that the material in this collection will contribute to the information needed.

This volume is one of the outcomes of Cooperative Research Project No. 2612 of the U.S. Office of Education, "Critical Reading Ability of Elementary School Children," which study was conducted at the Ohio State University by the three editors of this book and Charlotte S. Huck.

The editors want especially to acknowledge Charlotte Huck for her contributions to the content of their papers. They would also like to acknowledge the authors, editors, and publishers who have granted permission to include their articles in this volume.

December, 1966   M.L.K.
Columbus, Ohio   B.D.E.
                                                                        W.W.

Contents

PART THREE

PART FOUR

Research in Critical Reading

PART ONE

The Importance and Nature
of Critical Reading

INTRODUCTION

The development of critical readers has long been considered an important goal of reading instruction. However, this objective has remained more the subject of discussion than one of accomplishment. Evidence that critical reading continues to be a popular subject for discourse is to be found in the rapid rise in the number of articles published on the topic. During the first five years of the 1960's articles published on critical reading increased sevenfold over the number printed in the entire decade of 1940–50. On the other hand, critical reading ranks low in the priorities of reading skills to which teachers give instructional time. The Austin study of reading practices reported that more than one-half of the school systems devoted "little or no" time to teaching critical reading in the first and second grades and almost one-third indicated that teachers in grades 3 and 4 gave "little or no" instructional time to these skills.[1]

Conjecture about the reported neglect of critical reading suggests that teachers either do not consider these skills important content for the early grades of the elementary school or that they lack the concepts and techniques needed to accomplish the task. Part I of this book is designed to accomplish two purposes related to these inhibiting factors: (1) to confront the readers with the imperative need to

[1] Mary Austin. *The First R.* New York: Macmillan Co., 1963, p. 43.

1

teach critical reading skills and (2) to present data that will facilitate the formulation of concepts regarding this aspect of reading.

The first contributor, Francis Chase, implies that critical reading may have more significance for the survival of a free world than the atomic bomb. He identifies crucial social-political-scientific problems of the present generation which he believes can be solved only through reflective thought. Reflective thought, he maintains, is more likely to occur when one is reading than at any other time. Problems inherent in communication and the impact of mass media on human behavior is the concern of the writer of the next article. Hovland summarizes some of the principal research studies in communication from which he develops basic principles of communication. He then illustrates how these principles operate in various media, such as pamphlets, magazines, and newspapers.

A major deterrent to greater accomplishment in critical reading has been the lack of agreement among educators as to what critical reading is. Discrepancies in concepts of critical reading are to be found in the way it is related to critical thinking, to creative reading, to the total reading process, and to the interpretation skills, specifically. Some writers have described critical reading narrowly and negatively, limiting the concept to the selection and rejection of material. Others have defined the term broadly enough to include many skills that are frequently classified as literal comprehension or interpretation skills. Still other writers have categorized critical reading as one level in a hierarchial order of reading skills and placed it above literal comprehension and interpretation but below assimilative or creative reading.

The articles in the second section of Part I will help to clarify the nature of critical reading, both from the standpoint of the reader and the nature of the task. The first contribution by Edgar Dale is a lively, succinct statement in which he lists nine characteristics of critical reading and comments on the role of the teacher in developing critical readers. In the next article, Robinson brings together the contributions of over one hundred other sources in formulating a concise yet comprehensive definition of critical reading. DeBoer's article of more than two decades ago is included because of the similarity between his ideas and those found in more recent publications. Although he includes such skills as "the search for relevant data, the evaluation of data, the comparison of sources, and the synthesis of findings," he strongly implies that *experience* is highly important in critical reading.

The many issues, conflicting views, and ambiguities that are imbedded in critical reading are carefully researched and clarified in the contribution of Sochor. She makes the point that the thinking process has not yet been structured into a hierarchial order and that critical and literal reading cannot be differentiated on the basis of thinking processes or language-experience relationships. The differentiation that can be made is on the basis of the reader's purpose. The next writer, Triggs, also stresses the importance of purpose in reading. He states that reading is a one-, two-, or three-way process depending upon the purpose for reading. Critical reading, according to his view, is a process that requires the active participation of both the author and the reader in an interplay that usually goes beyond the contributions of the two and results in new understandings. The final article by Piekarz concentrates on one aspect of critical reading behavior: the role of attitudes. She emphasizes that "people differ in critical reading performance as much because of variations in attitudes as because of variations in intelligence."

Although agreement about the definition of critical reading has not yet been reached, there are common elements in the various lists of skills. The point that has been agreed upon is the urgency for teaching children and youth to evaluate what they read.

M.L.K.

1.   Demands on the Reader in the Next Decade

Francis S. Chase

Modern man carries a burden of anxieties inherited from generations of struggle to survive, to gain identity, and to derive joy from his own achievements and the society of his fellows. He has added to these accumulated anxieties a few new ones, including a nightmare of total annihilation for mankind and another, almost as frightening, of total replacement by the machine.

Through science and technology, man within the span of a single lifetime has produced changes so profound and set in motion forces so powerful as to be unmanageable within the framework of existing institutions and accustomed modes of thinking and acting. The rapidity of change, the mobility of populations, and the world-wide conflict of cultures produce feelings of rootlessness and helplessness. Moreover, the spread of aspirations to a "good life" among populations to whom means of achieving the aspirations are remote arouse resentments in the dispossessed, and fears and guilt in the favored nations and groups. The resulting tensions make rational solutions difficult, and now and again they erupt in hate, oppression, and violence.

PROBLEMS ON THE AGENDA OF MANKIND

A few centuries hence such men as are then on earth will look back on the present century either as a period when the forces unleashed by man became unmanageable or as a period in which the foundation was laid for the creative enjoyment of new freedoms. The demands on man today, and more especially on man the reader, may be summed up in the necessity of dealing with present conflicts and anxieties so as to win through to higher ground. It is not necessary to indulge in prophecy in order to discuss the demands which man must somehow contrive to meet in the next decade. We cannot know in detail what conditions will confront particular men or nations or foresee exactly what problems will become most urgent on the agenda for mankind in five or ten years; but we can identify the demands now pressing upon mankind which give every indication of becoming intensified within the next decade.

Among the conditions which cast a shadow on the future of civilization

"Demands on the Reader in the Next Decade," by Francis S. Chase, *Controversial Issues in Reading and Promising Solutions*, Supplementary Educational Monographs, No. 91, 1961, 7–18. Reprinted by permission of the University of Chicago Press.

are the tendency of population increase to gobble up social gains, if not, indeed, the means of subsistence; the lack of a world political structure able to control the instruments of destruction which modern science and technology have put at the disposal of nations and of political adventurers; the helplessness of the world's great cities in dealing with such menaces as slums, crime, transportation paralysis and pollution of water and air; the lack of opportunity for millions of persons to equip themselves either for genuinely productive work or for effective participation in their own governments. These are demands which can be dealt with by known means and through the use of resources either actually or potentially available. Yet the solution of the underlying problems calls for the creation of new political, economic, and social institutions and for wisdom beyond that which man has yet displayed. To illustrate some of the conditions which formerly would have been regarded as matters of local concern but which today have become high priority concerns of all nations, I would like to evoke a few scenes on the world stage.

For the first scene, I choose Pakistan, a country with which I have had the privilege of working in a small way in the past four years. I choose it as representative of the developing nations with great aspirations to move swiftly into industrial plenty and to establish governments under which the will of the people can prevail and the welfare of the people be advanced. This is one of many countries in Asia and elsewhere which are making strenuous efforts to strengthen the economy, reduce the ravages of disease, increase the food supply, and extend the benefits of education widely; but in which there are so many problems to be met at once that the resources of developed talent and material fall dangerously short of the goals set. Thus it happens that, in spite of significant advances, the increase in population tends to outrun the gains in food production and the social gains of various kinds, including the attempts to improve education.

The next scene revolves around Cuba and is one which touches our national pride on a spot recently rubbed raw by our own miscalculation and ineptitude. Here, too, are people pressing toward realization of aspirations to which access has been denied; but, in this case, choosing a path to their desires that may lead to a new servitude. The salient point of this scene, however, is that for many in this country, including some in high places, aversion to personalities and procedures has produced blindness to the character of the needs behind the disliked actions. It highlights the danger of underestimating the Communist threat; but it also carries a warning against viewing other peoples through the screen of our own interest and desires.

The third scene is cast in the southern part of our own country. It throws the spotlight on a people who for generations hardly dared to aspire to equal access to education and to employment, to a full voice in the making of national policy, or to the other good things which we have boasted as the birthright of Americans everywhere. It portrays a people who, in now aspiring to the full stature of citizenship, encounter resistance from those who see their own interests threatened. Here, again, one may note on the part of many actors on the scene, and of many spectators as well, an inability to relate constructively to the aspirations of a disadvantaged people and a corollary impulse to deny the need for any change.

The fourth and final scene shows Chicago, a representative metropolitan conglomeration, unable to solve its own problems but daily drawing into its vortex new residents from the South, from Puerto Rico, and elsewhere; and daily pushing out into the suburbs those who can no longer tolerate life in what the city has become. Here abound unsolved problems of political organization, housing, transportation, health, safety, social amenities, and education. Here, too, one notes a lack of vision and of decisiveness in dealing with the underlying causes of all too evident anxieties, frustrations, dislocations, and social alienation.

These four scenes, if viewed in full perspective, will bring to mind most of the problems and factors which man must deal with boldly in the next decade. Other scenes set in Berlin, the Congo, South Africa, and Laos might be added to round out the world picture. The polarization of the world between great powers championing competing ideologies is part of the backdrop of each of these scenes. In the near or far distance, as the case may be, is heard in each the rumble of impending nuclear conflict; and entering into each of the dramas is the competition for uncommitted nations, for economic supremacy, and for political power. Advancing science's promise of new abundance and new knowledge lights up the sky at intervals in each scene; and the signals of orbiting satellites are heard through the clash of terrestrial conflict.

Two Kinds of Illiteracy Threaten Civilization

The conditions confronting us in the next decade call for the application of knowledge and wisdom rather than force. Therefore, I hold that the values which thoughtful men cherish are more endangered by illiteracy than by the atomic bomb and its offspring. The illiteracy which threatens civilization may be said to be of two kinds: simple illiteracy or the inability to receive and express ideas through reading and writing; and the higher illiteracy or the inability to relate the content of verbal communication to events which at each moment are shaping the future.

Simple illiteracy operates to keep out of the reach of millions of persons the objects which even the most humble have learned to demand. One of the most interesting manifestations of our age has been the spreading aspirations of men. Even a few years ago, there were large masses of men in many parts of the earth who saw the good things of life as being so far out of their reach that they had not the energy or the will even to desire them. Today there is no village so isolated, no population so illiterate that the people have not come to look for a better life and to aspire to a part in determining their own destiny. Yet, to a large extent the tangible goods, such as food and shelter, and the intangible goods, such as self-esteem, esteem by others, and a sense of some control over one's destiny, are out of reach for those who are the victims of simple illiteracy. With every advance of science and technology the good life, however defined, becomes increasingly inaccessible to the poorly educated.

In modern societies there is a continuing replacement of occupations making small demands on literacy or on the higher mental abilities with jobs requiring precise communication, skill in quantitative thinking, and the exercise of judgment. The recent development of machines to control other machines has further accelerated the demand for trained intelligence in industry and business; and the industrial demands for highly literate manpower are paralleled in government, in the military service, in the professions, and in service occupations.

Tomorrow those with low levels of literacy and limited ability to think will be virtually unemployable. In our own and in other industrialized societies, access to work, and, therefore, to self-respecting participation in other important aspects of life, is being withdrawn steadily from those with limited ability to read, to estimate, to weigh evidence, and to reach and test conclusions.

The clear implication of the increasing demand for specialized abilities and highly developed talents is that we must find means of developing, in the majority, powers previously required only by a small proportion of the population. Our provisions for education must be such as to enable higher and higher proportions of the world's population to acquire the capacity to continue learning through reading and reflection, to become effective in speaking and writing, to understand scientific concepts, and to enter more fully into humane studies and the appreciative understanding of other cultures and peoples.

In the developing, but still impoverished, nations of Africa, Asia, and Latin America, illiteracy is a bar not only to individual satisfactions but to the attainment of national goals. The unattainability of ardently desired goals causes restlessness and mounting tensions which threaten to break down the institutions of organized society and to destroy civilization itself. It is too late to crush the desire, even if one were callous enough to propose such a solution.

The only remedy is for those who have access to the good things of life to assist others to gain access; and the means lies through educational provisions so far superior to those now prevailing as to challenge the ingenuity of creative men everywhere. The undertaking is formidable even within the most prosperous and highly educated nations; and for the world as a whole, with its millions of people who are unable to read in any language, the task appears all but impossible. Yet I see no other humane, and therefore no other acceptable, means through which we may hope to adjust population and food supply, develop the machinery and practice of self-government, and move toward peace and a community of mankind.

The Higher Illiteracy Compounds the Simple

While simple illiteracy is an easily recognizable barrier to the good things of life for a large part of the world's population, what I have designated the higher illiteracy is a serious compounding factor. The higher illiteracy is a characteristic of those who see, hear, and even read, but will not understand. They cannot, in fact, understand because they have not developed the ability to carry on a transaction between the world of ideas imbedded in language symbols and the world of real persons, objects, and events. They cannot entertain ideas which seem to threaten their own narrowly preconceived view of the world and they cannot enter sympathetically into the aspirations of peoples of other classes, races, and cultures. The higher illiterates, therefore, maintain the barriers (or at best do nothing to lower them) which stand between disadvantaged populations and the attainment of their aspirations.

The higher illiterate can absorb and repeat ideas found on the printed page but he has not developed the ability to relate these ideas to the life around him. He does not engage in the kind of dialogue which will test the relevance of what he has read to his own personal experience, to the lives of those he meets, or to the behavior of individuals and social groups in general. He does not know how to bring about the conscious interplay between ideas previously encountered and the content of what is being read at the moment. He does not raise the sharp questions which probe the content of reading for meaning, test it for accuracy and penetration, and weigh its implications for himself and for society. He cannot entertain ideas which are at variance with his preconceptions of the "nature of things," or see other other individuals, groups and nations in any light except that of his own self-interest. He lacks the courage to consider ideas which seem threatening to cherished beliefs or vested interests. He is unable to enter appreciatively into values, modes of behavior, and points of view arising in cultures other than that in which he has been nurtured. In short, for the higher illiterate reading is not an invitation to reflective thought. It does not arouse an active process of relating the abstractions on the printed page to persons, events, and institutions of the real world; it does not lead to an internal reorganization of ideas previously received or the establishment of receptivity to other new ideas; and it does not become a seizing of the present moment to extract from past experience insights into the future.

Examples of the operation of higher illiteracy are not difficult to find. The Sophists would qualify for membership among the higher illiterates on the basis of Plato's description of them as having "a sort of conjectural or apparent knowledge only of all things." [1] leading to speculations which are at variance with the facts of life.

A more recent example may be found in a speech by Archibald MacLeish to a conference of the American Library Association in 1942. Mr. MacLeish, deploring the failure of scholars and men of letters to oppose the rising Fascist revolution, said:

> Down through the thirties a considerable number of American intellectuals preached and practiced an intellectual isolationism which was at least as frivolous, and certainly as blind, as the political isolation of political counterparts.[2]

They could read the story of Nazi philosophy, plans, and behavior but they could not make any application of what they read to themselves or to the fate of humanity.

The heightened awareness that seems to be an accompaniment of social revolution does not penetrate the shield of the higher illiterate. On the committee of five appointed by the Continental Congress to draft the Declaration of Independence was Chancellor Robert R. Livingston, a man whose prominence and ambition might have been expected to give him a leading role in the building of the new nation. Livingston was a learned man, he was a reader, and yet as Professor Daniel J. Boorstin remarked in his review of a recent biography of Livingston:

> He was living and thinking on a historical island. The main stream of American history was passing him by. His was a world of vast landed estates, of feudal dues, of monopoly, of genteel aristocracy, of contempt for the people.[3]

Alfred North Whitehead may have been right when he observed that: "The dawn of brilliant epochs is shadowed by the massive obscurantism of human nature." [4] Whitehead defines obscurantism as "refusal to speculate freely on the limitations of traditional methods" [5] and goes on to

---

[1] "Sophist," *The Dialogues of Plato* (trans. by B. Jowett), II, 239. New York: Random House, 1937.

[2] *The New York Times*, June 27, 1942, p. 11.

[3] Daniel J. Boorstin, "He Swung Louisiana Purchase" (review of George Dangerfield's *Chancellor Robert R. Livingston of New York, 1746–1813*), *Saturday Review*, June 17, 1961, p. 53.

[4] Alfred North Whitehead, *The Function of Reason*, p. 34. Princeton, New Jersey: Princeton University Press, 1929.

[5] *Ibid.*

imply that the refusal to speculate and the denial of the importance of such speculation is related to a kind of vested interest in the existing order. He notes that while a few generations ago the clergy tended to be among the obscurantists, today the new dominant group, the scientists, tend to become the obscurantists. What Whitehead calls obscurantism seems to me one of the more dangerous forms of the higher illiteracy.

The term "unawareness" may be applied to other manifestations of the higher illiteracy. Ralph McGill, editor of the Atlanta *Constitution*, in a recent syndicated article, said,

> What produces so much agony of spirit for those who love the South is the incredible gulf which exists for so many persons between this reality [that is, the inevitable disappearance of segregation] and their understanding of it.[6]

Mr. McGill cites an editorial in a Texas paper comparing the freedom riders with a hypothetical invasion of Harlem by the Klu Klux Klan as a "masterpiece of irrelevancy" and concludes that "the quality of unawareness is at times almost unbelievable."[7]

It may seem that the definition of higher illiteracy is stretched to cover all forms of blindness and stupidity. It is my intention, however, to limit it to behavior which results not from lack of information but from inability to relate information to the behavior of other persons and to the course of events. We shall miss the point entirely if we do not recognize that all of us at times and in some degree are higher illiterates. All, therefore, need to cultivate the processes of reflective thought in order that what is seen and read may lead us to a more accurate perception of the world and its people.

REFLECTIVE THOUGHT AS A MEANS OF ESCAPE

If man is to become at home in this world and to reduce the chaos in his mind and in the social order, he must first see the world as it is. This means to see it in a moment of time caught between past and future, for it cannot be seen as it is unless it is also seen as it was and as it may become. Man must learn to encompass the past and future in the present, to see the threads that bind the three in culture-time sequence.

Escape from anxiety can be sought either through non-thought or through the kind of reflective thought which brings new understandings and, hence, new power. Non-thought takes one into a fantasy world and lulls the critical sense, whereas reflective thought merges the ephemeral

[6] Ralph McGill, "Bankrupt Leadership Is South's Big Problem." Reprinted by permission of the *Chicago Daily News* and the Hall Syndicate, Inc. All rights reserved.
[7] *Ibid.*

present and its apparently insoluble problems with a wider perspective of human struggle, human achievement, and human tragedy.

Reflective thought seems to me more likely to occur when one is reading than in most other contexts in the modern world. Television has become the supreme means of escape through non-thought—largely replacing the movies, the dime novel, and the pulp magazines for this purpose. It is a wonderful medium for shutting out reality by substituting a spurious but vivid world in which problems are solved neatly and finally. We need to remember that reading also can be a way of non-thinking and to recall that possibly the highest level of reflective thinking ever reached occurred some 2400 years ago among a people who could and did read, although they had not the printing press, but who used other forms of social discourse to provoke the dialogue which has been called the essence of reflective thought. We might dream of creating the modern equivalent of Plato's Academy, in which through the interaction of great minds in personal contact the relevance of ideas to the issues of the day would be deeply probed. The majority of even our more literate citizens of the present day can scarcely hope to share such experiences with any frequency; although certain television programs such as the National Broadcasting Company's "Meet the Press" and Irving Kupcinet's "At Random" suggest that it is possible to enable large audiences to hear penetrating conversations on important issues. The latter program, which is one of the most stimulating television programs that I have yet seen, is scheduled in the early morning hours and only on Chicago's Channel 2. As public taste improves, more such programs may appear in the hours now dedicated to escape through non-thought. Regardless of what television may bring, every person with any skill in abstracting ideas from the printed page can, through this means, seek the company of the great; and, in his own fashion, carry forward the dialogue through which he may come to a fuller understanding of himself, his fellows, his culture, and his time in history.

The great advantage of reading over listening as a means of provoking internal dialogue is that the reader can set his own pace, mark passages for future reference, and return at will to those portions most capable of evoking ideas previously encountered and stirring the imagination to reassemble the assorted ideas and to project one's own.

An example from recent periodical literature will serve to illustrate a few of the almost unlimited variety of reactions that reading may elicit. The *Saturday Review* of January 21, 1961, is devoted largely to the growth of the Soviet economy and the meaning of this growth to the free world. The material in the issue is adapted from off-the-record talks in which six distinguished economists presented to the Committee for Economic Development their impressions of a month's study in Russia.

One reader might go through this material very rapidly picking up information to be added to his repertoire of "facts" on the Soviet Union. The facts that such a reader would elicit would depend not only on his skill in gleaning ideas from the printed page, but also on his understandings of economic concepts and processes, and on his general cultural orientation. A reader thus motivated probably would not be inclined to "waste" much time on attempting to relate to the American scene Gregory Grossman's [8] description of the Soviet problem of attempting to create organizational forms which will combine the benefits of central supervision with those of decentralized decision-making. He would be even less likely to speculate on this as a dilemma presenting itself in one form or another in all industrialized societies and, indeed, in the administration of all large-scale enterprises, including education. The fact-finding reader thus might read the entire series without seeing any implications for the American economy, society, or education; and without attempting to relate the matters discussed to problems appearing in other societies, ancient and modern. In his eagerness to pin down the exact facts regarding the Soviet Union, such a reader might gain dubious knowledge and lose the opportunity to enlarge his own understanding of human behavior.

Another reader might be concerned primarily with reassuring himself that our economy is superior to that of the Soviet Union. This reader might give great weight to Leon Herman's conclusion that the annual growth rate in labor productivity in the Soviet Union "has been moving fairly steadily downward" [9] but pay little attention to Hans Heymann's point that even if there is a significant slowing up in the Soviet rate of economic growth, this represents "a retardation from an extraordinarily high present rate." [10] The wish-fulfilling or ego-bolstering reader thus would assimilate statements reinforcing his own opinions and screen out ideas likely to disturb settled sentiments. This type of reading can contribute to dangerous self-deception. The point is that not only is it possible to read with an eye to acquiring knowledge which is not applied significantly to the problems of one's own society; but that it is equally possible, and psychologically probable, that only those facts will be garnered which contribute to one's own predilections.

A reader with an inquiring mind would want to examine the observations on the Soviet Union made by each of the six economists in such a way as to increase his understanding not only of Soviet economy but of some of the unsolved problems in our own economy. He would engage in a process of checking the statements for internal consistency and for con-

[8] Gregory Grossman, "Planning: Backbone of a Nation," *Saturday Review*, January 21, 1961, pp. 23–25.
[9] Leon Herman, "The Labor Force: Who Does What," *Saturday Review*, January 21, 1961, p. 60.
[10] Hans Heymann, "Storm Signals for the West," *Saturday Review*, January 21, 1961, p. 41.

sistency with knowledge previously acquired, and he would formulate questions which would provide the starting point for further inquiries. A reader of this type could not fail to be intrigued by T. W. Schultz's question: "How has the Soviet managed to win so large an increase in production despite . . . substantial mistakes" [11] in allocation of resources and in other ways; and he would want to probe further the same author's evident concern with the relationship between the development of "human capital" and economic growth.

The reader who treats reading as an invitation to reflective thought would find ample range for speculation in Herbert Stein's observation that the life of the Soviet citizen "seems drab, dull, tasteless, graceless, conformist, devoid of individuality, creativeness, or independence" [12] and his conclusion that "the release of the individual human spirit to express and enjoy itself is the great thing the West has to offer the World." [13] For the reader thus inclined, Stein's statement would lead not to self-congratulation, but to a searching examination of his own society. He might ask: Is the release of which Stein speaks really more characteristic of the West than of the East? If so, how many individual human spirits have experienced the release in the history of Western civilization? He might wonder whether any considerable proportion of the population has experienced any compelling sense of release to express and enjoy in any deeply creative sense except in certain brief periods in particular locales such as Plato's Athens, Renaissance Italy, and Elizabethan England.

Other questions might arise such as: How much release does the illiterate Brazilian Indian have to express and enjoy himself? How free is the individual human spirit of the white man in our Southern states to express itself in opposition to segregation? How free to express and enjoy themselves are the insecure, anxiety-ridden children of our vast urban slums? Then, he might wonder: What of those in the West who can read, raise questions and propose answers, without serious danger to life, property, or social status? Are they released only to find their spirits have not the zest to express and enjoy themselves? Is the atmosphere of our society such as to provoke inquiry? Does it challenge the individual spirit to be itself, to express itself, and to enjoy the prospect of change?

The reflective reader might be led to speculate also about what the human spirit has to be released from and by what means, if it is to be free "to express and enjoy itself." He might ponder the possibility of releasing the human spirit from ignorance, which laps a heavy bondage still on the majority of mankind, and begin to consider what would have to be done to remove the bars of illiteracy which make access to knowledge

[11] T. W. Schultz, "Human Capital: A Growing Asset," *Saturday Review*, January 21, 1961, p. 37.
[12] Herbert Stein, "Americans on Tour," *Saturday Review*, January 21, 1961, p. 25.
[13] *Ibid.*

impossible for many millions in many lands. He might reflect that removal of ignorance alone would not give release to express and enjoy, unless accompanied by release from blind prejudice and superstition, from unrelenting pressures to conformity, and from fears and anxieties.

It would be easy to add other types of readers, and reading, to the three categories of fact-finding, wish-fulfilling, and inquiry-provoking; but the intent is not to illustrate the innumerable uses and varieties of reading so much as to focus attention on the importance of reading as reflective thought. One of the most disturbing aspects of the higher illiteracy is this failure to read reflectively.

IMPLICATIONS FOR THE TEACHING OF READING

We have long known that learning how to decipher words is a minor part of reading and recognized that the ability to recall ideas read is not the major objective of reading. We have not as yet, however, developed any great skill in teaching reading as reflective thought, carried on through an active internal dialogue. Moreover, much of the reading material used in our schools is not well adapted to this purpose, for the content of ideas is not sufficient to sustain a dialogue or to provoke inquiry. Many of the basal readers seem designed primarily to develop word recognition and vocabulary without much attention to extending the experience of the reader and encouraging him to carry on a transaction in ideas. Even in the upper grades and in high school, many of the textbooks and recommended readings are not sufficiently challenging to encourage active interaction between the abstractions that appear on the printed page and the experiences recorded in memory traces or projected in imagination.

Some of the currently advertised methods of teaching reading seem to treat reading primarily, if not entirely, as a process of abstracting quickly what the author has to say. This is a useful and essential skill; but, if we stop there, we are continuing the production of higher illiterates whose ability to absorb and recall may be very great, but whose capacity to understand themselves and the world in which they are living may be very small.

We need to learn how to help readers raise the fruitful questions, i.e., questions that establish interrelationships among items of information and lead to a search for added knowledge and deepened understanding. We can be betrayed into bad decisions either through inadequacy of information or through inability to assess and use information. Improving the adequacy of information is a task for communication and one that needs attention; but improvement in communication will avail little unless accompanied by improvement in the ability to assess and use information. There are many indications that our miscalculations about the Russian potential for producing atomic bombs, jet planes, and space satellites were due not so much to lack of adequate information as to unwillingness or inability to draw correct conclusions from the data available. The same thing might be said of our miscalculation with regard to the abortive Cuban invasion or the situation in Laos. It is equally true of our failure to understand developments on the domestic scene. Those who told themselves that the Negro did not want access to white schools and other facilities were overlooking evidence of his desire for access to opportunities to achieve his own identity and realize his own potential. They disregarded the information showing that what was being denied was not something pertaining peculiarly to the whites but rights to self-realization pertaining equally to all citizens.

I believe that the way in which reading is taught, the content of ideas available to the reader, and the encouragement given to rational inquiries —especially in the social domains which up to now have been little influenced by such inquiries—offer means to unraveling the great perplexities of the sixties. It is not too much to hope that someone may discover shortly a way of recording the range and quality of the dialogue which the reader carries on with what is read. With the insights thus provided, we could hope to learn how to develop in learners of all ages and from all types of backgrounds an increased capacity to ask relevant questions and to carry on the vitally important transaction between the world of abstractions and the world of events.

The creation of world order under a rule of law and the building of a community of mankind have moved out of the category of utopian dreams into the category of imperatives for survival. The technological advances which make effective international organization mandatory also may bring about a shift in emphasis from learning how to make a living to learning how to live in the Greek sense of occupying one's self with public affairs and with the sense of truth and beauty. This is more than a question of dealing with increased leisure and becomes a fundamental question of the ends of life.

These challenges and the problems referred to in the early part of this paper can be met, and to a considerable extent solved, in the next decade provided we can find ways to offer every child in the world a fair chance to learn those things which will make it possible for him to continue learning; and to provide a quality of education which will enable larger and larger numbers of the citizens of this and other countries to deal rationally with the problems threatening civilization; and to apply advancing knowledge and technology to the realization of man's higher aspirations.

The demands of the next decade are for action of many kinds—to ward off impending disaster and to open up wider vistas to human aspiration and achievement. Action, unless guided by understanding, will be futile when it is not self-defeating and dangerous. To act intelligently, man needs understanding of himself and his culture, other cultures, the method of science, and the potentialities of rational inquiry applied to all the affairs of men.

CONCLUDING STATEMENT

We can undertake no more important task in the next decade than that of developing among the people generally such qualities as:

1. The ability to read—and to listen and observe—reflectively, that is, to carry on a dialogue through which what is read is probed for its relevance to the events of the day and used to sharpen perception of the world about us and the peoples who inhabit it;

2. The power to comprehend the mathematical and scientific concepts and modes of inquiry which are reshaping the modern world;

3. The capacity to enter understandingly and appreciatively into values, modes of behavior, and points of view arising in cultures different from our own;

4. A willingness to consider ideas even when they seem threatening to cherished beliefs or vested interests;

5. A disposition to carry on steadily, through reading and other channels, inquiries directed toward the extension of knowledge and the cultivation of understanding.

These tasks and the means of managing them deserve the energies of the most creative members of our society. We can no longer settle for an attempt to develop the higher literacy only in persons for whom the doors of learning are opened wide by favorable early environment. In the future these powers and these values will be made available on equitable terms to all, or they may not for long be available to any. In this context research to increase our understanding of learning and how it may be enhanced, takes on fresh urgency; and, surely, one promising focus for research is on the development of reflective thinking through reading.

2. Effects of the Mass Media of Communication

Carl I. Hovland *

One of the most striking characteristics of the twentieth century is the fact that we live in an age of mass communication. Newspapers, radio, television, motion pictures, cheap magazines, and pocket-sized books have become the principal purveyors, in our society, of fact, fiction, entertainment, and information.

The technological revolution in production and distribution that has made mass communication possible on such a scale is of relatively recent origin. Fifty years ago three of the most potent of the mass media were practically unknown; and the other, the cheap press, had not yet reached the proportions it has presently assumed.

The rapid rise of the mass media, their ubiquity, and their potential influence have led many to wonder about the actual role they play in social life and behavior. Some writers suggest that mass communications are all-powerful, that they determine thought and action to a major degree. These persons cite the tremendous impact of propaganda during World War I, when the newspapers "got us into war." They also point out that advertising, via the mass media, has become a vital factor in our way of life.

Other analysts, however, are inclined to minimize the effects of the mass media. They point to the fact that many political candidates, enthusiastically supported by the press, are not actually elected to public office and, in general, they regard many interpretations of the power of the mass media as being quite extreme.

The existence of widely differing opinions concerning the effects of the mass media highlights the pressing need for further objective research. Indeed, the editors of the most recent book of readings in this field believe that investigation of "effects" is "the most neglected area in communication research" (Berelson and Janowitz, 1950, p. 395).

Considerable research on the effects of communication has already been done, but much of it is of a practical rather than of an analytical or theoretical character. At the same time there is a growing body of data on basic principles of communication that are relevant to the effects of

* The author wishes to acknowledge the helpful criticism and suggestions of Leonard W. Doob, Fred D. Sheffield, Irving L. Janis and Edmund H. Volkart. He also wishes to thank Gerald Wiener for his generous assistance in procuring books and journals from the various libraries and Ruth Hays for her careful editing of the next-to-final draft of the manuscript.

"Effects of the Mass Media of Communication," by Carl I. Hovland, is reprinted by permission from Handbook of Social Psychology, G. Lindzey (ed.). Cambridge, Mass.: Addison-Wesley, 1954.

mass media. The purpose of this chapter, then, *is to summarize some of the major studies and to relate the large number of empirical findings to basic principles of communication analysis.* In the first section there will be a brief review of some of the principal studies of the *major media* during the last decades. In the second section analytical studies attempting to assess the major influences affecting the impact of communications will be discussed. Here the concern will be with the nature of the communicator, the communication, the medium, and the audience. This section will conclude with a brief review of the variety of different types of behavioral change subsumed under the rubric "effects."

Numerous definitions of mass media have been advanced. Wiebe (1952b) restricts the term to media which are readily available to *most of the public,* "including a sizable number of people in all major subgroups," and whose "cost is so small to the individual that they are available to these same people in a financial sense" (pp. 164f.). For many purposes this is a useful definition. But for purposes of analyzing and interpreting the effects of mass media it does not appear desirable to limit the coverage of studies to those which have been done on extremely large audiences. What does appear critical is that the results bear on methods which could be utilized with mass audiences. Accordingly, we shall follow Klapper (1949) in including researches done with impersonal transmission media regardless of the size of audience. Studies done with radio, movies, books, newspapers, and magazines are included by this definition, but those involving personal address, the drama, and other face-to-face communications are excluded. It must be emphasized, however, that principles may often be uncovered in the latter situations which will enable us to understand better the type of communication which is involved with mass media. Studies of psychotherapy, for example, may help illuminate general problems of communication. But because they are complicated by methodological difficulties of controlling the interaction effects between communicator and communicatee, they cannot be directly generalized to mass media problems.

The emphasis in the present review will be on the analysis of the "effects" of communication. This results in the omission of discussion of content analyses of the various media, methods of control of communication, the economic and social characteristics of major communicators, and similar topics which must be included in a complete analysis of the communication process. A second emphasis is on empirical quantitative investigations. This involves the exclusion of a large number of brilliant essays by communication experts suggesting hypotheses not backed by research results. References to some of these other phases of communication will be found in the excellent bibliography of Smith, Lasswell and Casey, *Propaganda, Communication, and Public Opinion* (1946), and in the supplementary bibliography by Fearing and Rogge (1951).

In addition to the inevitable overlap between the several sections of the chapter, there will be some overlap between the present discussion and other chapters in these volumes. This is a reflection of the fact that the variables influencing the effectiveness of communication represent almost the entire range of problems studied by social psychologists.

SURVEY OF GENERAL STUDIES

Before proceeding to a discussion of the-specific factors influencing the impact of communications, a brief review of some of the major studies of the over-all effects of the principal mass media will be presented. These studies, primarily done within the last two decades, indicate some of the general effects on behavior produced by reading, movies, and radio. The relatively few studies done on the newest medium—television—will also be briefly reported.

EFFECTS OF BOOKS, MAGAZINES, AND NEWSPAPERS

What Reading Does to People, by Waples, Berelson, and Bradshaw (1940), summarizes the major studies concerning the effects of printed media. It is disappointing to find how few solid quantitative data are available here. But there are such formidable difficulties in the way of accurate analyses of the effects of reading books and newspapers—created by problems of evaluating exposure over the long period of time during which effects are produced and of determining the interaction between the effects of reading and other media—that one must be patient and not expect quick research answers.

Waples, Berelson, and Bradshaw have provided a very useful analysis of the types of effects which reading may produce. They distinguish five broad categories of effects: (1) *Instrumental*. These are primarily concerned with the utilization of information in print for a variety of the individual's practical and personal problems. (2) *Self-esteem or prestige*. Articles praising the group to which the reader belongs are avidly read for this reason. Sometimes the reading results in the mitigation of guilt and inferiority feelings, and at other times it invites identification with those who have achieved goals toward which the individual is striving. (3) *Reinforcement*. Support is sought for a position already taken on controversial issues. Conversions are rare and are more extreme responses to controversial reading. (4) *Enriched aesthetic experience*. (5) *Respite*. This is a transient type of response to reading which is characterized by such terms as "forgetting worries," "having a good laugh," and "killing time." The authors also present a number of interesting suggestions for research in this little-investigated area.

The five principal classes of print upon which research has been conducted involve (1) books, (2) newspapers, (3) magazines, (4) comic books, and (5) leaflets.

Books. We are all aware of the profound effects which certain books have had upon society; this may particularly be observed in the case of such books as the *Bible, Uncle Tom's Cabin,* and *Das Kapital.* The task of evaluating these effects is largely in the realm of the social historian. An excellent example of this type of analysis is found in *Books that Changed Our Minds,* edited by Malcolm Cowley (1939). A summary of the historical studies, with appropriate references, is provided by Waples, *et al.,* as follows:

> Reinforcement of their own function and position in society was a result of the reading done by the bourgeoisie in Elizabethan England. The influence of London was extended throughout Britain with the growth of a reading public in the provinces in the late eighteenth century. The radical ideas of the French Revolution were brought to the attention of the working classes through popular pamphlets, and opportunities for such readings are supposed to have stimulated an interest in reading among them. The specific titles read by the Victorians reinforced many of the political, moral, and religious attitudes of the time.
>
> The literary culture and literary production of early colonists in the United States are reflected in and explained by their reading. Propaganda in early American fiction, an outgrowth of the propaganda pamphlets of the Revolutionary War, was directed at various social reforms. The extension of the American reading public in the middle nineteenth century, documented in both general histories and specialized studies, is attributed to the democratization of education and the introduction of cheap and inviting mass publications. (pp. 105f.)

Newspapers. The effects of newspapers have also been studied from a historical standpoint by a number of writers (cf., e.g., Bent's *Newspaper Crusades,* 1939). A frequent concern is the effect of newspapers on voting. One of the earliest attempts to secure an assessment of the influence of the press on political behavior was made by Lundberg (1926). He interviewed a random sample of 940 residents of Seattle concerning their views on four public questions which had been given prominent press discussion during the preceding eight months. In a different connection each individual interviewed was asked what newspaper he read most frequently. Only a very slight relationship was found between the stand taken on each issue by the newspaper and the opinion of the reader of that newspaper. The slight relationship could readily be explained by selective factors working in the reverse direction; i.e., some readers selected papers with whose editorial position they agreed rather than that the editorials influenced their position. Lundberg concluded from the data he assembled that: "A modern commercial newspaper has little direct influence on the opinions of its readers on public questions. It probably seeks to discover and reflect that opinion rather than to make it." . . . "The stand of a newspaper on public questions is a negligible factor in the reader's estimation in selecting his newspaper" (pp. 712f.).

More recently, Mott (1944) has made an extensive analysis of the position of newspapers in presidential elections from 1792 to 1940. Wide discrepancies between newspaper support and popular voting were frequently found. Mott's conclusion is that "there seems to be no correlation, positive or negative, between the support of a majority of newspapers during a campaign and success at the polls" (p. 356).

While there may be no gross correlation between the position of the newspapers and voting in these studies, it appears to the reviewer that the conclusion that newspapers have no effect on opinion is clearly unwarranted. First of all, the studies are set up on the expectation of the effects being so pronounced that they will show up in the gross figures. From what is known about the mass media we should expect the effects to be of a magnitude which would require more careful and detailed analysis to test the relationship. In the second place, the election issues which have been studied are typically major ones, concerning which the public is usually moderately well informed. It is possible that on minor issues and local candidates the effect of the newspaper is considerably greater. Finally, editorials and news stories within the same newspaper often do not agree and hence there may be cancellation of effects. Separate analyses of the influence of editorials, news reports, and syndicated columnists would be most interesting.

The impact of the newspaper on behavior is a major concern of Lazarsfeld, Berelson, and Gaudet (1944). Much of their discussion and analysis is devoted to the problem of who reads the material in the newspapers dealing with the election issues. Their most general finding is that newspaper reading is done by those most interested in the campaign, and these are people who have already made up their minds long before the election. ". . . People with most interest were most likely to make their vote decision early and stick to it throughout the campaign. What we now find is that the people who did most of the reading about and listening to the campaign were the most impervious to any ideas which might have led them to change their vote. Insofar as campaign propaganda was intended to change votes, it was most likely to reach the people least susceptible to such changes" (p. 125). No definitive data are presented of the effects on individuals exposed and not exposed to the newspaper, but interviews did show that at least two-thirds of the voters mentioned that the newspaper was a source from which they obtained much information leading to their voting decision.

While the number of researches in naturalistic settings concerning the effects of reading have been few, there are a number of studies in which the reading of material has been controlled by the experimenter and the effects determined on information and opinion. Swanson (1951) presents a preliminary report of research carried out in this manner. A sample of 209 Minneapolis residents was interviewed on four successive occasions. On the first interview demographic and biographical data were secured. During the second interview a "before" test of information and attitude was administered, together with a five-item disguised intelligence test. During the third interview the respondent was asked to read several sections from the newspaper. "After" tests of the material read on the third interview were secured on the fourth interview. On the basis of the results obtained to date Swanson advances a number of hypotheses as to factors influencing the learning and retention of items concerning government contained in the daily press. The data indicate that there is considerable consistency, over a period of time, in an individual's habits of reading, and that on the basis of verbal ratings of interest one can effectively predict patterns of information acquisition. Those of his results bearing on the assimilation of information by men as compared with women and by brighter as compared with less bright members of the audience will be discussed below in connection with individual differences.

A frequently cited early study of the effect of reading on attitude was conducted by Annis and Meier (1934). Stories were "planted" in the university daily concerning a little-known Australian prime minister. To ensure exposure, the planted articles were included with other material read by the students during class sessions. Some of the students were exposed to material favorable to the prime minister, Mr. Hughes, while others were given statements which were uncomplimentary to him. The material read had considerable potency in influencing the attitudes of the students. Ninety-eight per cent of those who read the favorable editorials were biased in the favorable direction and 86 per cent of those who read the unfavorable editorials were biased against Mr. Hughes.

Another study using newspapers as the stimulus material is by Britt and Menefee (1939). Reports of the Dies Committee were read in newspaper form by students. Attitudes toward various individuals cited in the reports were strongly influenced by the reading.

Magazines. While there have been numerous surveys of who reads which magazines, the effects produced on those who do read them have not been extensively studied. Investigations of the effects of magazine advertising on sales are numerous but seldom made available publicly. It is doubtful that there are many distinctive effects associated with magazines which are not also characteristic of books and newspapers. One difference noted by Lazarsfeld, Berelson, and Gaudet (1944) is that magazines may be quite effective in reaching specialized audiences. Thus small specialized magazines may have considerable influence. It was found that the *Farm Journal* was mentioned as a concrete influence upon changes in vote intention as frequently as *Collier's*, despite the considerable discrepancy in circulation; and the Townsend publication was referred to as frequently as *Life* or the *Saturday Evening Post*.

Comic books. A new influence in the American pattern of reading is that of the comic books, which have skyrocketed in circulation. Seldes (1950) states that the number of copies printed is 700 million per year. They have been widely decried as injurious to morals and reponsible for the lowering of tastes. But little research on their effects is available, and the results reported are conflicting. Wertham (1948) refers to extensive "clinical studies" carried out by himself and associates which indicate that "comic books represent systematic poisoning of the well of childhood spontaneity" (p. 29) and set the pattern for later aggressive crimes. Wolf and Fiske (1949), on the other hand, report that the child finds in animal comics "subjects for his early projective needs, and later, in invincible heroes, he finds subjects for ego-inflation" and from comic classics material to "supplement the facts and insights he gains from more formal reading of history and current events and from experiences with real people" (p. 20). Objective research in this area is greatly needed.

Leaflets. In a number of investigations the effects of leaflets have been evaluated. The study by Hartmann (1936) on the use of political leaflets to influence voting is discussed elsewhere in this chapter. Leaflets have been extensively used in psychological warfare and there is keen interest in their effectiveness for this purpose. The problem of determining their impact in this situation is a difficult one methodologically. The kinds of data which may be secured and some of their implications are discussed by Herz (1949). Evidence concerning effectiveness was based on such criteria as the number of leaflets found on prisoners, the recall of the content by the prisoners, comments on allied leaflets by the enemy, etc. Simple ideas were judged to be much more effective than more complicated ideological discussions. Additional work on leaflets with better experimental procedures is currently being done by the military services but is still in the classified category.

A number of other studies of the effects of reading have been done with specially prepared material read by the subjects, usually with attitude scales for the measurement of effect. Some of these are cited elsewhere in this chapter. They include the investigations of Bateman and Remmers (1941), Bird (1927), Cherrington and Miller (1933), Hartmann (1936), Hovland and Weiss (1951), Knower (1936), Sims (1938), and Wilke (1934).

[Editor's Note: This article continues to discuss other media of communication, i.e., motion pictures, radio, and television, and concludes with an analysis of the influencing effects of all mass media.]

REFERENCES

A. D. ANNIS and N. C. MEIER, The induction of opinion through suggestion by means of "planted content." *J. soc. Psychol.*, 1934, V, 65–81.

R. M. BATEMAN and H. H. REMMERS, A study of the shifting attitude of
high school students when subjected to favorable and unfavorable
propaganda. *J. soc. Psychol.*, 1941, XIII, 395–406.

S. BENT, *Newspaper crusaders.* New York: McGraw-Hill, 1939.

B. BERELSON and M. JANOWITZ, *Reader in public opinion and communication.* Glencoe, Ill.: Free Press, 1950.

C. BIRD, The influence of the press upon the accuracy of report. *J. abnorm.
soc. Psychol.*, 1927, XXII, 123–129.

S. H. BRITT and S. C. MENEFEE, Did the publicity of the Dies Committee
in 1938 influence public opinion? *Publ. Opin. Quart.*, 1939, III, 449–
457.

B. M. CHERRINGTON and L. W. MILLER, Changes in attitude as a result
of a lecture and of reading similar materials. *J. soc. Psychol.*, 1933, IV,
479–484.

M. COWLEY (ed.), *Books that changed our minds.* New York: Doubleday,
Doran, 1939.

F. FEARING and GENEVIEVE ROGGE, A selected and annotated bibliography
in communications research. The Quart. of Film, Radio, and Television,
1951, VI, 283–315.

G. W. HARTMANN, A field experiment on the comparative effectiveness of
"emotional" and "rational" political leaflets in determining election results. *J. abnorm. soc. Psychol.*, 1936, XXXI, 99–114.

M. F. HERZ, Some psychological lessons from leaflet propaganda in World
War II. *Publ. Opin. Quart.*, 1949, XIII, 471–486.

C. I. HOVLAND and W. WEISS, The influence of source credibility on communication effectiveness. *Publ. Opin. Quart.*, 1951, XV, 635–650.

J. T. KLAPPER, The effects of mass media. New York: Columbia Univ.
Bureau of Applied Social Research, 1949. (mimeo).

F. H. KNOWER, Experimental studies of changes in attitude. II. A study
of the effect of printed argument on changes in attitude. *J. abnorm. soc.
Psychol.*, 1936, XXX, 522–532.

P. F. LAZARSFELD, B. BERELSON, and HAZEL GAUDET, *The peoples' choice.*
New York: Duell, Sloan and Pearce, 1944.

G. A. LUNDBERG, The newspaper and public opinion. *Soc. Forces*, 1926,
IV, 709–715.

F. L. MOTT, Newspapers in presidential campaigns. *Publ. Opin. Quart.*
1944, VIII, 348–367.

G. SELDES, *The great audience.* New York: Viking Press, 1950.

V. M. Sims, Factors influencing attitude toward the TVA. *J. abnorm. soc. Psychol.*, 1938, XXXIII, 34–56.

B. L. Smith, H. D. Lasswell, and R. D. Casey, *Propaganda, communication, and public opinion.* Princeton: Princeton Univ. Press, 1946.

C. E. Swanson, Predicting who learns factual information from the mass media. In H. Guetzkow (Ed.), *Groups, leadership and men.* Pittsburgh: Carnegie Press, 1951.

D. Waples, B. Berelson, and F. R. Bradshaw, *What reading does to People.* Chicago: Univ. of Chicago Press, 1940.

F. Wertham, The comics . . . very funny! *Sat. Rev. of Lit.*, 1948, *31*, No. 22, 6–7; 27–29.

G. D. Wiebe, *Mass Communications.* In E. L. Hartley and Ruth E. Hartley, *Fundamentals of social psychology.* New York: Knopf, 1952b. Pp. 159–195.

W. H. Wilke, An experimental comparison of the speech, the radio, and the printed page as propaganda devices. *Arch. Psychol.*, N.Y., 1934, No. 169.

Katherine M. Wolf and Marjorie Fiske, The children talk about comics. In P. F. Lazarsfeld and F. N. Stanton (Eds.), *Communications research,* 1948–1949. New York: Harper, 1949. Pp. 3–50.

3.   The Critical Reader

Edgar Dale

Nearly everybody sees that the future is unpredictable, that blindly following the habits and routines of the past will court disaster. But everybody doesn't see that providing alternatives to stereotyped habits requires creative, critical thinking—requires critical reading.

Reading can be roughly divided into three levels. The first level is simple, uncritical reproduction, a duplication of what has been read. It is *reading the lines*—literal comprehension. The reader knows what the author "said," no small accomplishment. But what did he mean?

The second and higher level of reading involves drawing inferences from what is read—discovering the implications. It is *reading between the lines*. It requires critical thinking, an analysis of what the writer really meant. Did he write ironically with tongue in cheek? Was his tone hopeful? cynical? an exaggeration for effect?

"The Critical Reader," by Edgar Dale, is reprinted by permission from *The News Letter*, XXX, 4 (January 1965), pp. 1–4.

A third level of reading involves evaluation and application of what is read and requires vigorous, critical judgment. It is *reading beyond the lines*. One asks—what relevance does this reading have to my ongoing work? How can I put these ideas to work?

Here are some characteristics of critical reading and comments about the role of the teacher in developing the critical reader.

Critical reading is independent reading. It is independent in the sense that thinking—like loving or appreciating—is an individual, personal affair, not a group process. The critical reader is on his own—self-directed, not teacher-directed. Obviously there can be some group teaching of critical reading as a preparatory measure, but finally the student is on his own with no teacher, no parent to help him. He is becoming an independent learner, one who has learned how to learn, and loves learning.

Critical reading is problem-centered. One of the key tasks of critical reading is to find and state the problem, the key issues. Poverty or unemployment or automation are umbrella terms which indicate a problem area, but to discover and clearly state what is at issue requires disciplined study. Without critical analysis we are likely to treat symptoms, not causes.

Further, the critical reader knows that great issues cannot be adequately stated on an either/or basis. He knows that this world is a complicated one—the *London Economist* says it is "untidy, ungrateful, and unjust." The critical reader knows that in dealing with great issues you can't really divide people into the good guys and the bad guys, the cops and the robbers, the saints and the sinners. You must learn to face both ambiguity and complexity.

The trouble with the good guy-bad guy approach is that in time these roles may be reversed. A few years ago the Japanese and the Germans were the bad guys and the Russians and the Chinese were the good guys. Now apparently the situation is reversed. Is De Gaulle a good guy or a bad guy? Perhaps he is blazing a new trail to a needed arrangement of world affairs.

The critical reader knows that there are no simple, easily-arrived-at solutions either to great global problems or indeed to some of our classroom problems. For example, if you know exactly how reading should be taught, you should get into touch with the experts. They need your help.

Critical reading is analytical and judgmental. A literary critic analyzes a book and then passes judgment on it, notes its strengths and weaknesses. He indicates either directly or inferentially whether this book is worth reading. He probes hidden assumptions, evaluates the logic or illogic of the writer. He must present his best judgments and demonstrate his awareness of critical standards.

A good critic can't say with a shrug of the shoulder, "There's a lot to be said on both sides." He can't be like the young woman who went to the psychiatrist for advice. When the psychiatrist asked, "Are you indecisive?" her answer was, "Yes and no."

The judgments that students make on a book or a magazine article will not usually be profound, although occasionally they may be. Students will either recommend the book to others or they won't. And they may tell why they liked it (they don't always know) and what parts pleased them most. They may also compare the book with others by the same author, giving judgments as to similarities and differences.

Critical reading is based on a stubborn effort to get at the truth. The critical reader must be aware of all the barriers to the truth, many of them in his own mind. He must learn that we see the world through the lenses of our own experience. Perceptions are personal. "The eye sees what it knows."

Here is where common sense may lead us into error. Common sense tells us (and every fool can see it) that the sun rises in the morning. But it doesn't rise, and it took Copernicus to show that common sense and the great astronomer Ptolemy were wrong. Common sense says that two balls of different weight will fall at different speeds—the heavier faster than the lighter. This application of common sense is wrong, as Galileo proved. The philosopher Alfred North Whitehead has written:

> Nothing is more curious than the self-satisfied dogmatism with which mankind at each period of its history cherishes the delusion of finality of its existing modes of knowledge. At this moment scientists and skeptics are the leading dogmatists. Advance in details is admitted: fundamental novelty is barred. This dogmatic common sense is the death of philosophic adventure. The Universe is vast.

Critical reading is creative, imaginative, non-conformist. Here we can contrast training and education. Reading can be taught as training—with fixed limits and predictable responses. Genuinely educational experiences, however, have no ceiling, no fixed boundaries, no neat terminal points. They are creative, not routine.

The critical, creative reader is willing to modify previous beliefs, is flexibly open to change. He thoughtfully examines his stereotyped notions about Protestants, Catholics, Jews, the Republican or Democratic Party, fluoridation, Cuba, China. He has learned to live with uncertainty, to tolerate ambiguity. He believes with Socrates that "the unexamined life is not worth living."

The critical reader associates with the best minds of all generations. The best way to do this is to read thoughtfully, analytically, judgmentally, critically. Ezra Pound once said: "Literature is news that stays news." Certainly the wisdom of Shakespeare remains news for four hundred years. The insights of Cervantes or Boswell or Thoreau have present-day applications.

To be ahead of the times, not twenty-five years behind, we must read critically what the great minds are saying or have said. Note this illuminating comment:

> There are at the present time two great nations in the world, which started from different points, but seem to tend toward the same end. I allude to the Russians and the Americans. . . . . All other nations seem to have nearly reached their natural limits, and they have only to maintain their power; but these are still in the act of growth. . . . . The principal instrument of (America) is freedom; of (Russia), servitude. Their starting-point is different and their courses are not the same; yet each of them seems marked out by the will of Heaven to sway the destinies of half the globe.

This is what the thoughtful reader of Alexis de Tocqueville learned more than one hundred years ago. The critical reader tries to discover the prescient minds of today.

Critical reading is an involving, participatory experience. Walt Whitman once said: "Books are to be called for and supplied, on the assumption that the process of reading is not a half sleep, but in the highest sense, an exercise, a gymnast's struggle; that the reader is to do something for himself."

The word "dialog" is overused today but it does have rich meaning. In critical reading you have a dialog with the author. You ask him tough questions, and sometimes you feel that he answers them well and sometimes he may answer them badly. The critical reader may ask the age-old questions that everyone faces and tries to answer: Who am I? What am I here for? What is worth doing? How responsible am I for my neighbor, and who is my neighbor? What really makes a difference?

The critical reader is sensitive to words and has acquired an excellent vocabulary. To read critically we must savor the flavor of words, make subtle discriminations between meanings of words—e.g., irony, sarcasm, and satire; or burlesque and farce. The critical reader is sensitive to metaphor, a way of making words do extra work. Think of how most fruits can be metaphorized: peach, top banana, apple, lemon, prune. Or animals: cat, tiger, lion, weasel, badger, bull. Or vegetables: tomato, string bean, corn, cabbage head.

The critical reader also enjoys figures of speech such as the oxymoron—the use of two apparently incongruous words to produce an epigrammatic effect. Examples are: broadly ignorant, wise foolishness, troubled joy, sweet sorrow, concise misinformation, trained incapacity, educated ignorance, successful failure, arrogant humility.

Meager vocabularies betray our failure to read widely and critically. For example, a young woman approached a noted speaker after a lecture and said, "You were simply superfluous. I've never heard such an enervating speech." "Thank you," the speaker replied. "I'm thinking of having it published posthumously." "Wonderful," replied the young woman, "and the sooner the better."

The critical reader reads to remember, not to forget. What the critical reader selects to read is not only worth remembering; it is worth talking about. Knowledge unshared is knowledge forgotten. We won't do much critical reading unless we engage in lively conversation about what we have read—not the stereotyped, unevocative reporting of thin experiences, but telling what hits us hard and makes us think, noting our doubts and possible disagreements with the author.

The uncritical reader often reads to erase experience. The critical reader tries to make a mentally indelible record of what he has read. The uncritical reader wants to get from suppertime to bedtime with the least amount of thinking—to kill time. The critical reader wants to fill time, not only with rich memories but also with fruitful, forward-looking experiences. Critical reading is disciplined reading by persons who have convictions about something.

4.   Teaching Critical Reading

John J. DeBoer [1]

The term "critical reading" holds a variety of connotations for students of the reading problem. To some it means simply the active rather than the passive approach to the printed page. To others it involves the ability to distinguish relevant from irrelevant data in finding the solution to a problem or the answer to a question. To still others it implies the existence of a spirit of skepticism in the reader, a disposition to evaluate carefully the reliability of evidence or the soundness of a conclusion.

If we may judge the schools by their product, we have abundant evidence of their failure to teach critical reading. College students who dare or care to challenge a textbook or to verify a fact in supplementary sources, or who know how to locate and organize material from a variety of sources, are relatively rare. Most students have leaned for so long on the textbook crutch that they are unable to walk.

[1] Professor of Education, Roosevelt College. This article is adapted from a paper read at the State College, Pa., Conference on Reading, Aug. 12, 1946.

"Teaching Critical Reading," by John J. DeBoer, *The Elementary English Review*, XXIII (October 1946), 251–254. Reprinted with the permission of the National Council of Teachers of English and John J. DeBoer.

Roma Gans discovered[2] that children who scored well on the usual standardized tests in reading performed poorly on a test of critical reading. She concluded that the ability to read critically requires systematic teaching. In another controlled study, carried on shortly afterward, Edward Glaser[3] found that systematic teaching definitely improved high school students' ability to think critically. He found a close relation between critical reading and critical thinking.

We may conclude, therefore, (1) that critical reading is important, (2) that the ability to read critically can be developed through teaching, and (3) that critical reading receives little attention in the majority of schools.

WHAT CRITICAL READING INVOLVES

Critical reading involves the search for relevant materials, the evaluation of the data, the identification and comparison of sources, and the synthesis of the findings. It involves the capacity for suspended judgment and the interpretation of the writer's motive. But chiefly it involves a sufficient background of knowledge to provide a sound basis for judgment. Critical reading implies the existence of appropriate criteria in the mind of the reader.

Much of the literature on critical reading has neglected the need for the development of criteria. It has emphasized the cultivation of the demand for evidence, the discounting of emotion words, and the insistence upon clear and objective referents, but it has tended to by-pass the problem of establishing criteria. Yet there can be no judgments without standards of judgment, no criticism without criteria.

KIND OF CRITERIA

Types and levels of criteria can best be identified by a series of illustrations. On *the simplest level,* a criterion may be merely a question of fact. In Miss Gans' study, for example, the children wanted to know what a colonial kitchen looked like, so that they could plan certain stage properties correctly. They rejected material which did not contribute somehow to the answer to their question. They approved of passages which threw light on their question. The criterion of acceptance was the relevancy of materials to the specific question at hand. No other consideration was

[2] *Critical Reading Comprehension in the Intermediate Grades.* Bureau of Publications, Teachers College, Columbia University, 1940.
[3] *An Experiment in the Development of Critical Thinking.* By Edward M. Glaser. New York: Bureau of Publications, Teachers College, Columbia University, 1941.

raised in the reading experience. It is to be noted that even on this simple level of criticism many otherwise good readers performed poorly.

On a somewhat more complex level, children are often called upon to evaluate the accuracy of an item of fact or the reliability of a source of information. An article in a popular magazine is usually less reliable than a paragraph in a cyclopedia article, and a description of a rocket ship in a comic magazine is usually less reliable than a chapter in a science textbook. Boys and girls should learn to distinguish between a Hearst newspaper and a report of the Department of Agriculture as to relative reliability.

Much more difficult and complex, however, is the ability to appraise the validity of a conclusion reached by the author. In this type of reading, the reader is called upon, not only to estimate the relevancy, accuracy, and validity of facts and arguments, but to decide whether or not any relevant facts or considerations have been overlooked or suppressed. Moreover, the reader must interpret what he reads in the light of generalized understandings previously reached. This is by far the most difficult kind of critical reading, but in a democratic society it is also the most significant.

This type of critical reading comes into play in connection with any newspaper editorial, any magazine article, radio play, photoplay, biography, short story, or novel. It is the kind of literary criticism that every consumer of printed matter is called upon to exercise. It involves such questions as these: Is the action of this character plausible, is that incident typical, is the author's evident intention justified? An article on Russia in *Life* magazine or the *Reader's Digest*, an editorial in the Chicago *Tribune* or the *Daily Worker*, a leaflet distributed on a street corner, presents a problem of the greatest complexity for critical reading.

It is a common observation that we approve of the play, the story, the editorial, or the article that re-inforces our basic beliefs or flatters our prejudices, and we disapprove of materials based on assumptions with which we disagree. The semanticists and the pragmatists insist that we approach each new selection with open mind, ready to weigh with Jovian impartiality each new generalization and hospitable to any conclusion to which the evidence presented may lead. Actually, the completely open mind is present, among people above the moron level, only in certain highly specialized situations, and only rarely in relation to the determination of social policy.

In the reading of history, whether in the examination of primary sources or of a historical treatise, we tend to accept or reject on the basis of a social philosophy previously formed. There is no other way of reading history. The data of history are infinite in number and yield no meaning to us until we have made a selection in harmony with some defensible principle. We modify, revise, or even completely reverse the guiding principle as the evidence demands, but the process of interaction goes on continually, the data modifying or clarifying the principle, and the principle in turn giving significance to the data.

The Formation of Criteria

How are the guiding principles or basic criteria formed in the mind of the average reader? Are they the result of careful reasoning, of generalizations derived from observation of the evidence? Actually they are the product of the culture and subject to the prevailing influences within the culture. As the cultural patterns change, the reader's standards of judgment change. When cultural patterns conflict, the reader chooses his pattern as a result of one pressure or another and evaluates the subject matter in relation to it. The reader who is caught in the center of the conflict is compelled to suspend judgment on what he reads—that is, he postpones the process of critical reading until such time as he can adopt some criterion.

Responsibility of the Teacher

If this analysis of the development of criteria is correct, what is the responsibility of the teacher in cultivating critical reading? First, the teacher helps the reader to clarify his own thinking, to identify his own assumptions. Second, the teacher helps the reader to analyze the issues and asssumptions in the reading material. Third, the teacher helps the reader to broaden the background of knowledge out of which adequate standards of judgment may emerge.

We can probably make the greatest contribution to the effectiveness of the school in the teaching of critical reading by providing constantly, in every unit of instruction, a wide variety of reading materials. The variety should be great enough to embrace a wide range of interests and ability levels, but if possible it should include also a wide range of viewpoints. Comparison of diverging viewpoints will compel a degree of critical reading which is impossible when the children's chief source is a single textbook.

In the world of books, magazines, and newspapers we can find every variety of viewpoint with respect to the nature of the world and of man and with respect to the kinds of social organization most desirable for man. In the United States there are few if any legal restrictions upon the dissemination of widely divergent ideas and types of information. Nevertheless, the vast majority of the people of the United States are effectively shielded, by an iron curtain of you wish, from all but the narrowest range of viewpoint on questions involving everyone's happiness, if not survival.

It is no accident, for example, that 95 per cent of the major newspapers in American cities opposed Franklin D. Roosevelt in his campaigns for re-election. Whether they were justified in opposing him is beside the point; the important thing is that they were nearly unanimous. During the San Francisco Conference, at which the United Nations came into being as a world organization, the headlines of nearly all newspapers of this country daily screamed their prophecies of doom for the infant organization. The newsmagazines, the digest magazines, the popular story magazines, the major press services, the newspaper chains, the majority of columnists, and the majority of news commentators unite in a systematic campaign to create antagonism in this country toward the Soviet Union. The stereotypes of racial and religious minorities which shape the public attitudes toward those minorities are carried in the mass media of communication. The same unanimity may be found with respect to the subject of labor and management relations, price control, subsidies, and other equally important public questions.

RESTORING COMPETITION IN IDEAS

For most citizens, including probably also most teachers, truly critical reading under such circumstances is impossible, because the standards of judgment which readers bring to the printed page have previously been shaped by a quasi-monopoly of the means of communication. It becomes the responsibility of the school, in a free society, to restore in the library and the classroom the free competition in ideas which is essential not only to critical but to any intelligent reading. Introducing materials of limited circulation representing the widest range of viewpoint and belief may be a dangerous undertaking, but it is an inescapable responsibility for the school that takes the reading task seriously.

Just how early in the school program can we begin to teach critical reading? In the sense in which it has been discussed in this paper, we can and should begin when the reading process begins. The child who reads his first line of connected discourse on the printed chart recording a group experience should be confronted with the question, "Is it true?" If he repeats the words correctly, if he comprehends the sense of the line, but fails to consider the truth of the statement, he is not learning to read properly. Indeed, the foundations of dangerously bad habits of reading are being laid. His judgment with respect to the people and events in the primer and first reader should be constantly challenged with respect to his own firsthand experience with people and events. By the time the child has reached the fifth grade, he should be able to compare and evaluate two divergent interpretations of a news event as reported in the newspapers, or two contrary interpretations of the Chinese character as found in text- or reference books.

Critical reading does not imply the spirit of indiscriminate skepticism. It implies the use of judgment and the adoption of defensible criteria. For our day, it should not be difficult to formulate some of the criteria which a democratic school system could approve. Certainly we can ask of the things we read today, "Is this designed to strengthen cooperation and promote world peace, or is it intended to divide and to lead us down the road to war and disaster? Is this designed to promote the well-being of all people, regardless of race, religion, or national origin, the humble as well as the privileged? Is this material written in behalf of some special-interest group capable of buying expensive advertising, or for partisan political purposes, or for the exploitation of the consumer? If this material has a bias, as nearly all printed matter has, is it a bias in favor of human beings in general or for a narrow group?"

The development of the critical attitude as one of the objectives of the reading process is not simply one skill to be added to the long list of reading skills found in the yearbooks and the textbooks. It demands a new kind of curriculum, one that is based on real pupil purposes, one that is in touch with real life. If we ever really taught critical reading in school we should be face to face with a transformation which would be far-reaching not only in its effect upon the growth in perception and power of individual children, but in its effect upon the very structure of our society. Small wonder that most schoolmasters continue to prefer the safer routines of uncritical acceptance of the printed page, the grammar period, the geography period, the spelling period, the penmanship period, the history period. They know that critical reading is dangerous. But they should know also that without it neither our free institutions nor we ourselves will long survive.

5. Developing Critical Readers

Helen M. Robinson

Most teachers and reading experts agree that critical reading is one of the significant goals of reading instruction. Some educators use other terms and descriptions as did Chase [1] when he referred to "higher illiteracy" as the inability to relate the content of verbal communication to events which at each moment are shaping our future. He stated that "I hold that the values which thoughtful men cherish are more endangered by illiteracy than the atomic bomb and its offspring."

Among the characteristics Chase attributed to higher illiteracy are two which have pertinence for this paper: "the higher illiterate can absorb and repeat ideas found on the printed page, but he has not developed the ability to relate these ideas to the life around him. He does not engage in the kind of dialogue which will test the relevance of what he has read to his own personal experience, to the lives of those he meets, or to the behavior of individuals or social groups in general." [2]

While few others have related the significance of critical reading to the atomic bomb, many have rated this ability as essential for the survival of a free world.

WHAT IS CRITICAL READING?

A cursory examination of approximately a hundred references reveals that critical reading is usually mentioned, included in some sequence, or described; but it is seldom defined. At times it is lumped with the "higher level" reading skills or designated as critical thinking applied to what is read. One who plans to do research on critical reading or a teacher who wishes to teach this ability may be confused by reading many of these references because of the vague descriptions of the process and skills or because of sharp differences in opinions about the definition.

Some examples of definitions of critical reading which reveal the differences are offered in the following paragraphs.

Fay wrote that "the essential element in critical or evaluative reading

[1] Francis S. Chase. "Demands on the Reader in the Next Decade," in *Controversial Issues in Reading and Promising Solutions.* Supplementary Educational Monographs, No. 91. Chicago: University of Chicago Press, 1961, p. 9.

[2] *Ibid.,* p. 11.

that distinguishes it from literal comprehension is that the critical reader must react to what he reads. He must do something more than merely absorb what the author is telling him." [3] After an extensive review of the literature on the nature of critical reading, Sochor [4] concluded that literal and critical reading could be differentiated only on the basis of the reader's purpose—to understand what is stated or to deal with the ideas in some way. Later she differentiated the two types of reading by defining literal reading as "the ability to obtain a low-level type of interpretation by using only the information explicitly stated"; while critical reading was described as "the ability to obtain a level of interpretation higher than that needed for literal interpretation." [5] Both of these definitions or descriptions are vague and offer little direction in determining the unique characteristics of critical reading as opposed to *inferring meanings, arriving* at *conclusions,* and other similar abilities.

Part of Critical Reading?

A more precise, but narrow, definition was given by Gans [6] who considered critical reading comprehension as the selection or rejection of reference material for use in solving a problem. Russell included critical reading, along with other skills, in creative reading, which he defines as "the process of integrating and organizing materials in order to come to some conclusion or synthesis or to solve some problem." [7]

The next two definitions come to terms with the more specific aspects of critical reading.

DeBoer stated that "critical reading involves the search for relevant materials, the evaluation of the data, the identification and comparison of sources, and the synthesis of findings. It involves the capacity of suspended judgment and the interpretation of the writer's motives. But chiefly it involves a sufficient background of knowledge to provide a sound basis for judgment. Critical reading implies the existence of appropriate criteria in the mind of the reader." [8] In DeBoer's description of what is involved

[3] Leo Fay, *Developing the Ability to Read Critically.* Reading Promotion Bulletin, No. 28. Chicago: Lyons and Carnahan, p. 1.

[4] E. Elona Sochor. "The Nature of Critical Reading," *Elementary English,* XXXI (January, 1959), 47–58.

[5] E. Elona Sochor. "Literal and Critical Reading in Social Studies," *Journal of Experimental Education,* XXXVII, (September, 1958), p. 50.

[6] Roma Gans. *A Study of Critical Reading Comprehension in the Intermediate Grades.* Teachers College, Columbia University. Contributions to Education, No. 811. New York: Bureau of Publications, Teachers College, Columbia Univ., 1940.

[7] David H. Russell. *Children Learn to Read.* Boston: Ginn and Company, 1949. P. 305.

[8] John DeBoer. "Teaching Critical Reading," *Elementary English Review,* XXIII, (October, 1946), p. 251.

in critical reading, there is a distinct implication that to read critically one must have experience sufficient to develop criteria for judging the validity or worth of the materials read.

Gray developed a conceptual framework for the total reading act which includes critical reading. He referred to the four major aspects as: 1. perception of words, including both recognition and meaning; 2. grasp of meaning of continuous discourse, both stated and implied; 3. thoughtful reaction to ideas gleaned; and 4. assimilation, or fusion of the new ideas with those already acquired. In this framework, Gray included critical reading in the third aspect—thoughtful reaction. He described it as "the evaluation of what is read in the light of sound criteria or standards." [9] He added that critical reading involved the wise selection of facts or standards needed in making specific evaluations. Of primary importance are clear thinking, weighing of values, and rigorous checking on the validity of the conclusions reached. He added that the reader will accept or be guided by that which is sound and meritorious, and reject or disapprove that which is untrue or of questionable value.[10]

The dictionary definition of *critical* suggests harshness of judgment, but states that "in precise use, critical implies an effort to see a thing clearly and truly in order to judge it fairly." [11] Based on the precise use and the definitions and descriptions already given, a definition of critical reading has been adopted for this paper. It is judgment of the veracity, validity, or worth of what is read, based on sound criteria or standards developed through previous experiences.

Skills and Abilities Basic to Critical Reading

Most investigators and theorists agree that critical reading is based on, or is an instance of, critical thinking. In this respect, there is great similarity to critical listening. For this reason, there is some objection to including this ability as a part of reading. Nevertheless, reading offers tremendous opportunities for insuring the development of critical thinking. Although thinking has been defined many ways, the description used in this paper is "to exercise the powers of judgment, conception, or inference, to reflect for the purpose of reaching a conclusion." [12] Acceptance of such a choice is in contrast to imagining, planning, envisioning, and realizing. The assumption is frequently made that critical thinking and by implica-

[9] William S. Gray. "Sequence of Reading Abilities," in *Sequential Development of Reading Abilities*, Supplementary Educational Monographs, No. 90. Chicago: University of Chicago Press, 1960, p. 17.

[10] *Ibid.*, p. 19.

[11] *Webster's New Collegiate Dictionary*. Springfield, Mass.: G. & C. Merriam, 1951, p. 197.

[12] *Ibid.*, p. 883.

tion, critical reading, is closely related to intelligence level as measured by tests. In Russell's [13] review of the research as well as in more recent investigations, the coefficients of correlation between intelligence test scores and critical thinking have not exceeded .50 and most have been considerably lower. The discrepancy may be based on the (1) nature of the tests used, or may be due to (2) lack of development of critical thinking abilities on the part of those who are capable of learning critical thinking. The consensus of writers is that critical thinking and critical reading are greatly facilitated by intellectual maturity but that even persons of below average intelligence may learn the simpler levels of critical reading.

Several types or levels of complexity of abilities basic to critical reading have been given. Gray proposed three requisites. The first "is an attitude of inquiry concerned with such items as the soundness or worth of the ideas expressed, the actions of a character or the literary quality of the material read." The second "is an adequate background or basis for evaluation which includes information, specific facts and established principles. . . ." [14] A third requisite "is ability on the part of readers to make sound judgments, in evaluating what they read." [15]

DeBoer recognized three general levels of critical reading, each successive one implying more complex abilities than the others. First is the relevancy of materials to a specific question or topic. At the second level is evaluation of the accuracy of an item of fact or the reliability of a source of information. Third is the ability to appraise the validity of a conclusion reached by an author. This level calls for not only the relevancy, accuracy, and validity of facts and arguments but also a decision as to whether pertinent information has been overlooked or suppressed.[16]

Russell suggests four conditions as essential to critical reading: 1. a knowledge of the field in which reading is being done; 2. an attitude of questioning and suspended judgment; 3. some application of the methods of logical analysis or scientific inquiry; and 4. taking action in light of the analyses or reasoning.[17]

Heilman proposed that "Almost all of the prerequisites for, and obstacles to, critical reading are related to the two skills of discerning a writer's purpose and drawing inferences. The presence or absence of bias, a lack of background, the habit of accepting that which is in print or that which is allegedly backed by authority, and the lack of experience in dealing with controversial topics, all help to determine whether critical reading can take place." [18]

[13] David H. Russell. *Children's Thinking*. Boston: Ginn and Company, 1956. P. 292.
[14] Gray, *op. cit.*, p. 17.
[15] *Ibid.*, p. 19.
[16] DeBoer, *op. cit.*, p. 252.
[17] Russell. *Children Learn To Read, op. cit.*, p. 308.
[18] Arthur W. Heilman. *Principles and Practices of Teaching Reading*. Columbus, Ohio: Charles E. Merrill Books, 1961, p. 312.

An interesting description of many skills and abilities called into use comes from Strang. The following quotation is illustrative: "In reading to obtain proof on any point the student will first formulate the assumptions which are to be studied. Then he will select, as he reads, the ideas significantly related to the assumptions. He will search for evidence in support of or opposed to the assumptions and weigh each bit of evidence as he reads. If evidence accumulates against one of his original assumptions, he will change it." [19]

So far, in this paper, little attention has been given to the familiar reading skills requisite to critical reading. Many of the writers already mentioned have detailed the skills and abilities needed. Some writers separate the skills and list ten to twenty. Others group them into classes. For example, Heilman lists ten abilities, but in summary says that "the reader must know the meaning of the words used and the different shades of meaning words have in different contexts. He must separate main thoughts or ideas from qualifications; he must detect the author's purpose, bias, and intent." [20]

In one of his last publications, Gray [21] brought together, in diagramatic form, the essential skills. To summarize his views, he said that it is necessary to perceive words accurately, knowing both the proper pronunciation and the appropriate meaning in a given context. Comprehension calls for fusing smaller meanings into larger ideas and noting the relationship and organization of the ideas. Both literal and implied meanings must be secured. The type of material must be recognized and inquiries appropriate to it should be made. The inquiries include identifying the author's purpose, mood, and attitude toward his topic. These abilities are often known as reading the lines, reading between the lines, and reading beyond the lines. Furthermore, these reading skills must be sufficiently developed so that they can be applied automatically with major attention given to the mental processes suggested earlier in this section.

The intellective and reading skills and abilities must be supplemented by a consideration of the attitudes of the reader. McKillop [22] found that, among eleventh grade students, attitude had very little effect on literal meaning. However, when judgment, evaluation and prediction were required, attitude was a very significant factor.

In Grades VII–X, McCaul found that the stronger the pupils' attitudes the greater was the effect on interpretation. He concluded that "he (man) is not purged of emotion, prejudice, and attitudes just because he has a

[19] Ruth M. Strang. *Problems in the Improvement of Reading in the High School and College.* Lancaster, Pennsylvania: Science Press, 1938, p. 190.

[20] Heilman, *op. cit.,* p. 313.

[21] Gray, *op. cit.*

[22] Anne Selley McKillop. *The Relationship Between the Reader's Attitude and Certain Types of Reading Response.* New York: Teachers College, Columbia University, Bureau of Publications, 1952.

book in his hands. When he reads he is as much a dupe of his attitudes as he is under any other circumstances." [23]

At the adult level, a plethora of studies have been made of the effects of strongly held beliefs (biases) on understanding an author's argument or reasoning.

Thus, attitudes combine with experience to contribute to individual differences in critical reading.

Therefore, to develop critical readers, it is essential that the skills and abilities in reading for complete understanding be combined with: 1. an inquiring attitude; 2. a background to supply knowledge about the topic, field, or area to provide standards or criteria for evaluation; 3. the ability to suspend judgment until the writer's message is fully secured; 4. the ability to follow the organization or logic of the presentation, recognizing what is included and what is omitted; 5. awareness of the author's qualifications and intent; and 6. recognition of the publishers commitments. Inductive and deductive reasoning, analysis of language, and appreciation of quality of writing seem to be essential ingredients. All of these abilities will be influenced by the reader's attitudes.

Conditions for Critical Reading

The first essential condition is a commitment on the part of the school or school system to develop critical readers. Such a commitment will be reflected in the aims and goals of reading instruction and in all content areas in which reading is used.

Second, the materials provided for reading must be appropriate for children and youth to use at various levels of maturity. For example, a single textbook, selected by the teacher as authentic, is not conducive to critical reading. Books, magazines and newspapers presenting different points of view and kinds of writing are helpful in developing critical reading. For example, Engle [24] stated that "A curriculum for reflective thinking is one which selects and organizes instructional materials and experiences in such a way as to maximize the opportunities for students to make intelligent and thoughtful decisions with respect to what to hold valuable, what to believe, what guiding ideas or principles to accept as true and what courses of action to follow. . . . In contrast, a curriculum antithetical to reflective thinking selects and organizes materials on principles which emphasize the memorization of specific pieces of information in relative isolation from other similar data. . . ."

[23] Robert L. McCaul. "The Effect of Attitudes Upon Reading Interpretation," *Journal of Educational Research*, XXXVII (February, 1944), p. 456.

[24] Shirley H. Engle. "A Curriculum for Reflective Thinking," *The Indiana Social Studies Quarterly*, XIV (Autumn, 1961), p. 21.

Third, the teachers must be able to read critically, must value an inquiring attitude, and be ready to foster the kinds of discussions which reflect differing views. Austin et al [25] found that there was general agreement that critical reading should be one of the goals of instruction, but that few college teachers felt secure in guiding classroom teachers so as to reach the goal.

A fourth requisite is the ability on the part of teachers to ask the right kinds of questions. In this connection, there is general agreement that reproducing isolated facts deters critical reading. The questions must be appropriate to the selection, calling for critical evaluation of the materials. Teachers should be prepared to expect differences among responses, especially those based on value-judgments. In each instance, teachers should consider both the response to the selection and the standard or criterion for making the judgment. When children and young people become adept at answering a wide range of questions requiring critical judgment, they should be led gradually to formulating their own questions before they read, while they are reading and after they have finished. This step is greatly facilitated when teachers foster an inquiring attitude throughout the school years.

A fifth requisite is willingness to take the time necessary to help pupils develop adequate criteria for critical reading, for reading slowly enough to weigh the evidence, for discussion which helps clarify similarities and differences in conclusions reached. In other words, it is essential to "uncover the ground rather than cover it" as others have said.

WHEN TO TEACH CRITICAL READING

The discussion so far has emphasized the need for a broad background of experiences and a fund of information. Obviously, background is built from infancy, in the home; and it is a continuous function of the school. In addition, background needs to be related to what is read at all developmental levels.

Preschool children are capable of critical thinking before they read, according to Smith.[26] To be sure, the critical level is simple and the topics are sufficiently familiar that they have information so as to judge validity or worth. It follows then, that beginners in school may be taught to read critically as soon as they have acquired sufficient competence in the undergirding skills. They may learn to compare and contrast ideas as soon as they are sufficiently mature to identify clearly likenesses and differences.

[25] Austin, *op. cit.*, p. 48–50.
[26] Madorah E. Smith. "The Preschool Child's Use of Criticism," *Child Development*, III (June, 1932), 137–41.

At the primary grade level, McCullough [27] compared pupils' abilities to answer questions of detail, main ideas and sequence, with those requiring creative reading. At this level she used questions requiring pupils to draw conclusions, pass judgments, and see relationships. She found significant relationship among the skills with no special difficulty in what she called creative reading.

As pupils progress in school and read many easy books, they can learn to be critical of the materials selected for their personal reading, going beyond the responses that they like or dislike the story or informative material.

Nearly a quarter of a century ago, Gans [28] demonstrated that middle-grade children could judge relevancy and authenticity of materials, especially when relationships were close or fairly obvious. They were less successful with remotely related materials. Other aspects of critical reading can be taught at this level, but we have just begun to explore the possibilities.

A great deal of attention has been given to propaganda analysis, sometimes in the middle grades, but more often in junior high school. Perhaps the reason is that more than 20 years ago, the Institute of Propaganda Analysis reported seven sly techniques used to influence readers: 1. "bad names," 2. "glad names," 3. "transfer," 4. "the testimonial," 5. "plain folks," 6. "stacking the cards," and 7. "the band wagon." [29] The simplicity and structure of this list seems to help teachers "get hold of" this aspect of critical reading.

Even though sixth-grade children learn to identify propaganda devices, Nordelli [30] found that the pupils did not change in their abilities to resist the propaganda. Osborn [31] showed that knowledge of the methods of propaganda was not enough to provide resistance to them.

To some writers, teaching propaganda devices is the essence of critical reading. It would be exceedingly unfortunate if instruction stopped at this level, using only a small segment of the range of possibilities. But this example suggests the necessity for clearly identifying other areas of critical reading so that they, too, may be taught.

In the secondary school, all of the content of the curriculum offers tremendous opportunity for teaching critical reading. Literature is an ex-

[27] Constance M. McCullough. "Responses of Elementary School Children to Common Types of Comprehension Questions," *Journal of Educational Research,* LI (September, 1957), p. 65–70.

[28] Roma Gans, *op. cit.*

[29] "How to Detect Propaganda," Propaganda Analysis I. Publication of Institute of Propaganda Analysis, (November, 1937), p. 1–4.

[30] Robert R. Nordelli. "Some Aspects of Creative Reading," *Journal of Educational Research,* L (March, 1957), p. 495–508.

[31] Wayland W. Osborn. "An Experiment in Teaching Resistance to Propaganda," *Journal of Experimental Education,* VIII (September, 1939), p. 1–17.

ample, because as Gainsburg [32] points out, critical reading is the foundation of appreciation. Social studies provides a rich source of materials for critical reading. In science and mathematics, critical reading becomes essential.

College and graduate schools are likely to expect critical reading, often in areas where students lack the background to read critically. In fact, in my own doctoral courses to which only excellent students are admitted, critical reading of research must be developed. This is done by exposing graduate students to excellent and poor research, making comparisons and contrasts, evolving standards for judging research, redesigning published reports to improve them, and offering a great deal of practice in the application of all of these abilities.

It seems clear to me that if an attitude of inquiry is fostered and if the techniques of critical reading are taught, this ability may increase throughout life as background and experience develop ever higher standards against which to judge what is read.

TEACHING CRITICAL READING

Three general approaches to teaching critical reading were pointed out by Huelsman.[33] The direct approach is one in which teachers plan systematically to develop the attitudes, skills and abilities of critical reading.

The second approach may be called incidental in that teachers are developing critical reading as a by-product of the inquiry into content. Using the unit or topic in which many references are read requires some aspects of critical reading.

The third is the functional approach which emphasizes the evaluation of primary source material rather than securing information from secondary works.

So far, no evaluation of the relative effectiveness of the three approaches has been made. In fact, few studies to determine how well the elementary and secondary schools combine efforts to develop critical reading can be found.

One study seems worth a brief reference at this time. Rogers used for her subjects 30 high school sophomores and 30 seniors. She compared their performances in an undirected reading situation, reading a magazine as

---

[32] Joseph Gainsburg. "Critical Reading is Creative Reading and Needs Creative Teaching," *Reading Teacher*, XV (December, 1961), p. 185–92.

[33] Charles B. Huelsman, Jr. "Promoting Growth in Ability to Interpret when Reading Critically in Grades Seven to Ten," in *Promoting Growth Toward Maturity in Interpreting What is Read*. Supplementary Educational Monographs, No. 74. Chicago: University of Chicago Press, 1951, p. 149–153.

one would in a dentist's office, with that of a school assignment where questions about the selection were anticipated. Articles were paired from three issues of the *USSR* Magazine for reading level, human interest and content interest. A descriptive rating scale for level of competence permitted her to ascertain the level of the use of critical reading as revealed by the responses. She reached the following conclusions:

1. "There tended to be a focus on 'remembering facts' to the exclusion, in many instances, of evaluative thinking about what was read." For example, students were asked to tell what they thought about an article but responded with the content of the article.

2. "There was little awareness of the need for evaluative response." This behavior was exhibited especially when direct questions were not asked. The students showed no curiosity about the purpose of the magazine, or its publisher, but accepted its slanted content fully.

3. "The subjects demonstrated question-answering skills rather than reading skills." The subjects attempted evaluation of the selections, with varying degrees of skill, only when questions triggered this response. Without the teacher or a test, critical reading did not appear to function.[34]

From this study, it seems clear that the teachers' emphasis and the kinds of questions used will markedly influence the development of critical reading.

A second study by Smith[35] using high school seniors revealed that they set purposes for reading by their teachers' tests and the questions or the ones students anticipated.

The limited evidence available strongly suggests the necessity for direct instruction, for the frequent use of questions which promote critical reading, and for developing independence on the part of students in reading critically.

TESTING CRITICAL READING

Undoubtedly one of the greatest deterrents to critical reading has been the nature of standardized tests. Most of the elementary reading tests, as well as the bulk of high school reading tests require reproduction of material stated, with few of the evaluative or critical types of questions. Because students rank high on these tests, teachers are not moved to the difficult task of teaching critical reading.

Judging from the problems reported by those who have attempted to

[34] Bernice Rogers. "Directed and Undirected Critical Reading Responses of High School Students," Unpublished Doctorial Dissertation, Department of Education, University of Chicago, 1960, p. 209.

[35] Helen K. Smith. "Research in Reading for Different Purposes" in *Changing Concepts of Reading Instruction,* International Reading Association Conference Proceedings, VI. New York: Scholastic Magazines, 1961, pp. 119–122.

construct tests of critical thinking, it will not be easy to add tests of critical reading to our present survey tests. Yet without them, few teachers will do more than express their opinions that critical reading is important. Furthermore, experiments and practices in teaching reading will be difficult to appraise without tests.

Concluding Statement

Critical reading is one of the least understood, and most elusive of the reading skills and abilities. At the same time critical reading is reported to be basic to appreciation of literature, to arriving at sound conclusions concerning personal and social problems, to scientific investigation—in short—to the educated man. Piecing together the scanty reports, there is evidence that critical readers can be developed but that time and effort must be directed toward instruction for this purpose throughout the school years. Self-understanding of biases and an independent inquiring attitude may contribute to continued development of critical reading throughout life.

6. The Nature of Critical Reading

E. Elona Sochor

For the past ten years, the term "critical reading" has been appearing with growing frequency in educational literature. This phrase refers to something; words always do. What does "critical reading" represent? What is its nature?

The term "critical reading" is used by authorities in three ways: (1) as a major heading under "comprehension" with one or two other headings of relatively equivalent value, each heading including a number of stated or implied skills (10, 14, 63), (2) as a higher-level comprehension abilities in general (32, 40, 43, 50), or (3) as a rather specific comprehension ability (21). Regardless of how the term is used, it invariably represents reading comprehension that involves (1) the facts as presented in the selection and (2) the use of higher-level mental processes.

Thus, reading authorities who use the term critical reading do not

"The Nature of Critical Reading," by E. Elona Sochor, *Elementary English*, XXXI (January 1959), 47–58. Reprinted with the permission of the National Council of Teachers of English.

necessarily agree on what it includes. On the other hand, there are those who use other labels for what seems equivalent to critical reading: "creative reading" (70, 75), "analytical reading" (97), and "critical evaluation" (63, 85), all referring to major headings under comprehension. "Study or work type reading" frequently includes analytical and evaluative as well as organizational abilities such as getting the main idea, relating details, and coordinacy (32, 62, 63, 85). Some writers prefer to list comprehension abilities of different types with no differentiation between higher and lower-level abilities (16, 21, 32, 37, 40, 50, 63, 80, 85, 95).

Much of the variability in what constitutes "critical reading" is due to insufficient research evidence on the reading abilities themselves and on basic and related factors which might contribute. Research workers have been unable to clarify sufficiently the nature, independence or difficulty levels of comprehension abilities in reading. Consequently, those concerned with reading abilities resort to a logic for a definition of critical reading. Even though it produces inconsistency, the current dependence on logical analysis of these abilities is a pragmatic one; the need for comprehension beyond what is explicitly stated becomes more obvious daily.

There is complete agreement on the importance and basic nature of "getting the facts" as presented in the material. Opinions seem to vary, however, as to the school-level at which this ability should be initiated and where in the school program the ability is best developed, i.e., some feel subject matter areas or "everyday living situations" provide better opportunities.

Such variability is even more pronounced with critical reading. Those authorities that discuss thinking abilities in relation to reading stress the need to lay the foundation for understanding what is read, not only in terms of facts, but also in terms of evaluating, organizing and concluding from facts, in readiness for beginning reading. They recommend emphasis on reading for meaning as soon as reading begins and in all activities involving reading (10, 70). Research evidence that five- and six-year olds can use all thinking abilities supports their stand.

As with critical interpretation, various terms in the literature refer to grasping "what is stated": "literal reading" (70), "cursory or observational reading" (97), "assimilative reading" (10, 97), "understanding details" (63). Although the terms are not necessarily synonymous in how much understanding they include, they are used to differentiate between (1) grasping what is presented and (2) going beyond what is stated, or critical reading.

COMPLEXITY OF READING COMPREHENSION

I

Research workers, beginning with Thorndike in 1917 (82), have unquestionably established the complexity of reading comprehension. Yet to be determined are how many abilities and skills are involved and specific information on their nature and development. Studies using the correlational technique have yielded helpful but limited information. Studies based on factor analysis have indicated what appear to be general language and thinking factors.

Davis (26), Langsam (56), and Hall and Robinson (42) all conducted factor analysis studies of reading comprehension with college students. Anderson (2) used secondary level students; and Gans (36) and Mazurkiewicz (61), intermediate grade pupils.

Attempting to combine the factors reported in these studies is challenging, the limitations of language and statistical figures being what they are. Likewise intriguing are (1) factors that appear to be present but elude identification (36, 42) and (2) the attitude of comprehension accuracy (42). Some of the identified factors are very general in nature: reading comprehension (36), reasoning (61) and intelligence (2); others are more specific. If the factors are interpreted and grouped, three seem to emerge.

A "word factor," dealing primarily with individual word forms and their meanings appears to be one (2, 26, 42, 56). This factor would operate most obviously in the typical vocabulary test.

A second might be a "verbal factor" which contributes to the ability to see interrelationships among ideas represented by words in context but which would not involve too much abstract reasoning. Langsam reported such a factor separate from a word factor and reasoning (56). It could include Davis' ability to grasp explicit statements but not the implicit ones, the ability to get detailed statements and possibly the ability to follow the organization of a passage (26). Langsam's factor of noting details (56) and Mazur's verbal comprehension (61) would also fall here. Hall and Robinson's factor of rate, when considered in light of their other factors, might be classified under this factor (42) as well as Gans' delayed recall factor (36). Such a factor would be substantiated by the fact that even the simplest literal interpretation involves more than isolated word meanings.

The third factor, "abstract reasoning," appears in all the studies. Davis identified abstract reasoning as such as well as main idea synthesis (26). Hall and Robinson found an inductive factor (42); Mazurkiewicz reported deductive thinking and problem solving (61); Gans, a selection-rejection factor (36); and Anderson, an analysis-synthesis factor (2). Langsam's factor of seeing relationships might also be included.

The above three groupings of factors in reading comprehension are hypothesized on what is admittedly insufficient evidence. On the other hand, language, meaning, and thinking continua seem to operate together among the factors. Language (words and meanings) assumes a proportionately greater role in the "word factor," but some thinking occurs. In the third factor, the language (words in context, style of writing, punctuation, typographical aids, etc.) still supplies direction to and influences the thinking, but the thinking may go far beyond the meanings of the individual or groups of printed symbols. Language factors vary from the very familiar to the completely unfamiliar to the reader. Meanings vary from the specifically concrete to the most abstract concept (as used by the writer), from the already known to the unknown for the reader, and from possible to impossible to reconstruct because of the presence or absence of appropriate experiences in the reader. The thinking necessary for comprehension would vary from the simple to the complex, depending on the first two factors, the reader, his ability to use the thinking processes needed, and his purpose for reading. The three continua operate in an interrelated manner at all times in any given reader, each influencing the others in a constantly changing pattern.

What would critical reading include in terms of the language, the meanings, the thinking processes, and the reader? Or even in terms of the word, verbal, or abstract reasoning factors? Only further research can supply the answers.

II

The factor analysis studies discussed above attempted to identify basic factors in reading comprehension that would influence or contribute to specific skills and abilities. The results indicated the complexity of the reading process.

A related problem is research evidence on the differentiation between literal (understanding what is stated explicitly) and critical reading. A number of studies reveal that literal reading and evaluating, inferring from or applying facts, though related positively, are not the same (9, 28, 36, 52, 57, 86). Studies (60, 79) investigating literal reading comprehension and a number of specific "critical reading" skills have also indicated that the relationship between literal and critical reading, though substantial, is not high enough to assume they are the same abilities. A comparison of correct responses further indicates differences in performance on the literal and critical parts of the test, with the former being substantially higher.

Literal and critical reading, as treated in these studies, do differ. Moreover, the first (understanding the facts) appears to be basic to (60, 61, 79) and probably an integral part of critical reading.

THINKING: A BASIC PROCESS

I

Thinking as an inherent part of reading was pointed out by Thorndike in 1917 when he stated, ". . . 'to read' means 'to think' . . ." (84, p. 114). After analyzing subjectively the responses of elementary-school children in paragraph interpretation, he compared the thinking processes necessary to that of solving a problem in mathematics (83). In other words, he found evidence of typical problem-solving behavior in paragraph comprehension.

Horn likewise concluded that understanding what was read was similar to problem solving (51, p. 154) and that any understanding involved selection, evaluation, inference and organization (51, p. 123). Although he did not refer to or discuss thinking directly, it is implicit in what he says.

The unanimous acceptance by educators of mental maturity as a contributing factor to readiness for beginning reading indicates recognition of thinking ability needed for reading (78). The use of mental age as a criterion of expectancy of achievement in reading at any level is another indication of such acceptance (10, 43). That reading authorities are beginning to discuss the thinking processes as such (10, 70) and that one has recently published a text on children's thinking (71) point to what seems to be growing attention to this particular and crucial aspect of the reading process.

Research evidence supports the premise that reading is a thinking process. The relationships between reading performance and intelligence (8, 94), particularly when the latter is controlled (60, 79), and the ever-present factor of reasoning in reading comprehension discussed earlier are but two examples.

If reading comprehension involves thinking, then critical reading must involve thinking. To understand the nature of critical reading would necessitate the understanding of thinking in general and possibly of "critical thinking."

II

One of the first and most important premises which must be kept in mind constantly is that thinking takes place in an individual. At any particular time he is functioning from a total internal context, a dynamic,

fluid and complex pattern of nervous system activity, conscious and unconscious. His thinking will be a product of and will be affected by the
number and kinds of past experiences he has had; it will involve his particular organization of these experiences (concepts). His general level of
maturation in all respects (physical, social-emotional, language, motor,
etc.) and his physical status will have their influences. His feelings, needs,
and attitudes, varying from time to time (sometimes from moment to
moment) and from topic to topic are inextricably interrelated with and
affect what he thinks about and how he thinks.

Two recent publications have dealt with thinking, one concentrating on
children and adolescents (71) and the other more general in nature (88).
Although the approaches vary, the discussions are similar as well as com-
plementary in a number of ways.

Vinache (88), in surveying the variety of human thought processes,
emphasizes the "wholeness" of the individual. He points out (1) each
process is in a dynamic relation to every other process (not limited to thinking) and (2) the importance of past experiences to thinking and their interrelatedness with all other aspects of human behavior. Russell (71), on
the other hand, structures thinking primarily in terms of direction and
organization, although he, too, recognizes personalizing factors. Direction
varies ". . . from rather random association to specific channeling toward
specific ends;" organization moves from the relatively simple to an abstract
level involving complex relationships (71, p. 18).

Both authors conclude that the term "thinking" has no clearly established meaning, ". . . in large part, perhaps, because the processes involved
in it are so elusive and, apparently, incapable of direct observation" (88,
p. 2). However, the two definitions formulated independently by these
writers agree in essence.

Vinache defines thinking as mental activity, not predominantly perceptual, that is ". . . an interplay of response to outer, or realistic and
inner, or imaginative . . . forces which occurs in relation to the mental
context, or personalizing factors" (88, p. 358). "Reasoning," which includes logical thinking, concept formation, transfer, and problem solving,
is more likely to be a product of outer (realistic) determinants. Inner
determinants are more likely to prevail in imagery, imaginative thinking,
autistic thinking, and creative thinking, all grouped under "imagination."
Russell defines thinking as "a determined course of ideas (which may vary
greatly in the extent to which it is determined), symbolic in character,
initiated by a problem or task (or other environmental factors including
the personal ones) and leading to a conclusion (or solution)" (71, pp.
4–5).

Russell discusses first what is used in thinking, the "materials of thinking," beginning with percepts which "grow out of sensations resulting
from environmental stimuli." The percepts, together with mental "images"

and memories from prior percepts, "develop into understandings and generalizations in the form of verbalized concepts" (71, pp. 65–66). He then discusses "processes in thinking" which occur as a product of needs and are not separate from the "materials." These processes differ ". . . in such ways as the amount of (goal) direction involved, the extent to which organization of materials is needed, and the type of final organization or conclusion that is reached" (71, p. 28). Of particular interest here is his use of the term "critical thinking," one of the thinking processes, which he reports "usually . . . implies appraisal in terms of some norm, standard, or value" (71, p. 13) and which is, at times, described as a part of problem solving and of creative thinking, two other higher-level thinking processes. Critical thinking involves the inspection and comparison of facts, and it includes arriving at some conclusion. Of interest, too, are the inductive-deductive thinking processes which lead to the formation of concepts or the formulation of conclusions.

One other recent publication dealing essentially with thinking and the use of knowledge structures educational goals from the simple to the complex (13). The accumulation of all kinds of knowledge is recognized as basic; higher levels of functioning include manipulating, seeing relationships and applying known facts and generalizations in increasingly more abstract and more complex ways, the simpler being incorporated in the more complex. Thus the structure is subdivided into (1) knowledge and (2) intellectual abilities and skills (listed in the order of increasing complexity).

These three sources dealing with thinking have a number of views in common. Vinache differs from the other two in that he does little specific ordering of processes or abilities.

All three agree that thinking utilizes what are commonly called "experiences," past and present; moreover, these experiences are related and organized into concepts and generalizations, and applied as needed. They see thinking as abstract or symbolic, i.e., dealing with objects and events not present in the immediate environment. All three include inductive and deductive thinking, evaluating, problem solving, and creative thinking. They accept the fact that thinking for everyday life draws on all thinking processes to constantly varying extents and in ever shifting combinations.

Other research workers dealing with the thinking processes agree that "thinking" refers to a complex group of abilities (31, 39), that the term is not synonymous with intelligence (30, 39, 54), that thinking is specific to the situation (27), and that many factors influence thinking and the development of the ability to think (15, 38, 58, 66, 67, 77). Furthermore, evidence of thinking as defined begins in infancy (71); the ability to generalize from meaningful and concrete experiences begins to be apparent by three years of age (41, 59, 89, 90); and the ability to reason and form concepts develops gradually with accumulated experiences, learning, and age (24, 48, 53, 55, 64, 87). Although the young child may have difficulty expressing himself (41, 44, 49, 59), his thinking is the same qualitatively as that of adults (44).

III

The term "critical thinking" appears at times in the literature as differentiated from thinking in general. As stated before, Russell uses the term to denote one of the more complex thinking processes which involve high-level evaluation; Betts (11) appears to agree. The Taxonomy places evaluation at the top of its hierarchy. Some research studies, by virtue of the abilities they incorporate, draw on a broader use of the term (39, 60, 61, 79). The studies investigating inferring (9, 86), judging relevancy (36), applying facts (52), concept formation (59, 92), reasoning (48, 64) and generalizing (24, 90) are also often quoted as dealing with "higher-level" thought processes, or critical thinking.

As with "thinking" in general, "critical thinking" has been found to be relatively independent of general intelligence and knowledge of subject matter (20, 35, 39, 71, p. 292). Instruction in these abilities does not appear to change the relationship (35), although at least some critical thinking abilities can be improved by instructional guidance (3, 12, 22, 34, 39, 54, 72, 96). Moreover, the ability to do critical thinking in its broadest sense (evaluating, generalizing, problem solving, etc.) is present by the time the child enters school.

Although "critical thinking," when used, designates one segment of thinking in general, the nature and number of thinking processes included varies infinitely. Research evidence to delineate it clearly is lacking. Again its definition becomes one that is a result of (1) logic or (2) pragmatic considerations in order to stress the need for thinking that is more complex in contrast with the superficial.

IV

One of the questions commonly asked about thinking refers to a hierarchal order of processes to be used in developing them with students. Vinache makes no attempt to do this systematically; Russell does, pointing out that his six types of thinking differ in terms of complexity. Welch in one of his studies concludes that going from simple to complex problem solving necessitates the use of more mental processes simultaneously and consecutively and with greater efficiency; however, he reported it was impossible to determine which mental processes were functioning at any given moment (91).

What originally appeared to be a child's inability to generalize or solve problems (a possible indication of a hierarchy) now appears to be due to the lack of experience; within the limitations of his experiences a child thinks in the manner an adult does (44). Chronological age and number of years in school for a child appear to be very important in this respect (27, pp. 10–11) and both of these have a direct bearing on accumulation of experiences. Yet there is evidence that primary level children do not appear to be ready to deal with much more than is in their immediate environments even with instruction and with the ability to use all the thinking processes (70, p. 59).

There is substantial research evidence that concepts (an end product) vary in difficulty (13, 71, 88). Those closer to the object-level are acquired earlier and are basic to those more abstract. There is no evidence, however, that the abstracting and generalizing processes themselves vary.

Thus, proposed hierarchies for thinking abilities, to date, are primarily the product of logical thinking rather than research. If we could study the emergence and development of thinking processes in the very young child, as has been done for language development, we might find some answers to this question of relative difficulty. Unfortunately for investigations on thinking, language is more directly observable. General physiological maturation could be basic to dealing with any thinking process at a particular point in growth as it seems to be in vision and motor skills and as it has been suggested by Welch in regard to thinking (89). Hereditary, environmental, and personality factors might affect such levels for any individual.

The conclusion is: a hierarchy of difficulty for thinking processes or within thinking processes has not been established. Such a structure has been identified for concepts and it may well be that the number of concepts which are or must be manipulated, their familiarity and abstractness, the state of the individual and the complexity of the situation requiring thinking produce increasing levels of difficulty and complexity rather than the thinking processes themselves.

V

There are several important implications for reading comprehension and its development that can be drawn from the available information on thinking. First and foremost, thinking refers to a complex group of mental processes which utilize experiences. Furthermore, thinking is basic to living. It becomes imperative, then, that varied experiences be provided and that all thinking abilities be fostered and developed at every school level and in many activities. In order to do this, one must begin with the learner and with what he has already acquired; this will vary in different situations. Until the reader-to-be has learned to think, he cannot read and comprehend.

Thinking abilities cannot be assumed to exist. Intelligence, knowledge of subject matter, language facility, age: none of these can be used for prediction. Specific attention must be given to both evaluation and development of thinking.

The research indicates that, other things being equal, five- and six-year-olds can use the thinking processes. Thus, they are ready to profit from guidance in developing better thinking abilities. Moreover, beginners in reading are ready to infer, evaluate, organize, and apply what is read.

EXPERIENCES, CONCEPTS, AND LANGUAGE

Thus far in this paper, thinking has been stressed as one basic factor operating during reading. That one must have actual, direct experiences with which to think has already been pointed out. Moreover, both experiences and thinking abilities need to be developed prior to their use in reading, a process which imposes additional responsibilities on the reader.

In the reading task, one specific type of situation involving thinking, not only must the reader have experiences and concepts on which to draw and with which to think but these must be appropriate, i.e., enable him to reconstruct what the author is saying or implying. If the reader can build up a total structure of experiences with interrelationships and organization similar to the author's, he can interpret more accurately the author's presentation.

Reading has long been recognized as a "taking to" process and there is much evidence on the extreme importance of a background of experiences of innumerable kinds which are related, organized, and reorganized as needed (1, 4, 17, 23, 69, 74). Having experiences refers to "experiencing": anything an individual receives through his senses, his emotional reactions to these percepts, his use of them in thinking or any other activity, become a part of his experiential background.

Experiences, when related in some way, volitionally or otherwise, result in concepts. Any concept exists only in the nervous system of an individual; it may or may not be associated with a verbal symbol. Moreover, since concepts are formed under varying conditions (individual and situational) by everyone, a concept is personal; no two people will have identical concepts of any object, event, situation, or generalization. The more abstract (i.e., more inclusive and further removed from the concrete) the concept is, the more this becomes true. The concepts of "honesty" and "democracy" are examples.

Research evidence on concepts is accumulating (19, 71, 88). Development begins in pre-school years (44, 89) with direct experiences (46, 47, 65). For any given concept, the development moves in a gradual manner (27, 41) from concrete and simple to abstract and complex levels, depending on the number and kind of experiences (18, 45, 68, 91, 93). Learners enter schools with concepts of many kinds developed to varying degrees of abstractness. One of the important responsibilities of a teacher at any school level is to further the growth of clear and accurate concepts which can then be used in reading or any other activity.

Reading is a communication process using printed symbols. Since reading entails language, it must also be considered in terms of its nature and its development.

The prevalence of verbalism, or the use of language which does not refer to experiences and concepts, has been pointed out and discussed repeatedly (17, pp. 7–14, 25, 29, 51, 73). One reason for such widespread verbalism is the confusion that has existed between the language symbol and the internal cognitive system it represents. The concrete object, the concept, the conclusion, or thinking processes used are not language but are referred to through the use of language labels. Language is symbolic and refers to experiences; without the latter, language is meaningless. Thus, language ability, such as pronouncing the words in reading, cannot be used as proof that meaning exists in the individual. The fact that it has been so interpreted has helped to produce a wide-spread problem. Overemphasis on the use of language in evaluating understanding and learning has also contributed. As the meanings become more abstract, the problem becomes greater. Verbalism interferes with literal interpretation; critical interpretation by its nature breaks down further.

Language development (69, 78) as well as the interdependencies and the interrelationships among language abilities have received much attention in the literature (4, 5, 6, 11). The reader will recall that there was confusion about pre-schoolers' ability to think because of their inability to express themselves verbally; the thinking was present, the language development was not. Sufficient language facility is a prerequisite for reading. However, if the ability to interpret printed language literally is present, critical reading can and should be fostered.

LITERAL AND CRITICAL READING

Earlier in this paper, two premises were developed. First, reading is thinking with experiences and concepts in relation to printed language. Second, literal and critical reading are not synonymous.

The question arises: Is thinking related in any particular manner to literal reading as contrasted with critical reading? The latter has been hypothesized as necessitating "higher-level" mental processes, at times called "critical thinking." Is the differentiation between the categories of reading directly related to the level or nature of thinking necessitated?

In the discussion of thinking, it was concluded that, with the available research knowledge on thinking, it is not possible to structure a hierarchy of thinking processes. If such a structure exists, it has yet to be identified.

Is the reading task of such a nature that it demands particular thinking processes in a relatively pure form, like inductive thinking? There is no evidence to support such a conclusion.

The reading task involves first and foremost the reconstruction of the author's ideas (goal-directed thinking). The reader then may go beyond what the author states; he may apply the ideas to some problem or he may evaluate authenticity, to mention two possibilities. The thinking processes necessary to understand what one author says (literal reading) may be far more complex than the evaluation of what another author states (critical reading). If after difficult literal interpretation the reader must proceed to what is known as critical reading, the situation becomes even more complex.

Research indicates that literal reading involves at least some aspects of higher-level thinking. Problem-solving processes appear in the interpretation of a paragraph. Selecting what is relevant from one's experiences and rejecting what is irrelevant (evaluation) is a constant process in reading to "get the facts." Locating antecedents, interpreting punctuation or figurative language, determining sequence (particularly if inverted), or analyzing an unknown word may produce situations that call for problem solving. Deciding at which level of abstraction an author's concept falls or reorganizing personal experiences to reconstruct a writer's concept will involve inductive and deductive processes, evaluation and arriving at a conclusion. Understanding one sentence in a particular context may call for thinking of the most complex order, depending on the reader and the sentence.

Logically, reconstructing the facts represented by words is a relatively easy task compared to reading tasks that require more than understanding what is stated explicitly. However, the nature and complexity of the "facts" together with their language representations (language-experience relationships) vary from author to author, and may even vary from one piece of printed material to another by the same author. Familiarity with the facts as a result of (1) experiences and (2) the organization of these experiences in relation to the author's language will vary from reader to reader and from material to material with the same reader. All of these might necessitate more complex thinking; yet for any one reader with a given selection, getting the facts will be relatively easier than "reading between lines" or using the ideas to solve a problem.

Thus, for all practical purposes, literal and critical reading cannot be differentiated either on the basis of thinking processes or the language-experience relationships. Both will vary with the materials and the reader. Attempting to combine the two in some pattern for differentiation does not appear possible at the present time.

The differentiation can be made on the basis of the reader's purpose for reading, i.e., his need to understand what is stated (literal reading) as contrasted with his need to deal with the facts in some way (critical reading). In order to accomplish his goal, he must adjust to the nature of the facts and the language, and he must use whatever thinking processes he finds necessary. To the extent that he is helped to accumulate the necessary experiences and to acquire all the thinking and language abilities needed, to that extent he will be a successful reader.

References

1. MILLIE C. ALMY, *Children's Experiences Prior to First Grade and Success in Beginning Reading*, Contribution to Education, No. 954. New York: Bureau of Publications, Teachers College, Columbia University, 1949.
2. C. C. ANDERSON, "A Factorial Analysis of Reading," *British Journal of Educational Psychology*, 19 (1949), 220–221.
3. D. L. ARNOLD, "Testing the Ability to Use Data in the Fifth and Sixth Grades," *Educational Research Bulletin*, 17 (1938), 255–259, 278.
4. A. S. ARTLEY, Chairman. *Interrelationships Among the Language Arts*, Research Bulletin of the National Conference on Research in English. Champaign, Illinois: National Council of Teachers of English, 1954.
5. ——, "Oral-Language Growth and Reading Ability," *Elementary School Journal*, 53 (1953), 321–328.
6. ——, "Research Concerning Interrelationships Among the Language Arts," *Elementary English*, 27 (1950), 527–537.
7. ——, *A Study of Certain Relationships Between General Reading Comprehension and Reading Comprehension in Specific Subject Matter Areas*. Unpublished Doctoral Dissertation. State College, Pennsylvania: The State College of Pennsylvania, 1942.
8. W. BARBE and W. GRILK, "Correlations Between Reading Factors and IQ," *School and Society*, 75 (1952), 134–136.
9. R. C. BEDELL, *The Relationship Between the Ability to Recall and the Ability to Infer in Specific Learning Situations*. Unpublished Doctoral Dissertation. Kirksville, Missouri: University of Missouri, 1934.
10. E. A. BETTS, *Foundations of Reading Instruction*. New York: American Book Company, 1950.
11. ——, "Guidance in the Critical Interpretation of Language," *Elementary English*, 27 (1950), 9–22.
12. BLOOM, B. S. and BRODER, L. J. *Problem-solving Processes of College Students*, Supplementary Educational Monograph, No. 73. Chicago: University of Chicago Press, 1950.
13. BLOOM, B. S., (ed.). *Taxonomy of Educational Objectives*. Handbook

I: Cognitive Domain, New York: Longmans, Green and Company, 1956.

14. G. L. BOND and E. B. WAGNER, *Teaching the Child to Read.* New York: The Macmillan Company, 1950.

15. K. W. BRALY, "The Influence of Past Experience in Visual Perception," *Journal of Experimental Psychology,* 16 (1933), 613–643.

16. M. E. BROOM, M. A. DUNCAN, D. EMIG, and J. STUCBER, *Effective Reading Instruction.* New York: McGraw-Hill Book Company, Inc., 1951.

17. W. A. BROWNELL, Chairman. *The Measurement of Understanding,* 45 Yearbook of the National Society for the Study of Education, Part I. Chicago: University of Chicago Press, 1946.

18. W. A. BROWNELL and G. HENDRICKSON, "How Children Learn Information, Concepts, and Generalizations," in Anderson, G. H., Chairman, *Learning and Instruction,* 49th Yearbook of the National Society for the Study of Education, Part I, pp. 92–128. Chicago: University of Chicago Press, 1950.

19. J. S. BRUNER, J. J. GOODNOW, and G. A. AUSTIN, *A Study of Thinking.* New York: John Wiley and Sons, Inc., 1956.

20. N. M. BUCK and R. H. OJEMANN, "The Relation Between Ability in Scientific Thinking and Behavior in Situations Involving Choice," *Journal of Experimental Education,* 11 (1942), 215–219.

21. W. H. BURTON, *Reading in Child Development.* Indianapolis: The Bobbs-Merrill Company, Inc., 1956.

22. R. P. CARROLL, *An Experimental Study of Comprehension in Reading with Special Reference to the Reading of Directions,* Contributions to Education, No. 245. New York: Bureau of Publications, Teachers College, Columbia University, 1926.

23. R. W. CHAPMAN, *The Effect of Readiness Activities Prior to Reading at Selected Grade Levels.* Unpublished Doctoral Dissertation. Pullman, Washington: The State College of Washington, 1951.

24. W. C. CROXTON, "Pupils' Ability to Generalize," *School Science and Mathematics,* 36 (1936), 627–634.

25. E. DALE, "Relation of Reading to Other Forms of Learning," in W. S. Gray, Editor, *Reading in General Education,* pp. 45–76. Washington, D.C.: American Council on Education, 1940.

26. F. B. DAVIS, *Fundamental Factors of Comprehension in Reading.* Unpublished Doctoral Dissertation. Cambridge, Massachusetts: Harvard University, 1941.

27. JEAN M. DEUTSCHE, *The Development of Children's Concepts of Causal Relations,* Institute of Child Welfare, Monograph No. 13. Minneapolis: University of Minnesota Press, 1937.

28. J. C. DEWEY, "The Acquisition of Facts as a Measure of Reading Comprehension," *Elementary School Journal,* 35 (1935), 346–348.

29. ——, *A Case Study of Reading Comprehension Difficulties in American History*. Unpublished Doctoral Dissertation. Iowa City: State University of Iowa, 1931.

30. A. E. DICKINSON and F. T. TYLER, "An Experimental Study of the Generalizing Ability of Grade Two Pupils," *Journal of Educational Psychology*, 35 (1944), 432–441.

31. E. R. DOWNING, "The Elements and Safeguards of Scientific Thinking," *Scientific Monthly*, 26 (1928), 231–232.

32. D. D. DURRELL, *Improving Reading Instruction*. Yonkers-on-Hudson, New York: World Book Company, 1956.

33. L. C. FAY, "The Relationship Between Specific Reading Skills and Selected Areas of Sixth Grade Achievement," *Journal of Educational Research*, 43 (1950), 541–547.

34. FRANCES L. FERRELL, "An Experiment in the Development of Critical Thinking," *American Teacher*, 30 (1946), 24–26.

35. E. J. FURST, "The Relationship Between Tests of Intelligence and Tests of Critical Thinking and Knowledge," *Journal of Educational Research*, 43 (1950), 614–625.

36. ROMA GANS, *A Study of Critical Reading Comprehension in the Intermediate Grades*, Contributions to Education, No. 811. New York: Bureau of Publications, Teachers College, Columbia University, 1940.

37. A. I. GATES, *The Improvement of Reading*. New York: The Macmillan Company, 1949.

38. J. A. GENGERELLI, "Mutual Interference in the Evolution of Concepts," *American Journal of Psychology*, 38 (1927), 639–648.

39. E. M. GLASER, *An Experiment in the Development of Critical Thinking*, Contributions, Teachers College, Columbia University, 1941.

40. LILLIAN GRAY and DORA RUSE, *Teaching Children to Read*. New York: The Ronald Press Company, 1957.

41. OLIVE GRIGSBY, "An Experimental Study of the Development of Concepts of Relationships in Preschool Children as Evidenced by Their Expressive Ability," *Journal of Experimental Education*, 1 (1932), 144–162.

42. W. E. HALL and F. P. ROBINSON, "An Analytical Approach to the Study of Reading Skills," *Journal of Educational Psychology*, 36 (1945), 429–442.

43. A. J. HARRIS, *How to Increase Reading Ability*, New York: Longmans, Green and Company, 1956.

44. VICTORIA HAZLITT, "Children's Thinking," *British Journal of Psychology*, 20 (1930), 354–361.

45. EDNA HEIDBREDER, "The Attainment of Concepts: III, The Process," *Journal of Psychology*, 24 (1947), 93–138.

46. ——, "The Attainment of Concepts: VI, Exploratory Experiments on

Conceptualization at Perceptual Levels," *Journal of Psychology*, 27 (1949), 3–39.

47. ——, "Language and Concepts," *Psychological Bulletin*, 33 (1936), 724.

48. ——, "Problem Solving in Children and Adults," *Journal of Genetic Psychology*, 35 (1928), 522–545.

49. ——, "A Study of the Evolution of Concepts," *Psychological Bulletin*, 31 (1934), 673.

50. KATHLEEN B. HESTER, *Teaching Every Child to Read*. New York: Harper and Brothers, 1955.

51. E. HORN, *Methods of Instruction in the Social Studies*, Chapters V and VI. New York: Charles Scribner's and Sons, 1937.

52. J. E. HORROCKS, "The Relation Between Knowledge of Human Development and the Use of Such Knowledge," *Journal of Applied Psychology*, 30 (1946), 501–508.

53. KAI JENSON, "The Social Studies," in *Child Development and the Curriculum*, Thirty-Eighth Yearbook of the National Society for the Study of Education, Part I, pp. 325–360. Bloomington, Illinois: Public School Publishing Company, 1939.

54. A. JEWETT, "Detecting an Analyzing Propaganda," *English Journal*, 29 (1940), 105–115.

55. J. I. LACEY and K. H. DALLENBACK, "Acquisitions by Children of the Cause-Effect Relationships," *American Journal of Psychology*, 52 (1939), 103–110.

56. R. S. LANGSAM, *A Factorial Analysis of Reading Ability*. Unpublished Doctoral Dissertation. New York: New York University, 1941.

57. W. T. LOFLAND and B. T. RITTER, "The Relation Between Reading Ability as Measured by Certain Standardized Tests and the Ability Required in the Interpretation of Printed Material Involving Reason," *Elementary School Journal*, 24 (1924), 529–546.

58. L. LONG and L. WELCH, "The Influence of Levels of Abstractness on Reasoning Ability," *Journal of Psychology*, 13 (1942), 41–59.

59. L. LONG and L. WELCH, "Reasoning Ability in Young Children," *Journal of Psychology*, 12 (1941), 21–44.

60. ETHEL S. MANEY, *Literal and Critical Reading in Science*. Unpublished Doctoral Dissertation. Philadelphia: Temple University, 1952.

61. A. J. MAZURKIEWICZ, *An Investigation of the Nature of Reading Comprehension*. Unpublished Doctoral Dissertation. Philadelphia: Temple University, 1957.

62. P. MCKEE, *The Teaching of Reading in the Elementary School*. Boston: Houghton Mifflin Company, 1948.

63. MARGARET G. MCKIM, *Guiding Growth in Reading*. New York: The Macmillan Company, 1955.

64. THOMAS V. MOORE, *The Reasoning Ability of Children in the First Five Years of School Life*. New York: Williams and Wilkins, 1929.

65. M. E. OAKES, *Children's Explanations of Natural Phenomena.* Contribution to Education, No. 926. New York: Bureau of Publications, Teachers College, Columbia University, 1947.
66. W. W. OSBORNE, "An Experiment in Teaching Resistance to Propaganda," *Journal of Experimental Education,* 8 (1939), 1–17.
67. H. B. REED, "Factors Influencing the Learning and Retention of Concepts: I. Influence of Set; II. Influence of Length of Series; IV. Influence of Complexity of Stimuli," *Journal of Experimental Psychology,* 36 (1946), 71–87, 166–179, 252–261.
68. S. REICHARD, M. SCHNEIDER, and D. RAPPAPORT, "The Development of Concept Formation in Children," *American Journal of Orthopsychiatry,* 14 (1944), 156–162.
69. D. H. RUSSELL, Chairman. *Child Development and the Language Arts,* A Research Bulletin of the National Conference on Research in English. Champaign, Illinois: National Council of Teachers of English, 1953.
70. D. H. RUSSELL, *Children Learn to Read.* Boston: Ginn and Company, 1949.
71. ——, *Children's Thinking.* Boston: Ginn and Company, 1956.
72. RACHEL SALISBURY, "A Study of the Transfer Effects of Training in Logical Organization," *Journal of Educational Research,* 28 (1934), 241–254.
73. J. S. SEEGERS, Chairman. *Interpreting Language: An Essential of Understanding,* Research Bulletin of the National Conference on Research in English, 1951.
74. MARY C. SERRA, *A Study of Fourth Grade Children's Comprehension of Certain Verbal Abstractions.* Unpublished Doctoral Dissertation. Philadelphia: Temple University, 1951.
75. W. D. SHELDON, "Children's Experiences in Reading," in V. E. Herrick and L. B. Jacobs, Editors, *Children and the Language Arts.* Englewood Cliffs, N.J.: Prentice-Hall, Inc., 1955.
76. J. H. SHORES, *Reading and Study Skills as Related to Comprehension of Science and History in the Ninth Grade.* Unpublished Doctoral Dissertation. Minneapolis: University of Minnesota, 1940.
77. J. H. SINCLAIR and R. S. TOLMAN, "An Attempt to Study the Effect of Scientific Training upon Prejudice and Illogicality of Thought," *Journal of Educational Psychology,* 24 (1933), 362–370.
78. NILA B. SMITH, Chairman. *Readiness for Reading and Related Language Arts,* a Research Bulletin of the National Conference on Research in English. Champaign, Illinois: National Council of Teachers of English, 1950.
79. E. ELONA SOCHOR, *Literal and Critical Reading in Social Studies.* Unpublished Doctoral Dissertation. Philadelphia: Temple University, 1952.
80. RUTH STRANG, CONSTANCE M. McCULLOUGH, and A. TRAXLER, *Prob-*

lems in the Improvement of Reading. New York: McGraw-Hill Book Company, 1955.

81. ESTHER J. SWENSON, *The Relation of Ability to Read Materials of the Type Used in Studying Science to Eighth Grade Achievement.* Unpublished Master's Thesis. Minneapolis: University of Minnesota, 1938.

82. E. L. THORNDIKE, "The Psychology of Thinking in the Case of Reading," *Psychological Review,* 24 (1917), 220–234.

83. ——, "Reading as Reasoning: A Study of Mistakes in Paragraph Reading," *Journal of Educational Psychology,* 8 (1917), 323–332.

84. ——, "The Reading of Sentences," *Elementary School Journal,* 18 (1917), 98–114.

85. M. A. TINKER, *Teaching Elementary Reading.* New York: Appleton-Century-Crofts, Inc., 1952.

86. W. L. TYLER, "Measuring the Ability to Infer," *Educational Research Bulletin,* Ohio State University, 9 (1930), 475–480.

87. W. E. VINACHE, "The Investigation of Concept Formation," *Psychological Bulletin,* 48 (1951), 1–31.

88. ——, *The Psychology of Thinking.* New York: McGraw-Hill Book Company, Inc., 1952.

89. L. WELCH, "The Genetic Development of the Associational Structures of Abstract Thinking," *Journal of Genetic Psychology,* 56 (1940), 175–206.

90. ——, "The Span of Generalization Below the Two-Year Age Level," *Journal of Genetic Psychology,* 55 (1939), 269–297.

91. ——, "The Transition from Simple to Complex Forms of Learning," *Journal of Genetic Psychology,* 71 (1947), 223–251.

92. L. WELCH and L. LONG, "A Further Investigation of the Higher Structural Phases of Concept Formation," *Journal of Psychology,* 10 (1940), 211–220.

93. ——, "The Higher Structural Phases of Concept Formation of Children," *Journal of Psychology,* 9 (1940), 59–95.

94. L. R. WHEELER and V. D. WHEELER, "The Relationship Between Reading Ability and Intelligence Among University Freshmen," *Journal of Educational Psychology,* 40 (1949), 230–238.

95. P. WITTY, *Reading in Modern Education.* Boston: D. C. Heath and Company, 1949.

96. J. W. WRIGHTSTONE, *Appraisal of Newer Elementary School Practices.* New York: Bureau of Publications, Teachers College, Columbia University, 1938.

97. G. A. YOAKAM, *Basal Reading Instruction.* New York: McGraw-Hill Book Company, Inc., 1955.

7. Promoting Growth in Critical Reading

Frances Oralind Triggs

Critical reading is truly the interpretation of symbols. Historically, when there was little printed matter available, people's behavior was guided by interpretation of symbols, but the symbols were not the printed word. Learning came only from an individual's limited surroundings. In this day, when rich written sources are available, we tend to forget that all reading, especially critical reading, is based on interpreting symbols. It is apparent, when we carefully consider the matter, that a word or picture becomes a symbol only when meaning is attached to it. The meaning which is attributed to a symbol is not intrinsic within the passage or picture or experience but is there only when the reader supplies that meaning.

READING AS A THREE-WAY PROCESS

Conceivably and justifiably reading can be considered a one-way process, a two-way process, or a three-way process depending on the purpose for which the reading is being done. If a person is reading to get information only, then all he must do is to find a specific date, name or other fact, and his purpose is accomplished. If his purpose is to determine the accuracy of the fact, then reading becomes a two-way process for the information gained from reading must be checked against information the reader has or will obtain from some other source. If the purpose of reading is to gain knowledge, to modify or add to the information the reader already has, or to gain background for interpreting what the author says, then reading becomes a three-way process. The reader reads not only to add to understandings he has, but to modify and perhaps change those understandings. He also must judge as he reads whether the author's background and subject matter checks with his own previous knowledge gained from reading and other real and vicarious experiences; but more than that, he must check more than one author in this manner to make such judgments.

Critical reading then requires a contribution by both the author and the reader, and an interplay between these two contributions which usually results in a new understanding—something more than or different from the original contributions. Thus critical reading, at least in one sense, results in learning, in education itself.

Certain comprehension skills are necessary to critical reading: ability to

"Promoting Growth in Critical Reading," by Frances Oralind Triggs, *The Reading Teacher*, XXV (February 1959), 158–164. Reprinted with permission of Frances Oralind Triggs and the International Reading Association.

read for main ideas and details and to distinguish between the two, ability to recognize inferences and conclusions, and ability to adapt the rate at which materials are read to the situation met. In order to apply these comprehension skills, a reader must have, or gain as he reads, understanding of the words used by the author. These understandings of words are gained from actual experiences, or from vicarious experiences which often come from reading. Thus again the reading process leads to an apparent parallelism with learning in general, or with education itself as broadly conceived.

TEACHING OF CRITICAL READING

If this seeming parallelism between critical reading and learning or education seems confusing, perhaps examples from the process of reading done at the various levels of education will help to clarify this relationship. Reading and learning do overlap but they are not synonymous. "Critical" reading is critical only in terms of the background of the reader and is not confined to the reading of what would be considered by us all as markedly difficult material. The extent to which reading is "critical" reading is relative in terms of who is doing the reading and what is being read.

For example, the principle of "reading readiness" in its narrow meaning as applied to preschool and early formal education provides a parallel to growth in critical reading. All teachers accept the fact that a child, even if he can learn to recognize words, often cannot understand, cannot truly "read" these words. Thus the importance of his having in his auditory or meaning vocabulary the words he is learning to recognize at sight through application of word attack skills. And how does a child come to understand a new word? Through experiences, using reading, and avenues of learning other than reading, to supply meanings which are attached to words. These words then become the symbols of the experiences. This process is accomplished by stimulation through the various senses so necessary to education, especially in these early years: smell, taste, feel, sight, and hearing. And the ability of one sense to stimulate another or others should not be forgotten either. A child may say, "That story makes me think of . . ." The listener (later the reader) begins to react to the stimulus of words by calling up previous experience. Is this not a step toward his later doing so in critical reading?

LEARNING CRITICAL READING IN AN EXACT SCIENCE

We find another parallel in the laboratory experiment in the science class. The student has now learned many reading skills which he can apply, but he meets words technical to the subject which he does not entirely understand, and the good teacher realizes that to make the meanings of these words completely clear, they should be illustrated as well as discussed, and the ideas for which they stand should be described. Let's take, for instance, *chlorine*. There are many derivatives of this word. The teacher may do a simple laboratory experiment which has as its purpose illustrating the volatile characteristics of chlorine when free. Thus he takes some compound of chlorine, heats it, or uses some agent to release the gas. The students smell the chlorine. They are asked of what it reminds them. Most will say they have smelled something similar when they ran a bath, or when they went in swimming, or give other experiences which are stimulated by the smell apparent when chlorine becomes a free gas. Then the teacher will try to relate this experience with chlorine to other experiences by comparing the characteristics of this gas to other gasses with which the students may have had direct contact: ammonia, gasoline, and the pungent smell from solids such as wax. There will be discussion of the uses of chlorine in industry, medicine, and in everyday life, and the properties which make it valuable for these uses. Now the teacher has supplied "readiness," has made the symbol, i.e., the word *chlorine,* really meaningful to the student. Supposing now the student reads in the newspaper about the cost of water purification by the use of chemicals, one of which is chlorine, and by the use of other methods. As a voter now, he reads what is said critically and with interest because he brings to his reading previous knowledge. Again, he may get a sore throat while at camp and may remember the discussion of the disinfecting qualities of chlorine. He gargles a solution of table salt. Thus his real understanding of this symbol has twice contributed to his experience. And as his experience grows, his understanding becomes greater.

It is through such processes that a background is built up for critical reading. At this stage the student is able to add to his knowledge through reading about chlorine, for it is a meaningful symbol to him. He can also check what he reads not only against what one author says, but against combinations of what authorities say and what he knows. This is critical reading.

LEARNING TO READ CRITICALLY IN THE SOCIAL SCIENCES AND THE HUMANITIES

Critical reading in an area of exact science has been illustrated. Critical reading where human relations, feelings, affect, and emotions are involved becomes even more complex.

Again we go back to the readiness principle. In early years, the child's reading skills are not yet as mature as his feelings about a familiar subject. The teacher, therefore, uses pictures to convey broad connotations for words being introduced. "Reading pictures" is a familiar technique in the early grades. In one picture a child is crying (a symbol!) and a dog lies on the road. A man with a white jacket (a symbol!) and a black bag (also a symbol!) kneels beside the dog. The teacher asks the children how each person in the picture "feels." The children suggest such words as *sad, sorry, sick to the stomach, ache, cry, hurt.* These words are not parallel as suggested by the children, but they can be woven into a story which can be read and which may have as its purpose an illustration of how words express feelings. Children must grow in their understandings of such words as *love, hate, beautiful, wonderful, sorry,* and others like them which will make reading critically in the social sciences and humanities real to them, or such reading will be neither enjoyable nor profitable. Teachers know that the feeling expressed by the word *sorry* may not have been experienced in relation to the word. There is a time in a child's life when he does not know this word and until it is experienced, and is in some manner connected with the word itself, it almost defies explanation. In some manner the word itself must become the symbol for the feeling, and the feeling must be experienced many times to make the symbol a meaningful tool of critical reading. Perhaps the best example of *word* reading (the reader says the words but they stimulate no meaning or thought in the reader's mind) is seen when many students are prematurely, and without adequate "readiness" activities, pushed into reading some of our great classics. What does reading of *A Tale of Two Cities* mean to the student who literally knows nothing of the French Revolution and of the life and people of England at that time. He has never *felt* the oppression of a similar social situation and this may be his first exposure to it through reading. He has not lived through either recent great war; communism, fascism, and certainly oppressive monarchies are only words to him. Here television and discussion of the mob action in terms of passages read aloud become valuable readiness activities for reading critically. This is a sociological as well as an historical novel; it certainly was not put into the curriculum for the story itself. Students are supposed to grow in their ability to assess the effects of methods of governing people. One intended outgrowth is surely the fact that government of the people functions only so long as an informed citizenry makes it function. Another intended outgrowth is that it is dangerous to draw hard and fast conclusions which cannot be modified by experience. Students must learn that in the area of human values there are no final conclusions. Holding one's judgments in abeyance in order to gain enough information on which to be critical is an important learning. Citizens may revolt from oppression, but the degree of oppression is not the same to every person or to all groups of persons. Why have not predicted revolts taken place in Russia and China? Actually for many Russians and Chinese who have never known self-government, freedom of expression and action, present conditions may not seem like oppression. The reader must bring understandings of this kind to his reading if he is to read critically.

How does the student gain the background to read critically in the humanities and the social sciences? By making reading a three-way process! It can be three-way only when the reader's skills are so sharp that they are almost automatically applied. The skillful golfer need not be told what club to use or what stroke to try but senses it from the situation and can immediately call on the skills needed and shift to them automatically. Just so the *reader* must be able to shift from skill to skill, sometimes applying them in quick sequence, unconscious of the fact that this is what he is doing in order that his energies may all be on recalling, sorting, checking and seeking understandings. This is true of all reading skills: vocabulary, word attack, and comprehension skills.

Teaching Word Attack Skills and Learning to Read Critically

A great deal is being written and said concerning methods of attacking words and ways in which these skills are being taught. It is important for a student to understand these skills intellectually and to be able to use them so easily that he is unconscious of the fact that he is using them except where he needs consciously to call upon them when meeting a difficult, unknown word. These skills function to support the reader when reading critically as well as reading for other purposes. As the reader practices these word attack skills, they become automatic, partially at least, through what a psychologist would call cue reduction. At first, when a skill is learned, the user has to go through every step consciously, each step stimulating the next as one line of poetry calls to mind the words of the next line. Soon, as the reader's use of the skill progresses, the steps are applied in such close conjunction one to another that he is unaware of his use of the separate steps. He may even skip some steps because they are not needed to get to the end result, but he probably does not know this.

However, the student must learn word attack skills in meaningful context, for the purpose of all reading is understanding. There is no time when reading is merely word calling. Yet the rote learning of word attack skills tends to result in word calling, not reading. Previously in this article reading has been described as a one-way, two-way, or three-way process. These processes become increasingly complex but all are based on understanding of what is read. Word reading is none of these, and the learning of word attack skills without reference to the meaning of the words to which they are applied has two fallacies: first, there is no purpose for recognizing the word if it calls up no meaning, for without meaning the word cannot be used in reading, and second, the meaning of the context in which an unknown word is found should itself be used as a part of the attack the reader takes to make the word meaningful.

There is probably no more difficult problem met by a teacher than that of helping the "word reader" to make reading meaningful. Such a student can often parrot all of the word attack skills but cannot apply them. Research has established the importance of the teaching of all the reading *skills*, but they must be taught in meaningful context in order that they may be "transferred" and used in the reading of all materials and for all purposes. This is a most important principle. Early psychological research which resulted in the finding that transfer of training is not automatic, must in fact be taught, is the basis of this principle. If word attack skills are not so taught, then it is almost certain that the reader will not be able to use them to help him when reading for purposes much less demanding than critical reading.

CRITICAL READING OF BIASED MATERIAL

Another outgrowth of the ability to read critically is the ability of the reader to recognize the use of words weighted according to the result desired but not necessarily according to the facts presented, or those which are studiously not presented. The reader, aware that material presented in a biased manner is intended to sway those who are exposed to it, is able to check both what is and what is not presented. He will withhold judgment on critical issues, political and social, until he has adequate basis for coming to a considered conclusion. Propaganda can be either good or bad, often according to the bias of the writer, but it should be recognized for what it is, and the critical reader is in a position to interpret what is presented, checking from his own background of present knowledge or the knowledge he will obtain before acting on the basis of what he has read.

SPEED AND CRITICAL READING

Reading critically, that is, reading to check thoroughly what is written, illustrates well the fact that the reading process involves a close association of the writer, the reader, and the world around them. The impression that reading is a simple race of the eyes, excluding the mind, is a direct result of the putting a premium on speed of reading alone without regard to the effect of reading on the reader and the contribution the reader makes to the reading process. It is odd that the need for flexibility in using reading skills according to the purpose and background of the reader for reading and the material being read should have led to such overemphasis on speed. However, a careful consideration of the need for ability to read critically, which also involves flexibility (many rates of reading according to the need) will help to make the rates at which a reader reads little more than a symptom of his other skills and not a major point of attack in improving reading skills. This should be remembered especially when teaching adults to improve the efficiency with which they approach their reading tasks. These persons may be anywhere along the scale of proficiency in any of the reading skills. Teaching these adults to increase the rate at which they read without first diagnosing other skills is a very superficial approach to teaching them. Almost without testing, other difficulties of the adult reader become evident. The person who spells poorly, the man who can't concentrate, the person with careless speech characteristics, and the individual whose style of written expression is inaccurate, is exhibiting behavior related to his language skills and, therefore, symptomatic of the efficiency of his reading skills, just as the rate at which he reads may be symptomatic. No one of a person's reading skills can be treated without regard to others if a professional job of teaching reading is to be done.

SUMMARY

Critical reading is similar to the pinnacle reached after a steep climb. It involves the use of all of the reading skills the reader has, but it includes more; to read critically one must read *beyond* the material presented by the author and involve one's own experiences and previous learning. Critical reading also involves adding to the reader's knowledge. It is, therefore, evident that critical reading should be taught at every developmental level. The teacher of the first grade knows that teaching critical reading is as important as teaching word attack and comprehension skills. Thinking is the basis of critical reading and every child challenged to use his ability can learn to read what for his level of understanding is critical. It is the failure to emphasize at all levels the three-way reading processes, along with the teaching to the level of mastery of the basic reading skills, that causes some of our students to accept as truth whatever they see in print, failing to react personally in such a way that fallacies become apparent. They never have learned to read critically!

8. Attitudes and Critical Reading

Josephine A. Piekarz

There are many ways that attitudes can be related to reading. For example, self-concept as an attitude can be related to reading achievement; attitudes toward books, reading, teachers, and school can be related to various facets of reading, to the amount of reading engaged in, to reading success and failure; and so on. I have chosen to discuss the effects of readers' attitudes toward what they read on their reading performance. Therefore, this discussion should be applicable to all age and grade levels —whether you personally are concerned with reading in the primary grades, in the middle grades, in high school, or in college. Critical reading pertains to all these levels and can be carried on in some form from first grade through the adult years.

In order to make this discussion meaningful and in order to ensure that communication between you and me takes place, we need to establish what is meant by *attitudes* and what is meant by *critical reading*. More correctly, I should let you in on what I mean by these terms as I'm going to use them in my discussion today. Let's begin with *attitudes*.

Borrowing from the psychologist, Hilgard,[1] "An attitude represents both an orientation toward or away from some object, concept, or situation, and a readiness to respond in a predetermined manner to these or related objects, concepts, or situations." Both orientation and readiness to respond have emotional, motivational, and intellectual aspects. They may be in part unconscious. Attitudes denote bias, preconceptions, convictions, feelings and emotions, hopes and fears. They form the emotional screen through which we view the world. Opinions are the verbal formulations of attitudes. Attitudes tend to be stable and usually reveal a consistency among the feelings, beliefs, and overt actions called forth by the stimuli of these attitudes. If, for example, the source of an attitude, such as the United Nations, evokes pleasant and favorable feelings, it is also likely to elicit beliefs about its effectiveness and value—such as, world peace is possible only through the United Nations, and to lead to actions consonant with the belief—such as, contributing financial support to the United Nations.

Attitudes are acquired, over time, as by-products of one's experiences. Almost every thing or idea in a person's life-experience can become the source of an attitude, but not every person has a discernible or measurable attitude with respect to every possible thing or idea—either because some

"Attitudes and Critical Reading," by Josephine A. Piekarz, is reprinted by permission from *Dimensions of Critical Reading*, XI (1964), University of Delaware, 134–144.

things and ideas may simply not exist in his life-experience or because they are not psychologically significant enough to result in a crystallization of his emotional and motivational dispositions around them. Once an attitude is formulated, it functions as a filter through which all future things, ideas, and experiences are processed by that person, affecting both perceptual and cognitive processes.

Attitudes are private and unique to individuals. Each person's complex of attitudes differs from everyone else's. At the same time, similar attitudes may be shared by groups of people such as by the members of a family, by people living in various sections of a country, by people of a given nation, by members of political, religious, and social groups—or even by separated and unrelated people. Attitudes may be favorable or unfavorable and they range in intensity from extreme approval and whole-hearted acceptance through neutrality to extreme disapproval and complete rejection. In the presence of strong attitudes, people tend to act on an emotional level rather than on an objective and rational level. No effort is going to be made here today to distinguish among preferences, attitudes, prejudices, and complexes. Nor will we be concerned here with how attitudes are measured or how they are formed. Our only concern will be how attitudes, once formed, affect our reading.

Critical reading is the other term that needs amplification to ensure effective communication. Reading is the receptive end of the written communication process. It consists of many highly interrelated and simultaneously occurring subskills, involving primarily the reconstruction of speech from printed symbols and the concurrent reconstruction of the meanings represented by the speech—for written English is manually recorded speech and speech is a phonemic representation of reality. In the initial stages of learning to read, word identification or the reconstruction of speech from printed symbols is carried on at a conscious level. After adequate fluency in word identification has been achieved, this part of the reading process recedes to a subconscious level while attention is directed toward the meanings represented by the symbols—until an unfamiliar word is encountered and speech is again consciously reconstructed. The meanings symbolically represented via speech and recorded by writing must be understood by the reader if communication is to succeed.

Meaning can be analyzed and classified in many different ways. Try reviewing the literature on this topic and you will readily see what I mean. I'm taking the liberty of splitting it up into three segments—literal, interpretive, and evaluative. We usually get evidence of meaning, or more correctly stated, understanding in reading, from answers to questions, although free verbalizations can provide this information too. Meaning, of course, is not restricted to reading but relates to language in general. We stated earlier that writing represents speech and that speech represents reality wherein meaning exists or resides.

Literal comprehension involves merely the awareness or recognition of explicitly stated facts. It does not extend beyond the surface value of the words and punctuation. This kind of understanding is concerned with "What does it say?", not with "What does it mean?" Frequently, questions of the *who, what, when,* and *where* types are asked at this level and the answers, of course, are clearly right or wrong because the information is given and leaves no room for personal opinion or ambiguity. Included among these understandings are the identification of stated facts and details and the sequence of details, identification of referents, understanding of punctuation, association of quotations with speakers, recognition of person addressed, association of multiple word meanings in appropriate contexts, grasp of double negatives and unusual word order, understanding of simple, compound, and complex sentences, and so on. This kind of understanding is literal and mechanical and requires no imagination, creativity, or special reasoning ability. Since it is limited to the given facts, the only background information and knowledge it involves is that experience necessary to give basic meaning to language, to the particular language used in the selection being read. Essentially, all understanding is dependent upon experience—a person's experience at any time being the sum of everything he has seen, heard, felt, smelled, and tasted—and intellectually processed. Whatever a person has derived from these experiences and retained, equals his vocabulary and knowledge at any given time. In other words, neurologically processed, experience becomes knowledge and information expressed through words. It is in the light of this information and knowledge that a person understands whatever he reads. We cannot reasonably expect a pupil to understand something he has never experienced in some way or that cannot be deduced from what he has experienced. Experience, information and knowledge, and vocabulary are inextricably intertwined.

Interpretation refers to those meanings that are implied in the writing and which must be inferred by the reader. *How* and *why* questions are frequently of this order. This kind of understanding is concerned with "What does it mean?" rather than with "What does it say?" It involves what is often referred to as reading between or behind the lines; it involves reasoning with the facts that are recognized at the literal comprehension level. Now ability to note relationships and make associations between the stated facts and one's experience is vital—as is a vast fund of background information and knowledge. Still, these understandings are limited to the "ideational content" of the material. We take the facts that are given and reason with them in relation to everything else that we know. We are obliged, however, to accept the facts and information at face value and reason accordingly—whether we like them or dislike them, approve of them or disapprove of them, agree with them or disagree with them, accept them or reject them. Errors in this kind of understanding may be due to the misidentification of facts at the literal comprehension level, to the selection of wrong or inappropriate facts to reason with, to incorrect reasoning with the right facts, or to lack of adequate background information and knowledge—or to any combination of these things. Included among these understandings are likely to be inferences of all kinds, implications, conclusions, generalizations, comparisons and contrasts, assumptions, relationships of various kinds: anticipation of events, prediction of outcomes, identification of character traits and emotional reactions and motives of characters and so forth.

The evaluative category is that which involves the personal reaction of the reader to the material he reads—to the facts expressed and the ideas implied as well as to the writer and writing as author and composition. The reader weighs, judges, and evaluates against some sort of criteria and in the light of all that he knows. Evaluation cannot be carried on in a vacuum; it requires a vast fund of cumulated knowledge. Included among the many specific kinds of understandings in this category are judgments concerning accuracy, relevancy, authenticity, authoritativeness, validity, completeness, truthfulness, recency, recognition of fact and opinion, propaganda, slant, bias, prejudice, different points of view, ambiguities and discrepancies, omission of facts, irony and sarcasm, half truths, emotionally charged words, exaggerated claims; identification of the author's purpose, mood, tone, and intent. In addition, it includes evaluation of values presented, of the quality of writing and so on. In other words, for this kind of understanding the reader must get out on some vantage point outside the ideational content and react appropriately to the stated facts and implied ideas as well as to all the additional things that are an inherent part of the communication.

Critical readers are those who, in addition to identifying facts accurately as they read, engage in interpretive and evaluative thinking—they project the literal meanings against their own background of experience, reasoning with and evaluating the stated facts and implied ideas. Noncritical readers, on the other hand, are those who restrict their thinking to the identification of the clearly stated facts and accept these facts literally and unquestioningly.

We now finally come to the purpose of this paper—a consideration of the relationship between the attitudes of readers toward the content of the material they read and their reading performance. The process of reading involves perceptual abilities as well as conceptual abilities, the perceptual abilities operating more heavily in word identification and the conceptual abilities more heavily in the understanding of meaning represented by the language symbols. Research evidence indicates that attitudes can and do affect both the perceptual as well as the conceptual abilities in reading.

Visual perception, of course, is basic to the reading process—that is, in ordinary reading using ordinary printed material—for what we understand is dependent upon the printed words we see. It is disquieting to realize that the printed words we see are not necessarily the words that are printed in the book. I'm sure that you have all heard of the tired Wall Street broker who was commuting home to the suburbs at the end of a hard day of work. As he sat down in the train, he opened up his newspaper to read and was elated to see a big headline that said, STACKS OF BLONDES. He grabbed his briefcase ready to disembark before the train moved. However, a close second look revealed that the headline really said, STOCKS AND BONDS, so he relaxed and continued on home.

Experiments have been done which prove that we often see what we expect to see in the light of our attitudes, emotions, and expectations rather than what is actually there. A frequently cited study is the one in which a number of words were projected on a screen by tachistoscope to a group of students.[2] Among the words presented were six nonsense syllables. Half the students had been told previously that the words would be related to birds or animals; the other half had been told that they would relate to travel or transportation. As expected, the majority of students expecting to see words relating to birds and animals saw the six nonsense syllables as real words relating to birds and animals; those expecting to see words relating to travel or transportation actually saw real words relating to travel and transportation rather than nonsense syllables. Hence, *chack* was seen as *chick* or *check, sael* was seen as *seal* or *sail, pasrort* was seen as *parrot* or *passport,* and so on.

While all people supposedly seek to perceive things clearly and correctly, attitudes can distort what is actually seen. This is especially true when ambiguity is involved. For example, people who cannot tolerate ambiguity show it not only in their social attitudes but also in their perceptual responses in the laboratory. In one study [3] groups of people prejudiced and unprejudiced to minority groups were shown a series of pictures. The first picture was clearly that of a dog. The dog picture was followed by several other pictures, which by gradual stages made a transition to the picture of a cat. The prejudiced group held to the first object (that is, they interpreted the transitional pictures as a dog) significantly longer than the unprejudiced group. They were reluctant to let go of what was once clear. A similar reaction was elicited when a gradually changing series of numbers was used. The prejudiced group kept seeing the original numbers longer than the unprejudiced group. Thus, even at the perception level, attitudes affect reading. Despite high competency in the skills of word identification, it is possible to misidentify printed words because of tricks played on perception by the attitudes of the reader.

At the same time, it is possible to perceive printed words accurately and still misunderstand what is read because of interference of attitudes on the conceptual processes. It is in this respect probably that attitudes make their greatest impact on reading. Attitudes may operate in different ways depending on the kind of understanding and response expected from the reader. McKillop [4] explored the relationships between the reader's verbally expressed attitudes and his responses to different types of questions, ranging from those clearly and definitely structured to those less highly structured and therefore permitting greater opportunity for interpretation and evaluation. She found that the relationship between attitude toward a topic and response to reading passages dealing with the topic depended in part on the kind of questions asked. On questions of specific fact and detail a relationship was seldom found. On the other hand, on questions of judgment, evaluation, and prediction, it was regularly obtained. I found substantially the same thing to be true in my own doctoral study.[5] A strong negative parental attitude did not seem to interfere with accurate understanding at the literal comprehension level but it did prevent objective and rational understanding at the interpretation and evaluation levels. Those children with favorable attitudes towards their own parents appeared to grasp the author's intended neutral meaning easily and accurately and were able to answer all kinds of questions correctly. The children with strong negative feelings and attitudes towards their own parents answered literal comprehension questions dealing with the identification of clearly stated facts fairly successfully. Their answers to interpretive and evaluative questions, however, showed evidence of distortion and misunderstanding. It seems, therefore, that it is in those areas that distinguish critical from noncritical readers that attitudes play their most effective, and oftentimes pernicious, role.

Attitudes affect still another area closely related to reading—memory, or the retention of what is read. Studies show that readers tend to remember best those facts and ideas that confirm and reinforce their own views and attitudes and to forget material on other sides of an issue whether it be political, religious, racial, ethical, or purely personal. This kind of differentiated forgetting can occur even when the facts and ideas are acknowledged correctly during the reading.

Let's look at how attitudes function and in what ways they disrupt cognitive and retention abilities so that several people reading the same selection manage to derive different and often contradictory meanings from it and then remember and forget different things about it. Self-preservation appears to be a strong characteristic of attitudes. Having been formed, attitudes resist change; they fight to maintain themselves. Therefore a person with a strong attitude unconsciously struggles and connives to protect his attitude and keep it inviolate. He does so in several different and devious ways. By considering these different ways we can at the same time study their impact on understanding in reading.

One technique of self-preservation is withdrawal. A person with a strong attitude often withdraws himself, physically, from the necessity of facing contradictory evidence—much like the confirmed smoker who read so much about the harmful effects of smoking that he *gave up reading*. Attitudes, by encouraging this withdrawal behavior, drop a kind of silent curtain against the intrusion of possible embarrassing facts. The person pretends that facts contradictory to his attitudes simply don't exist. Therefore, attitudes influence what a person selects to read when given voluntary choice. When given no choice, he will read but will avoid thinking things through because he is afraid of what might be revealed. Obviously, this person can get only partial, incomplete, and distorted understandings from what he reads.

Selectivity is another means of defending attitudes from violation. As a person with a given attitude reads material that is contradictory to his attitude, he will notice and remember only the facts that are in harmony with his attitude and will fail to notice and remember conflicting facts. When confronted with the conflicting facts in discussion, he will quite innocently reply, "I didn't even notice that."—and to be sure, he didn't. Very soon after exposure, he will have forgotten the contradictory facts and his attitudes will remain unchallenged and he will be secure in the knowledge that he is right. He will answer questions solely on the basis of (from his point of view) the acceptable retained facts, a curtain of repression having denied the existence of all unacceptable facts.

People rarely deliberately misinterpret facts unless they are trying consciously to deceive—and people seldom consciously try to deceive themselves. However, much information is innocently reinterpreted by people as they read leading to all sorts of misinterpretations and misunderstandings and self-deceit. Facts rarely speak for themselves; they must be interpreted—that is, they must be neurologically processed through a screen of our attitudes and stored information and knowledge. Attitudes tend to color the facts. Thereby, a given fact may mean different things to different people depending upon their different attitudes and experiences with the concepts involved. This is unavoidable even when all these people may seriously and earnestly be trying to be objective about the facts. Denotations of words are one thing; connotations are another. The stronger that an attitude is, the more likely is correct understanding apt to be "derailed" by the attitude. As an example, the Cooper and Jahoda studies [6] undertook to find out what happens to a prejudiced person when he is involuntarily confronted with antiprejudice propaganda. In these studies prejudiced people were presented with a series of cartoons lampooning a character named "Mr. Biggott" who was depicted as holding the same prejudices as the subject. The producers of the cartoons assumed that the prejudiced person would perceive that Mr. Biggott's ideas were similar to his own; that Mr. Biggott was an absurd character; and that, therefore, the subject would reject or at least begin to question his own prejudices in order to avoid identifying himself with the absurd Mr. Biggott. But the results were quite different from those expected.

In one cartoon, Mr. Biggott is shown lying in a hospital bed saying to the doctor that he wants only "sixth-generation American blood" for his blood transfusion. This cartoon was shown to anti-Semitic subjects after which they were interviewed and asked what they thought of Mr. Biggott and his attitudes. One of the subjects said that obviously Mr. Biggott was a socially inferior person, and that anyone who was only a sixth-generation American had no right to pretensions! In this way the point of the cartoon was reinterpreted to deal with snobbishness rather than with prejudice, and thus the subject's own absurd racial prejudices remained unaffected by the absurd Mr. Biggott.

Rationalization such as this, where the disturbing element is placed in a context harmless to our beliefs, is even more likely to happen when reading material is unaccompanied by pictures since the abstract nature of words with their connotative overtones makes them more vulnerable to distortion than pictures which are more concrete representations of reality. If clearly stated facts can be misconstrued, how much easier it must be to misconstrue interpretations and evaluations. Explicitly stated facts minimize opportunities for distortion. Interpretations and evaluations depend upon personal opinions and experiences. They are more ambiguous. They can scarcely remain unaffected by attitudes. The more ambiguous that something is, the more it is perceived, conceived, and remembered in harmony with the reader's attitudes. It is precisely at the levels of understanding which differentiate critical from noncritical reading that attitudes play their most potent role.

There are also, of course, many instances in which people reading controversial material (and any material that is in conflict with preconceived notions is controversial to the reader) intellectually recognize the incongruity between the stated facts and ideas and their feelings and attitudes—and in the face of such evidence maintain their original beliefs anyway. The more intense that an attitude is, the more emotion is associated with it, and the less subject it is to change. How many people do you know who verbalize racial tolerance but who put their own homes up for sale the moment that the first Negro moves into their neighborhood? Incidentally, sticking to one's attitudes and convictions despite what we read is not necessarily undesirable. All written material, unfortunately, is not about things acceptable, beneficial, and good, and we certainly should be able to resist being persuaded by it. Cigarette advertisers are facing this problem now. People have been convinced that cigarette smoking can be deleterious to one's health so that no matter what the advertisers say, write, and picture about the pleasurable aspects of smoking (and TV screens are still crowded with lovely ladies and virile men in all sorts of idyllic settings inhaling the smoke of many different brands of cigarettes to the tunes of catchy songs), ever-increasing numbers of people are giving up their cigarette smoking habits.

Attitudes and emotions may have one other effect on critical reading. Because of their tension producing powers, they interfere with attention and concentration. Sustained focusing of attention is essential to critical reading. Mental energy that is tied up in emotional conflict cannot be freed and used for thinking and learning purposes.

In summary, we read with our feelings and attitudes as well as with our intellectual abilities. These emotional factors can facilitate or impede our intellectual functions. Attitudes provide us with a personal outlook on the world through our feelings, biases, inclinations, preconceived notions, ideas, fears, threats, and convictions, making each person's view of the world different from everyone else's. Negative attitudes are probably more influential than positive attitudes, but strong attitudes in either direction do affect our awareness and recognition of truth and reality—it isn't only people in love who see no faults in each other! Attitudes affect reading at the perception level by helping to determine the printed words we actually see, at the understanding level by coloring, twisting, and distorting ideas, and at the retention level by selecting those things that will be remembered and those that will be forgotten. Critical readers go beyond the identification of stated facts and ideas and engage in interpretive and evaluative thinking as they read. This makes them particularly susceptible to their own emotions, prey to their own attitudes. Successful critical readers recognize material which is emotionally loaded for them because of differences in viewpoint and resist, in so far as possible, giving in to their personal feelings and emotions and remain detached, neutral, and objective about what they read as they read. People differ in critical reading performance as much because of variations in attitudes as because of variations in intelligence.

REFERENCES

1. E. HILGARD, *Introduction to Psychology* (New York: Harcourt, Brace and World, Inc., 1962).
2. E. SIIPOLA, "A Study of Some Effects of Preparatory Set," *Psychological Monograph*, 46, No. 210, 1935.
3. E. FRENKEL-BRUNSWICK, "Intolerable of Ambiguity as an Emotional and Perceptual Personality Variable," *Journal of Personality*, 18, 1949, pp. 108–143.
4. A. McKILLOP, *The Relationship Between the Reader's Attitude and Certain Types of Reading Response* (New York: Teachers College, Columbia University, Bureau of Publications, 1952).
5. J. PIEKARZ, "Individual Differences in Interpretation," (Unpublished

Ph.D. Dissertation, Department of Education, University of Chicago, 1954).

6. E. COOPER and M. JAHODA, "The Evasion of Propaganda: How Prejudiced People Respond to Anti-Prejudice Propaganda," *Journal of Psychology*, 23, 1947, pp. 15–25.

PART TWO

Critical Reading in Relation to Other Kinds of Thinking and Creative Behavior

INTRODUCTION

As the study of critical reading developed it suffered from the lack of a precise definition and an intermingling with related areas. Emerging definitions of critical reading have frequently overlapped parts of the newly formed concept of creative reading. Since neither concept has been sharply delineated, many writers illustrate both critical and creative reading with similar examples of behavior. Recognizing the confusion, Helen Huus attempts to distinguish between critical and creative reading. She points out that critical reading requires evaluating material and comparing it to known standards or norms, whereas creative reading is concerned with the production of new ideas, the development of new insights, fresh approaches, and original constructs. She cites Russell's distinction that creative thinking involves the production of new ideas, whereas critical thinking involves reaction to another person's ideas or to one's own previous ideas.

Hester and Tronsberg use the terms critical and creative reading almost interchangeably in their articles. Creative reading embodies critical reading and critical thinking according to Hester. She lists the ability to distinguish between real and fanciful tales and the ability to make a distinction between fact and opinion as creative

reading skills. Tronsberg states that reading creatively involves analyzing, associating, organizing, interpreting, judging, and utilizing
the material read. Generally these skills appear on lists of critical
reading skills.

Torrance describes an experiment in which he asked one group of
students to read research reports critically and another group to read
them creatively. He describes the "critical set" as one in which the
reader *looks for defects* and the "creative set" as one in which the
reader *looks for new possibilities,* alternative hypotheses, and other
possible conclusions. In a subsequent paragraph he describes the
creative reader as one "who sensitizes himself to problems, gaps in
knowledge, missing elements, or something incorrect." These behaviors are similar to "looking for defects" and this makes the distinction between critical and creative reading difficult to maintain.

Commingling the concept of critical reading with related concepts
can be illustrated through a description of the critical and creative
processes. In the critical reading process there is a period of searching, gathering information, recognizing discrepancies or discontinu-
ities, then a period of generating possible hypotheses, collecting more
information and testing hypotheses, and finally the forming of a
conclusion. The process of the creative act includes sensing a gap,
searching for possible hypotheses, trying out alternative hypotheses,
and coming to closure. Similar steps or stages have been identified in
descriptions of the scientific process and the stages of reflective
thinking. Unquestionably, authors of articles in this section who speak
of creative reading are encompassing major portions of the same
skills that the editors have identified as critical reading skills. However, labels are not as crucial as having teachers who view both critical and creative reading as inseparable goals in teaching children
to read.

Although various interpretations of critical reading and critical
thinking are evident in articles appearing in this section, there is
general agreement among the contributors that critical reading involves thinking critically during the reading act. Ennis illustrates the
complexity of critical thinking with an extensive list of skills which
are applicable to thinking that occurs during reading or during oral
interaction. Relevance of the fundamentals of logic to the area of
critical reading is clearly shown in Ennis' work.

Karlin succinctly states that critical reading *is* critical thinking, and Russell says that critical reading does not exist in a vacuum but can be thought of as closely related to critical thinking. Russell places critical thinking with a group of overlapping categories including perceptual thinking, associative thinking, concept formation, problem-solving, and creative thinking. He believes that critical thinking is best described as a three-factor ability: an attitudinal factor of questioning and suspended judgment, a conative factor involving use of logical inquiry and problem-solving, and a judgmental factor of evaluating in terms of some norm or standard or consensus.

Taba identified some problems of teaching critical thinking in an early article and dispels several misconceptions about teaching children to think in the article included here. In the study she reports, there was an attempt to examine the relationship between teaching strategies and the development of cognitive processes. She questions whether or not formal thought can appear earlier than Piaget found if training for it occurs.

Ziller traces the origins of critical thinking from the child's earliest contacts with his environment. As the child is developing concepts and organizing them into some type of category system he is involved in the beginnings of critical thinking. He hypothesizes that a child with a more extensive verbal conceptualization of the world is capable of making finer qualifications of judgment or critical thinking. The interrelated nature of a child's level of concept development, his system of categorization, and his ability to think critically seems undeniable. Indeed, the relationship between critical reading and critical thinking is strong. It could be said, in fact, that they are both manifestations of the same mental processes.

B. D. E.

9. Critical and Creative Reading

Helen Huus

Anyone who has recently made even a brief survey of the literature on critical and creative reading has probably come to some of the following conclusions: (1) that critical and creative reading mean different things to different people; (2) that critical reading emphasizes a negative approach and consists of trying to catch the author in error of tact, logic, or judgment; (3) that critical reading is most often applied to propaganda material; (4) that critical reading and problem solving, that critical reading and creative reading are synonymous; and (5) that all reading is creative because the reader is reconstructing an experience that is, for him, unique. However, not all of these reflect the best thinking in the field.

DEFINITIONS

To bring some order out of this confusion, let us begin by first defining both critical and creative reading.

"Critical reading" requires the evaluation of the material, comparing it with known standards and norms, and concluding or acting upon the judgment. Russell, in his classic work entitled *Children's Thinking*, points out that critical thinking is comparative and that a knowledge of the field is a prerequisite.[1]

"Creative reading," on the other hand, is concerned with the production of new ideas, the development of new insights, fresh approaches, and original constructs. Russell, too, emphasizes that creative thinking involves new ideas, "whereas critical thinking . . . involves reaction to other's ideas or to one's own previous ideas. Critical thinking can be creative in that it can produce new insights for the individual, but those insights are concerned with previously established conditions."[2]

CRITICAL READING

If students are expected to read critically, what are some of the necessary skills? Those needed could be classified into two broad categories—

[1] David Russell. *Children's Thinking*. Boston: Ginn and Company, 1936, pp. 283 ff.
[2] *Ibid.*, p. 306.

"Critical and Creative Reading," by Helen Huus, was presented as a paper at the International Reading Association, Detroit, Mich. (May 1965). Reprinted with permission of Helen Huus and the International Reading Association.

inference and evaluation. The critical reader swings from one to the other as he reads, first inferring, then evaluating his inference against his experiences and other data, then inferring and judging again.

THE AUTHOR

A reader ought to be concerned with the person who has written the material, and, therefore, he must make certain inferences about the author. He ought first to ask, "Why did the author write this? Was it to advertise, to propagandize, to present information, to promote a point of view, or to entertain?" In an article entitled "The Power and the Glory of the Word," Nance puts it this way:

> Writers throughout the centuries have had many different goals: To recover the past, to record and conserve for the future, to interpret, comment, report, arouse, condemn, defend, entertain, annoy, or to obtain personal or institutional publicity.[3]

A related question ought to be, "How competent is this author to write an article on this topic for this purpose?" To answer this, the author's background, education, reputation, vested interests, and professional position need to be investigated. Practical exercises for doing this are included in the 1948 edition of *The Teaching of Reading in the Elementary School*. Here McKee suggests finding biographical information for each author, then comparing his qualifications with the subject on which he is writing. It is often not difficult, even for quite young children, to recognize that one or the other seems to be best qualified.[4] Sometimes locating information about living authors, however, poses a problem, for often the only source of information is the dust jacket of a book, the comment column in a periodical, the advertisement from a publisher, or the reputation of the publishing house.

Nance has this additional comment:

> The writer is a human being and a citizen. The scope and content of his material will be conditioned by his major interests, his outlook on life, his responses to life, and his experience, knowledge, abilities, and opportunities.[5]

When expressing an idea or a point of view, it is difficult for an author to escape from himself and create an impression different from the kind of individual he really is. His competency becomes particularly important when facts disagree and students look for help from recognized authorities. At any rate, knowing the author is an important factor in criticism.

---

[3] E. C. Nance. "The Power and the Glory of the Word," *Vital Speeches*, XXIII (March 1, 1957), 381.

[4] Paul McKee. *The Teaching of Reading in the Elementary School*. Boston: Houghton Mifflin Company, 1948, Chapter 14.

[5] Nance. *op. cit.*, p. 381.

THE CONTENT

A second aspect to be evaluated is the content itself—its adequacy or completeness, its accuracy and recency, its inherent logic and consistency, its suitability to the purpose at hand. Questions to be asked here include: "Are *all* the facts presented? Are the facts presented *true?* Are the facts presented in perspective?" Exaggerated statements abound in advertising; willful distortion of facts is rampant in propaganda; and assertions are made directly or implied, occasionally from ignorance, but sometimes, too, from lack of proper checking.

Obviously all facts cannot be presented in a short selection nor is it easy to determine the total body of fact, but the perspective implied by the relative importance given to various topics should be preserved so that tentative conclusions can be made from the data available, with necessary modifications when additional data warrant it.

McKee also describes exercises for checking the validity of the printed statement and uses an example about the asking of paper. But I am re-minded of my own childhood, when I had learned at home the glory of the Viking expeditions to Greenland and Vinland, only to find in school that Columbus was getting all the credit. Quickly, I learned to give the proper answers at school, but it has cheered me no end to read of the recent discoveries in Newfoundland by Ingeted.[6]

Children can learn to delete irrelevant sentences in a paragraph, to note the omission of important information needed for an understanding of the whole, to recognize ideas placed out of logical order, to separate factual statements from one of opinion. And perhaps you might encounter a wise young one, such as I did once, who was reading up on birds' nests in the encyclopedia. When making her report, she cited her source, then calmly stated, "In this encyclopedia, it says that the oriole's nest is the most beautiful of all birds' nests. Now I realize this is just the author's opinion, and this is my evaluation of what I have been reading." Would that all readers could locate statements of opinion; they could be kept very busy with the front page of some newspapers!

THE STYLE

In addition to the competency of the author and the quality of the content, the manner in which the material is written—its style and "tone"—also influence the critical reader. "Style" refers to the precision of vocabu-lary, its range and vividness; to the cadence of the sentences; to the subtle use of modifiers and figures of speech; to such techniques of elab-

[6] Helge Ingeted. "Vinland Rules Prove Vikings Found the New World," *National Geographic Magazine*, CXXVI (November, 1964), 708–734.

oration as analogy, description, anecdote, or exposition; to the organization—the "unity, coherence, and emphasis" so dear to the hearts of English
teachers. These elements, when combined, lend an appropriate tone to the
total—solemn and dignified, lighthearted and gay, clear and simple, or
whatever the topic demands. The reader should be able to join in with
the spirit of the work and to lose himself as he identifies with it. He is
truly "there," and when this occurs, he knows he has met an artist with
words. While he may not always be able to locate the various techniques
that cause him to feel so involved, nevertheless he recognizes that this
piece of writing approaches his standard and, therefore, is a better work
than one which leaves him cold as last night's dinner.

The influence of the connotation of words upon the tone of writing is
well exemplified in this historical example that quotes a few headlines in
the Paris newspapers from March 9 to 22 in the year 1815:

March 9:   The Anthrapophagus Has Quitted His Gun
March 10: The Corsican Ogre Has Landed at Cape Juan
March 11: The Tiger Has Arrived at Gap
March 12: The Monster Slept at Grenoble
March 13: The Tyrant Has Passed Through Lyon
March 14: The Usurper is Directing His Steps toward Dijon
March 18: Bonaparte is Only 60 Leagues from the Capital; He has
           Been Fortunate Enough to Escape His Pursuers
March 20: Napoleon Will, Tomorrow, Be Under Our Ramparts
March 21: The Emperor is At Fontainebleau
March 22: His Imperial and Royal Majesty Arrived Yesterday Eve-
           ning Amid Joyful Acclamations of His Devoted and Faith-
           ful Subjects [7]

Another aspect of tone, especially important in the materials written
for elementary school children, is the approach that authors take when
writing for children. Condescension and a patronizing air is unacceptable,
and children are quick to spot it.

These three—author, content, and style—all must be considered in critical evaluation of reading material. Each of these must be analyzed in
depth; only the briefest of introductions can be indicated here, but it must
be remembered that points of quality as well as weaknesses should be
noted.

CREATIVE READING

A reader who has learned to judge what he reads, both content and
manner of presentation, still fails to obtain the greatest pleasure, enjoy-

[7] Carl Warren. *Radio News Writing and Editing*. New York: Harper & Brothers,
1947, p. 272.

ment, and even knowledge from his efforts unless, in the doing, he gives something of himself. He must integrate the total into his own background of information, what the psychologists call his "apperceptiveness," and reorganize his ideas to accommodate his new learnings, his new attitudes, or his new feelings. In this reorganization, he gains new insights—sees the same things from a different point of view, sees aspects hitherto not noticed, senses the color and texture of a word or phrase, stores away a new visual image, or feels apathy with characters he has previously ignored or misunderstood. Russell puts it aptly when he says that, in creative reading, "the solution or conclusion (to a problem) represents a bit more of the child himself, is fresher and more personal than a routine solution." [8]

Creative reading requires, then, certain skills of comparison and synthesis; comparison to see relationships between parts of sentences, paragraphs, and longer sections, in order to arrive at the total, between causal factors and their accompanying results, between juxtaposed events, and between the actions of a character of different times; and comparisons of time and space, place and sequence. From these understandings, the creative reader can produce his own combinations, his own syntheses of ideas, and anticipate what the outcome will be. That it is not the same as the author's need be of little consequence, and occasionally children have a much more logical ending to a story than has the author himself.

Creative reading thus calls into play the child's imagination, his flow of ideas, his ability to see comparisons where no obvious one exists, to relate what he is reading to his own peculiar background of remembered activities, and to make the new learning so much his own that it has always seemed a part of him. This is the real contribution which reading makes to personality development, to the development of attitudes and ideals, to the making of the "educated man." And this is the goal of education, at whatever level.

But for teachers and others to know what lies behind the interested look, the quick nod, the perceptive twinkle requires that the child express the ideas he has been accumulating. Thus we see full circle in the language arts—from the receptive (reading) through evaluation and assimilation to the expressive (speaking or writing).

Creative reading ultimately resolves itself in the development of "taste," the "power of discerning and appreciating fitness, beauty, order, congruity, proportion, symmetry, or whatever constitutes excellence, especially in the fine arts and belies letters; critical judgment, discernment, or appreciation." [9] As each reader makes up his own mind and follows his own judgment, individuality is preserved. He has no need for "tastemak-

---

[8] Russell. *op. cit.*, p. 13.
[9] *Webster's New International Dictionary of the English Language.* Second edition. Unabridged. Springfield, Mass.: G. & C. Merriam Company, Publishers, 1957, p. 2585.

ers," for he has confidence in his own ability and need not wait for some-one to decide for him. He can interpret situations in the light of his experience and understand analogies, allusions, figures of speech, connotations and denotations, and he can reorganize the ideas he receives into a pattern that is unique and personal. He can express his reorganized learning through various media—word and song, gestures and actions, materials and composition. The actual product may be as fleeting and transitory as spoken language or as lasting a monument as the Statue of Liberty.

Conclusion

If reading has produced real conviction, then the reader must be willing to meet all comers and defend his ideas, which must be firmly based on the integrity of this interpretation, on accurate factual data, and on his unique approach. But he remains able to "live with uncertainty" and to revise his ideas to another and still another plane of uncertainty as new information and experiences are acquired.

The skills of critical reading require an interpretation and evaluation of the author's qualifications and purpose, of the internal consistency, accuracy, recency, and perspective of the content, and of the style and tone of the presentation.

Creative reading requires skills of comparison and synthesis. It implies that the reader places facts into a new organization and gains new insights that contribute to his development of taste. By these means do teachers create literate, discriminating, and appreciative readers.

10. Creative Reading: A Neglected Area

Kathleen B. Hester

Creative Reading: A Neglected Area

One must be an inventor to read well. . . . When the mind is braced by labor and invention, the pages of whatever book we read become luminous with manifold allusion. Every sentence is doubly significant, and the sense of our author is as broad as the world.

Emerson

"Creative Reading, a Neglected Area," by Kathleen B. Hester. Reprinted from the May 1959 issue of EDUCATION. Copyright 1959 by The Bobbs-Merrill Company, Inc., Indianapolis, Indiana.

Dictatorship or Democracy! Are we making "rubber stamps" of our children? To many people, reading is recognizing words and understanding what an author says. "Parroting back" thoughts an author gives us is the goal of many readers. Children are not encouraged to think or to react to the content of a story or an article. Challenging ideas is discouraged. For living a story there is no time. An atmosphere of "We must hurry on. We have books to cover," prevails in many classrooms. Yet those same people worry about the future of our country.

The future of a democracy is dependent upon ability of its readers to read critically and creatively. Passive and uncritical reactions to what a person reads is perilous. Advancements of science are dependent upon students' skill in reading creatively. Our chief protection against propaganda lies not in constructing better missiles and bombs, but in ability of our people to react to and to evaluate ideas encountered in reading, radio, television and motion pictures.

WHAT IS CREATIVE READING?

Creative reading means active reading. It is not the casual, indifferent, effortless type. In creative reading, the reader becomes a co-author. He visualizes, recalls experiences from his own life that verify or refute statements, sees relevance to current conditions, and decides what he is willing to accept. Understanding depends not only upon what an author says but also upon the reader's responses of thought and feeling that he himself contributes (4, p. 7).

Creative reading requires capacity to understand something that has depth, the ability to appreciate that which has beauty, skill to evaluate controversial material, and competency to read aloud any material in a way which will make words leap from a page and live for the listener (4, p. 6). It embodies critical reading and critical thinking.

WHY PUPILS FAIL TO READ CREATIVELY

The problem of teaching children to read creatively is not confined to elementary schools. This is a complex skill which cannot be perfected in six years.

Our high school graduates are markedly deficient in ability to read creatively for two reasons. First, because of the complex aspects of this skill, systematic, sequential instruction frequently is not provided.

Second, our achievement tests generally fail to measure progress in this skill. Most widely used standardized tests in reading measure simple reading skills such as vocabulary, comprehension of main ideas, details, and certain study skills. A student may be competent in vocabulary attack but poor in recognizing use of emotive words; outstanding in finding main ideas but slow in differentiating fact from opinion. Yet he rates high on a standardized reading test and his teacher acclaims him a good reader.

Fostering Growth in Creative Reading

How, then, do we achieve this higher level of reading? How does a teacher set up a plan of instruction for creative reading in his classroom?

First of all, a teacher must learn to read creatively. Then he can lead his students. He must recognize that this skill is not only for talented readers but that average readers are entitled also to satisfactions accruing from creative reading. Every pupil has some creativity within him. According to Woolf and Woolf (9, p. 53), "Creativity belongs to all of us, and should be encouraged in all, including the potential geniuses."

Teachers must re-examine their definitions of reading. To many, the task of reading is done if a student can recall the words of an author. Reading a book is a mechanical, undiscriminating task. In schools where value is placed upon "number of books covered," creativity tends to decline. Great emphasis is placed upon conformity, little is given to spontaneity, new ideas, and freedom of response (9, p. 52). Teachers are afraid of original ideas and shun questions which involve responses that may differ from student to student. Time cannot be spared for critical and evaluative thinking. Yet a century ago Macaulay, the great English statesman and poet said,

A page digested is better than a volume hurriedly read.

Lastly, a teacher must understand that this higher level of reading is not acquired easily or suddenly. Reading skills, whether mechanical, study type, or creative, must be taught systematically. Each component subskill must be developed to the highest degree possible at each maturity level.

Simple subskills of creative reading should be taught in lower elementary grades, beginning at kindergarten level; more complex aspects should be taught in secondary schools because a certain degree of maturity is necessary for depth of comprehension.

Alert teachers will become acquainted with this hierarchy of skills and provide an instructional program to encourage pupils to read creatively.

Suggestive Classroom Activities

Space does not allow a discussion of all the facets of creative reading, but an imaginary visit to a few classrooms may spark your thinking. Look into these classrooms to see what is being done to foster several important subskills of creative reading.

Understanding Cause and Effect in Relationship to Pupils and Events

Through literature children become aware of moral issues. They discuss "good" and "bad" behavior of story characters. Join Mrs. DeWaters' class of primary children. They have just finished reading "Goldilocks and the Three Bears." A child has made the statement, "Goldilocks was a 'bad' girl for going into a house without being asked." There was a difference of opinion within the group. Then Mrs. DeWaters suggested they "think through the story" before making a decision. The following account shows how she guided their thinking.

> Run with Goldilocks. Run into the forest. Run around among the trees until you are tired. You are out of breath, your legs are tired, you are thirsty. Then you discover you do not know the way out of the forest. How do you feel about it?
>
> Wander on trying to find your way home. Discover the little house in the woods. Tap on the door and wait. Do you hope someone will come to the door, ask you to come in and rest, and then tell you the way home?
>
> How do you feel when no one answers the door? Push the door open and peep into the room. How do you feel about what you see? Do you feel curious about the house, tired enough to walk in and sit down for a while?

With this directed discussion the children experienced the whole story. Then they were asked to "pretend you are telling your mother all about your adventure." Recounted tales showed that real creative thinking had been done about the moral issue. This story to these boys and girls will always be rich and meaningful. Words became alive.

Cause and effect in relationship to events is important also. Questions such as, "Could this story have happened here? What might have happened if one event had been substituted for another within the story?" encourage creative thinking.

Understanding Power of Words

Emotive words which highlight feelings of an author are recognized by a good reader. Throughout the grades there are many opportunities for teachers to help pupils become proficient in detecting words and phrases which are used to create feelings, words, and impressions. Pupils analyze words, phrases, and placement of ideas for emphasis to see how impressions are created. They learn to interpret figurative expressions. Literary stories and newspapers lend themselves well to the development of this skill.

A junior high school class had read "Singing Family" by Jean Ritchie. They were discussing the power of words. The question arose, "How did Jean Ritchie create an impression that food she had as a mountaineer child was good tasting?" Pupils were locating phrases which "made their mouths water." They had already listed "hot, crusty corn pone, browning 'taters, thick pieces of home-cured ham." And now they were describing some of their favorite foods in a similarly vivid way.

School integration was the topic of discussion in another class. Pupils were discussing two versions of a new story. One account of the event was taken from a northern newspaper, a second account from a paper printed in the south. Although facts were identical, the two stories gave very different impressions. The pupils were interested in discovering how meaning had been changed through use of emotive words and placement of phrases within sentences.

EVALUATING A STORY OR ARTICLE

A very important aspect of creative reading is ability to distinguish between real and fanciful tales, and to differentiate fact and opinion. Is this a true story? What makes you know the story could or could not be real? Which statements in an article reflect feelings and biases of the author?

A fifth grade class was having a stimulating discussion of fact and opinion. Each member had brought in a statement heard on a television commercial the previous evening. Statements were listed on the blackboard and the class was "head over heels" into the problem. Of each statement or commercial they were asking: Is the statement true? Is it partly true? Is the statement misleading because of the part-truth? What did the speaker say to make you think the way he wanted you to think? Was his reasoning good? What evidence did he offer to support his statement? Why do people make such statements?

Within a story evaluation of a character and his actions is valuable also in developing creative reading.

A junior high school group was grappling with the question, "Does a person have a right to do as he pleases or must he consider the effects of his actions on others?" This problem arose from an attempt to decide whether the boy in the story "High Lonesome Places" by Fred Gilpin was justified in doing what he pleased. This question was real and alive to these pupils. They were doing creative thinking and reading.

There are other subskills which are important in developing creative reading but perhaps the few discussed here will serve to convey an understanding that creative reading can be fostered on all levels. Teachers cannot expect all pupils to attain the highest level of creative reading but with systematic instruction they will find every child has some creativity within him.

REWARDS OF CREATIVE READING INSTRUCTION

Teachers who become proficient in developing this higher type of reading will find their pupils more excited and more enthusiastic about reading than they ever have been previously. It is a thrilling experience to watch children develop a depth of understanding and an ability to respond intelligently to a printed page. As Gainsberg (2, p. 25) has said of critical and creative reading,

The added understandings are well worth the time it takes.

When children, with stars in their eyes, have caught the joys of adventuring and creating with an author, and have realized the stimulation of thinking, with both prose and poetry, they become "readers."

To quote from Coleridge, the noted English poet,

There are four kinds of readers. The first is like the hour-glass; and their reading being as the sand, it runs in and runs out, and leaves not a vestige behind. A second is like the sponge, which imbibes everything, and returns it in nearly the same state, only a little dirtier. A third is like a jelly-bag, allowing all that is pure to pass away, and retaining only the refuse and dregs. And the fourth is like the slaves in the diamond mines of Golconda, who, in casting aside all that is worthless, retain only the pure gems.

REFERENCES

1. OSCAR S. CAUSEY, *The Reading Teacher's Reader*. New York: The Ronald Press Company, 1958, pp. 107–119.
2. JOSEPH C. GAINSBERG, "Critical Reading Is Creative Reading and Needs Creative Teaching," *The Reading Teacher*, Vol. VI (March, 1953).
3. VIRGIL E. HERRICK and LELAND B. JACOBS, *Children and the Language Arts*. Englewood Cliffs, New Jersey: Prentice-Hall, Inc., 1955, pp. 336–361.
4. KATHLEEN B. HESTER, *Teachers' Manual for use with New Horizons through Reading and Literature*, Book 1. River Forest, Illinois: Laidlaw Brothers, 1958.

5. C. W. HUNNICUTT and WILLIAM J. IVERSON, *Research in the Three R's.* New York: Harper & Brothers, 1958, pp. 134–146.

6. CONSTANCE M. McCULLOUGH, "Creative Reading," *Ginn and Company Contributions to Education in Reading,* No. 15. Boston, Massachusetts: Ginn and Company.

7. PAUL McKEE, "Creative Writing," *McKee Language Service Bulletin.* New York: Houghton Mifflin Company.

8. RUTH STRANG and DOROTHY KENDALL BRACKEN, *Making Better Readers.* Boston: D. C. Heath and Company, 1957.

9. MAURICE D. WOOLF and JOANNE A. WOOLF, *Remedial Reading.* New York: McGraw-Hill Book Company, 1957.

11. Creative Reading at all Grade Levels

Josephine Tronsberg Benson

You have thought of reading as being either silent or oral, developmental or functional, recreational or corrective, but have you thought of it as creative? "How can reading be creative?" you ask. Certainly, we have creative writing, but that is something one formulates in his own words and therefore we say it is creative. But in reading you must read the words as they are; you cannot change the printed words into your own words and call it reading. What then do we mean when we say children should be taught to read creatively?

Russell [1] regards creative reading as "any reading which goes beyond superficial understanding and literal interpretation of the material read." It is a "process of integrating and organizing materials in order to come to some conclusion or synthesis or to solve some problem." Mere recognition and understanding of the symbols is not creative reading. Some interpretation or judgment of the meaning must be included and some use must be made of the material if it is to be considered as such. Reading creatively involves analyzing, associating, organizing and utilizing the material read. It requires thinking, imagination and the ability to tie in one's experiences with what is being read.

Since creative reading depends upon good thinking ability, let us review

[1] Russell, David H. *Children Learn to Read,* p. 305, Ginn and Company, 1949.

"Creative Reading at All Grade Levels," by Josephine Tronsberg Benson, is reprinted by permission from *Reading in Relation to Mass Media.* Donald Cleland (ed.). Report of 14th Annual Conference and Course on Reading. Pittsburgh: University of Pittsburgh (July 14–25, 1958), pp. 145–150.

what we know about the thinking process and how it develops in children. All of you are familiar with the six steps which Dewey [2] lists in his description of how we think: (1) the awareness of a problem, (2) the collection and classification of data related to the problem, (3) the formulation of a tentative hypothesis, (4) the judging of the worth of the hypothesis by mental tryout, acception or rejecting, (5) actual test of the hypothesis, (6) possibly some conclusion or some solution of the problem.

Children, however, do not always use all of these steps. They may proceed from an awareness of the problem immediately to a conclusion. Some of the thinking required of them as they read is concerned with forming ideas, associating meanings, seeing relationships between cause and effect and making generalizations rather than with problem-solving.

Much research has been done on children's ability to think. Their perception, memory, ability to concentrate and to reason have been scientifically investigated. First grade children appear to have some ability to generalize about scientific experiments. By the time they enter third grade they can make self-appraisals in a group situation which is an important aspect so far as critical reading is concerned. Although adults have a wider experiential background to check their hypotheses and conclusions there apparently is no real difference in how they think.

Reading creatively requires two types of thinking: (1) recognizing a problem and working towards a solution of it; (2) organizing ideas to reach a decision.

Every child can think creatively, but not all children can think on the same level because of individual differences. It is the teacher's responsibility to find the level at which a child can read with understanding and to group the children accordingly. To find the child's level of thinking ability the teacher can administer a standardized test in which she reads successively harder stories and the child is required to answer questions about the stories. Some teachers select paragraphs from several graded readers and have the child answer questions about the material.

Creative reading activities may be divided into two main types:

1. The child's own experiences, thinking and imagination will be integrated with the ideas of the printed material.

2. The printed material will be used to solve some problem.

The first activity may be the result of the child asking himself, "What do I think about this?" The second activity may be the result of his asking himself, "What should I do about it?" These two divisions simply represent different stages and the child may incorporate the material in his store of information rather than apply it immediately in solving some problem.

From their earliest reading experiences children can be called upon to make thoughtful and critical judgments. The teacher might ask, "How do you think Tom felt when his dog got lost?" As these children develop

[2] Dewey, John. How We Think. Heath, 1933.

reading ability they should be aided in relating what they read to the task at hand. They must be given an opportunity to choose reading materials so they can learn to be selective.

Children can learn to evaluate reading materials in the primary grades, too. They are quick to comment that "this book tells us a lot about bears but doesn't say how big they are." These children are reading creatively as they visualize what they read, recalling similar experiences from their own lives. They enrich the material with the meanings they bring to it. They speculate on the outcome of the story.

Each teacher must select and adapt activities which are suitable to the abilities of the children within her grade. Some of the following activities can be utilized with skilled first graders while others may be more appropriate for third graders:

1. Read a story to decide if it is real or fanciful.
2. Discuss the accuracy of the illustrations in a story.
3. Choose from a group of stories the one most appropriate for sharing with other children.
4. Verify the information gained from a story with that obtained on an excursion.
5. Select answers to questions on a worksheet.
6. Complete sentences on a worksheet.
7. Select material pertinent to a topic.

Primary children who have been given a wealth of experiences soon learn to relate what they read to what they know. Ideas gained from reading materials in the form of instructions are applied to the tasks at hand. As the first graders build experience charts, they are getting practice in deciding which ideas are relevant and which are not. They are constantly asked to predict the outcome of a story they are reading. Third graders should be guided in their reading so that they acquire the skill to understand why they like or dislike what they read. Ask them if they would like to experience the incidents about which they have read.

With the greater variety of reading materials at the intermediate and junior high school level, the purposes for reading become more extensive. The pupils should be more skillful in evaluating what they read in terms of their purposes. They now have a wider acquaintance with author's differences in writing style and should show more ability in selecting books for varied purposes. They should be more discriminatory in selecting information appropriate to their problems. They must learn to recognize the difference between finding the answer to a specific question and merely locating a general statement bearing on the subject as a whole.

The need for pupils to read reference materials selectively and critically is already recognized. As they read social studies or science materials, specific questions frequently arise. They should be referred to reference material for pertinent data. They may then check sources outside of books and compare the information. If some of the questions are vague, the pupils may question if the author really knew what he was talking about. This, in turn, should lead them to find out if the author or authors of the material were actually authorities on the subject.

Pupils should be encouraged to require evidence to support a conclusion they are asked to accept. Teach them to see relationships between related facts and draw valid generalizations. Have them collect and organize facts into a unit and then show how their conclusions follow logically from these facts. Teach them to be tolerant of new ideas and to consider now evidence with an open mind. Encourage them to be on the alert for ambiguous words or vague phrases and to demand meaning from everything they read. Teach them to consider negative as well as positive evidence on any question they discuss. Give them practice in appraising the accuracy of what they read. They should be able to distinguish fact from fiction and editorial writing from news reporting. Have them decide which of a series of stories is the most exciting or the most humorous. They should be able to decide which of several books is the most helpful in supplying needed information.

Some of the suggestions for creative reading may be too difficult for elementary pupils because they require a certain amount of maturity. The more complex aspects of the skill may be taught at the secondary level. For example, deciding upon authoritative sources is difficult and perhaps only a beginning can be made in the elementary grades. High school students can gain an awareness of self and others through their reading of books. Teachers should help them to develop a critical appreciation of books, magazines and newspapers. They should be given opportunities to discuss the reasonableness of what they read and, through their experiences, be able to confirm or reject the conclusion of an author.

High school students should be made aware of the tremendous influence of certain propaganda techniques on public opinion. Radio, movie and television advertising often infer that certain products are approved by doctors and dentists. Students need practice in detecting overstatements and unfounded claims which appear often in magazines and newspaper editorials. They need help in interpreting certain cartoons on world affairs. While some cartoons do not require any thinking, there are many others drawn by able cartoonists which merit our consideration.

High school students should be encouraged to make suggestions for improving an article or selection. Perhaps the selection has a great many descriptive passages, but is not very exciting. Have them make suggestions which they think would make it more exciting. Ask them to read an article and to express their opinions about it either orally or in writing. Give them practice in recognizing the difference between fact and opinion. This can be done effectively by calling their attention to certain statements heard on the radio or seen on television or in advertisements in newspapers and magazines.

Reading creatively at the college level means that the college student must not only read extensively, but must be more selective about his reading. As he weighs evidence for conclusions, makes judgments and inferences he is thinking critically. He must develop the ability to compare sources, noting the purposes, bias and accuracy of several authors; to trace the development of ideas; to note points of similarity between doctrines. Different subjects demand different kinds of critical reading. Reading philosophy requires a different kind of skill than reading history.

Critical or creative reading means forming judgments and opinions, interpreting feelings, making comparisons and inferences and reflecting on what has been read. It can also be concerned with choice of vocabulary, sentence organization, paragraph structure, illustrations or general quality of writing.

Training in thinking critically and creatively must be included in the reading program at all levels if we hope to make an adult population capable of evaluating the printed word.

BIBLIOGRAPHY

LILLIAN GRAY and DORA REESE, *Teaching Children to Read.* Second Edition. New York: The Ronald Press Company, 1957.

MARGARET G. McKIM, *Guiding Growth in Reading.* New York: The Macmillan Company, 1955.

DAVID H. RUSSELL, *Children Learn to Read.* New York: Ginn and Company, 1949.

RUTH STRANG and DOROTHY KENDALL BRACKEN, *Making Better Readers.* Boston: D. C. Heath and Company, 1957.

12. Developing Creative Readers

E. Paul Torrance

WHY BE INTERESTED IN DEVELOPING CREATIVE READING?

I know that many of you must be genuinely skeptical about the desirability of developing creative readers! How many times have you been told that this is none of the school's business? Is it not the school's purpose to teach realistic facts? Is it not the purpose of the school to give children a realistic view of the world in which they live?

I wonder, however, if we might not accomplish more successfully this goal by doing a better job of developing creative readers. I would like to read you a poem written by an eighth-grade girl who *is* a creative reader. I believe this poem shows that she is achieving a more realistic view of the world by being a creative reader.

> A book is a magic carpet; it crosses every sea;
> It flies above the highest cloud, carrying me.
> I look down on skycrapers, and all the city life.
> I look down on people's joys, their happiness and strife.
> I can see the fluffy clouds, dusting off the sky.
> I can see New England herring, brown bread, and Boston pie.
> I can see a western rodeo; miles and miles of prairie.
> Hear the shrieks of witches and ghosts, and everything that's scary.
> A book is a magic carpet, it carries me afar;
> See the planet Saturn, the moon, and every star.
> New and old ways of living; aye, what treasures I gain!
> By gathering and storing knowledge, wisdom, from every terrain.
> Deep as the earth is the secret, old as the Sphinx; you see,
> That a book is a magic carpet that crosses every sea.

> By Diane Badman [1]

Yes, it takes a creative reader to achieve a realistic view of the world. Betts [2] has pointed out that many children can pronounce astronomical numbers and yet cannot estimate the coast-to-coast distance across the United States. The mere pronunciation or memorization of words leads to the use of empty words which contribute nothing to the attainment of a realistic view of the world.

Even achieving this goal is not enough! You want your pupils to use reading as a source of thinking materials in solving problems and in cop-

"Developing Creative Readers," by Paul E. Torrance, is reprinted by permission from *Dimensions of Critical Reading*, XI (1964). Compiled by Russell G. Stauffer. University of Delaware, Newark, Del., pp. 59–74.

ing with the stresses in their lives. As Betts points out, one's ability to think is limited primarily by his personal experiences and the uses he makes of them in problem solving, in abstracting, and generalizing, in judging, and in reaching conclusions. The creative reader increases his personal experiences through his reading because he uses the ideas he gains in reading as he would firsthand experiences. In solving problems and reaching decisions he is just as likely to see the relevance of a story situation or biographical account as he is the relevance of a firsthand experience. What he reads becomes real to him and he can use it.

Not only does it take a creative reader to grasp the meaning of what one reads, but it takes a creative reader to ferret out the truth from what one reads. This is why I think it is so essential that we teach the children the nature of the intellectual processes known as historiography and something of the scientific spirit of historiography. This requires, of course, that one be both a critical and a creative reader. Being a critical reader would only make one aware of the biases in records and accounts of witnesses. It takes a creative reader to understand the reasons behind discrepant accounts and reach sound conclusions about what is true. Children catch the spirit of historiography and develop with amazing rapidity skills in the intellectual processes involved. Vincent Rogers [3] at the University of Minnesota has been developing some fascinating materials in elementary social studies to develop such skills from the first grade upwards. I have also been having some exciting experiences in teaching some of the skills of historiography to high-achieving sixth graders. [4]

It even takes a creative reader to remember in a meaningful way what is read. It is interesting to note that most of the special memory courses make considerable use of evoking either visual or auditory imagery regarding what is to be remembered. You might be interested in trying an exercise devised by Hayes [5] a well-known teacher of memory courses. Listen carefully as I read a list of the errands you must accomplish on a certain day. Do not write them down. Try to remember them. Here is the list:

Purchasing a pound of bacon,
          a package of tape,
          a box of matches,
          a bouquet of flowers,
          a bottle of ink,
          a flashlight,
          a jar of mustard,
          a mousetrap;
Getting your glasses adjusted,
Paying the telephone bill.

Now that you have read this list, see how many of them you can remember without looking back. Write them out.

How many could you remember? The average person remembers about six. Let's try Hayes' method and see how many you can remember. He suggests that you group the items and visualize them in combinations.

> Visualize a pound package of sliced bacon with lighted matches standing between the slices. The entire package is held together by a large adhesive tape. This looks rather strange, but in the strangeness of it lies an important clue toward the ability to recall at once almost anything that you care to remember.
>
> Next, visualize a beautiful bouquet of flowers standing alongside the previous package. Standing by the flowers is a good friend holding a flashlight over the flowers. As the person tilts the light an amazing thing happens: jet black ink comes from the flashlight and pours all over the lovely bouquet. Some of the ink spatters on the bacon. Now, you have two groups of items. Let us add a third.
>
> As you were wondering how to clean up the mess you heard a loud snap and, glancing around, you see a mousetrap closed over your eyeglasses. It has a broken lens. The lens has been smeared with mustard. Just as you are reaching for the mousetrap, you hear a tinkling sound and are startled to find coins falling out of your telephone.
>
> Now the articles are grouped by three's, with the additional odd item of the telephone rounding out the things you are trying to remember. Turn away from the page now and see how many items you can recall. You should remember ten. If you do, then I have "proved a point." [6]

I should pause at this point, however, to caution that it is not the amount of information per se that one possesses which enables him to think creatively, but the way in which he has stored his information and the attitude he has towards it. I have demonstrated this point by having students read research articles creatively as opposed to reading them critically and by having them read textbook materials with different reading sets.[7,8] Hyman [9] in the field of industrial research has also shown that a constructive rather than a critical attitude towards information results in solutions both on related and unrelated problems which were rated significantly more creative.

WHAT DOES IT MEAN TO READ CREATIVELY?

In a number of the experiments we have conducted I have tried to describe some of the essentials of reading creatively. I would like to offer as an example, the instructions I gave in the experiment involving the use of different reading sets in mastering textbook assignments.[10]

> When you read, it is important that you think about the many possible uses of the information which you are reading. It is especially im-

portant that you think of the various ways in which the information could be used in your personal and professional life. In reading, do not just ask, "What is the author saying." Also ask, "How can I use what the author is saying." Do not stop with just one use. Think of as many uses as you can of the important ideas presented. Jot down some of these uses for future reference. It may take some practice before you are really successful in assuming this set or attitude towards your reading, but do not be discouraged. By the third day, you should find it easy to assume this set.

In the experiment involving the critical and creative reading of research reports, those reading the reports with a critical set were required to describe the *defects* in the statement of the problem and its importance, the underlying assumptions and hypotheses studied, procedures for collecting and analyzing the data, the conclusions and interpretation of the findings, and a critical appraisal of the worth of the research. The *creative* readers were asked to think of new possibilities suggested by the problem, other possible hypotheses related to the problem, improvements which could have been made in collecting and analyzing the data, other possible conclusions and interpretations of the findings, and an appraisal of the possibilities stemming from the findings. Students reading research reports creatively produced new ideas of their own which were judged to be more creative than were those of their peers who read critically.

These examples do not tell us just what happens to the thinking of the creative reader. What mental operations [11] are involved in reading creatively? One way of conceptualizing the mental operations which occur when one reads creatively is in terms of the mental abilities involved in creative thinking. In other words, the creative reader sensitizes himself to problems, gaps in knowledge, missing elements, something incorrect. This calls for the formation of new relationships and combinations, synthesizing relatively unrelated elements into a coherent whole, redefining or transforming certain elements to discover new uses, and building onto what is known. In this search for solutions, there is the operation of ideational fluency (the production of a large number of possibilities), spontaneous flexibility (the use of many different approaches or strategies), originality (the production of bold new ideas off the beaten path), and elaboration (the development of the idea, filling in the details, making the idea attractive or embroidering it).

Many suggestions have been made about how the reader produces these ideas. Almost all agree that the creative reader must be open to his experiences and that he must reflect upon what he reads, discovering the relationships among the ideas presented and seeing them in the light of his own experiences.[12] He must react to new concepts, playing with the possibility that the new idea might be correct and trying to see what its consequences might be. In this way, the new concept becomes a center of vivid concrete images and feeling reactions. The creative reader has an inquiring attitude about what he reads and seeks to make rational evaluations. McCullough [13] suggests that the creative reader will identify with the author or with the character in a story, play, or novel. Through the imaginative process of identification, the creative reader can guess what is going to happen next and what might have happened instead. This leaves the creative reader with a desire, perhaps a need, to discuss the material in his own unique terms or to transform the experience into a poem, a song, a dance form, or a drama. Carl Rogers,[14] among others, maintains that this desire to communicate is a highly important part of the creative process. He maintains that "it is doubtful whether a human being can create, without wishing to share his creation." A person may not create *in order to communicate* but having created something he *desires to communicate* what he has discovered or produced.

How Do Creative Readers Develop?

I would like to try to develop two ideas for developing creative readers. The *first* is to keep alive expectation and anticipation as a reading task is approached. The *second* is to do something with what is read, either at the time it is being read or after it has been read.

Expectation and Anticipation

The creative process itself embodies the tension of anticipation or expectation, and individuals who distinguish themselves in artistic, scientific, and entrepreneurial creation exemplify this tension quite vividly. It has variously been described as the warming-up process, the ability to rise to the occasion, or attraction to the unknown, the strange, and the puzzling.

I am sure that all of you can think of materials and methods for heightening the tension of expectation from kindergarten through graduate school. I would like to introduce a few examples, beginning at the kindergarten level and proceeding upwards.

One of my favorite sets of material at the preschool or primary level is a series of books by an Italian artist and story-teller, Bruno Munari.[15] They are published in the United States by World Publishing Company. An interesting one entitled, *Who's There? Open the Door!* is good for developing both the imagination and the evaluation or judgment abilities. The cover of the book is like a big door with the eye of an animal peeking out. You can have the child guess all of the things he can think of that would be so big that it would take a room for them to stand up in. The child might guess an elephant, a camel, a giraffe, a pony, and the like. You open the door and it's actually "Lucy the giraffe with a large crate come all of the way from Lisbon." It might also have been some of the other things guessed. You might accept such large ones as elephant, camel, and some others. You might point out, however, that a pony would not take this much space. Next, the question becomes "What's in the crate?" Again, he might guess pony, bear, hippopotamus, pig, cow, and the like. It is actually "Peggy the zebra with a trunk come all the way from Paris." Again, other things similar in size to the zebra can be accepted and those larger and smaller can be eliminated. The game continues. We have Leo the lion with a valise come all the way from London. Next we have "Romeo the cat with a package wrapped in tissue paper, come all the way from Rome." In the package we have "Bertha the blackbird with a basket come all the way from Berlin." In the basket we have "Dick the cricket with a small parcel come all the way from Dublin." In the parcel we have "a little ant with a grain of wheat for the winter."

With such materials you are doing more than developing the imagination, you are developing the ability to think in terms of possibles, to make judgments about size, and to gain a more accurate picture of the world in which we live. Incidentally, children might on later occasions be stimulated in their curiosity to ask about the places from which these animals and insects have been shipped: Lisbon, Paris, London, Rome, Berlin, and Dublin.

Another of the Munari books that I like is *The Elephant's Wish*. The story begins: "The elephant is bored with being a big heavy animal. He wishes he could be something else. What do you think he would like to be?" This starts the guessing game. The child is asked to look into the mind of the elephant, to imaginatively put himself in the place of the elephant and think what he would want to do if he were to be tired of being an elephant. Then he is given a look into the elephant's mind by the artist and author. "He wishes he could be a little bird who flies and sings." The bird, however, has his problems. "The little bird is bored with flying and singing. He is wishing too. What does he wish?" After some guessing on the part of the child, he can be given a look into the bird's mind. The bird "wishes he could be a fish and swim under water." But the fish is bored too. He is bored with swimming under water. "What does he wish?" He wishes he could go on land. How tempting it must be to him to want to go on land! "He wishes he could be a lizard sitting on a stone in the sun." The story continues. The lizard wants to be a fat, lazy ox. The ox wants to be an elephant. Thus, we return to the place where we started. Everything wants to be something else. Our problem is to accept creatively our limitations and use our ability and resources. If we do, we will not be bored. Life will always be exciting.

Somewhat the same effect can be obtained when reading new material in the primary and intermediate grades by asking, before you turn the page in the middle of a story, "What do you think will happen now?"

Later you can encourage children to ask questions which will lead them to find relationships among certain facts and thus come to a logical conclusion.[16] This same technique can be used in history, geography, and science. Children can be given enough facts to enable them to make predictions and then asked to make guesses about the consequences. Later, they can check their guesses against documentary sources or established facts and try to determine wherein their theorizing went wrong. We have used this technique in some of the experimental materials we have created and are testing in the fourth grade. In these materials, the atmosphere of expectation is created through brief dramas of great moments of scientific discovery, geographical discovery, and historical achievement, as well as fantasies. An example from the fantasy series is our use of the famous Italian story of *"Giovanni and the Giant."* [17] In the dramatization, the tape recorder is stopped each time Giovanni gets himself into a predicament. The pupils are asked to think of as many solutions as possible for extricating Giovanni. By the time the tape is completed, each pupil has enough material for another version of the story. After this kind of experience, pupils may also be invited to expand the story or put it into a here-and-now setting. Or, they may be invited to write newspaper articles dealing with selected parts of the story from an "I was there" viewpoint. This, in turn, might lead to reading creatively more material about 12th-century Italy, the Crusades, city-states, and the like. This technique is also used in the geography series in "Polar Pilot," [18] the story of Admiral Richard E. Byrd. Several of Byrd's "close calls" are dramatized and as each is reached the tape is stopped for the pupils to formulate their solutions which are in turn checked against the solutions which Byrd and his men developed.

In the intermediate grades and in the high school years, something of the same effect can be achieved by giving the title of a book and asking students to guess what the book is about. Josephine Shotka [19] has suggested a list of questions which can be used to stimulate creative reading. Hers are designed for stories but might be adapted to biographies, history, and other kinds of reading materials. Here are some of the questions she suggests for use before the story is read:

From the name of the story, what do you think it will be like?
What experiences do you think the characters will have?
Do you think this will be a funny story, a sad story, a make-believe story or an exciting story? Why?
What do you think the characters will be like?

The following is her list of questions for use during the reading of the story:

Where does our story take place?
Have you ever been to a place like this?

Who are the characters and what kind of persons are they?
Have you ever met a person like the character in the story?
Are the characters ones you would like to have for your friends?
Have you any friends like the characters in our story?
What is the author trying to give us to think about in the story?

For use after the reading of the story, she suggests the following:

Why did you like or dislike the story?
What would you have done if you were in the same position as the character or characters in the story?
What do you think was the main idea of the story?
How do you think the character or characters felt? Have you ever felt like that?

Thus, we see that creative reading involves reactions to the reading material before, during, and after the actual reading. Then, there is the matter of doing something further with what has been read but this will be discussed in the next section. One of the major problems in arousing anticipation and expectation is to lead the reader to see the fundamental relationships among the facts, ideas, and events which constitute the reading materials and between them and the experiences and problems of the reader.

Doing Something with What Is Read

I was amazed when I first began giving examinations in the courses I teach at the University of Minnesota that required that students do something with the theories and research findings that had been studied. One device I used was to give some important research finding and ask students to list all of the educational uses they could think of for this finding. Student after student would come to me and say, "What do you mean by 'uses'? The only thing that I can think of is to tell it to somebody." This experience helped me to begin understanding why courses in education, psychology, and the other behavioral sciences have so little impact on what happens in classrooms. I found that students were struggling with courses and learning facts which they did not intend ever to use. *Indeed* it had not occurred to them that such information *could* be useful in any very concrete or real sense! I would like to suggest now some ways by which creative readers can be developed by "doing something with what is read."

REPRODUCING WHAT IS READ WITH IMAGINATION

Even if one's goal is only to "tell it to someone," as in the case of my Educational Psychology students, it can and should be done with imagination. If you are having difficulty in getting your pupils to read orally with imagination, I believe John Ciardi might help you in this task. I have been fascinated by his recording "I Met a Man" by Pathways of Sound, Inc. This recording grew out of Ciardi's attempt to teach his own daughter how to read with meaning and imagination when she was in the first grade. His aim in the recording is to encourage children to put meaning into their reading instead of mouthing the words, whether the mouthing be slowly or rapidly. He encourages the young listener to make poems "sound like the thing happening."

ELABORATING WHAT IS READ

Next to reproducing what is read comes *elaborating what is read*. There are many ways of elaborating upon what one reads and in so doing developing creative readers. Durrell and Chambers [20] predict that "it will probably be found that well-designed exercises in elaborative thinking in reading will produce higher permanent retention and greater availability of knowledge to new situations." One of the most common means of doing this is to have children illustrate what they read. A recent innovation in the field of children's books is the *Poetry-Drawing Book* [21] that consists of poems for children to illustrate and color. Other media, such as music, songs, rhythmic movement, and dramatics can also be used in elaborating what has been read. Also valuable are modifications of what is read: writing a different ending, changing a character in some specific way and seeing what else this would change, expanding upon a certain episode in a story.

I suspect that some children who are having difficulty in learning how to read at all would learn to do so, if given experiences in elaborating what is read. I would like to tell you about one very striking case that has come to my attention through one of my students, Miss Joy Alice Holm. [22] I would like to describe this case in Miss Holm's own words:

> Bob was nervous, withdrawn and sad. He was failing every subject except gym and art and could not read well enough to keep up his work. He was not high school material according to his teachers . . . he was becoming more antisocial and unhappy and less able to participate in anything that involved being with other people. He felt inadequate and began to withdraw, even in basketball games. He had been a fine athlete but, losing self-respect in situations that demanded reading and talking, he soon lost his confidence altogether. He painted football games with no players on the field and made many sketches of boys huddled in blankets on the bench, watching the game . . .
> Fortunately, Bob was in my English class so in addition to having reading drills after school, he illustrated the stories we read to show he had understood the material. The poetry which was read aloud in class

he envisioned richly and his clarity of visual images was a revelation. It showed that he understood the thoughts and transformed them into vivid pictures. He could not write a quiz on the meaning or details of a poem or story, nor could he talk about them. . . . In Robert Frost's poem "Mending Fences," Bob drew the neighbor ". . . like a stone savage armed" with determined expression, while he pictured Frost with his head to one side in sad contemplation of the unfriendly act of mending the fences. Even the details of the kinds of trees each man had were pictured. Frost's trees were apple and his neighbor's were pine, which made an important point to emphasize the meaningless-ness of the wall. All this Bob visualized but could not express in words. The pent-up ideas and feelings and the strain of failing for lack of ability to use words were wearing Bob down. . . . His grade school teachers said he was "sweet but dumb," but at this point he was too sad to be sweet.

Finally, after his illustrations were exhibited first in the English class and then in the art class, he realized he was doing something im-portant. Other students admired his work, expressed envy for his talent and bolstered his morale . . . after almost a year of illustrating his way through English class and drawing and painting away his conflicts by externalizing them, he was able to increase his skills in reading and participate again in sports. He got back into "the crowd" and became "himself" again, a quiet, good-natured boy with more than his share of artistic ability.

There are a number of remarkable facets of Miss Holm's encounter with Bob. She was willing to embark with him on an untrodden path. What teacher would have thought of letting Bob take his English examinations using visual rather than verbal symbols? Most teachers would be afraid that they could not "grade" or "correct" such an examination paper. By "going along with" in this unorthodox fashion, a "hopeless case" learned to read and perhaps escape a life of pathological withdrawal.

I offer this rather lengthy example, because I imagine that there are many of you who believe that a child must be a *good reader* before he can be a *creative reader*. In the first place, I would say that a child can-not be a good reader unless he is also a creative reader. Furthermore, I have a very strong hunch that some children will not learn to read at all unless they have a chance to become creative readers, as in the case of Bob. Marjorie Hourd and Gertrude Cooper [23] describe an interesting case in which creative writing was used in somewhat the same way as drawing was used in Bob's.

TRANSFORMING AND REARRANGING WHAT IS READ

Third in my scale of doing something with what is read is the trans-formation or rearrangement of what is read. Shakespeare's creativity was of this type. It never occurred to Shakespeare that a playwright should invent a plot and characters. Today, of course, many students in playwriting courses feel that they must invent a plot, usually with some half-demented and/or tormented characters. With all of the great stories we have in history, science, geography, and government—with all of the myths and fables available—with all of the great biographies—there are plenty of plots and characters waiting to be brought to life in dramas, songs, paintings, murals, and other forms by creative writers. Of course, in bringing these plots and characters to life in such a way, students will need to read creatively from a number of sources. What results will be a creative recombination and transformation of what has been read.

The book report assignment or report on other outside reading can also be made a transformation of what has been read. Mauree Applegate,[24] Robert Wilson,[25] and others have given an exciting variety of suggestions for such assignments. The following are some of Applegate's suggestions:

1. What was your favorite character like? Make a drawing and point out passages in the story which make you think this is the way your character looks.

2. Before you read the book, write the story the title makes you think of; then when you read the book, write the report of the real story and chuckle at the difference. (You may feel that you have a better story.)

3. Write an interview between a character in the book and the author, between you and the author, between two characters in the book, between you and a character in the book, or between you and a friend about the book.

4. Write your book report in verse.

5. You have just finished reading a biography. Pretend you visited the person when he was your age. Tell about the fun you had.

6. Choose a lively scene from a book you and your friends have read and either dramatize it or make a puppet's play of it.

7. Have a friend interview you about a book of which you pretend to be the author.

8. Make a hand-rolled movie of a book you have read.

9. Make a radio or television play of your favorite book.

I am sure that you and your pupils can think of many others that are even more exciting than the ones Mauree Applegate suggests.

GOING BEYOND WHAT IS READ

In the creative process one thing must be permitted to lead to another. Creativity begets creativity. Your own Dr. Stauffer[26] has written that "a good story is likely to evoke many ideas and questions which can send the reader beyond the story." He considers going beyond a basic reader story a natural and integral part of all group-directed reading. Oppen-heim [27] and Zirbes [28] have offered a variety of suggestions for stimulating children to go beyond what they read.

It is to be anticipated that there will in the very near future be sets of basal readers specifically designed to develop creative and critical readers, giving practice in doing something with what has been read. The very recent series from Edinburgh, Scotland, is thus far one of the most deliberate attempts of this kind.[29]

I might emphasize that the idea of permitting one thing to lead to another is the very essence of the experimental materials which we have been producing for the fourth grade. Basic to our strategy is to generate enthusiasm, interest, and curiosity through the tape-recorded drama and then to use this warm-up to get pupils to produce something. They are then encouraged to produce something on the basis of what they have already produced. Additional reading may come in at any one of several stages in the process and we believe that such reading is rather certain to be creative reading. Let me cite an example from one of our lessons based on "Eyes at Their Fingertips," the story of Louis Braille.[30] The instructions for the first step go something like the following:

One of the big reasons why Louis Braille thought of and worked out a way for blind people to read and write better was that the old way really bothered him. It really got under his skin that little blind children had to read out of books that were so big that they couldn't carry them around. And besides, reading raised or embossed writing wasn't very accurate. Try to think of as many things as you can that really bother you and get on your nerves—things that bother you so much that you would like to change them or invent something new to make them less annoying. List as many of them as you can.

Immediately after this list has been produced, we go ahead to the second stage with the following instructions:

Of all of the things you listed, what bothers you most? What really gets you down? Is there any one of the things you listed on the first page that towers over all of the others and makes them seem small? Pick out one of the things you have just listed and write it down.

Then follows:

Now, think of all of the things you can about this annoyance or "thorn in your flesh" that makes it annoying and list them below. What is there about it that bothers you?

After this pupils are told:

Now list as many things as you can think of that would make it less annoying or remove the annoyance from your life. It doesn't have to be something that is now possible. Play being a magician and list all of the things that would make it ideal.

After thinking this through, they are asked to continue with the following instructions:

Now, think of something you could invent or some plan that would remove some of the things that bother you about this annoyance and would have as many as possible of the characteristics you just listed.

After this, we definitely have a phase which calls for creative reading. The orientation for this is as follows:

Louis Braille was helped in developing his kind of writing because he was familiar with sonography which had proved unsuccessful. Do you know of any unsuccessful attempts to solve the problem you selected? If you do, write them below. If you don't know of any, how could you find out if there have been any?

The next phase is introduced as follows:

If you thought of some unsuccessful attempt to solve your problem, what would have to be changed about it to make it successful?

Following this step, pupils are encouraged to draw a picture or diagram of the invention, plan, or procedure which they have in mind or to describe it as fully as possible. As a final step, they are asked to think of the possible consequences of their invention or plan. This activity is introduced in the following words: "If you were to succeed with your invention or plan, it would change many things. Think of as many things as you can that would probably be changed, if your invention or plan becomes successful."

You will note that we have tried to reproduce essentially the same thinking process through which Louis Braille went in working out a system of writing and reading for the blind. In each of the great moments of discovery, an effort is made to distill in the drama as much as possible the essence of the thinking of the scientist or inventor. Benjamin Franklin's thinking processes were motivated in quite a different way from Braille's. He was sensitive to the needs of other people and he kept inventing and discovering things which would solve problems for other people, things like bifocals, lightning rods, electricity, coal stoves, mail-delivery service, police and fire departments, political cartoons, Poor Richard sayings, street lights, and the like. Thus, instead of starting with personal concerns, with the Benjamin Franklin story we start children by having them observe what things bother other people. Even in the manuals for *Eyes at Their Fingertips* and *All-Around American* we offer dozens of alternative activities which might take pupils beyond their reading and bring them back again and again to read creatively.

Conclusion

I hope that I may have said enough to start you thinking creatively about the reasons why we shoud be concerned about developing creative readers, what it really means to read creatively, how teachers can create situations which will increase the chances of your pupils becoming creative readers. I hope that you will become creative in finding ways of heightening expectation and anticipation and in doing something with what has been read. I hope that some of you will be challenged to create and evaluate new materials and methods for developing creative readers, because I feel that this is indeed a promising area of development. If I have succeeded to this extent, I know that the remainder of your teaching career is going to be exciting and satisfying.

References

1. Mauree Applegate, *Easy in English* (Evanston, Ill.: Row, Peterson, 1962).
2. E. A. Betts, "Reading Is Thinking," *Reading Teacher*, 1959, *12*, pp. 146–151.
3. V. R. Rogers, "History for the Elementary School Child," *Phi Delta Kappan*, 1962, *44*, pp. 132–135.
4. E. P. Torrance and R. E. Myers, *Teaching Gifted Elementary Pupils How To Do Research* (Minneapolis: Perceptive Publishing Co., Box 4086, University Station, 1962).
5. O. W. Hayes, *Your Memory: Speedway to Success in Earning, Learning and Living* (New York: Exposition Press, 1958).
6. *Ibid.*, p. 21.
7. E. P. Torrance, "Effects of Induced Evaluative Set on the Development New Ideas Among Graduate Students," *In Creativity: Second Minnesota Conference on Gifted Children* (Minneapolis: Center for Continuation Study, University of Minnesota, 1959), pp. 136–140.
8. E. P. Torrance and J. A. Harmon, "Effects of Memory, Evaluative, and Creative Reading Sets on Test Performance," *Journal of Educational Psychology*, 1961, *52*, pp. 207–214.
9. R. Hyman, "On Prior Information and Creativity," *Psychological Reports*, 1961, *9*, pp. 151–161.
10. Torrance and Harmon, *op. cit.*
11. J. P. Guilford, "Frontiers of Thinking That Teachers Should Know About," *Reading Teacher*, 1960, *13*, pp. 176–182.
12. W. S. Gray, "Reading and Experiencing, Thinking, and Learning," *California Journal of Elementary Education*, 1959, *27*, pp. 135–149.

13. C. M. McCullough, "Characteristics of Effective Readers in the Elementary School," in Helen M. Robinson (ed.), *University of Chicago Conference on Reading*, 1959, *21*, pp. 3–8.

14. C. R. Rogers, "Toward a Theory of Creativity," in S. I. Hayakawa (ed.), *Our Language and Our World* (New York: Harpers, 1959), pp. 172–185.

15. B. Munari, *Who's There? Open the Door* (New York: World Publishing Co., 1957), and *The Elephant's Wish* (New York: World Publishing Co., 1959).

16. J. Oppenheim, "Teaching Reading as a Thinking Process," *Reading Teacher*, 1960, *13*, pp. 188–193.

17. B. Cunnington, Pearl Buckland, and R. Peterson, *Giovanni and the Giant* (Minneapolis: Bureau of Educational Research, University of Minnesota, 1962).

18. B. Cunnington, R. Peterson, Pearl Buckland, and R. E. Myers, *All-Around American* (Minneapolis: Bureau of Educational Research, University of Minnesota, 1963).

19. Josephine Shotka, "Creative Reading," *Education*, 1961, *82*, pp. 26–28.

20. D. D. Durrell and J. R. Chambers, *Reading Teacher*, 1958, *12*, pp. 89–91.

21. W. Cole and Julia Colmore, *The Poetry-Drawing Book* (New York: Simon and Schuster, 1960).

22. E. P. Torrance, *Guiding Creative Talent* (Englewood Cliffs, N.J.: Prentice-Hall, 1962), pp. 176–177.

23. Marjorie L. Hourd, *Coming Into Their Own* (London: Heineman, 1959).

24. Applegate, *op. cit.*

25. R. C. Wilson, "Creativity," in *Education for the Gifted*. Fifty-seventh Yearbook, National Society for the Study of Education. (Chicago: University of Chicago Press, 1958), pp. 108–126.

26. R. G. Stauffer, "Productive Reading-Thinking at the First-Grade Level," *Reading Teacher*, 1960, *13*, pp. 183–187.

27. Oppenheim, *op. cit.*

28. Laura Zirbes, *Spurs to Creative Teaching* (New York: Putnam's, 1959).

29. A. Elliott-Cannon, *Reading and Thinking*, Books I and II (London: Oliver and Boyd, 1963).

30. B. Cunnington, R. E. Myers, Pearl Buckland, and R. Peterson, *Eyes at Their Fingertips* (Minneapolis: Bureau of Educational Research, University of Minnesota, 1962).

13.   A Definition of Critical Thinking

Robert H. Ennis

As a root notion, critical thinking is here taken to mean the correct assessing of statements. This basic notion was suggested by B. Othanel Smith (3): "Now if we set about to find out what . . . [a] statement means and to determine whether to accept or reject it, we would be engaged in thinking which, for lack of a better term, we shall call critical thinking." Since Smith's definition does not use any words like "correct," his notion is slightly different. Smith's concept of critical thinking, however, permits us to speak of "good critical thinking" and "poor critical thinking" without redundance or contradiction. Though this is an accepted manner of speaking, the predominant manner of speaking presumably builds the notion of correct thinking into the notion of critical thinking. Though the latter interpretation is used in this paper, it would be easy to restructure what follows and use Smith's concept. "Good critical thinking" in Smith's sense means the same as "critical thinking" as used in this paper.

Since there are various kinds of statements, various relations between statements and their grounds, and various stages in the process of assessment, we can expect that there will be various ways of going wrong when one attempts to think critically. In view of this fact, the aspects of critical thinking about to be presented, which may be looked upon as specific ways to avoid the pitfalls in assessment, are bound to make a rather heterogeneous list.

This list and the accompanying criteria for judging statements are based in a large part upon a study of the literature in education, philosophy, and psychology.* The list of critical thinking aspects is also based upon an analysis of a number of specimens of alleged justifications of statements, and a consequent realization of the places where these justifications can go wrong. One may look upon this list as a statement of a number of items that, if taught to students, will result in a greater likelihood that they will be critical thinkers. Further refinement of this list is a continuing task, and of course much remains to be done.

* References that were of help can be found in Robert H. Ennis, "A Concept of Critical Thinking," *Harvard Educational Review*, 32 (Winter, 1962), 81–111; the present article is a streamlined version of that article. The theoretical analysis of critical thinking and the proposals for needed research in that article have also been omitted here. The latter feature is expanded in an article entitled "Needed: Research in Critical Thinking," *Educational Leadership*, October, 1963.

Major Aspects of Critical Thinking

A critical thinker is characterized by proficiency in judging whether:

1. A statement follows from the premises.
2. Something is an assumption.
3. An observation statement is reliable.
4. A simple generalization is warranted.
5. A hypothesis is warranted.
6. A theory is warranted.
7. An argument depends on an ambiguity.
8. A statement is overvague or overspecific.
9. An alleged authority is reliable.

Although the root notion calls for its inclusion, the judging of value statements is deliberately excluded from the above list. This exclusion admittedly weakens the attractiveness of the list, but makes the job more manageable. So long as we remember that this exclusion has occurred, we should not be confused by the truncated concept. Perhaps this gap can at some future time be at least partially filled.

The exclusion of other important kinds of thinking (creative thinking, for example) from this basic concept of critical thinking does not imply that the others are unimportant, nor does it imply that they are separable from it in practice. This exclusion is simpy the result of an attempt to focus attention on one important kind of thinking.

Another aspect which has deliberately been excluded from the list is proficiency in judging whether a problem has been identified. This is excluded not because it is unimportant, but because it resolves into one or another of the items on the list (or the judging of value statements) in each of the various meanings of "identifying a problem." This point will be developed later.

Each of the listed aspects of critical thinking will be examined and, if possible, criteria will be presented, clarified, and, when it seems necessary, at least partially justified.

JUDGING WHETHER A STATEMENT FOLLOWS FROM THE PREMISES

The concern of most logic books is with whether a statement follows *necessarily* from the premises. This is the judging of deduction. Reasoning in mathematics, "if-then" reasoning, and syllogistic reasoning all exemplify deduction.

The basic criterion is this: "A conclusion follows necessarily if its denial contradicts the assertion of the premises." Various rules have been developed for different types of deduction, but all see to it that this requirement is fulfilled. Well-developed sets of rules include:

1.1 The rules for handling equations and inequalities.
1.2 The rules of "if-then" reasoning:
    1.21 Denial of the "then-part" requires denial of the "if-part," but not necessarily vice versa.
    1.22 Acceptance of the "if-part" requires acceptance of the "then-part," but not necessarily vice versa.
    1.23 Instances of an "if-then" statement are implied by the "if-then" statement.
1.3 The rules for categorical reasoning. These rules may be summarized by the following: "Whatever is a member of a general class is also a member of whatever that general class is included in, and is not a member of whatever the general class is excluded from."

A number of cases of reasoning are parallel to strict deduction, but are different in that the generalizations in use as premises do not hold universally under any conceivable circumstance; they have exceptions and limits, not all of which can be specified. To extend Waisman's term (5), they are "open-textured." Reasoning from principles and hypotheses to the world of things, men, and events is inevitably of this sort. Sometimes the exceptions and limits are so far removed that we do not have to worry about them, and in such cases we can proceed as in deduction without fear of going wrong. Sometimes the limits and exceptions are close by, in which case, still approximating the deductive model, we use words like "probable," "likely," "barring unforeseen circumstances," etc., in the conclusion.

For an example of the latter case, consider the application of that standard law of economics, "If the supply is constant and the demand for a product decreases, the price will decrease." Two of the limits of the application of this law are within the knowledge of all of us. It is intended to apply to an economy free of government control and to a sector of it that is free of monopolistic control. Mention of these limits will suffice for present purposes, although there are others.

Now let us apply this law to a situation in which there is a decrease in demand for microscopes. Applying the law deductively, we are unalterably committed to a prediction of a price decrease. But it is not wise to be unalterably committed to such a prediction. For one thing, the well-known limits of the law might be breached: the government might decide to maintain the price of microscopes and pay for the destruction of the extras; or a monopoly might be formed to maintain the price.

But secondly, other things that are not yet explicitly built into the limits might go wrong. The makers of microscopes might form a trade association and decide incorrectly that with good advertising they *can* create a demand much greater than ever before, so that they can afford to raise prices. They therefore raise prices in anticipation of a nonexistent demand.

It is because of considerations like these that qualifiers like "probable" must be included in the application of many principles. The application of that law in that situation might be, "It is probable that there will be a lowering of price." But the application would not be this at all if it can be seen that a known limit is breached or that there is some other extenuating circumstance. The point is that the application of such principles should often not be stated any more strongly than this, even though the steps in reasoning parallel those of deduction.

Thus there are two kinds of following: strict necessity and loose following. The critical thinker can do both.

JUDGING WHETHER SOMETHING IS AN ASSUMPTION

This topic is complicated because there are various logically-different abilities that go under this title. These can be best approached through an examination of various uses of the word "assumption": the deprecatory use, the concluding use, the premise use, and the presupposition use.

2.1 *The deprecatory use and the concluding use.* The deprecatory use implies the charge that there is little or no evidence to support a given belief and that the belief is questionable. Here is an example: "You're just assuming that Frank didn't read the assignment." This deprecatory use is often found to be incorporated in the other uses, but sometimes it stands alone. As such its appearance is tantamount to a judgment that the view should prehaps be rejected, or at least be held in abeyance because of lack of support. No further discussion of the evaluation of this kind of assumption-claim is necessary here, since this is a general charge and is covered under discussion of the various other abilities.

In the concluding use, the term "assumption" is used to mark a conclusion, but the deprecatory use is involved too, since the conclusion is implied not to be fully established. Here is an example: "My assumption is that Hissarlik is at the site of Troy" (a statement made at the completion of a presentation of the evidence bearing on the location of Troy). We need not be concerned with discussing whether something is an assumption in the concluding sense; the important question is whether such an assumption is justified and that question is covered elsewhere in this paper.

The first two uses of "assumption" were specified in order to keep them out of the discussion of the next two; the following discussion does not apply to them.

2.2 *The premise use.* This kind of assumption stands anterior to a conclusion in a line of reasoning, whether the conclusion be inductive or deductive. To call something an assumption is to say that the conclusion depends upon it, and that if the conclusion is to be accepted, the alleged assumption should also be accepted. Thus the location of assumptions (in this sense) is a useful step in the evaluation of conclusions.

Here are criteria for premise-type assumptions:

2.21 Of the various possible gap-fillers, the alleged assumption should come closest to making the completed argument, proof, or explanation, a satisfactory one. (This criterion is necessary and sufficient.)

   2.211 The simplest gap-filler is ordinarily the one to choose.

   2.212 If there is a more plausible gap-filler among the more complex ones, it should be chosen. Plausibility, however, requires fitting in with existing knowledge—not being a special case.

2.22 Other conditions remaining the same, the state of affairs that is predicted could not occur (or probably would not occur) if the alleged assumption were false. (This criterion applies only to alleged empirically-necessary assumptions, but for them it is necessary and sufficient.)

2.23 The community of experts in the field would not accept the position, conclusion, or argument without first believing the assumption to be true. (This criterion is neither necessary nor sufficient, but is a good ground.)

What is a gap-filler? Consider this piece of reasoning: "Since the demand for microscopes has decreased, the price may be expected to decrease." A gap-filler here would be:

1. When the demand for a commodity decreases, the price will decrease. (It fills a gap in reasoning from the decrease in demand for microscopes to a decrease in price.)

It is not the only way to fill the gap, however. Consider these alternatives:

2. When the demand for goods and services decreases, the price decreases.

3. When the demand for optical instruments decreases, the price decreases.

4. When the demand for optical instruments (other than field glasses) decreases, the price decreases.

Since all four of these will fill the gap, it should be clear that being a gap-filler is not by itself a sufficient condition for being an assumption. The simplest gap-filler is ordinarily the one to attribute, thus ruling out No. 4. Simplicity might also be a ground for not accepting No. 2 as the assumption, since there is a conjunction of two things (goods and services) mentioned. But if the prevailing knowledge in economics admits no basis for distinguishing goods from services in the context of this principle, then simplicity is counter-balanced by the need to fit into existing knowledge. The first two gap-fillers would then be equally defensible (or indefensible) and either could be called the assumption.

Gap-filler No. 3 introduces a new twist, talking only about optical instruments. It is as simple as No. 1 but is not as general. Other things being equal, generality is to be preferred. A system of knowledge is better if it covers more cases. But if the more general gap-filler (1) should be false, and the less general one (3) true (or more likely to be true), the less general gap-filler is the one to choose.

Assumption-finding then is the locating of a gap-filler, the simpler the better, provided that it fits into and contributes to a system of knowledge. The assumption-finder should try to be generous to the person whose assumptions he is locating, generous in that he should try to find the best candidate for participation in a knowledge system. He should not accept a false gap-filler as the assumption until he has searched for one that fits into an acceptable body of knowledge. Put more simply in a way that covers most cases, he should search for one that is true.

While discussing gap-filling it would be well to note that there is one sometimes used criterion that is inapplicable: *logical* necessity. As exemplified by the four gap-fillers previousy discussed, there is no single significant premise-type gap-filler which is logically necessary. It is always *logically* possible (though it may be extremely implausible) to complete an argument in more than one way, a point I have developed elsewhere (2).

Empirical necessity (2.22) is different. To the extent that empirical statements can be necessary, there can be empirically necessary assumptions. For example, a statement which predicts that the pressure in a fixed cylinder of confined air will increase is assuming that there will be a temperature increase. Since an increase in temperature in that situation *is* necessary for there to be an increase in pressure, the assumption is empirically necessary and can be pinned on the argument with confidence.

Criterion 2.23 mentions the experts. Although their considered opinions can be wrong, they do ordinarily know what fits into their body of knowledge. And they do know what is used successfully in the field to back up arguments and conclusions. So they can ordinarily be expected to know what an argument would need in order to be a good one.

2.3 *The presupposition use*. Presuppositions are sentences which must be true for a given statement even to make sense. This is the meaning of the term "presupposition" presented by P. F. Strawson (4). The claim, "The governor's mistakes have caused our present plight," presupposes that the governor has made mistakes. His not having done so would make nonsense out of either the affirmation or denial of the claim. If the governor has made no mistakes, it does not even make sense to say that his mistakes have caused our plight; nor does it make sense to say that his mistakes have not caused our plight.

Presupposition-finding is useful in avoiding being swayed by false presuppositions (if the governor has made no mistakes, we should be able to react to the presupposition that he has). And presupposition-finding is useful in grasping a verbal picture, and a part or the whole of a theory.

Judging whether something is presupposed by something else is simply a matter of stating the meaning of the "something else."

JUDGING WHETHER AN OBSERVATION STATEMENT IS RELIABLE

An observation statement is a specific description. Over the years, those fields most concerned with accuracy of observation have built up a set of rules for judging the reliability of observation statements. Here is a combined list of principles from the fields of law, history, and science:

3.1 Observation statements tend to be more reliable if the *observer:*
    3.11 Was unemotional, alert, and disinterested.
    3.12 Was skilled at observing the sort of thing observed.
    3.13 Had sensory equipment that was in good condition.
    3.14 Has a reputation for veracity.
    3.15 Used precise techniques.
    3.16 Had no preconception about the way the observation would
       turn out.
3.2 Observation statements tend to be more reliable if the *observation conditions:*
    3.21 Were such that the observer had good access.
    3.22 Provided a satisfactory medium of observation.
3.3 Observation statements tend to be more reliable to the extent that the *statement:*
    3.31 Is close to being a statement of direct observation.
    3.32 Is corroborated.
    3.33 Is corroboratable.
    3.34 Comes from a disinterested source with a reputation for ve-
       racity.
3.4 Observation statements, if based on a record, tend to be more reliable if the *record:*
    3.41 Was made at the time of observation.
    3.42 Was made by the person making the statement.
    3.43 Is believed by the person making the statement to be correct—
       either because he so believed at the time the record was made,
       or because he believes it was the record-maker's habit to make
       correct records.
3.5 Observation statements tend to be more reliable than inferences made from them.

JUDGING WHETHER A SIMPLE GENERALIZATION IS WARRANTED

A simple generalization is a statement which covers a number of instances and holds that they share some trait. For example, that red-headed people tend to have hot tempers is a generalization. It holds that red-headed people share the trait of tending to have hot tempers. A generalization is warranted:

4.1 To the extent that there is a bulk of reliable instances of it. The greater the variability of the population, the greater the bulk needed.

4.2 To the extent that it fits into the larger structure of knowledge.

4.3 To the extent that the selecting of instances is unbiased.

    4.31 A pure random sample is unbiased.

    4.32 A systematic sample is unbiased if a careful investigation suggests that there is not a relevant cycle or trend followed by the sampling procedure.

    4.33 Stratification of a population on relevant variables and unbiased sampling within the strata, is likely to be more efficient than 8.131 or 8.132 alone.

    4.34 An unbiased sampling of clusters of the population and unbiased sampling (or complete enumeration) within the clusters is likely to be an efficient way of sampling when access to separate individual units is difficult.

4.4 To the extent that there are no counter-instances.

The generalization that red-headed people tend to have hot tempers would be warranted to the extent that there is a large number of reliable instances of red-heads with hot tempers, to the extent that we are able to account for red-heads being hot-tempered, to the extent that our instances of red-heads are picked without bias, and to the extent that there is a lack of reliable instances of red-heads with even tempers.

JUDGING WHETHER A HYPOTHESIS IS WARRANTED

Though the word "hypothesis" is often used to refer to a simple generalization, for purposes of marking off an important kind of statement which has a different relationship to its grounds than a simple generalization I will restrict the word "hypothesis" to the job of referring to this other kind of statement. Under this usage a hypothesis is a statement which is fairly directly related to its support by virtue of its power to *explain* this support, rather than being related by virtue of the support's being composed of instances of the hypothesis, as is the case for simple generalizations.

The hypothesis can be either specific (as is the case in law and usually in history) or it can be general (as is ordinarily the case in physical sciences and the social sciences of economics, sociology, and psychology).

Here is an example of a specific hypothesis: "Hissarlik is located at the site of Troy."

Here is an example of a general hypothesis: "The pressure in a liquid varies directly as the depth, assuming the pressure at the surface to be zero."

A hypothesis is warranted to the extent that:

5.1 It explains a bulk and variety of reliable data. If a datum is explained, it can be deduced or loosely derived (in the fashion of the application of principles) from the hypothesis together with established facts or generalizations.
5.2 It is itself explained by a satisfactory system of knowledge.
5.3 It is not inconsistent with any evidence.
5.4 Its competitors are inconsistent with the evidence. This principle is the basis of controlled experiments.
5.5 It is testable. It must be, or have been, possible to make predictions from it.

For purposes of illustration let us consider the bearing of each of the criteria on each hypothesis of the above two examples of hypotheses:

Explaining a bulk and variety of reliable data (5.1). Since Hissarlik is only an hour's walk from the sea, the Hissarlik hypothesis explains the reported (in the *Iliad*) ability of the Greeks to go back and forth from Troy several times a day. It explains why there are ruins at Hissarlik. These explained reports, it should be noted, can be derived from the Hissarlik hypotheses together with established facts or generalizations:

Hissarlik is at the site of Troy.
Hissarlik is one hour's walk from the sea.
People are able to walk back and forth several times a day between places that are one hour's walk apart.
Therefore it is probable that the Greeks were able to go back and forth from Troy to the sea several times daily (the explained fact).
Hissarlik is at the site of Troy.
A large city when abandoned tends to leave ruins.
Therefore it is probable that there are ruins at Hissarlik (the explained fact).

Of course explaining only those two pieces of evidence is not enough to establish the hypothesis. More evidence of different types must be provided.

The pressure hypothesis explains why water spurts farther from a hole near the bottom of a tank than from a hole in the middle of a tank. It also explains the proportional relationships between the following sets of readings of pressure gauges attached to the supply tank in a water system:

Distance from Top of Tank (in ft.)	Pressure Reading (in lbs./sq. in.)
0	0
5	2.1
10	4.2

These data can be derived from the hypothesis together with established facts or generalizations:

> The pressure varies directly as the depth.
> The greater the pressure at a hole, the farther the liquid will spurt.
> The bottom hole is at a greater depth than the middle hole.
> *Therefore*, the water spurts farther from the hole near the bottom
> (the explained fact).
> The pressure varies directly as the depth.
> The depth at 10 ft. is twice that at 5 ft.
> *Therefore*, the pressure at 10 ft. (4.2 lbs./sq. in.) is twice that of 5 ft.
> (2.1 lbs./sq. in.), (the explained fact).

Again the explanation of these data alone does not establish the hypothesis. More explained data of various types are needed.

Being explained by a satisfactory system of knowledge (5.2). If the
Hissarlik hypothesis could itself be tentatively explained by established
facts and generalizations, it would then be more acceptable. For example,
suppose it were possible to show that the traits of the Trojans and the
facts about the geography, climate, and nearby civilization at the time
make it probable that the Trojan city would have developed at Hissarlik
at the time that Troy was supposed to have existed. If it were possible
to show that, the Hissarlik hypothesis would thereby receive support.

Similarly the pressure hypothesis is supported by showing that it can
be explained, and thus derived, as follows:

> Pressure in a liquid is the numerical equivalent of the weight of a
> regular column of liquid extending to the top of the container.
> The weight of a column of liquid varies directly with its height.
> *Therefore*, the pressure in a liquid varies directly with the depth.

Not being inconsistent with any evidence (5.3). The Hissarlik hypothesis would be weakened if no springs could be found in the area of
Hissarlik, since the *Iliad* mentions two springs in the area, one hot and
one cold. The reasoning might go:

> Hissarlik is at the site of Troy.
> There were probably at least two springs at Troy, one hot and one
> cold.
> Springs tend to remain in existence over the years.
> *Therefore*, it is probable that there are at least two springs at His-
> sarlik, one hot and one cold.

Note that in using the absence of springs as evidence against the hypothesis, we are assuming that springs tend to remain and that the report
of the *Iliad* is reliable. Either of these could be wrong. The less dependable these auxiliary assumptions are, the less dependable is our counter-
evidence.

The pressure hypothesis would be weakened by the discovery that water spurted out the same amounts at the middle and the bottom, since the hypothesis implies otherwise. That is, it would be weakened if we did not previously have so much by way of other evidence built up in favor of the hypothesis—so much that, in this case, one would have a right to suspect such data.

Its competitors' being inconsistent with the data (5.4). A competitor of the Hissarlik hypothesis is the hypothesis that Bunarbashi is at the site of Troy. This competing hypothesis is not consistent with the data that Bunarbashi is a three-hours' walk from the sea and that the Greeks were able to go back and forth several times daily, if we assume that the Greeks walked.

A competitor of the earlier-stated pressure hypothesis might be one to the effect that the pressure increases directly as one gets closer to the surface of the earth. This hypothesis is inconsistent with pressure gauge readings on two independent tanks, one over the other, when the top tank has the pressure gauge at its bottom, and the bottom tank has its gauge at the top. The alternative hypothesis implies that the gauge in the upper tank would give the smaller reading. The data are just the opposite.

A controlled experiment is designed to rule out competing hypotheses by producing data inconsistent with them. When we test the hypothesis that a new fertilizer will increase the growth of corn, we put the fertilizer in a corn patch, develop a companion corn patch, the control, identical in every respect possible except for fertilizer, and watch the results. If there is a difference, the fertilizer hypothesis can explain it. But it would not be explained by heavy rainfall, warm weather, sunlight, etc., since both patches supposedly received the same amount. These alternative hypotheses would justify a prediction of no difference and would thus be inconsistent with the data.

It is, of course, impossible to develop a perfectly controlled experiment, since the perfect isolation and variation of a single variable is not possible. The important thing might be a *combination* of weather and fertilizer, or the important thing might have slipped by unnoticed. But we can still see in the controlled experiment an attempt to approximate the logical goal of eliminating hypotheses by turning up data that are inconsistent with them. The controlled experiment is an efficient way of eliminating hypotheses by this method.

It should be noted that there is an implicit assumption of standard or familiar conditions in the reasoning that leads to judgments of explanation and inconsistency. For example, the inconsistency resulting from Bunarbashi's being a three-hour walk from the sea is an inconsistency only if Bunarbashi was a three-hour walk from the sea at the time of the Trojan War. In declaring the data to be inconsistent with the competing hypothesis one is gambling that the sea was not at a significantly different level at that time.

This feature of reasoning from hypotheses fits in with the notion of loose reasoning presented under Aspect No. 1. There are always possible qualifications when we apply principles to the world of things, men, and events.

Being testable (5.5). This is a logical criterion, not a criterion of practicality or even physical possibility. The criterion requires only that it must be possible to *conceive* of what would count as evidence for, and what would count as evidence against, the hypothesis. We have already seen that this is possible for each of our hypotheses. The fact that some conceivable tests are not practically possible is not important so far as this criterion is concerned. A conceivable, though presumably physically impossible, test of the pressure hypothesis would involve swimming to the bottom of the ocean with pressure and depth gauges, recording readings at various points along the way.

An hypothesis that appears untestable is this one: "Airplane crashes are caused by gremlins," since it does not appear possible to conceive of something that would count as evidence for and to conceive of something that would count as evidence against the hypothesis. The word "appear" is used deliberately, since the conceiving of evidence for and evidence against would immediately make the hypothesis testable—and would reveal to some extent the meaning of the hypothesis.

Most hypotheses that we consider are testable in this logical sense, so this criterion does not often discredit an hypothesis. But its fulfillment is absolutely essential for hypotheses about the world of things, men, and events.

JUDGING WHETHER A THEORY IS WARRANTED

The difference between a theoretic system and an hypothesis of the type we have been considering is that the former is an involved network of relations between concepts, many of which are abstract and technical, while the latter is a simple relation between two or a small number of concepts, often less abstract and technical. Examples of theoretic systems are the kinetic theory of matter, the atomic theory, Gestalt psychology, the theory of evolution, Keynesian economics, Turner's frontier theory, and classical English grammar. Obviously evaluation of theories is a demanding task. It demands more than we can ordinarily expect of elementary and secondary students. Undergraduates are sometimes better equipped, and graduate students are expected to become equipped to perform this task.

Evaluating theories is comparable to evaluating hypotheses, but much more complex. In general the same criteria apply but on a broader scale.

Two modifications should be noted: the addition of the criterion of simplicity and the weakening of the effect of contrary evidence.

The criterion of simplicity calls for choosing the simpler of two competing systems, other things being equal. The classic example of the application of this criterion is the preference of the Copernican system, which considered the sun the center of the universe, to the Ptolemaic system, which looked upon the earth as the center. The Copernican system was simpler since it needed fewer cycles and epicycles to explain the movements of the planets.

Since theories have so many parts, contrary evidence does not usually result in outright rejection, but rather in adjustment to fit the contrary evidence—until the whole system becomes more complex than a competitor. The criterion of simplicity then functions.

Following are the criteria for theoretic systems. There will be brief comments, but no attempt to exemplify the operation of each will be made, because to do so would be a monumental task and would make rather laborious reading for those not versed in the fields chosen. You are invited to provide examples from a theoretic system in a field you know.

A theoretic system is warranted to the extent that:

6.31 It explains a bulk and variety of reliable data. Within the system, furthermore, the less abstract statements should be explained by the more abstract ones.

6.32 It is explained by broader theories. Some theories are so broad already that, with our present state of knowledge, to demand fulfillment of this criterion is often to demand speculation.

6.33 It is not inconsistent with any evidence. As indicated earlier, occasional inconsistency can be handled by adjusting the theory. Sometimes the inconsistency must just be accepted for lack of a better theory, and we say, "The theory does not hold for this kind of case."

6.34 Its competitors are inconsistent with the data. Again a single inconsistency does not destroy a competitor, for it too can be adjusted, but a larger number of inconsistencies damage it.

6.35 It is testable. When adjusting a theory to fit the data, people are sometimes tempted to make the theory impregnable by making it untestable. Freudian psychology is sometimes accused of being untestable.

6.36 It is simpler than its rivals. As theories are adjusted to fit new data, they may become extremely complicated, as had happened to the entire Ptolemaic system at the time of Copernicus.

JUDGING WHETHER AN ARGUMENT DEPENDS ON AN AMBIGUITY

The ambiguity can appear anywhere in an argument, but most frequently it appears in a shift of meaning from the sense in which the conclusion is proved to a sense in which it is applied. There is such a shift in the following line of reasoning:

> There are people who sincerely believe on religious grounds that medication is wrong. They believe this because they believe that any treatment of human beings with medicine is a violation of their religious principles. "Medication" means anything intended for the prevention, cure, or alleviation of disease." Since the chlorination of water is intended for the prevention of disease, it is medication. To chlorinate water is thus to violate their religious principles.

The statement, "Chlorination is medication," is proven when the statement has one meaning: "Chlorination is something intended for the prevention, cure, or alleviation of disease." And it is applied with a different meaning: "Chlorination is treatment of human beings with medicine."

Obviously arguments that depend on ambiguities are to be rejected. No criteria can be given that will serve as guides to students in detecting ambiguities, although you can exhort them to be alert with such statements as, "Make sure that the key words are used in the same sense throughout," or "Check the argument using the key word in its ordinary sense, and if it fails, check it using the word in any technical senses that might be employed."

JUDGING WHETHER A STATEMENT IS OVERVAGUE OR OVERSPECIFIC

For the purposes of a given situation, a particular statement might be too vague to provide guidance. In such situations the statement should be rejected or inquired into, since in its condition its truth or falsity is irrelevant.

The statement, "Education has disappeared from the schools" (or, "There is more education in the schools than ever before") is useless in decision-making about curriculum and school finance until the terms, "education," "disappeared," and "the schools," are clarified. The statements are not specific enough to be tested and applied. They are too vague.

On the other hand, in a war-ravaged country it might be quite meaningful to say that education has disappeared from the schools (since they are now used for hospitals or housing). In this situation, "education," even loosely defined, has disappeared from the schools.

This aspect requires consideration of the purpose of the discourse and requires the judgment, "This is (or is not) specific enough for our purpose." If the purpose is to come up with curriculum and budgetary recommendations for a school system long in existence, the statement is not specific enough. If the purpose is to make a report to the leader of a war-ravaged country, it is specific enough.

It might be thought that this aspect of critical thinking is one in which people do not make mistakes. In concrete situations this tends to be true, but in abstract situations it is easy to go wrong by forgetting to put questions and answers in the context of situations with purposes. Crawshay-Williams develops this point well (1).

JUDGING WHETHER AN ALLEGED AUTHORITY IS RELIABLE

In order to assess the statements made by an alleged authority, one must appraise his credentials. Certainly other aspects of critical thinking should also be applied, if one is able to do so. But there are times when one must make a judgment about a statement solely on the basis of the credentials of the person making the statement. An alleged authority should be accepted to the extent that:

9.1 He has a good reputation.

9.2 The statement is in his field.

9.3 He was disinterested—that is, he did not knowingly stand to profit by the results of his statements (except that he may have stood to have his reputation affected).

9.4 His reputation could be affected by his statement and he was aware of this fact when he made his statement.

9.5 He studied the matter.

9.6 He followed the accepted procedures in coming to his conclusion (although there are legitimate exceptions to this requirement).

9.7 He was in full possession of his faculties when he made the statement.

THE REDUCTION OF PROBLEM IDENTIFICATION TO THE OTHER ASPECTS

Different kinds of judgments go under the label, "problem identification":

1. Judging that a want has been identified, as when someone says, "My problem is to learn to appreciate poetry." In this sense the judgment that the speaker has identified his problems is tantamount to the judgment that this is something the speaker, who might also be the judge, really wants to do. Problem identification here is identification of wants, either one's own, or someone else's. If they are one's own introspected wants, then critical thinking is not involved. For a person to know his wants (felt needs) is something that he cannot fail to do.

If they are someone else's wants, then identifying problems is the same as establishing explanatory hypotheses, as is the case for all subconscious wants, one's own or someone else's, for example, "Mark's problem is to get attention." Judging the identification of someone else's problem and

of subconscious wants are then critical thinking of a type already discussed—judging hypotheses.

2. Judging that a valuable goal has been selected. Here is such a
problem identification: "Our problem in Culver City is to increase respect
for law and order." Insofar as that is a statement of an end rather than
a means, the judgment that it is an adequate identification of a problem
is a value judgment. For reasons indicated earlier, this type of judging,
though important, is excluded from this analysis of critical thinking.

3. Judging that a means decision is adequate. For example, if the
broader objective were respect for law and order, the following might
be a statement of a means decision: "Our problem in Culver City is to
establish a youth bureau." The judgment here that the problem has been
identified does at least these two things: (1) implies endorsement of the
goal of respect for law and order (this part of the judgment then is a
value judgment); (2) says that the means selected will facilitate achievement of the goal and that they will be at least more likely to facilitate
it than any other course of action, within the limits of existing resources
and goals. These limiting goals, by the way, are another instance in which
values are impressed on problem identification. To judge that the problem
has been identified is to judge that no unjustified goal violation would
take place if the problem were solved.

To apply the means interpretation to our example: it is there implied
that establishment of a youth bureau would increase the likelihood of winning respect for law and order, and would be more likely to do so than
any other course.

Judging a means decision is judging the application of a principle and
judging the acceptability of the principle. To judge whether a youth
bureau in Culver City would result in increased respect for law and order
is to judge whether a principle about the effectiveness of youth bureaus,
applied to this situation, gives us this statement with sufficient probability;
and to judge whether the principle is acceptable. Judging principles comes
under judging generalizations, hypotheses, or theories, depending on the
principle in question.

In summary, problem identification is many different things and often
a combination of them. Elements capable of being treated under the
proposed notion of critical thinking are (1) judging the alleged identification of the wants of others and of subconscious wants (explanatory hypotheses), and (2) judging the assertion of a means of reaching a goal
(judging the application of principles and judging the principles themselves). Each of these types of judging is treated elsewhere.

Summary

There has been presented a root notion of critical thinking: the correct assessing of statements, and the presentation and clarification of a list of nine major aspects of critical thinking, which are based upon the root notion. These aspects get at the most important ways people can go wrong in assessing statements and can serve as a statement of elementary and intermediate goals in the teaching of critical thinking.

It has not been the purpose of this paper to suggest how to teach critical thinking, since that would vary so much from one level to another and one subject to another. Perhaps the examples will suggest teaching ideas.

References

1. Rupert Crawshay-Williams, *Methods and Criteria of Reasoning.* London: Routledge and Kegan Paul, 1957.
2. Robert H. Ennis, "Assumption-Finding." In B. Othanel Smith and Robert H. Ennis (eds.), *Language and Concepts in Education,* pp. 161–178. Chicago: Rand McNally, 1961.
3. B. Othanel Smith, "The Improvement of Critical Thinking," *Progressive Education,* 30 (Mar. 1953), 129–134.
4. P. F. Strawson, *Introduction to Logical Theory.* London: Methuen, 1952.
5. F. Waisman, "Verifiability." In Antony Flew (ed.), *Logic and Language.* Oxford: Basil Blackwell & Mott, 1952.

14. Critical Reading Is Critical Thinking

Robert Karlin

The following basic elements may be regarded as major cornerstones in critical thinking, which has been defined as "the process of examining . . . verbal materials in the light of related objective evidence, comparing . . . the statement with some norm or standard and concluding or acting upon the judgment then made." [1] It is the writer's belief that critical thinking

[1] David Russell, *Children's Thinking* (Boston: Ginn & Co., 1956), p. 285.

"Critical Reading Is Critical Thinking," by Robert Karlin. Reprinted from the September 1963 issue of *Education.* Copyright 1963 by The Bobbs-Merrill Company, Inc., Indianapolis, Indiana.

and critical reading have much in common. Thinking must accompany reading; otherwise, reading is futile.

"Fact vs. Fancy"
"Truth vs. Half-Truth"
"Accuracy vs. Distortion"
"Discrimination vs. Persuasion"
"Reservation vs. Acceptance"

We do recognize that the printed word rather than the spoken one serves as an intervening variable, and it is not impossible that this difference produces effects which are not found in the latter. Printed words seem to have a mystical power for many persons in our culture in much the same way that other visual symbols dominate the behavior of people in primitive societies. Nevertheless, children and youth can be taught to deal with printed ideas.

It has been estimated that approximately seventy per cent of what we learn is obtained through visual means; reading is a major force for obtaining the information upon which critical thinking can be based. Within this framework, reading serves two purposes: to provide a source for ideas and to trigger reactions to ideas. These are the essence of critical thinking. Critical reading, then, *is* another form of critical thinking.

FACTORS IN CRITICAL READING

Attitude and Ability. Many children and older students have the ability to read critically. In fact, they have been *thinking* critically, though not always clearly, for a number of years prior to their entrance into first grade. Slow and even mentally-retarded learners show that they are capable of making judgments and evaluations on the levels that are meaningful for them.

Thinking critically is not so much a question of ability as it is a matter of *attitude*. Young people can learn to read narrative and expository materials with an inquiring mind. They can do so only in a classroom climate that encourages creativity and participation and under enlightened leadership that nourishes one's right to be wrong.

However, no one suggests that intellectual ability is not tied in any way to critical reading. Brighter children may be expected to respond to ideas in more and varied ways than their lesser-endowed age-mates. But the mere possession of high intelligence does not guarantee equally high performance in weighing ideas. The promotion and development of appropriate attitudes toward them are responsibilities which each of us must assume.

Knowledge. A reader cannot evaluate statements unless he is ready to compare them with known standards. It is obvious that knowledge is a prime element in critical reading. The reader must possess not only information but also the background and understanding against which he can weigh the writer's statements and views.

Meaningful experiences which lead to the formation of solid concepts constitute the foundation for making judgments and reaching decisions. It is unrealistic to expect anyone to react prudently unless he has the means to do so.

Careful analysis is dependent upon prior learnings. Teachers hold the keys to the doors of knowledge. They must help young people unlock them if the latter are to be prepared for roles associated with maturity and responsibility.

Feelings and Values. Personal factors such as the reader's feelings and values may affect the degree to which he responds judiciously to ideas of others. Statements and topics that contain emotional overtones can produce reactions that might not otherwise occur.

Readers have been known to misinterpret the purposes and views of writers and even to fail to "listen" to them, not because of any failure to understand but because of an inability to receive. Younger children as well as older ones are subject to such adverse influences.

We must try to remove any obstacles which interfere with clear thinking. Some authorities believe that it is important to help readers understand on what grounds they may be evaluating ideas. Students can be encouraged to review their beliefs in order to determine whether their judgments are being influenced by them.

CRITICAL READING IN THE LOWER GRADES

Many teachers have directed activities which required children to make judgments and decisions, but a smaller number have planned systematic programs that were designed to treat critical reading in more than an accidental way. This section and the following one enumerate a series of activities which teachers who are known to the writer are using to foster the spirit of evaluative reading and refine the quality of pupils' responses.

Even though most children in the primary grades do not read complex materials, there are ample opportunities for judging content. Basal readers, trade books, subject-oriented books, and newspapers and magazines are being used in well-organized programs to develop critical reading skills.

For example, children examine pictures in order to evaluate them. They compare one with another to decide which they prefer to use as an illustration for a report or an experience story. They look at pictures which accompany narrative and expository selections and compare their features with what they personally know about them. They decide whether a picture is an accurate or fanciful statement by using their own knowledge as the criterion of measurement.

Children also examine different views about pictures, accept or reject them, or withhold judgment until they can be verified. They discuss and compare the quality of pictures and suggest changes or additions to them. They decide whether a black-and-white or colored illustration better serves the reader's and author's purposes.

In short, they examine pictures critically, thereby building an attitude toward them and developing standards to judge them.

Young children respond to stories in similar ways. They ask themselves whether the story thread is plausible. They are interested in discussing the characters and comparing them to the children they know.

Children consider such questions as, "Would you have done what the children in the story did?" and "In what ways might the story have ended differently?" They discuss events and behavior in relation to their own standards. They often decide that they need to complete the story in order to reach firm judgments.

Informative writing presents other opportunities for evaluating material. Children separate facts from opinions. They understand the difference between "I know" and "I think" and classify statements accordingly. They are alert to differences in explanations of events in science and social studies.

Children seek confirmation from more than one source by comparing accounts and selecting appropriate ones. They want to know who the author is. Is he qualified to write about the topic? How old is the material? Have new discoveries changed matters? Answers to these and related questions are being sought by children who are learning to read with an inquiring attitude.

CRITICAL READING IN THE UPPER GRADES

The foundations of critical reading laid in the primary grades are reinforced and extended in the middle and upper grades. As children reach greater maturity in reading and understanding they are inspired and challenged to use their abilities creatively. The ability to react thoughtfully to the acts and ideas of others is a major objective of a sound reading program for the intermediate and higher grades.

Wider reading is encouraged. Older children who are active instead of passive learners sample a variety of materials and have opportunities to draw comparisons between them.

For example, they study factual information obtained from several different textbooks, encyclopedias, and current sources such as newspapers and magazines. They note differences and similarities among them, select relevant portions, and reject others.

They also determine how different newspapers and magazines handle selected stories and seek reasons for variations among them. They analyze the content of newspaper editorials and relate it to the ways in which papers present the news. They point out in books and periodicals statements of fact and of opinion.

Literature becomes a vehicle for developing critical evaluation. Students read short stories, plays, poems, essays, biography, and novels and study them for meanings and messages. They compare fictional characters with people they know and explain similarities and differences in character and behavior.

They also observe how identical themes are treated by different authors and indicate why some writers are preferred to others. They examine literary styles in relation to authors' purposes and decide which are effective. They review complete works and compare their own evaluations to those of professionals.

More mature students are alerted to biased and distorted statements. They seek to identify them as well as provide explanations for them. They are as much concerned with a writer's purposes as they are with his ideas. They relate an author's background and associations to what he writes.

Furthermore, they learn to recognize rhetorical devices that are designed to create impressions and mold opinions. They study their own and others' reactions to language and the ways in which words are used to generate feelings for or against ideas. They become wise in the ways of propaganda and persuasion. They recognize the "soft" as well as the "hard sell." They are encouraged to practice a healthy skepticism and at the same time avoid intemperate behavior.

Conclusion

Anyone who has the ability to think critically can learn to read critically. Intelligence, background of experiences, feelings, and values are factors known to influence the level and quality of the reader's responses to printed ideas. Of equal if not greater importance are the attitudes the individual brings to material he reads. A teacher's major responsibility is to stimulate all readers to react as thoughtfully as they can to reading matter.

Teachers can guide young children and older students to read critically by suggesting activities which require them to make evaluative judgments. Questions of "how" and "why" sharpen their thinking. Discussions assist them to understand the basis for accepting or rejecting points of view. Carefully planned lessons in critical reading are likely to help boys and girls achieve one of reading's major objectives.

15.   The Prerequisite: Knowing How to Read Critically
David H. Russell

Censorship usually involves a decision by a person or group about what others should read; ability in critical reading suggests that the individual himself makes the choice. Should the screening be done by the Lord Chamberlin, by the Watch and Ward Society or by the person doing the reading or viewing? The primary concern of NCTE is not with the banning of materials at the source. We must have competence and established procedures in dealing with censorship by individuals or groups in our local districts but our first concern is with the critical abilities of children and youth. We want to help young people to reject for themselves the vulgar, the meretricious, the fallacious. We want students who can decide for themselves whether there is Communism in *Robin Hood,* pornography in *The Good Earth* or *Drums Along the Mohawk.*

Critical reading does not exist in a vacuum by itself but can be thought of best as closely related to critical thinking. Recent statements of the aims of education and psychological studies of cognition made during the last thirty years both give us leads to a consideration of critical thinking.

The importance of the idea has been expressed in the last bulletin of the Educational Policies Commission entitled "The Central Purpose of American Education." The writers of the bulletin put it this way: "The purpose which runs through and strengthens all other educational purposes—the common thread of education—is the development of the ability to think." In another place the bulletin discusses ethical character in relation to thinking. "Character is misunderstood if thought of as mere conformity to standards imposed by external authority—(It has) meaning to the extent (it represents) affirmative, thoughtful choices by individuals. The ability to make these choices depends on awareness of values . . . and this awareness of standards or values is an integral part of critical thinking."

This brings us to the question of what we mean by "thinking" and "critical thinking." As currently used the word *thinking* is an omnibus term carrying too heavy a load, such a heavy load that it sometimes becomes meaningless. We say a child is thinking when he builds a bridge with blocks, a housewife when she is following a recipe, a poet when contriving a sonnet. The same confusion exists in defining the type of thinking called

Dr. Russell is Professor of Education at the University of California at Berkeley and President of the National Council of Teachers of English. This paper was presented at the Miami Beach meeting of NCTE, November, 1962.

"The Prerequisite: Knowing How to Read Critically," by David H. Russell, *Elementary English,* Vol. XL (October 1964), 579–582. Reprinted with the permission of the National Council of Teachers of English.

"critical thinking." One of my doctoral candidates has recently compiled no less than thirty-five descriptions of critical thinking in educational journals. It is probably time we became critical about the definitions of critical thinking.

If I may be critical of the Educational Policies report on "The Central Purpose" I would say that it tends to regard thinking as one thing. Sometimes as teachers of English we are urged to teach youth to think as if thinking were some single, unitary ability. The research evidence in psychology is against this single-mindedness. Different psychologists use different terms, but it is my own belief that the kinds of thinking we do in school or business or the rest of the world's work can be divided into some six overlapping categories. Elsewhere I have called these: perceptual thinking, associative thinking, concept formation, problem solving, critical thinking, and creative thinking. We see, then, that critical thinking is only one of the kinds of thinking we want children to learn and adults to practice.

What is critical thinking? I believe it can be best described as essentially a three-factor ability. It includes an attitude factor of questioning and suspended judgment, a conative or functional factor which involves use of methods of logical inquiry and problem solving, and a judgment factor of evaluating in terms of some norm or standard or consensus. The attitude factor, for example, may be represented by "I'm from Missouri" or "Show me." It means checking on the assumptions of the author—a difficult task, especially in some fiction. The conative or action factor may include selecting significant words and phrases in a statement, identifying emotion and bias, picking out stereotypes and clichés. We can all have fun recognizing an emotional appeal to something sacred like home or mother or identifying what E. E. Cummings calls a "duck-billed platitude." The third judgment factor may include distinguishing the relevant and irrelevant, assessing literary merit, and looking for evidence in any conclusion drawn by speaker or writer.

All these sound like formidable accomplishments which we all need to practice. They appear difficult to us adults so how can they be started with children? We might as well face the facts that critical thinking abilities are difficult and they are slow agrowing. And yet the need to use them is all around us.

May I state four reasons why I believe critical thinking must be stressed from kindergarten through college—why I believe teachers, and curriculum committees must give development of abilities in critical thinking a continuous place in the curriculum.

1. The mass media of communication influence us to think and act alike. Conformity, not individuality, is stressed in our listening and much of our reading. In 1962, the date farmer in Southern California, the lumberman in Washington, and the owner of the cranberry bog in New England read

the same columnists, hear the same radio news reporters, watch the same TV shows. We know that elementary school children, millions of them, watch television on an average of over 20 hours a week. As one man has said, television is a cookie cutter shaping our minds all in the same mold. Wiser men than I have written about the dangers of conformity in our society. These dangers are particularly great, and insidious, in relation to the impressionable minds of children. The effect of our mass culture is to make little bands of conformists—only the home and the school can help children think for themselves, reject the unworthy, resist the blandishments of the "guy with a bill of goods for sale."

2. High performance on an intelligence test does not guarantee high scores on a test of critical thinking. Good mental ability does not guarantee strong critical thinking abilities. The relationship between general intelligence and critical thinking is positive but not high. Critical thinking abilities are not acquired automatically as a part of general mental growth; specific provision must be made for their development in all curricular areas.

3. Attitudes are learned. The first of the three components of critical thinking I have mentioned is an attitude of questioning, a suspending of judgment until the facts are all in. Youth do not develop a questioning attitude automatically. Instead, teachers and schools have to work to develop the attitude. I do not believe that teacher and class must always be suspicious. Some of you saw the *New Yorker* cartoon of an instructor and his class. On the chalkboard was written $2 + 2 = 4$. The caption on the cartoon was only one word but the instructor was saying, "However . . ."

The facts in a single book on science or in a fictionalized biography may be questioned, just as doubts can be expressed about some news story in a newspaper or the words of the speaker. An attitude of questioning and criticism is sometimes relevant. Such attitudes are learned partly by imitation, for attitudes may be caught as well as taught.

4. The third component of critical thinking I have described as judgment or evaluation. Judgment in terms of some norm or standard or consensus implies a background of experience which sometimes the school must supply. Knowledge and experience are prerequisite to critical thinking in the area in which the thinking is done. We cannot ask children or adults to be critical in a vacuum. In these days when many chidren have never seen a farm, when rural children may never have entered an apartment house, the school must help supply a broad background of experience before problem solving or creative thinking or critical thinking can be attempted. But from the first grade on, let us not stop just with the experience—teacher and group must discuss, contrast, and compare, and then the teacher moves imperceptibly into questioning and judgment. (*Why* are trains and railways losing out these days?)

Here, then are four reasons why school people must take definite steps to develop critical thinking abilities: (1) The whole force of mass culture is toward conformity rather than individuality. (2) Good mental ability does not guarantee some of the specific skills needed in critical thinking. (3) Attitudes of critical thinking can be learned, at least in part, by imitation of the procedures of the teacher and other adults; and (4) The school must often help supply the background of experience, the familiarity and know-how, which is the necessary basis for critical thinking. Each of these reasons, and especially the fourth, relate to the question of self-censorship instead of outside censorship.

Some of you, and especially those of you who work with older adolescents or college students, may think I am pretty optimistic when I recommend beginning work with young children in critical thinking. You know that some students come to high school or even college who have difficulty in reading for literal meaning, much less being critical of what they read or hear. Can the ten-year-old or the fifteen-year-old really exercise the judgment necessary for evaluating the newspapers, films or novels he sees? In partial answer here are nine statements of things we know or believe which have been at least partly verified by research. I give them in rapid-fire order but each can be expanded in your own thinking:

1. Some children have acquired abilities in critical thinking before they enter school. (One five-year-old said to me smilingly, "*All* the TV ads say they have the best breakfast cereal.")

2. Activities in critical thinking begin in the primary grades—not with the "rational" adult. (A first grade recently distinguished fantasy and reality after they heard the story "The Day It Rained Cats and Dogs.")

3. Critical thinking depends less upon specific techniques and more upon attitude and experience. (In the words of Don Marquis, we can detect the speaker who "strokes a platitude until it purrs like an epigram," but we must be able to discover the platitude.)

4. Part of the attitude factor in critical thinking is the objectivity which comes from the ability to shift perspective—to see one's own behavior and ideas as they may be viewed by others. (This may be part of developing the self concept, especially crucial in the junior high school years.)

5. The experience factor in critical thinking involves considerable participation in the social and linguistic community. A chance to talk things over or explore the effects of action produces a validation by consensus which is prerequisite to making sound judgments.

6. Although probably not so important as attitude or experience, there are hundreds of skills in the conative or operational phase of critical thinking. These include the ability to read for exact details, to relate cause and effect in a speaker's statement, and to detect a propaganda device such as "glittering generality." In relation to Communism the favorite device is name calling. Long ago a political opponent said that FDR was

substituting the hammer and sickle for the stars and stripes in the American flag. This device is not dead today.

7. The evaluation phase of critical thinking is closely related to the ability to check one's own thinking against some social norm or consensual validation. This means that the child or youth must know the habits and customs of the group and the school must be aware of possible differences between home and community values.

8. Irrationality in thinking occurs when the challenge to the individual is too severe, when he does not have the resources to meet the questioning of an idea close to the heart of his own personality or philosophy. If we are threatened by a statement or idea it is hard to consider it unemotionally and critically.

9. Critical thinking about materials which may be labeled "lewd" or "obscene" or "pornographic" by certain censors is probably related to the reader's standards or tastes. Many teachers have reported successful efforts to raise their students' tastes in literature and in cinema. If this is accomplished the knowledge and attitude may provide the best bulwark against undesirable material.

These nine principles have been partly validated by research and indicate action for each of us.

I have suggested this morning that, ever so often, we have to dynamite some educational debris out of the way and replace it with the high priorities, the essentials for today. In English and other curricular areas we need greater emphasis on thinking abilities. At least six different thinking abilities can be identified and one of the most important of these is critical thinking. Most of the influences of modern life are against such skill and so the school has a peculiar and unique responsibility for developing it, from the first grade onward. It is not enough to be *against* Communism or sadism or hedonism, we must be *for* the development of skills in critical thinking about any "ism." In one of my children's group-written newspapers recently appeared this epigram, "Many a good story has been ruined by over-verification." Fortunately for us, many a bad story can be ruined by it too when we have the time and skill to check it critically.

In our pluralistic culture, there are many extreme voices. We must be able to resist some of the statements of a Senator Joseph McCarthy, a Texas oil millionaire, or a high-riding labor boss. We must be able to decide for ourselves that this writer has something to say but that one is merely filthy. Socrates, facing death, told his accusers that "The unexamined life is not worth living." The ability to examine complex community affairs or personal problems begins in childhood and develops slowly over the years. As a product of our schools we do not want bulging-jawed squirrels crammed with knowledge. We want not sheep but curious, questioning people; not thoughtless conformity, but thoughtful appraisal;

not parrotting back but reflecting and judging; not prohibiting but evaluating.

16.   The Teaching of Thinking

Hilda Taba

Educators have long said to themselves and to others that the proper
business of school is to teach students to think. Yet this objective has remained a pious hope instead of becoming a tangible reality. A variety of
factors have militated against developing a serious and well thought out
strategy for helping students to become autonomous, creative, and productive thinkers.

Perhaps the most serious inhibiting factor has been the hazy conceptualization both of what is meant by teaching and what thinking consists
of. Thinking has been treated as a global process which seemingly en-
compasses anything that goes on in the head, from daydreaming to constructing a concept of relativity. Consequently, the problem of defining
thinking is still before us. The distinctions between the various types of
thinking have been defective also. Even the more serious educational
thinkers fail to distinguish the strategies of thinking, such as problem
solving, from the basic cognitive process and skills, such as generalizing,
differentiating, and forming concepts. These processes are the necessary
ingredients of problem solving if this strategy is to amount to anything
beyond sheer formality.

Implementation of thinking as an educational objective also has been
handicapped by several questionable assumptions. One rather widely accepted assumption is that reflective thinking cannot take place until a
sufficient body of factual information is accumulated. Teaching, which follows this assumption, stresses factual coverage and burdens the memory
with unorganized and, therefore, rather perishable information.

An equally unproductive assumption is that thought is an automatic
by-product of studying certain subjects and assimilating the end products
of someone else's disciplined thought. Some subjects are assumed to have
this power independently of how they learn or are taught. Inherently,
memorizing mathematical formulae or the steps in mathematical processes
is assumed to be better training than memorizing cake recipes, even

"The Teaching of Thinking," by Hilda Taba, *Elementary English*, XLII (May
1965), 534–542. Reprinted with the permission of the National Council of Teachers
of English and Hilda Taba.

though both may be learned in the same manner and call for the same mental process—rote memory (15).

The analysis of teaching suffers from similar difficulties. Teaching is still viewed largely as communication of knowledge, and often knowledge is equated with descriptive information—the "what," "who," and "when" questions are the main diet of classroom instruction. As a consequence the current methods of teaching tend to be shaped by this emphasis. Research on teaching has skirted the actual process of teaching and has concentrated instead on such matters as personal characteristics of good teachers and *a priori* criteria for rating effective teaching (6).

It is no wonder, then, that despite the widespread acceptance of thinking as an educational objective little consideration has been given to the ways in which learning to think differ from the ways in which students learn knowledge or content of various sorts.

Recent research is producing changes in both of these areas. Studies of cognition are under way, which promise a more precise analysis of the processes and of the psychological dynamics of the mental activity we call thinking. Some of these studies are concerned with styles of labeling (12), others with strategies of concept formation (2), and still others with what amounts to the styles in strategies of thinking (7, 10) important as these studies are, as yet their results cannot be easily translated into the methods for modifying the ways of thinking. But at least they are opening up the possibility of a scientific approach to the analysis of thinking.

The development of thinking has received renewed attention also, as exemplified by the recent interest in the work of Piaget and his followers. Piaget's theories regarding the nature of thought and the sequences in the transformation of the patterns or modes of thinking have influenced such enterprises as Bruner's (3) analysis of the process of education and Suchman's (13) experiments with inquiry training.

Some progress is being made in the study of the teaching process also. Recent studies of teaching have focused on teaching as it occurs in the classroom instead of inferring its effectiveness either from *a priori* notions of good teaching or from the characteristics of good teachers. Studies by Hughes (8), Flanders (5), and Bellack (1) focus on describing and cataloguing the teaching acts and on inferring from these descriptions their impact on learning in general, on classroom climate, and on achievement.

This article is a description of a study of classroom interaction designed to examine the relationship between teaching strategies and the development of cognitive processes (16). The study, conducted under a grant from the Cooperative Research Branch of the U.S. Office of Education, focused on several hypotheses. The central hypothesis was that it is possible to train students in the processes of thinking, provided that the trainable cognitive skills could be identified.

The studies of thinking cited above seemed to have one difficulty in common as far as the application of their findings to instruction in the classroom is concerned. The findings regarding the styles of thought fail to shed light on the processes by which these styles are acquired or to describe the skills on which these styles are founded.

Another hypothesis was that under optimal conditions this training would result in an acceleration of the usual developmental sequence, such as the appearance of abstract or formal thought. The studies of the development of thought and intelligence by Piaget and the Geneva school (9 *, 11, 14 **) suggest that the evolution of thought takes place in three stages, essentially: 1) the sensory-motor stage or the preverbal intelligence; 2) the stage of concrete operations or thinking with objects and concrete events, which stage lasts from around two to eleven years of age; and 3) the stage of conceptual or formal thought which is established between eleven years of age and adolescence. There is a question, however, whether training would alter these age placements since the available data recorded the performance of untrained children, or those with only a minimum of training, such as in the study by Ervin (4). It seemed reasonable to assume that if both the curriculum and teaching strategies were addressed to the development of thought, formal thought could appear earlier.

The third hypothesis was that with adequate teaching strategies the possibility of abstract thought would be opened to students who are now considered to have too low an IQ to be capable of higher levels of mental activity.

The study was conducted in elementary classes which were using a curriculum in social studies that systematically stressed the development of an ability to generalize and to use generalizations productively. What remained to be done was to specify the necessary teaching strategies and to train the teachers in their use, in order to become adept at these processes themselves, and to learn how to induct children in the mastery of the required cognitive skills.

The Concept of Cognitive Tasks

In an effort to arrive at teachable and learnable aspects of thought, three cognitive tasks were identified: 1) concept formation, 2) the development of generalizations and inferences through interpretation of raw data, and 3) the explanation and prediction of new phenomena by applying known principles and facts.

* Chapter 6.
** Pp. 107–112.

CONCEPT FORMATION

In its simplest form, concept development may be described as consisting of three processes or operations. One is the differentiation of the properties or characteristics of objects and events, such as differentiating the
materials of which houses are built from other characteristics of houses.
This differentiating involves analysis in the sense of breaking down global
wholes into specific properties and elements.

The second process is that of grouping. This process calls for abstracting
certain common characteristics in an array of dissimilar objects or events
and for grouping these on the basis of this similar property, such as
grouping together hospitals, doctors, and medicine as something to do
with health care or according to their availability as an index to the
standard of living. Naturally, the same objects and events can be grouped
in several different ways. For example, hospitals, X-rays, and surgical
equipment can be grouped together as health facilities, as type of services,
or as indices of standard of living, depending on the purpose of the grouping.

The third process is that of categorizing and labeling. This process calls
for the discovery of categories or labels which encompass and organize
diverse objects and events, such as evolving the concept of a unit measurement from measuring with a cup, a yardstick, a plain stick, and a rubber
band. It also involves the process of super- and subordination; that is, deciding which items can be subsumed under which category.

In classrooms this cognitive task occurs in the form of enumerating or
listing, such as identifying a series of specific items noted in a film or
reported by a research committee, then grouping similar things, and,
finally, labeling the groups.

INTERPRETATION OF DATA AND INFERENCE

Essentially this cognitive task consists of evolving generalizations and
principles from an analysis of concrete data. Several subprocesses are
involved. The first and the simplest is that of identifying specific points
in the data. This process is somewhat analogous to the listing or enumeration preceding grouping. The second process is that of explaining specific
items or events, such as why ocean currents affect temperature, why
Mexico employs the "each one teach one" system in eradicating illiteracy,
or why the way of life in California changed when its harbors were
opened for free trade. This process also involves relating the points of
information to each other to enlarge their meaning and to establish relationships.

The third operation is that of forming inferences which go beyond that which is directly given, such as inferring, from the comparison of the data on population composition with data on standards of living in certain Latin American states, that countries with predominantly white populations tend to have a higher standard of living.

Interpretation of data and formulation of inferences takes place in the classroom whenever the students must cope with raw data of one sort or another, such as comparing the imports and exports of several countries or analyzing and synthesizing the factors which determine the level of technological development in a given culture by examining the tools and techniques used in the production of goods.

APPLICATION OF PRINCIPLES

A third cognitive task is that of applying known principles and facts to explain new phenomena or to predict consequences from known conditions. For example, if one knows what a desert is like, what way of life it permits, and how water affects the productivity of the soil, one can predict what might happen to the desert way of life if water became available.

This cognitive task requires essentially two different operations. One is that of predicting and hypothesizing. This process requires an analysis of the problem and of the conditions in order to determine which facts and principles are relevant and which are not. Second is that of developing informational or logical parameters which constitute the causal links between the conditions and the prediction and, in fact, make a rational prediction or explanation possible. For example, if one predicts that the presence of water in the desert will cause cities to be built, one needs also to make explicit the chain of causal links that leads from the availability of water to the building of cities. These chains may consist of logical conditions, such as that the presence of water is the only condition to make the soil productive, or from factual conditions, such as whether the desert soil contains salt or not.

These predictions and explanations are of different orders of generality and complexity: for example, the prediction that cities will be built as a consequence of a water supply represents a greater leap than does the prediction that grass will grow.

In order to develop criteria for effective teaching strategies it was necessary to evolve a theoretical construct. In the light of this construct these processes and their development were viewed.

Space permits the description of only a few principles in this theoretical construct. First, the learning of thinking was viewed as essentially an active transaction between the individual and his environment. The nature of this transaction is only partly controlled by the nature of the immediate stimulus. Partly, it is controlled by whatever mediation is available either in the form of models offered or of guidance that is available. Chiefly, however, the individual must develop for himself both the conceptual schemes and the processes of using them. In other words, the environment and training become available to the individual only to the extent that he performs certain operations on what he receives. These operations cannot be "given" in the ordinary sense of the word. An individual may, for example, imitate a model of the "if-then" reasoning. But this model remains unproductive unless he internalizes and elaborates this process himself.

Second, the development of thought follows a sequence in which the simpler and the more concrete operations must precede and prepare for the more complex and the abstract. The elementary school child, for example, must work out the idea of cause and consequence on concrete material before he can evolve an abstract concept of causes and consequences. It appears also that the elementary school years are the period during which the concrete thinking, or thinking with concrete objects and events, is being transformed into formal thinking or thinking with symbols. For this reason an emphasis on the development of certain basic cognitive skills on this level is crucial.

The idea of a sequential order applies also to the mastery of the skills involved in the cognitive tasks described above. As a matter of fact, the skills as described above could be seen as a series of sequential steps in which each preceding one is a prerequisite for the success in mastering the next one. For example, in interpreting data the differentiation of specific points is a prerequisite to comparing and contrasting these points or to seeing relationships between them. The latter is, in turn, a prerequisite for making inferences, and so on.

Finally, the conceptual schema undergo a constant reorganization. The dynamics of this reorganization can be visualized as a rotation of intake of information into the existing conceptual scheme and the extension or reorganization of the scheme whenever the problem or the information received creates a dissonance because it does not fit the scheme. For example, a child whose concept of relationship of altitude and temperature is that the higher one goes the colder it gets is jarred into modifying this concept when faced with the fact of high altitude combined with high temperature. He now needs to extend this concept to include the concept of geographic zones.

Piaget (11) calls these two processes "assimilation" and "accommodation," and these terms will be used in the discussion that follows. This rotation of assimilation and accommodation seems to describe the psychological dynamics or mechanism for the gradual maturation of thought, and, as such, is extremely important in the strategy of training.

Hunt (9) points out, in addition, that this rotation requires a proper match between the existing conceptual scheme and that which is required by the new information or task. When the requirements of the accommodation are too far beyond the existing conceptual scheme it is impossible for the child to make a leap. When it is too close there is no challenge for reorganization.

Teaching Strategies for Cognitive Growth

The concepts of the cognitive tasks together with the principles which govern the development of the cognitive skills have interesting implications for the formulation of teaching strategies.

First, the concept of thinking as essentially an active process, in the sense that it can be learned only by doing, sets the process of teaching into a new perspective. If students are to develop a cognitive structure by their own efforts, the usual role of teaching and of the teacher has to be reversed. Instead of teaching consisting primarily of communication of information, with the role of the teacher as a fount of that information, he needs to become an adroit guide of the heuristic process. In this kind of teaching strategy the art of asking questions assumes a crucial role. Questions, furthermore, need a double focus: on the substance of what is being discussed and on the cognitive operations. A question such as, "What materials do we use in building houses?" focuses on the materials and excludes other characteristics of building houses such as tools and labor. This question also asks for enumeration of these materials rather than explanations of why these materials are used. Other questions are addressed to explanation, such as why women in certain primitive tribes carry things on their heads or why some countries fail to use the natural resources they have.

The concept of sequence and of the rotation of assimilation and accommodation suggests, further, that teaching acts, such as the questions, need to be programmed to foster an appropriate sequence of learning. If the learning to apply knowledge to explaining new phenomena involves mastering certain modes of thinking in a certain order, then the questions the teacher asks and the remarks she makes need to follow that order. If there is to be rotation of intake of new information with tasks that require changing the conceptual structure, then the teaching acts need to be organized to stimulate such a rotation. If time and pacing of transitions from one mode or level of thinking into another is essential, then the teaching strategy must manage this pacing. In other words, teaching needs to be addressed first to the objective of thinking; second, seen as a series of acts, each of which has a specific pedagogical function; and, finally, viewed as a strategy or organization of these functions.

In the study described above, *Thinking in Elementary School Children* (16), two groups of teaching functions were identified which seemed to affect the development of cognitive skills, either positively or negatively.

First are questions or statements made by the teacher or the students which are psychological or managerial in their function and unrelated to the logic of the content. Statements of this type included approval, disagreement, disapproval, management, and reiteration. Second, are teacher questions or statements which give direction to discussions and are related to the logic of the content and of the cognitive operations sought. This group of functions included focusing, refocusing, change of focus, deviating from focus, extending thought on the same level, lifting thought to a higher level, and controlling thought (16 *).

Focusing questions or remarks establish both the content topic under consideration and the cognitive operations to be performed. They set the cognitive task. For example, a question by the teacher such as, "If the desert had all the water it needed what would happen to the desert way of life?" establishes the central content topic for discussion and calls for prediction of consequences. However, to prevent students from indulging in associative thinking which follows a single line and opens up new dimensions, a change of focus may be needed. Refocusing may be necessary to bring the discussion back to the original topic.

Extending thought on the same level fulfills the requirement of allowing a sufficient amount of assimilation before thought is lifted to another level, such as making a transition from description of specific points noted in a film, to explaining why certain events took place in the film or from prediction to establishing its validity. This is essentially a strategy in which a number of students are induced to respond to the same question instead of proceeding from an answer by one student to a question to the same one, as is usual. Extension of thought on the same level also assures the participation of the slower students. This engages them in the initial step of the process and thus prepares them for participation in the next step.

Lifting of the level of thought occurs when the teacher or child either gives or seeks information that shifts the thought to a level higher than the previously established one. Thus, making a transition from enumeration to grouping and from grouping to labelling represents lifting of thought. However, pursuing each of these steps by engaging more students or by seeking clarification and elaboration would represent extension.

Controlling thought occurs when the teacher gives what the students should do for themselves, such as suggesting a category or classification or giving explanations of phenomena observed instead of seeking explanation from the children.

The examples below illustrate the function of focusing, extending, and lifting thought:

(1) C Malobi took the money home with her. (Child gives specific information.)

* Chapter 7.

(2) T What did Malobi do with the money? (Teacher seeks specific information.)

(3) C She saved it. (Child extends thought on the level of specific information.)

(4) C She put it underground. (Child extends thought on the level of specific information.)

(5) C She puts sticks and tin over it. (Child extends thought on the level of specific information.)

(6) C Before she did that she put it in a little pot. (Child extends thought on the level of specific information.)

In the following example the teacher attempts to lift the level of thought from the giving of information to explanation:

(1) C They carried things in baskets on their heads. (Child gives specific information.)

(2) T Explain why. (Teacher lifts thought to the level of explanation.)

(3) C I suppose they can carry more things that way. (Child gives an explanation.)

The combination of these functions together with the pacing of assimilation and the timing of lifting thought to a new level is what constitutes the teaching strategy. This strategy is determined by recognizing that it takes time to learn the skills involved in these cognitive tasks. They are not in the class of instantaneous learning. Furthermore, presumably there are individual differences in the speed with which these skills can be mastered. Some students may make a clear distinction after a few attempts at enumeration, while others need to "mess around" for a longer time to discover what is at stake and what the model of differentiation is. Teaching strategy, to be effective, must allow variation in pacing each step, determining how long to continue on the plateau of each step, and when to make a transition to the next one.

In order to assess the effectiveness of these pedagogical functions, the verbal remarks of students were rated as to level of thought in each of the three cognitive tasks. In effect, these ratings described the successive cognitive operations involved in each of the tasks described previously. Presumably the process of making inferences is a more complex one and of a higher order than is identification of the points in the information presented, the latter being a prerequisite to the former. In the task calling for inferring from data, a teacher may seek, first, specific information. She may then attempt to lift the level of thought to that of explanation, and follow with questions designed to elicit inference, *etc.* The success in eliciting appropriate responses constitutes the measure of the effectiveness of the teaching strategy.

The charting of this flow of teaching acts and of the level of students' responses describes visually the relationship of the two. For example, when the teacher attempts to raise the level of thought too early in the discussion, this typically results in the children's returning to a lower level and in their inability to sustain discussion at the higher levels of thought. On the other hand, an effective strategy of focusing, extending, and lifting thought, combined with appropriate pacing of extensions and properly matched lifts, will result in a gradual movement toward higher levels of mental operation by the majority of the students. A frequent change of focus produces an alternation between several levels, a lack of sustained thought at any level, and a gradual return to the most primitive one. The same result occurs when the teacher inserts controls of thought by giving students what they should be doing for themselves. The figure on Levels of Thought illustrates some of these strategies:

LEVELS OF THOUGHT

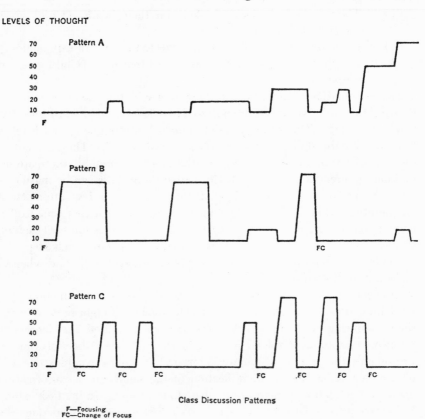

Class Discussion Patterns

F—Focusing
FC—Change of Focus

Pattern A represents a strategy in which the transitions are paced appropriately, with the result that the class follows the transitions from one level of thought to the next and sustains the thought on each. In Pattern B the lifting of thought occurs too early, with the result that when the few students who could follow it have exhausted their ideas the class settles down to the lowest level. Pattern C illustrates a discussion in which the focus is lost, and the teacher is forced to keep the discussion alive by constantly changing the topic without being able to sustain thought of any.

What, then, can be said about the merits of this approach to teaching thinking? First, the specification of thinking as an object of educational effort permits a clearer analysis of the appropriate pedagogical functions necessary to make this objective both more realistic and attainable. A more clearly focused target together with more articulated pedagogical functions may also permit a more effective training of teachers than is possible when both the nature of cognitive processes and of the appropriate teaching strategies for them are vague and obscure.

Second, it seems that a similar analysis of other educational objectives, such as the enhancement of the ego concept, the growth in affective domain, and the development of a creative approach to literature and art, might eventuate in the kinds of description of instructional processes which may provide the material for the development of a generic and a functional theory of learning and teaching.

Finally, such an approach to teaching thinking may reach students who are now relatively untouched by instruction. The results of the study described here indicated a lack of correlation between the performance on the test of Inference in Social Studies and the students' IQ. Analysis of tapescripts suggested that a careful structuring of the sequential steps in mastering the basic cognitive skills and an appropriate timing and pacing of the transitions from one level of thought to another are the chief ingredients to opening the possibility for a higher level of mental functioning to students of low ability (as measured by tests of intelligence). Analysis of a few individual cases indicated the possibility that among the so-called slow students are many who are only slow absorbers. Evidently, when the amount of information to be assimilated is reduced and opportunity is provided for systematic processing of that information, such students can function on abstract levels of thought.

BIBLIOGRAPHY

1. A. BELLACK and J. R. DAVITZ, *et al.*, *The Language of the Classroom.* New York: Institute of Psychological Research, Teachers College, Columbia University, 1963.
2. J. S. BRUNER, JACQUELINE J. GOODNOW, and G. A. AUSTIN, *A Study of Thinking.* New York: Wiley, 1956.
3. J. S. BRUNER, *The Process of Education.* Cambridge: Harvard University Press, 1960.
4. SUSAN M. ERVIN, "Training and Logical Operation of Children," *Child Development,* 31 (1960) 555–563.

5. N. A. FLANDERS, *Teacher Influence, Pupil Attitudes, and Achievement*. Prepublication manuscript of a proposed research monograph for the U.S. Office of Education, Cooperative Research Branch, Washington, D.C. 1960.

6. N. L. GAGE (ed.), *Handbook of Research on Teaching*. A Project of The American Educational Research Association. Chicago: Rand Mc-Nally and Company, 1963, Chap. 11.

7. J. P. GUILFORD, "Basic Conceptual Problems in the Psychology of Thinking," *Annals New York Academy of Science*, 91 (1961) 9–19.

8. MARIE HUGHES, *et al., Development of the Means for the Assessment of the Quality of Teaching in Elementary School*. (Mimeo.) Salt Lake City: University of Utah, 1959.

9. J. McV. HUNT, *Experience and Intelligence*. New York: Ronald Press, 1961, Ch. 5–9.

10. E. A. PEEL, *The Pupil's Thinking*. London: Oldbourne, 1960.

11. J. PIAGET, *The Psychology of Intelligence*. New York: Harcourt, 1950.

12. I. SIGEL, *Cognitive Style and Personality Dynamics*. Interim report. Merrill-Palmer Institute, 1961.

13. J. R. SUCHMAN, *The Elementary School Training Program in Scientific Inquiry*. U.S. Office of Education, Title VII, Project 216. Urbana: University of Illinois, 1964.

14. HILDA TABA, *Curriculum Development. Theory and Practice*. New York: Harcourt, Brace & World, 1962.

15. HILDA TABA and F. F. ELZEY, "Teaching Strategies and Thought Processes," *Teachers College Record*, Vol. 65, No. 6, March, 1964.

16. HILDA TABA, S. LEVINE, and F. F. ELZEY, *Thinking in Elementary School Children*. U.S. Office of Education, Cooperative Research Branch Project No. 1574. San Francisco: San Francisco State College, 1964.

17.   The Origins of Critical Thinking

Robert C. Ziller

Once upon a time, in Reno, Nevada, a little first-grade girl lived across the street from my family and me. In school one day, the youngster drew a picture. The picture consisted simply of a slightly distorted circle with a

"The Origins of Critical Thinking," by Robert C. Ziller, is reprinted by permission from *Dimensions of Critical Reading*, XI (1964). Compiled by Russell G. Stauffer, University of Delaware, Newark, Del., 13–19.

short line against the white paper as background. The teacher happened by and inquired, "What is that?" The girl responded, "Why, that's an apple." Teacher: "That doesn't look like an apple; an apple isn't white." First Grader (after a pause): "I peeled it."

In some respects this illustrates two components of critical thinking. The child's concept of the apple was more highly differentiated than that of the teacher. Probably more directly, the child did not respond passively to authority figures.

Critical thinking is a protean term, signifying many things to many people. Some [1] have suggested that the term implies selecting and organizing relevant facts, making inferences, distinguishing fact from opinion, and recognizing insufficient evidence. One of the basic references with regard to critical thinking in the educational subculture [2] includes in the term "(1) an attitude of being disposed to consider in a thoughtful way the problems and subjects that come within the range of one's experience, (2) knowledge of the methods of logical inquiry and reasoning, (3) some skill in applying these methods." Indeed, this definition of critical thinking might include most of the area of thinking in general.

Outside the education world, the term "critical thinking" is rarely encountered. In Guilford's now classic article on the "Three Faces of the Intellect" [3] in which he describes 120 independent kinds of thinking, critical thinking as it is described above is discussed under the rubric of evaluative abilities. In this paper, we shall employ Guilford's definition. Evaluative abilities, or critical abilities in the present context, are described as judgments as to the accuracy, goodness, suitability, or workability of information. Several of the items suggested by Guilford as measures of evaluative abilities are whether the idea expressed in one sentence is the same as that idea expressed in another sentence; items of the type: "What is wrong with this picture? Which of five solutions to a practical problem is most adequate or wise? What are some needed improvements in toasters or the telephone?"

It is only for purposes of analysis, however, that we are justified in considering evaluation, or critical thinking, if you will, as an independent mental process. Thus, within Guilford's cubical model representing the structure of the intellect, he includes five thinking processes: cognition, memory, divergent thinking, convergent thinking, and evaluation. It is apparent, however, that divergent thinking (creativity in popular terms) and convergent thinking (problem solving), necessarily involve the evaluation process at some stage. For example, in creative thinking, after an idea or a number of ideas have been generated, they may be evaluated for their appropriateness or superiority with reference to other proposals.

Anderson [4] has proposed that critical thinking is involved in varying degrees in all types of thinking. He arranged types of thinking along a continuum ranging from night dreams, reverie, day dreams, imagination, thinking, and problem solving. With regard to this continuum, he proposed that freedom of association is restricted by critical thinking as the mental activities move from night dreams to problem solving. In this same regard, many psychologists working in the area of creativity advocate the suspension of criticism during the initial free association processes of creative thinking. This is referred to as brainstorming. It is assumed here that the flow of associations is stemmed through premature criticism.

Finally, not only must critical thinking be considered as an integral part of all the thinking processes but also as part of the personality of the child within the social environment in which he finds himself. Indeed, we will argue that critical thinking is, in part, a cognitive style or a way in which impinging stimuli are structured which includes, necessarily, personality and social components. Thus, when we attempt to change the child's thinking processes we are necessarily involved in therapy as well as teaching. We shall now attempt to trace the development of these response dispositions.

As the receptor systems of the child develop, the number of stimuli to which the child may attend is astronomical. Through selective attention, the child ignores all but an infinitesimally small fraction of the potential stimuli. Initially, the child attends to the objects in the sensory field in a concrete manner; objects are perceived individually without relation to one another. At this stage, the objects themselves operate as concepts. For example, when the child sees any man, he will refer to him as "Daddy." "Daddy," here, is used as a crude category or concept and all other men are sorted into this category. Even at this stage, then, it may be said that the child is engaged in critical thinking; he has discriminated man from woman. This discrimination process requires, at a very fundamental level, a judgment of the accuracy, goodness, suitability, or workability of information. It also involves a comparison among stimuli before rendering a judgment.

Increasingly, the concepts or categories of judgment employed by the child become at once more differentiated and abstract. Thus, a "man" category is formulated of which "Daddy" is but an example. Hierarchical constructs are formulated, as, for example, Daddy-men-people. It has been estabished that this latter stage of cognitive development begins at about 26 months.[5]

In describing the development of cognitive processes, it has become necessary to introduce language processes. This does not mean to imply that thinking is impossible without language. It is assumed, however, that language facilitates thinking, and especially, critical thinking. For example, object identification, memory, and learning have been shown to be affected by grammatical classification, and conceptual categories. It has been demonstrated [6] that a child who has learned the names of a wide variety of colors performs better in a task in which he is shown a particular color and is required to locate that same color among a display of 120 colors. Thus, since language and concept formation are inextricably related, it is hypothesized that the child with the more extensive verbal conceptualization of the world is capable of making finer qualifications of judgment or critical thinking.

In this sense, language may serve as a nemonic or category system which enables the child to organize concepts for ready recall, reformulation, and application; that is, language facilitates information storage and retrieval. Similarly, writing, which is a superior recall system, may be expected to facilitate critical thinking processes through the sharpening of concepts and categories. Parenthetically, it may also be proposed that encouraging the child to learn to typewrite at an early age facilitates critical thinking. Having typewritten himself and recognized errors, he will learn to feel capable of critically evaluating the typewritten work which is usually associated with inviolable power figures.

The relative amount of information to which the child is exposed (experience) and the spread of sources of information also contribute to the child's need and ability to critically evaluate the information. Initially, the family is the only source of the child's information; and although the memory of the parents may be less than perfect, a rather consistent picture of the world is conveyed to the child. As the number of sources of information multiplies and the communication among these sources diminishes, the child is compelled to reconcile divergent points of view. The severity of the conflict will vary, of course, according to the heterogeneity of the sources of information.

To this point I have referred to at least four influences on the critical thinking processes of the child: language, information accumulation, sources of information, and social environment. We now propose, paradoxically, that the concepts themselves influence the critical thinking processes. As concepts are formulated these same concepts may act as mediators between the objects and the child's perception of them. Thus, once having formulated the concept of "sin" for example, the child's perceptions of other people and himself are colored, as it were, through the sin "filter." Moreover, since every concept is, to some extent, an abstraction of a number of concrete observations, necessarily the individual having developed a new concept has also developed a slightly distorted view. For example, once having formulated the concepts of man and woman, the child tends to perceive men and women as much different in all respects than they actually are. Indeed, one of the mechanisms facilitating concept formation is the exaggeration of contrasts. As information accumulates, however, the child may find it useful to modify the concept in order to achieve closer accord between the concept and the objects it represents. The process of concept formation and the subsequent critical thinking and reformulation of the concept are a continuous leveling and sharpening process in an effort to develop a workable cognitive structure. Initially, only crude categories or concepts are required in order to function adequately. However, increased control of the environment requires greater differentiation of the environment and closer evaluation of the concepts employed.

Thus, concepts serve as filters of information between objects and perception; and since concepts are more or less crude abstractions of the objects they are meant to represent, a critical thinking process must accompany the concept formation process as a self-correcting mechanism.

In this same regard, Piaget [7] describes thought as the outcome of the reciprocal effects of assimilation and accommodation. Here, he is referring to the incorporation of new elements into the existing conceptual framework and the subsequent modification of the framework. ". . . These two aspects of thought are inseparable: thought organizes itself in adapting to objects, and thought structure objects in organizing itself." [8]

Here we must introduce yet another influence on the child's critical thinking processes. The concepts which the child develops become integrated into a hierarchy of concepts of which the concept of the self is dominant.[9] It is proposed that as individual experiences accumulate they are abstracted and conceptualized much in the same way as other stimuli. This conceptualization of personal experiences becomes structured as the "self." This outline of self-oriented experiences enables the individual to describe boundaries that differentiate self from others, enables others to identify him, and furthermore, facilitates the prediction of his behavior in new situations.

The assumption of the need for stability of the self-concept is central to a large number of theories of personal adjustment.[10] These personality theories assume that the self-concept acts as a stabilizer and point of reference for the individual as he moves through time and experiences. In charging his behavior pattern under these new situations, the individual is disposed to act in a manner consistent with his past behavior or consistent with the concept of himself.

Now, returning to critical thinking, it is proposed that the concepts which an individual has formulated are the bases of the self-concept. If the stability of the self-concept is the bases of personal adjustment, alterations of the concepts through critical thinking may be presumed to pose a threat to the self-concept; particularly if the self-concept is only tenuously held. Thus, critical thinking is a process in which stable personalities may indulge with impunity.

Critical thinking then, necessarily involves self-criticism. Thus, perhaps, self-criticism is fundamental to critical thinking. In any case, the mechanisms of critical thinking and self-criticism are associated.

I believe that most of us entertain the notion that the child is characterized by complete acceptance of new information without critical evalua-

tion whereas the elderly approach complete cynicism toward new information. Again this poses the question of the appropriate stages and
intensity of critical thinking for optimal mental and personal development.
To critically evaluate before comprehension is like interrupting the
speaker after the first sentence. Not only must critical evaluation be preceded by knowledge and comprehension, but to some unknown degree,
the stability of the self-concept must be an antecedent of critical thinking.

Piaget [11] contends that the child is initially autistic in his thinking. A
child's interpretation of a story is most frequently consistent with his
wishes. He evaluates the story from a completely personal frame of reference. Critical thinking, on the other hand, is sometimes described as the
ability to objectively evaluate from outside the self or from another's
point of view. It is now proposed that in order to critically evaluate from
the point of view of another, the child must first be able to distinguish
the self from the other. In a sense this may be the basis of autistic thinking; the self and other are inadequately distinguished. Again, then, critical
thinking must be preceded by the development of a stable self-concept.

The last consideration involving critical thinking is the social environment of the child. Little research has been conducted with regard to this
question so we are forced to speculate. We do know, however, that what
the child of any individual accepts as "true" or "real" is that which society
accepts as "true" or "real." This is sometimes referred to as "social reality."
Thus, the extent to which the famliy or immediate social group of the
child accepts critical thinking, may be presumed to be a cogent factor in
the degree to which the child will indulge in critical thinking. Thus, when
we inculcate critical thinking, we are frequently attempting to oppose the
social pressures which the child faces from his family and perhaps the
personality of the child himself. Thus, considerations in the origin of
critical thinking include language, information accumulation, information
source, concepts, personality and concept of self, and the social environment.

To reiterate, in attempting to change the critical thinking processes of
the child, necessarily, we become involved in therapy as well as teaching.

REFERENCES

1. H. R. ANDERSON, F. G. MARCHAM, and S. B. DUNN, "An Experiment
   in Teaching Certain Skills of Critical Thinking," *Journal of Educational Research*, 38, 1944, pp. 241–251.
2. E. M. GLASER, *An Experiment in the Development of Critical Thinking* (Teachers College Contributions to Education, No. 843, 1941).
3. J. P. GUILFORD, "Three Faces of Intellect," *American Psychologist*, 14,
   1959, pp. 469–479.

4. J. E. ANDERSON, *Psychology of Development and Personal Adjustment* (New York: Holt, 1949).

5. L. WELCH and L. LONG, "The Higher Structural Phases of Concept Formation in Children," *Journal of Psychology,* 9, 1940, pp. 59–95.

6. E. H. LENNEBERG, "Cognition in Ethno-Linguistics," *Language,* 29, 1953, pp. 463–471.

7. J. PIAGET, *The Child's Conception of the World* (New York: Harcourt, Brace, 1929).

8. *Ibid.,* p. 186.

9. O. J. HARVEY, D. E. HUNT, and H. M. SCHRODER, *Conceptual Systems in Personality Organization* (New York: John Wiley, 1961).

10. P. LECKY, *Self-Consistency* (New York: Island Press, 1945).

11. PIAGET, *op. cit.*

PART THREE

Teaching Critical Reading

M any teachers who have had the desire to improve pupils' critical reading abilities have been handicapped by a nebulous defini- tion of the skills involved, inadequate instructional materials, and some disquieting controversy surrounding certain aspects of critical reading. The articles that follow help to clarify the specific reading skills that may be classified as "critical" and describe procedures and materials of instruction that have proven to be effective. Divergent points of view which reveal controversies in approaches to critical reading are represented.

Although the general skills of critical reading, such as "noting rele- vance," "determining authenticity," and "analyzing the logic of state- ments," have been identified as significant skills in critical reading, the specific components of the comprehensive skills have often been overlooked. The first four papers that follow present skills required for critical reading and relate how they might be taught in orderly ways. While none of the writers provides a comprehensive listing of the skills, the group of papers offers a wide range of skills with sug- gestions of many practical teaching techniques. Stauffer's article dif- fers from the others in that he emphasizes one important skill—the "educated guess" or prediction—that he thinks should underlie all critical reading.

One of the issues pertaining to critical reading has to do with the feasibility and appropriateness of teaching critical reading skills to children who are in the beginning stages of learning to read. The next four authors—Shotka, Stauffer, Petty, and Johnson—not only state the opinion that critical reading *should* be taught in the kindergarten and primary grades, but outline procedures to develop the ability in children at these levels.

Wolf, Eller, and Rasschaert emphasize instructional techniques for specific skills in semantics and logic. The component skills required for inductive and deductive reasoning, or logic, are delineated by Wolf, who not only illustrates how the skills are applied by the reader in complex materials, but suggests procedures for the initial instruction of these skills to elementary school children. Eller and Rasschaert identify semantic problems involved in reading critically and describe experiences that will help pupils become increasingly knowledgeable about the role of words in conveying meaning.

TEACHING CRITICAL READING IN THE CONTENT FIELDS AND LITERATURE

Study of the comprehensive nature of critical reading has revealed that there is no one set of critical reading skills that can be applied indiscriminately to all types of printed materials. Part of the growth in critical reading ability is knowledge of the appropriate skills to use. Burrows illustrates the application of a number of critical reading skills through reading, researching, and reporting in the social studies. Each subject area appears to have its own "pattern of writing" which requires some adaptation in the way that the material is read. The two articles by Smith describe different patterns of writing in literature, science, social studies, and mathematics.

The role of literature and literary analysis has not as yet been accepted as an essential part of the curriculum by many teachers. Huck suggests that we dare not stop with merely teaching children *how* to read but that we must be concerned with *what* they read. She illustrates how a comprehensive program of planned literature can enrich all areas of study and lead to discriminating reading. Jenkins' article follows with examples of application of reading skills to literature. Each author holds that enjoyment should be the primary purpose of reading literature and that critical analysis of literature can enrich and deepen that appreciation.

Usery and Ellinger and MacDougall describe structured approaches to the study of literature. Usery analyzes critical thinking processes and illustrates how they can be taught through the analysis of two books. Ellinger and MacDougall establish a framework for examining literature critically and give examples of techniques that have proven to be effective. Common to the three writers is the belief that increased enjoyment and appreciation of literature will result from more thoughtful and evaluative reading. A teacher who points out the elements of good literature can help children to appreciate aesthetic qualities that had previously gone unnoticed. The discussion of a picture book reported by Frazier and Schatz reveals critical responses by children as they examine the figurative language and theme of a picture book. The final paper in this section by Jeraldine Hill provides numerous selections from children's literature that may be used to develop general skills of critical reading, such as comparing and contrasting form, characterization, and theme.

Separately, the contributions in Part III will suggest ideas for specific lessons in critical reading; in their totality, they cover a broad range of critical reading skills and provide insight into some of the problems and issues in the field.

M.L.K.
B.D.E.

18. Critical Reading

Ruth K. Flamond

*All citizens of a democratic society need to be able to act critically.
With this ability, they can weigh public issues and make intelligent
choices; without it, they are too often at the mercy of demagogues.*
*What is required for critical reading? How is getting facts related
to critical reading? What kinds of classroom work develop critical
abilities?* *

In the past we have spent a great deal of time in developing the mechanical skills of reading—and have done a commendable job. But, since
reading is more than simply the sum of its parts, our students must be
equipped to do more than literal reading. Today, more than ever before,
higher-level reading skills are needed by every reader. Never before have
we been bombarded by so many words from so many sources attempting
to influence us—to persuade us to vote for this or that candidate, to want
this or that product, to accept this or that ideology, etc. The fact that it
appears so easy to bilk the American people of millions of dollars annually
would seem to imply a woeful lack of ability to think and read critically.

NATURE OF CRITICAL READING

What do we mean by critical reading? Since critical reading is not a
single or simple entity, no single definition seems adequate to include all
its ramifications. Rather than attempt to define critical reading per se, I am
going to discuss some of the skills and abilities involved in critical reading
and some of the ways teachers can develop critical reading skills.

If reading is defined as a special form of thinking, then critical thinking
may be considered a special form of reading and conversely, critical reading is an aspect of critical thinking. They are not entities. However, an
individual must learn how to think critically before he can read critically.
Perhaps the three conditions most important for critical reading are: first,
complete understanding of what is read; second, *a propensity to be skeptical, analytical, and inquiring;* and third, *the application of critical reading skills which have been specifically taught and developed. Evidence
from research would seem to indicate that most children do not become
critical thinkers and critical readers by themselves.* Neither high intelli-

* From *Explorations in Reading,* June 1962.

"Critical Reading," by Ruth K. Flamond, Albert J. Mazurkiewicz (ed.), is reprinted
by permission from *New Perspectives in Reading Instruction.* New York: Pitman
Publishing Corporation, 1964, pp. 256–261.

gence alone nor extensive knowledge about a subject will insure ability to think and to read critically. Children need help in becoming critical readers.

READINESS FOR CRITICAL READING

Currently some of the literature dealing with the linguistic approach to the teaching of reading suggests that children should first learn to read and after learning how to read they read to learn (meaning to get information). This approach certainly does not conceive of reading as thinking. All of the basal readers in use today stress comprehension from the beginning. *To develop critical readers we must stress critical thinking from the very beginning.* The kindergarten teacher lays the foundation for critical reading when she says, "I am going to read you a story about a dog named Prince and a cat named Fluff. The name of this story is *Prince and Fluff*. What are some things you think this story may tell us?" The children are thus encouraged to think about the story and to set up purposes for listening. The responses given will depend upon the children's experiences. At the conclusion of the reading, evaluation of what they heard or learned will be in terms of the purposes established prior to the reading. Next, the teacher is asking the children to make a judgment when she queries, "Is this a true story or a make-believe story? How do you know?" Before answering these questions, children must mentally review what they know (experience) and associate this with the story just heard (apprehension of relationships). Since one of the first steps in critical thinking is the organization of information and experiences through the recognition of similarities and differences, the teacher should read several stories which contain a similar pattern or theme. Then she can ask, "What other stories do you know that remind you of (or are like) this one?" As soon as children recognize that a story (or concept) is similar to others they have encountered, they can be led to generalize by asking, "In what way are these stories alike? How are they different?"

Before going any further, I want to emphasize that merely *getting the facts* is *not* critical reading. *The reader must first determine whether he is reading facts or merely opinions and/or assumptions.* Sensing the relationships among the facts, comparing the facts with experience, knowing when the facts are relevant, evaluating *these* facts against other facts to arrive at some conclusion, and going beyond the facts to get the inferred, but not explicitly stated, meaning are aspects of critical reading.

DIFFERENTIATION BETWEEN FACT AND OPINION

From the kindergarten, where children begin to differentiate between *fact and fancy*, we move into the distinction between *fact and opinion*. If someone says, "It is a nice day," is he stating a fact or an opinion? A fact is usually defined as a statement that can be verified universally. Before a statement can be evaluated, the meaning of all words must be clear. In this case, there must be a definition of the words "nice day" before we can determine if the statement is a fact or an opinion. If the sun is shining and the temperature stands at 68 degrees, and the reference is to weather, this sentence would be commonly accepted as fact (in the temperate zone). However, if the sentence refers to the way individuals *feel* on or about this particular day, it may only represent a limited number of opinions.

Skill in differentiating between fact and opinion can be developed by requiring students to verify or prove their statements. To say that an answer has been found in a story is not enough. Students should be required to support their statements of fact with verification. Verification can be derived by inference as well as by direct quotation. An illustration of verification by inference, in answer to the question "How do you know John's mother was angry?" might be derived from "His mother's eyes flashed fire when John came home an hour late." This statement requires the ability to interpret a figure of speech in order to get the inferred meaning of anger.

WRITER QUALIFICATIONS

Only looking at the facts is not enough for critical reading. A great deal of what we read in print comes from individuals with no particular authority to make the pronouncements. Therefore, students must also be taught to look into the qualifications of the person who is doing the writing. To illustrate, listen to this statement from the book *Why Johnny Can't Read* by Rudolph Flesch, a free-lance writer: "Mind you, I am not accusing the 'reading experts' of wickedness or malice. . . . All I am saying is that theories are wrong and that the application of those theories has done untold harm to our younger generation. . . . Our scientific educators simply don't want to know the truth."

Do the training, experience, and occasional random observations of this writer qualify him to tell teachers how reading should be taught? Would you say his writing represents an attempt to substitute his opinion for the research and study of many scholars over a long period of time?

CRITICAL READING APPLIED TO ADVERTISEMENTS

Advertising represents one of the biggest businesses in our country to-day. And advertising is the business of persuasion. *Since every individual in our country represents a potential buyer, students must be taught to examine critically the advertising claims made for various products, as advertisers make use of all the tricks and devices in the book.* Elementary school children can collect advertisements from magazines and newspapers. Classroom discussions can alert them to the risk in blindly accepting unsupported claims. Note some of the attention-getting devices used—Hexachloraphene (Stripe Toothpaste), Gardol (Colgate Dental Cream), and GL-70 (Gleem). What do these words mean? Is there any substantial evidence that they do marvelous things for the users or even fulfill their claims?

Can *these* claims be substantiated—"1225 paper sponges on each sheet" (Hudson paper towels), "43 beans in every cup" (Nescafé coffee), "21 great tobaccos make 20 wonderful smokes" (Chesterfield cigarettes), and "'Germ-Fighter' brand toothpaste won't pass along germs" (Dr. West's toothbrushes)?

Note the consequences implied if one doesn't use Pond's Cold Cream—"She's lovely, she's engaged"; in "Pepsi for those who think young"; and in "The Man Who Thinks for Himself Knows Only Viceroy Has a Thinking Man's Filter."

Note also, how certain words or ideas are associated with a product to create a particular impression. Yardley After-Shave Lotion is currently using "For the Man Who Won't Settle for Average." The ads for Cadillac cars use a necklace of fabulous gems to associate elegance, wealth, and discrimination with the car.

As students collect advertisements and examine them, there might be discussions on the following points:

To whom is the ad addressed?
To what need or desire does it appeal (health, popularity, comfort, security, etc.)?
What claims are not substantiated?
What attention-getting devices are used?
How is actual cost disguised or minimized ("cost only a few pennies a day")?
Why are "testimonials" used?
What words or ideas are used to create a particular impression?
What evidence do we want from advertisements?

Vance Packard in *The Hidden Persuaders* states that "astute persuaders always use word triggers and picture triggers to evoke desired responses. Once a response pattern is established in terms of persuasion, then you can persuade people in wholesale lots, because all of us are creatures of conditioned reflex."

Congressional investigations with regard to false advertising mention the confusion created by the tricky quantitative figures used on packaged goods. Few purchasers are able to determine whether they are getting a better buy in selecting two 8-oz. cans of a product at twenty-two cents a can or one 1 lb. 3 oz. can at fifty cents a can. Wouldn't it be a good idea to give our students practice in working out problems such as this, since price concerns their economic welfare?

PROPAGANDA DEVICES

At the secondary level, critical reading can be approached through examination of the propaganda devices used in current writing. Editorials can be examined for bias and slant. Critical reading, followed by discussion, can help students to identify the writer's purpose. Was the article written to inform or to persuade? Are facts presented or does the writing merely state the author's opinion? Certain words or expressions have emotional connotations (welfare state, democracy, left-winger, etc.) used to arouse certain feelings which lie below the surface in the human personality. The social status of an individual can frequently be inferred by noting whether the newspaper refers to the person as "Miss Smith" or "the Smith woman."

Newspaper and magazine articles can be used to have students look for and tabulate emotionally loaded words, overuse of superlatives, unsubstantiated "facts," questionable statistics, overgeneralizations (too little evidence to say this is true in every case). Various accounts of the same event can be studied to note differences of fact, differences of opinion, bias, etc.

Political speeches and campaign promises often represent the ultimate in sheer verbalization or language without a referent. Political speeches are generally filled with emotionally toned words. Students can practice rewriting such speeches, eliminating all verbalization (i.e., language which does not refer to either experiences or concepts), then compare the winnowed version with the original.

The Induced Hypothesis is one of the trickiest but most effective propaganda techniques in the business. Since the writer never formulates a hypothesis of his own, he is thus difficult to attack. He presents one-sided information, or *quotes wrenched from context*, in a slanted or biased manner. He thus induces the reader to make his own hypothesis on the basis of the account the writer presented. Once the writer can induce a hypothetical position in the minds of his readers, he makes *them* the defenders. Admiral Rickover used this technique in his article "The World of the Uneducated."

In solving a problem or attempting to test a hypothesis, we must collect all the available data and then use these data to either verify or reject the hypothesis.

19. Classroom Activities in Critical Reading

William Kottmeyer

In an attempt to find a solution to the reading problem in the St. Louis schools, effort has been made, in an extended in-service training program, to identify and to describe the stages or areas of developmental reading skills without regard to the grade placement of children. The purpose of the effort is, of course, to adjust reading activities and materials to individual differences in the wide range of abilities in reading which is to be found in most classrooms. In the reading of larger units of printed material, four basic areas of instruction have been isolated: assimilative or work-type reading, recreational reading, locational or fact-finding reading, and critical reading. This discussion is concerned with the last-mentioned type of reading ability and describes efforts in St. Louis to provide classroom activities to develop this ability.

By the term "critical reading skills" is meant those skills in which the reader projects his own judgments, attitudes, and appreciations into juxtaposition with the reading material. Critical reading is essentially the highest and the most complex form of reading. The physiological and the psychological processes involved in the reading act are, of necessity, so firmly habituated that they do not intrude into the realm of conscious effort, and the mind is enabled to judge, compare, evaluate, and criticize without the disruption of such mechanical interferences as difficulties of word recognition, word-by-word reading, unco-ordinated eye-movements, and so forth. This type of reading is thinking, and activity in such reading will tend to produce students who think—objectively and critically.

In other words, critical reading is differentiated from assimilative reading in that the latter enables the reader to receive the ideas conveyed on the printed page, to understand them, and to make them his own, whereas the former skill involves additional mental activity over and beyond the assimilation of ideas. Only when mastery of the assimilative type of skill has been achieved can the reader, simultaneously with his assimilation, evaluate and judge and make application of that material. Critical reading

"Classroom Activities in Critical Reading," by William Kottmeyer, *School Review*, 1944, 557–564. Reprinted by permission of the University of Chicago Press.

is independent thinking; assimilative reading is receiving and absorbing the thinking of others.

The need for training in critical reading, for those who are capable of objective and penetrating thinking, requires no elaborate exposition. An undisputed function of formal education is to teach students to think. Some evidence may readily be cited to demonstrate that educational programs have often been largely concerned with furnishing abundant subject matter to think about rather than with directing attention to the process itself.

The power of the newspapers in influencing political opinion, for example, no longer occasions surprise. Illustrations of the response of the public to movie and radio propaganda have often been cited and are taken for granted. Magazine advertisements, although they have been the objects of occasional jibes, pay generous returns—a fact which is amply attested by the space rates in popular magazines. If the functioning of a democracy is effective in proportion to the number of American citizens who analyze and think objectively about the verbiage with which they are deluged, then, it appears, educators may well view with proverbial alarm and point with less complacent pride to their educational products, many of whom too often conclude all controversy with the schoolboy's irrefutable argument: "But the book says so."

In the St. Louis experiments with various materials to provide a simple approach to the area of critical reading at the upper elementary-school level, we have found three units to be especially serviceable. One is on propaganda analysis, one on the reading of newspaper editorials, and one on the interpretation of newspaper cartoons. The nature of these activities and the materials which are employed are described in the following pages.

ANALYSIS OF PROPAGANDA

A few years ago the Institute for Propaganda Analysis directed considerable attention to the problem of analyzing propaganda. The basic information disseminated by certain writers on the subject proved in several instances to be so clear and coherent that adaptation and re-writing of the material at the elementary-school level was not a difficult task.[1] The seven basic propaganda techniques or types as identified and described

[1] Materials developed for this unit are wholly dependent on the following:

a) "How to Detect Propaganda," *Propaganda Analysis*, I (November, 1937), 1–4. (Also in *Essays of Three Decades*, pp. 45–52. Edited by Arno L. Bader and C. F. Wells. New York: Harper & Bros., 1939.)

b) Clyde R. Miller, "How To Detect and Analyze Propaganda," *A College Book of Prose*, pp. 261–73. Edited by Selma W. Schneider and J. A. Sanford. Boston: Ginn & Co., 1941.

by the Institute were therefore re-written in the form of guide sheets for small-group activity under teacher guidance at the junior high school level. Application of the principles outlined in the guide sheets was made to advertising material.

Advertising material appearing in current magazines was utilized because it falls readily and obviously into the patterns or types identified in the guide sheets and because the propaganda technique can be more readily perceived in the comparatively brief text which accompanies the usual advertisement illustrations than it can in extended prose material, where the approach is more subtle and complex.

In conjunction with the study and the discussion of the guide sheets, seven large bulletin boards were prepared, each devoted to illustrations of one of the seven types of propaganda. After assimilation of the basic principles by a small group, through careful reading of the guide booklet, discussion with the teacher, and assembling and identifying type samples from the magazines, the group completed a series of workbooks on the subject.

These workbooks consist merely of large numbered envelopes, each containing at least one sample of each of the seven propaganda types. The instructions on the envelope read:

> You are familiar with the seven common types of propaganda. In this envelope are several samples of propaganda used in advertising. Write the names of the advertisements, and after each one write the kinds of propaganda you think it is. Add any explanations which are needed.

Pertinent excerpts from the guide sheets are reproduced in the following paragraphs.

> We may define propaganda as the opinion of one group expressed for the purpose of forming or changing the opinion of others, usually from selfish motives. The seven common methods of propagandists are:
> 1. *Bad names.*—This is a method by which we are tempted to judge without looking at real facts or evidence. The propagandist tries to arouse our hate or our fear by using "bad" names. He does not give any real evidence. He simply calls someone bad names or uses words which are unpleasant. Because we use these words for things which we ourselves do not like, we often attach the bad meanings to the person or thing the propagandist wants us to hate or despise.
> On Bulletin Board Number 1 are some samples of bad names used in advertising. Read them carefully.
> In Figure 1 the most important bad word is "slacker," of course. The advertisement is careful not to say directly that you are a slacker, but it wants you to feel that way about yourself. Of course, you can keep from being a slacker by paying for a —— course. You can see that there

is no real evidence given to prove the advantages of the —— school. It is just another example of bad-name calling.

Now read the advertisement listed as Figure 2. There is some bad-name calling in this advertisement also. Note the words in the head-line: *guilty, fungus, athlete's foot.* Other bad names on the page are: *sufferers, complain, disease, fungus, organisms, infected, skin disease, peeling, cracks, soggy, itching, inflammation, perspiring feet, foot-odor.*

Notice in this advertisement that bad names can be suggested by pictures, too. By showing unpleasant pictures, such as the germ and shoe photographs, the disgust of the reader is made stronger.

Find the bad names in the other advertisements on the bulletin board.

2. *Glad names.*—This is another method of keeping a reader's atten-tion from real evidence by using "glad" names—pleasant words which are written so that the reader will attach them to the person or thing about which the propagandist is speaking or writing. He appeals to our feelings of love, friendship, or kindness. Words like *truth, freedom, honor, liberty, justice, beautiful, charming, lovely, delicate, handsome, alluring, unmatched, unequaled, highest grade, magic, amazing, fa-mous, delicious, noble, exciting,* and so forth are used to get effect. As bad names are used to get us to reject or condemn, so glad names are used to get us to accept or approve without examining the evidence. Read the samples carefully on Board Number 2. [Here follow refer-ences to specific examples of this type of propaganda.]

3. *Transfer.*—The transfer method in propaganda is one by which the writer tells us or reminds us of something which we admire and then about something which he wants us to admire or like. By putting the two things together, he tries to get our feeling of admiration to pass over, or transfer, from the thing we already like to the thing he wants us to like.

Suppose a soap manufacturer wants to advertise so that many women will want to buy his soap. He knows that women usually want to make themselves prettier, if possible, so, when he advertises, he puts the picture of a well-known beautiful woman, a movie star, for ex-ample, at the top of his advertisement. Then he tells how his soap makes women beautiful. If people do not think carefully about what they read, they see the picture of the movie star and transfer their feeling of admiration from her to the soap.

Or, suppose some politicians want their candidate elected to an office. They may tell in their speeches that, among other good things, he teaches in a Sunday school. Now most people have a good feeling for churches. By bringing in the church, these politicians try to transfer this good feeling over to their candidate.

Here are some samples of transfer in advertising. [Here follow ques-tions which stimulate observation of this particular technique in the bulletin-board samples.]

4. *The Testimonial.*—The testimonial method is somewhat like the transfer method. In the testimonial the propagandist gets some well-

known person to say that he likes or does not like something. If we like such a person, we often want to like what he likes or hate what he hates. If we do this, we do not look carefully for evidence, nor do we think for ourselves. We must remember that often such people are paid for saying what they do. Often they do not even use the product that they say is good. Read the advertising samples on Board Number 4. [Here follow questions which refer to these advertisements.]

5. *Plain folks.*—This is a method used especially by politicians, businessmen, and even ministers to win our confidence by appearing to be people like ourselves—just plain folks. In elections candidates for office shake hands with everybody they can, joke with people, ask about the wife and family, and kiss babies. They go to country picnics, they go to church, they pitch hay (when the photographers are there). They want to win our votes by showing that they are just as common as the rest of us, just plain folks, and therefore wise and good and honest. That is why candidates for office like to become known as "the workingman's friend." That is why many companies advertise over the radio by having hillbilly songs and Hoosier comedians. See how it is sometimes done:

a) In the pictures published in a magazine you will see that ——, the comedian, is shown stuffing some chewing tobacco into his mouth (Fig. 1). Why the chewing tobacco? Why is this good publicity for ——? In the other picture he is shown with his wife, who is knitting. What is the purpose of this picture?

b) In Figure 2 you see ——, dressed in an apron, cooking something at a stove. Why do you think this particular pose was chosen?

c) Figure 3 is the picture of ——, a big-league ball-player. What connection is there between his ball-playing and feeding his baby?

d) Read the —— advertisement. Explain how the *plain-folks* method is being used.

e) Explain how this method is being used in the wine advertisement, both by the words and by the picture.

6. *Stacking the cards.*—One way in which dishonest gamblers and cardsharps cheat their victims is by arranging the cards in the deck beforehand so that they themselves cannot lose. This is called "stacking the cards." We shall call this next propaganda device by this name because it is a method by which the propagandist does not give us full truth. He may try to direct all of our attention to one detail and to keep it from the rest. He may omit many important facts. He makes the unreal appear real and the real appear unreal. He lets half-truth appear as truth. So, for example, Japan attacks China and insists that she is doing it for the good of the Chinese and for the sake of peace. Hitler and his armies attack Russia and tell the German people that they are trying to stop the spread of communism. So, too, promoters will advertise a poor fighter and will call attention to only his good points so that, when he fights the champion, a large crowd will pay to

see the fight. So a worthless patent medicine will be shown to be a wonderful cure, and this will cause thousands to buy it.

Notice the advertisement for —— on Bulletin Board Number 6. The advertisement tries to center your attention on a picture of a scientist pointing to a tooth. The tooth shows an injury which, it says, is "risked by eight out of ten adults." There is a sworn statement by the scientist which says that what is said about the "brushing tests" is true. But notice that the scientist never says anything directly about ——. He says that you can cut cavities with dentifrices that contain "abrasives." Does that mean that —— contains none? The advertisement may all be true, but you cannot prove it because you haven't got the evidence. The cards have been stacked.

7. *The band wagon.*—This is a method to make us follow the crowd. The idea is "everybody's doing it." In order to use the idea, the propagandist gets a crowd or group to start doing the thing he wants them to do. Then he tells other people to "join the band wagon." This is often successful because people like to do what others are doing—they don't want to be different. If a candidate is up for office, his friends all go around saying that he is sure to win. In this way they hope to get others to vote for him because people like to vote for the winner. Often, if people think a man will win, they will vote for him without bothering to find out much about him.

The advertisements on Bulletin Board Number 7 show how advertisers sometimes use this method. The insurance company's advertisement shows a picture of many people following Uncle Sam. You immediately get the idea that many Americans are doing something; and you want to know what it is so that you, too, can do it. Therefore you read their advertisement and give them a chance to convince you of their argument.

The —— advertisement reveals its method in the line, "Nine out of ten said they wouldn't go back to their former shaving method for love nor money." You are to think that, if all those men like —— razors, you also ought to go out and buy one. What is the catch to the advertisement?

This work in propaganda analysis has been found to be unusually interesting for children who have adequate command of the assimilative reading skills. The advertising materials needed for the unit are, of course, available in discarded magazines, and a plentiful supply continues to appear each week. Teachers will find it convenient to type answer keys for the separate envelopes in order to facilitate the checking of answers.

READING EDITORIALS

Another source of reading material which can readily be presented in a manner to stimulate critical thinking by students is the editorial pages of the local newspapers. The teacher scans the pages for editorials dealing with subjects that show promise of at least several weeks of interest. Many of the editorials discuss municipal, state, national, and international problems of permanent significance. These items are then cut out and mounted in a durable folder.

The reading levels of the various editorials usually have a considerable range of difficulty. Some writers employ a difficult style or allude to personages or events about which youngsters know little or nothing. The editorial is, therefore, annotated by the teacher to make it meaningful for children.

On the opposite page of the folder is typed the silent-reading exercise in the form of questions to be answered by the pupil. Some of these questions may be assimilative in nature (that is, the answers to the questions may be found in the editorial text), but always included is a question, or several questions, which are calculated to induce on the part of the reader a judgment based on his own experience or on his own reasoning.

When such materials lose their quality of timeliness, they are discarded. The assembling of such work booklets in quantity is sometimes a laborious task, but, after the booklets are put into use, their maintenance does not require much effort. Each pupil in the small group engaging in this activity works at his own rate, and, as he need have only one editorial in his possession at a time, a great number need not be prepared before the work can be introduced. A typical editorial with its annotation is reproduced on a following page.

The following list of questions is an example of the type of exercise which is included in the folder on the page opposite the annotated editorial.

EXERCISE

1. What is Secretary Morgenthau's advice about raising money for the expenses of the government?
2. If Morgenthau's advice were followed, how much money would have to be raised by taxes for every $100 spent by the government? How much by borrowing?
3. For every $100 spent by the government, how much money is now being raised by taxation? How much by borrowing?
4. What fraction of the amount of money asked for by the Treasury did Congress provide for in their tax law?
5. What reason is suggested in the editorial for the failure of Congress to pass a law requiring higher taxes?
6. Do you think that the Congress did wrong by not passing a higher tax law? Why? Or why not?
7. If you were a congressman up for reelection and if you knew that

the voters would not like to have you vote for higher taxes for them, what would you do?

INTERPRETATION OF CARTOONS

Another classroom activity in the area of critical reading may be developed in the interpretation of political and social cartoons in newspapers which are provocative of logical reasoning and analysis. It will be understood that such material must be selected discriminatingly, with an eye for issues which involve genuine problems of objective thinking. Some cartoons do not make thinking necessary.

AN UNREALISTIC [2] TAX LAW

When the national defense program was well under way, Secretary *Morgenthau* [3] laid down a principle of *fiscal procedure* [4] which he strongly urged upon Congress as *essential*.[5] His principle was this: "We ought to raise at least two-thirds of our *expenditures* [6] by taxation and one-third by borrowing."

When actual war came, with all its necessarily huge expenditures, there was, of course, justification for some change in this *ratio* [7] of sound *economy*.[8] But where does it stand today? By official figures we are now raising 40.9 per cent of our expenditures by taxation and 59.1 per cent by borrowing. Taxpayers of the future are being counted upon to furnish almost half again as much of the war's costs as the taxpayers of today.

President Roosevelt in his recent message called on Congress to *enact* [9] "a realistic tax law." The Treasury had asked for 10½ billion dollars in new taxes. Instead of this, the *bill* [10] upon which *House and Senate* [11] *conferees* [12] have just completed action will raise only $2,315,800,000 in additional *revenues*,[13] less than a quarter of the Treasury figure. In an *election*

[2] That is, a tax law that does not do what it ought to do.
[3] Secretary of the Treasury, Henry Morgenthau, who is responsible for raising money for the government.
[4] A way of handling money affairs.
[5] Necessary.
[6] What we pay out.
[7] That is, how much money goes for different expenses.
[8] A system of dealing with money.
[9] Make into a law.
[10] A suggested law.
[11] The House of Representatives and the Senate, the two divisions of Congress.
[12] Those who confer or discuss the subject.
[13] Money coming in.

year,[14] Congress has not dared to enact the stiff tax measure essential for collecting their just share of the war costs from today's taxpayers, and for guarding against *inflation*.[15]

It's an unrealistic tax law if ever there was one.

Many thought-provoking cartoons are necessarily based on the assumption that the reader has a wide background of factual information which makes interpretation possible. Because the wide range of differences in the modern classroom precludes any such assumption, we have provided, with simple vocabulary, the background data necessary for intelligent interpretation. The cartoon, like the editorials, is mounted inside a folder. On the opposite side is typewritten the necessary information. Below this is provided a series of questions designed to elicit from the pupil a reasonably accurate interpretation of the message of the cartoon and a reaction from him to the message.

When such materials lose their element of timeliness, they may be discarded in favor of the new ones appearing daily. Some newspapers have unusually able cartoonists whose pictorial comments on world affairs are well worth consideration.

We are not able at this time to measure objectively gains made by pupils in critical reading as a result of working with these units. We feel, however, that we are providing for our superior readers a type of reading activity which is better adjusted to their needs than is further repetition of training in the assimilative reading in which they have already demonstrated mastery. We may also report that for such readers these materials are highly stimulating and that the pupils work at the exercises with enthusiasm and interest.

[14] That is, many members of Congress will be up for reelection this year, and they do not want to do anything which will lose votes.

[15] A time when wages are high but when prices are also high.

20.   Sequence in Thoughtful and Critical

Reaction to What Is Read

Robert Karlin

The purpose of this paper is to discuss the skills and abilities which should be developed to permit children and older students to react thoughtfully and critically to what they read. Before the reader can evaluate the content of a selection, it is essential that he perceive the words accurately and secure the meanings intended by the author. Sequential development of skills and abilities in these areas have been considered in the preceding chapters. The term critical is defined in *Webster's New World Dictionary of the American Language* as characterized by careful analysis; furthermore, the term implies an attempt at objective judging so as to determine both merits and faults. Applied to reading then, to be critical means to be discriminating or evaluative. A kind of judgment based on what is known is implied.

Those who have studied the process of reading emphasize the similarities to the process of thinking. The reader deals with printed language much in the same way as the listener deals with spoken language. In reading, the element of visual symbols must be introduced but once they are known, symbols trigger the orderly processes of thinking. If we regard the reading process as similar to the thinking process, then we may conclude that critical reading involves critical thinking. Therefore, Russell's definition of critical thinking appears to be appropriate. He explains it as "the process of examining . . . verbal materials in the light of related objective evidence, comparing . . . the statement with some norm or standard, and concluding or acting upon the judgment then made." [1] He refers to the use of concrete objects as well as verbal materials since he is not limiting the discussion to reading. With this frame of reference, let us examine some of the problems associated with the teaching of critical reading.

NEED AND PROBLEMS

Any reasonable group of educators would agree that the need for teaching critical reading is paramount. The authors of almost every modern

[1] David Russell, *Children's Thinking*, p. 285. Boston: Ginn & Co., 1956.

"Sequence in Thoughtful and Critical Reaction to What Is Read," by Robert I. Karlin, *Sequential Development of Reading Abilities*. Helen Robinson (ed.). Conference on Reading, University of Chicago, 1960, 74–79. Reprinted by permission of the University of Chicago Press.

textbook on the teaching of reading devote some space to developing this ability.

One of the problems in teaching critical reading has to do with the learner and the influence of teaching upon him. We know that children pattern their thinking and behavior upon models in whom they have confidence and with whom they feel a sense of security. These first models are their parents and other adults with whom they have some relation. When a pupil comes for the first time face to face with doubts that are cast upon his models' reliability, he has a difficult choice to make. Some children are not sufficiently mature to cope with this challenge and must not be forced by continuing pressures.

A second problem revolves around the issue of determining what kind of attitudes shall be fostered by the schools and who has the ultimate responsibility for deciding which these shall be. In some homes more than in others complete submissiveness to authority is demanded and ideas presented and pronouncements made are to be accepted without any reservations. The introduction and encouragement by the school of conflicting attitudes through the teaching of critical reading can be opposed to the training carried on in such homes. Obviously the schools must assume leadership roles in such situations but at times we are blinded to the consequences of our acts by our cause. By all means, teach children to read critically but be prepared to deal with exigencies which might result from this teaching.

Influencing Factors

Data have been accumulated showing that many students need help in improving their abilities to read and think critically. However, several factors may limit the extent of development in this area. Intelligence may prove to be a significant factor. Just as we ordinarily expect the child of normal or superior intellectual ability to surpass the school achievements of children with lesser endowments, so may we anticipate the degree to which a pupil is able to achieve in critical reading. Nevertheless, slower learners should be encouraged to react to ideas to the extent that they are able to do so. But our expectations of their achievements ought not be as high as for brighter children.

Although intelligence and ability to read critically appear to be related, investigators have found that high performance on an intelligence test does not guarantee equally-high performance in situations which require critical thinking. This fact has prompted many educators to point to the importance of providing instruction directed to improvement of critical thinking.

A second factor associated with ability to do critical reading is background of experiences. If we define critical thinking as comparing what is read with a known standard, then the standard arises from knowledge or understanding. "In general, the more a child knows about the circumstances surrounding a problem, the better his solution will be. Knowledge does not necessarily mean good thinking, but high-order thinking is dependent upon knowledge." [2] Knowledge is identified with concepts, and vague or tenuous ones may not be used as models for comparison. Since many of the ideas with which learners deal are abstract, then it follows that real experiences help to add substance to them. First-hand experiences are usually preferred to vicarious ones and should be provided. The student who is expected to evaluate a newspaper editorial must not only possess some information about the topic, but also understandings based upon his previous experiences.

A third factor which may affect ability to react critically is the attitude of the reader toward the content read. Prejudices toward or against persons, ideas or topics have been shown to interfere with the reader's performance in evaluating printed matter. The results of several investigations have demonstrated that the student's attitude toward the content which he is reading can influence his reactions to it. Among these is the study of Crossen [3] who reported a positive relationship between adolescents' ability to read material about minority groups critically and their attitudes toward these same groups.

There are indications also that the reader's understanding may be impaired when his attitude toward the subject matter is negative. Kendall and Wolf [4] reported the results of an experiment in which the individuals' predisposition toward the material read interfered with their understanding of it. Readers whose attitudes were favorably identified with the ideas expressed in cartoons were able to react positively to them while others whose views differed with those same ideas misinterpreted them. Psychologists have been categorizing patterns of behavior and have been able to identify persons who are likely to be swayed easily and others who are bound to resist.

SCOPE AND SEQUENCE

The over-all concept of readiness for learning is inherent in sequential learning. To start with the known, the simple, the concrete are guidelines that each of us may follow.

[2] *Ibid.*, p. 336.
[3] Helen Crossen, "Effects of Attitudes of the Reader upon Critical Reading Ability." Unpublished Ph.D. dissertation, University of Chicago, August 1946.
[4] Patricia Kendall and Katherine Wolf, "The Analysis of Deviant Cases in Communications Research." In P. Lazarsfeld and F. Stanton, *Communications Research*, pp. 152–179. New York: Harper & Bros., 1949.

Although there have not been systematic studies to determine in what order the skills of critical reading should be taught we have been able to extrapolate some hierarchy from the experiences of teachers. These empirical findings, however, remain to be tested under carefully controlled conditions. Students of critical reading have examined different aspects of the major ability in terms of the known and the unknown, the simple and the complex and the concrete and the abstract. Additional data have been drawn from our knowledge of some of the limiting factors that have been described earlier.

Several conclusions have been reached:

1. Some children have learned to think critically before entering school.
2. Critical reading has its earliest beginnings in the primary grades.
3. The level of critical reading achieved is controlled not so much by the nature of the process as it is by the experiences of the reader and his ability to deal with them.

On what skills of critical reading should the minds of six-, seven-, and eight-year-olds be stretched? One of the first might involve the reading of pictures which appear in their books. Illustrations may depict reality accurately or they may take liberties with it. It is not wholly a matter of accepting or rejecting them but rather recognizing them for what they are. Even though we see Jack climbing the beanstalk which towers over everything, we have no hesitation about going along with the story and picture.

Another ability is to select one picture among several, on the basis of its character and relationship to the highlights of the story. An extension of this ability would involve the recommendation of pictures which could be used to accompany original stories and poems.

The ability to accept or reject statements on the basis of authority can begin in the primary grades. A group studying the requirements of proper diet would be led to seek information from the school dietitian rather than from the school custodian. This ability to recognize the reliability of a source of information is built first upon gross discriminations and then finer ones. For example, to choose between the school nurse and school dietitian for authoritative information about food values would be more difficult.

Primary-grade children read fanciful tales as well as factual reports. The ability to discriminate between the two should be developed. Outright rejection may be tempered by tentative acceptance. But, here too, sequence demands simple distinctions first and more difficult ones later.

Children must learn to select sources which yield appropriate information for their purposes. Skilful evaluation of printed materials is reserved for higher levels but second and third graders can learn to choose a book or a magazine which is most likely to contain the knowledge they seek.

Sequential learning calls for judgments based in turn upon the pictures, titles, and tables of content.

The development of reading tastes involves discriminatory thinking. Preschool children are capable of making choices on the basis of some standard, and this ability may be strengthened in the primary grades. The ability to compare the worth of books and express a preference for better ones should be on our list of requirements.

Critical reading in the middle grades involves the strengthening and extension of skills that have been built in the primary grades. It also means the introduction of some higher-level skills for which older children are ready. The same type of critical attitude which is fostered in the lower grades will be encouraged in the higher ones; the materials with which the pupils deal, however, will be of a more difficult sort.

It is in the middle grades that wide reading of factual materials in textbooks, magazines and newspapers is encouraged. The solution to curriculum problems demands that children begin to use care in selecting and evaluating information from the above-mentioned sources. To determine the adequacy and accuracy of what purports to be a factual statement is an ability which calls for rather mature insights. Children are bound to meet different reports of the same event and must be prepared to evaluate each in terms of the authors' possible biases and qualifications, the audience for whom the information is intended and the recentness of the content. A viewpoint which depreciates the notion of space travel or the possibility of life on other planets may be seriously questioned in view of current scientific advances.

It would be well to note that most ten- or eleven-year-olds can hardly be expected to recognize biases which are masked by the use of subtle phraseology. But they surely can be taught to identify statements of personal opinion.

Another aspect of critical reading for pupils of this age involves questions of judgment based upon values to which they subscribe. For a child to be able to answer the question, "Was it the right thing to do?" as he studies the westward movement and the ultimate placement of the Indian on reservations requires the accumulation of more facts and fewer opinions and the weighing of issues. Of course he is able to relate such conduct only to his concept of fairness, and no effort should be made to have him struggle with moral issues that are beyond his present reach. But there is no question that this attitude of judging issues should be fed by careful guidance.

An adjunct to this ability is the restraint that should be shown in withholding judgments until the facts are available. It is tempting to base conclusions upon a minimal amount of information, but children must learn to curb this tendency. Later, learning to withhold judgment lays the foundation for dealing with propaganda and its techniques.

If we may assume that elementary school pupils have been participating in a developmental program in which provisions have been made for the sequential development of critical reading skills, the progression should continue through the high school and college. Obviously some students will be more advanced in their ability to react critically than others.

Though we may expect to deal with more complex skills, students' readiness for undertaking them can mean the difference between success and confusion. One would need to ascertain the point at which instruction should be initiated before plunging into areas which challenge even the ability of adults.

The ability to select sources which yield pertinent information and to determine the reliability of them should have been growing in the elementary grades. As students are surrounded by more advanced materials the exercise of these abilities becomes increasingly difficult. Instruction must continue if students are to respond satisfactorily.

Are students able to evaluate conclusions which have been drawn for them? Have they learned to examine the evidence which is cited to support these conclusions? Are they able to recognize that certain "evidence" is difficult to verify? Reading in the content fields provides a challenge to these skills.

Writers may merely present factual reports or they may be sharpening axes. The reader is in a better position to question if he recognizes the intent of the author. Then a written statement by the president of an organization known to have vested interests in an issue will not be viewed as another statement presented by an impartial observer. The reader should be able to answer a simple question: "Who would have me believe this?"

This ability to sense the author's purpose is tied to another one, the ability to discern and evaluate propagandistic or persuasive statements. Although one may not take issue with efforts to indoctrinate—and there are many causes for whose support we work—any attempt at deception or distortion is often regarded as unethical. The term propaganda has taken on these connotations, possibly because efforts to advocate particular practices or ideas have been accompanied by trickery and craftiness.

The techniques of propaganda have been analyzed and are well known. One which needs to receive special attention is the practice of citing quotations that have been deliberately removed from a larger context and as a result mislead the reader to believe what he would not ordinarily accept. A second device calls for truthful but incomplete statements, which cause the reader to react the way the writer desires. Other familiar techniques include the testimonial, band wagon and transfer. Students not only need to be alerted to these devices but also must have opportunities to respond to them as they read. The adolescent has demonstrated his readiness for learning suitable responses to exaggerated claims and partial truths; we must be ready to help him learn them.

The use of language and its influence upon reactions have been studied. There is no question about the power which words can generate. The specialists have responded intelligently: in economics, depressions have become recessions; and in ladies' wear, half-sizes are now B sizes.

Even writers of highly-regarded publications occasionally use words in such a way as to color the facts and influence the reader. A few years ago one of the leading newspapers of the country included a front-page account of the efforts of a "spinster ex-school teacher" to enact social legislation to which many persons were opposed. In this particular case straight factual reporting did not demand revelation of the marital status or previous profession of the bill's sponsor.

The reader must learn to separate words which have the power to produce feelings from words which merely serve to identify referents. The simple act of interspersing emotionally charged words among factual ones has led to reactions which the writer sought to cause. Readers must not be permitted to become slaves to words; our job is to lead readers to be masters of them.

CONCLUDING STATEMENT

To read critically is to read intelligently. Evidence which has been accumulated over the years reveals that such reading does not occur through osmosis nor does it result from chance. Efforts to develop this ability must be made by each teacher at every level of instruction. Only determined teachers can alter the reading behavior of students by helping each to become a thoughtful, careful, and critical reader.

21. Reading and the Educated Guess

Russell G. Stauffer

On the current scene it is likely that no one is exposed to more good-natured jostling than is the weatherman. It is not at all uncommon to hear

"Reading and the Educated Guess," by Russell Stauffer, is reprinted by permission from *Reading and Thinking*, A Report of the 17th Annual Conference and Course on Reading. Donald Cleland (ed.). Pittsburgh, University of Pittsburgh (June 12–23, 1961), pp. 27–33. References and page numbers in the text refer to the bibliography at the end of the reading.

a detailed weather report by a highly trained meterologist end on an apologetic tone. This is true in spite of the fact that today the U.S. Weather Bureau is using every kind of modern technological discovery to track down the weather. Yet, interestingly enough, the term "weather prediction," used to describe today's scientifically prepared reports, is also used to refer to the almanac annual forecasts. Neither time have the words "weather guessing" been used.

Should we encourage people to guess about the weather in the hope that eventually they may make intelligent guesses? Should such rules of thumb as "a red sky at night is a sailor's delight" be learned rotely or conjured up experientially? Should persons be asked to think of different weather variables and deduce potential relationships that might be verified or rejected by observation?

At an humbler level, predictions by a doctor take an "aura of awe" as he examines, classifies, and orders. The specialist sees certain conditions, hears reports about symptoms, and labels or classifies the illness. If he is right, he can tell about future conditions of the patient's temperature, substances in the urine, germs in the blood (1, p. 115), spots on the skin, and response to drugs. The inexperienced intern may need many clinical tests to predict the same condition. Before the prognosis of a case can have meaning, it must be related to the "right class" of illnesses and the meaning line of medical experience. Both approaches—that of the intern and that of the specialist—are useful. And we accept both with seldom a comment about "health predictions" or "health guessing."

Members of A. Conan Doyle societies are proud of their knowledge of how Sherlock Holmes examined evidence and made inferences. Constantly, as new facts came to light, hypotheses that Holmes had established earlier were subject to revision. Society members read mystery stories with this in mind—never stealing either a look ahead at a next page nor taking a last-chapter look.

To teachers of reading, I, then, address a question raised by Jerome Bruner: "Should we give our students practice not only in making *educated guesses* * but also in recognizing the characteristics of plausible guesses provided by others—knowing that an answer at least is of the right order of magnitude or that it is possible rather than impossible?" (2, p. 65)

Intelligent Guessing

Reading can be taught in such a way that the main channels of communication are between student and material being read (8). To do this the students must be encouraged to think, to ask questions, to find answers. One way to accomplish this is for students to be confronted with the same

* Italics are the present writer's

materials or stimuli and to be encouraged to extract information of predictive value. Then it soon becomes clear that in a free group discussion in which the main interchange of ideas is polarized towards the pupils and the material, different pupils may extract different information. They determine the predictive value of ideas by utilizing their own storehouses of experiences and knowledge. In such situations the tyranny of a right answer does not rest with the teacher as in common didactic methods, but resides in the material and the auditing of the group.

A group of six-year-olds reading in a First Reader was conjecturing about the plot of a story by using the title, "A Newspaper Helps." One boy said, "This story might be about a burning house. The people might put a notice in the newspaper about their burning house and then a fire company would come." To this another boy said, "That isn't logical. The house would have burned down in that time."

In another situation a group of seven-year-olds was reading a story about two dogs on a train. Halfway through the story, the children had learned that the dogs belonged to different owners and were headed for different destinations. When a next picture showed one of the two dogs being taken off the train, all the children were surprised. Story events had led them to think that the other dog would be the first to arrive at his destination. One girl speculated that perhaps the conductor had confused the tickets. All the children agreed with her and thought that this was what had happened. But the girl who made the speculation and who had obtained group consensus then changed her mind. "Conductors might confuse tickets," she said, "but I don't think this happened here because there were only two tickets."

A group of eight-year-olds reading a Third Reader level story about a dog-team race in the north country made two opposite predictions about the outcome of the race. According to the story this was the first time a girl had participated in the race. She was substituting for her sick brother. Six in the reading group said she would win; three said she would not. The six based their decision on four facts given in the story: Betty was tall for her age; she enjoyed outdoor activities; she could ice skate well; and she was fast on snowshoes. The three based their decision on the facts: Betty had not raced before; other entrants in the race had laughed when they heard about Betty; Red, the boy to beat, looked like a big, strong fellow.

A group of nine-year-olds was asked to conjecture about material entitled "The Two Mayflowers." With such limited information as provided by the title, the kinds of plausible conjectures could be quite varied, and they were. Ideas ranged from a new ocean liner named The Mayflower— to two May queens—to the making of a model of the original Mayflower. The article was about the trip of the second Mayflower in 1957. After the reading was done, the length of the ship (90 feet) and the width across the middle (25 feet) was compared with the classroom dimensions. The length of the main mast (100 feet) was compared with the school flag pole. The course followed by both ships was charted and compared. Trade winds, ocean currents, and calms were discussed, as well as the distance traveled: Mayflower I, 3,000 miles; Mayflower II, 5,000 miles; days traveled: Mayflower I, 66 days; Mayflower II, 53 days.

It is evident that in each of these situations some kind of guessing occurred. It should be evident, too, that in each instance the guessing was desirable. Patterns of meaning were being sought. The constructs provided by the stimuli (titles, pictures, maps, stories) were being tested by the children to see whether they were soluble in their old experiences. Creative responding was occurring in the sense that divergent thinking and original ideas were being obtained (4). Self-direction was being fostered as the children were encouraged to increase or decrease their exercise of choice of ideas: the burning house, tickets and conductors, winning a race, ocean liners, May queens, models.

It is evident, too, that the children were selecting relevant facts and gaining experience in recognizing the plausibility of their extrapolations or guesses. "The aim in scientific work is to extract information of predictive value from a given stimulus pattern." (1, p. 19) Of the many facts available about the dogs and their train adventure, the girl in episode two was selecting those she thought had most predictive value; and rejecting them when, upon reflection, they did not appear to be very soluble.

Similarly in the story about the dog race there were many other facts. Betty's brother had voiced confidence in her. It was a cold day. The dogs had been trained by the brother, and so on. Why were certain facts selected as support for guessing? Most likely they were selected because there were certain ways of structuring this episode that corresponded better with pupil experiences and purposes than did certain other ways.[7] At this early age these pupils were discovering that when they selected predictively fruitful facts, they were better able to make intelligent guesses. In other words, the pupils were learning to select evidence. Even though later in their school life they will learn scientific rules for being more precise about selecting evidence than common sense allows, they are already learning to select facts, how best to select facts, and how to use facts reflectively.

If the thinking mill is to produce grist that is well ground and relatively pure, it must be fed the grain of mistakes as well as successes. Any golfer knows this, as does any athletic coach, and any scientist. But all too often mistakes are outlawed in the classroom by the tyranny of a right answer, a teacher dominated by an "automatic pilot" Teachers' Manual, or the lure of primitive memory with its dazzling display of mental immobility. Students should not be protected from the discomfort of making mistakes, from the struggle to remain calm when their judgment is wrong, and from the need of resourcefulness when trying again. A mark of an educated man is his readiness to make honest mistakes and profit thereby.

Each pupil venturing a prediction faces the risk of being proved wrong. He may discover this himself as he reads or as others correct him if he misreads or misinterprets. The six-year-old who ventured the guess about the burning house and the newspaper could have been silenced by ridicule and condemnation. But this teacher handled her class in such a way that the child was not censored. Not only did she encourage the boy to make other conjectures but also, after the story had been read, they took another look at why calling a fire company needed to be done quickly. Similarly, the three pupils who made the wrong prediction about the outcome of the race were not stifled. They were learning to be open about their thinking and to be flexible, changing, learning persons.

In addition, they were learning how their own emotional reactions could stand in their way. They were discovering that there is a difference between an ignorant mistake and an intelligent mistake. Both sides agreed that the only way to prove which side was right was to read the story and get more facts.

The educated guess, then, is one that is based on the evidence at hand, is soluble in experience, and is as sound as one's knowledge permits. It is accomplished by creating, discovering, ordering, developing, and trying out ideas.

Values Pervading the Educated Guess

Each of the four illustrations exemplifies reading to learn through the creating and testing of meanings. Each story situation pointed the way to the development of conjectures. The subsequent reading provided the wherewithal to test the conjectures and accept or reject. This is undoubtedly a desirable outcome of sound reading instruction. It is the kind of approach toward knowledge that is essential—to create and to test.

Of almost equal importance is the resulting high respect for freedom and responsibility. Freedom to speculate has as its concomitant a responsibility to observe all available clues, order them, and draw forth guesses or speculations that are within the realm of plausibility (9). This is an intellectual challenge that encourages pupils to approach each opportunity with a zest for learning. Pupils soon sense the gravity of the privilege of trying out their ideas.

The responsibility is two-fold. First, pupils must diligently search for all the evidence that may be useful in declaring hypotheses and ordering them. Second, once a conjecture has been declared, it must be pursued until it is proved right or wrong. This may require the oral reading of lines to prove or disprove as the evidence is submitted to the group. The wild guess, the off-the-top guess, the guess based on one piece of evidence—these are soon recognized (6). The pupil held rigid in his examination of evidence by a bias or prejudice may learn to discover that his limited perspective caused him not only to overlook evidence but also to misinterpret that which he seized upon. The three pupils in the Third-Grade episode who believed the boy would win discovered that perhaps they had over-reacted to the evidence because they felt a boy should win.

Once a pupil has become involved in a reading situation by the use of his own ideas, he will want to move forward to test his ideas. This self-actualizing tendency to seek, to reconstruct, to reflect, to prove, has tremendous motivation potential (6). The pupil helps create a learning climate and strives to maintain it.

Few readers can remain withdrawn from the evidence of an unfolding plot and not make any choices until the final safe choice is apparent. Few people can remain withdrawn from decisions about experience until enough evidence is in to make a safe choice. Each proceeds by constructing and reconstructing, by speculating and testing—using the evidence at hand. So it becomes important to learn to select the possible rather than the impossible and the probable as well as the possible. "Hypotheses may range from very plausible answers to wild guesses, 'shots in the dark.' Both should be given a hearing. Many plausible guesses turn out to be only remotely related to the problem." (3, p. 64) It is through this process that making educated guesses can develop as a commitment to the ideal of objectivity and to the social circumstances that permit the process to carry on. The girl in Second Grade recognized that her idea about the confused tickets was possible but not probable. This she accomplished even though she had obtained the consensus of the group for her first conjecture. Their uncritical acceptance of her hypothesis and their social approval did not block her thinking.

Similarly, when pupils move creatively into a reading situation and produce a number of educated guesses, the impact of success and even intelligent mistakes is such that it promotes security and confidence. This, in turn, fosters a willingness to think, reflect, and hypothesize. The pupils reading about the two Mayflowers were ready to deal with the emerging facts about each ship's dimensions, the distances traveled, and the two courses pursued. Theirs was not a case of too easy acceptance of ideas but a checking and comparing that might yield better understanding. "Persistance, aggressiveness, objectivity, confidence, and rationability characterize effective thinking." (3, p. 251) And, as Bruner says:

> What is most important for teaching basic concepts is that the child be helped to pass progressively from concrete thinking to the utilization of more conceptually adequate modes of thought. But it is futile to attempt this by presenting formal explanations based on a logic

that is distant from the child's manner of thinking and sterile in its implications for him (2, p. 38).

THE ROLE OF THE TEACHER AND THE GROUP

In directing a reading activity so that intelligent guessing may occur, the teacher becomes the focal point in the act (8). The equipment a teacher needs is knowledge of the story being read or subject matter being dealt with; a lively imagination; a willingness to play with ideas; courage enough to direct thinking even though not knowing exactly where the questioning will lead; and a conviction that teaching is not telling answers or listening to rotely memorized answers. Where this facility occurs the teacher serves a double purpose: ". . . he not only leads the students through a process of thought to check the adequacy of their meanings, he also widens and enriches their conceptual activity by the range of information he brings to bear on the problem." (5, p. 198) Or again, as Bruner puts it:

It requires a sensitive teacher to distinguish an intuitive mistake—an interesting wrong leap—from a stupid or ignorant mistake, and it requires a teacher who can give approval and correction simultaneously to the intuitive student (2, p. 68).

A group provides a medium in which each individual can learn about the effectiveness of his thinking and reading. Pupils can learn that it is almost as useful to listen to others making guesses as it is to make their own; to agree, as to disagree; to criticize, as to approve; to prove, as to disprove. The aim of such free group reading and thinking is for the individual to learn ways of acting which will be useful to him when he is on his own.

The relationships between the group and the teacher, and between members of the group are of mutual regard, of fidelity to objective evidence, of emotional control, of dealing with successes and contradictions without embarrassment. "Sometimes the group works like a well-balanced orchestra . . ." (1, p. 74) Different members are featured in different compositions at different times. One member may repeatedly remind the group of the title and its possible significance: for example, "A Newspaper Helps." Some may follow the lead of others time and again, only to discover they were misled as in the "ticket confusing" episode. Others deal frequently on an emotional basis; sometimes they learn how this may be a successful intuitive leap, and other times may not be successful. The rate of contribution of guesses may vary from story to story according to individual interest and experience. Sometimes the difficulty of thinking and clear expression may result in frustration or anger.

The character of a group that deals in educated guesses should be but a reflection of the classroom as a whole. Effective thinking skills acquired and polished in a reading class should be recognized as the thread that unites all fields of instruction at all levels. The fact that texts used to teach reading have as their content, material from all the disciplines, gives the teacher the wherewithal to develop and refine scientific thinking skills. This means that effective reading-thinking skills should be taught and retaught as students progress through school. When the values of the processes of reflective thinking are recognized in their own right, the personal and social aim of education will be served.

To sum up, educated guesses are the crux of effective thinking and reading. They motivate and direct. They liberate the individual from the grip of the commonplace, the closed mind, the inflexible, the disregard for cause and effect, and intellectual dishonesty. They range from the crude and simple to the elaborate and highly sophisticated. "Since a hypothesis is essentially a 'guess,' it has its ultimate source in man's capacity to transcend imaginatively a group of given phenomena and to see possibilities of context and causation which will explain the 'facts.'"

References

1. M. L. Johnson Abercrombie, *The Anatomy of Judgment*. New York: Basic Books, 1960.
2. Jerome S. Bruner, *The Process of Education*. Cambridge: Harvard University Press, 1960.
3. William H. Burton, Roland B. Kimball, and Richard L. Wing, *Education for Effective Thinking*. New York: Appleton-Century-Crofts, Inc., 1960.
4. J. P. Guilford, "Frontiers in Thinking That Teachers Should know About," *The Reading Teacher*, Vol. 13, No. 3 (February 1960), pp. 176–82. Chicago: International Reading Association.
5. H. Gordon Hullfish and Philip G. Smith, *Reflective Thinking: The Method of Education*. New York: Dodd, Mead & Company, 1961.
6. Carl R. Rogers, "Significant Learning: In Therapy and In Education," *Educational Leadership*, Vol. XVI, No. 4 (January 1959), pp. 232–42.
7. David H. Russell, *Children's Thinking*. New York: Ginn & Company, 1956.
8. Russell G. Stauffer, "Productive Reading-Thinking at the First Grade Level," *The Reading Teacher*, Vol. 13, No. 3 (February 1960), pp. 183–87. Chicago: International Reading Association.
9. ——, "Reading and the Habit of Credulity," *The Science and Philosophy of Reading*, Vol. VIII, March, 1959. Newark, Del.: The Reading-Study Center, University of Delaware, 1961.

22.   Critical Thinking in the First Grade

Josephine Shotka

"Critical Thinking" sounds so profound that one is apt to question the posibility of a first-grader being capable of approaching an attitude toward it or developing skill in its use.

What does critical thinking mean? What is its value? It is the ability to think and to reason, whether it be a child experiencing reading readiness or a student in a higher learning situation. It means becoming familiar with the procedure in inquiring and discovering, developing skill in securing information, resolving the information gathered and then appraising the evidence obtained. It means also the ability to listen effectively and to retain and apply what one hears. Critical thinking stresses the necessity of being informed, of knowing how and where to get needed information, of developing ability to evaluate, discuss, and unify this information for the purpose of coming to a valid conclusion.

When a first-grade teacher studies an outline on critical thinking set up for use in junior high and high school, it is possible he might say, "This is beyond the mental capacity of a first-grader. Creative thinking, yes, but *critical* thinking I question."

Let's look at this outline:

1. Recognizing and defining the problem
2. Recognizing assumptions
3. Formulating hypothesis
4. Reasoning from hypothesis
5. Gathering evidence from: reading, observation, survey, and experimentation
6. Evaluating evidence: detecting bias, determining validity and reliability, evaluating significance
7. Organizing evidence
8. Generalizing and deciding

The outline usable in developing critical thinking in the first grade could look like this:

1. See and state a problem.
2. Recognize what can be taken for granted.
3. Assume what is true for the sake of testing.
4. Give reasons for testing.
5. Get evidence: reading (by teacher); looking about us for answers;

"Critical Thinking in the First Grade," by Josephine Shotka. *Childhood Education,* May 1960, Vol. 36, No. 9. Reprinted by permission of the Association for Childhood Education International, 3615 Wisconsin Avenue, N.W., Washington, D.C. 20016.

talking to parents and people in a position to help us; using pictures; experimenting (i.e., in science, numbers): seeing films.

6. Evaluate the evidence by: finding bias, validity, reliability.

7. Put findings together and organize them.

8. Draw conclusions.

First-grade teachers should teach the child to show good judgment, develop reasoning ability, and give academic content. As mental ability develops, the first-grader will learn to stay on the topic being discussed with less distraction and fewer irrelevant ideas. In time the child will come to listen attentively while others are talking and continue the topic without distraction.

We can encourage the child to express ideas in general terms as well as in concrete terms. A higher quality of thinking is attained when a first-grader can use such generic terms as *vegetable* instead of the series *peas, beans, corn*. We can encourage the child to give the reason for an idea he expresses. The child who learns to ask or to answer *why* will reach a higher level of mental growth.

We can also encourage the child to express his own ideas of evaluation and appreciation. To develop the ability to make comparisons in terms of something being suitable, appropriate, or accurate is of great help in thinking.

The study offers a splendid opportunity to develop, use, and improve critical thinking. My group is now working on the unit "The Home and the Community."

The flexible outline we set up is as follows:

1. What is a "home"? What is the "community"? Who are the "helpers"?

2. We can assume most homes, communities, and helpers—within certain bounds—are similar to our own.

3. For the sake of testing, get the idea of home, community, and helpers from each one in the group (with guidance by the teacher).

4. Reasons for testing: to get clear understanding, to get group interest and participation, to broaden our knowledge and experience, to get enjoyment, to increase our vocabulary.

5. Where can we get the information needed? Reading (by the teacher for the first part of the year), looking around us for answers, talking to people who can give us reliable information, using pictures, taking trips, seeing movies.

6. Evaluate the evidence by asking: Is it true? Is it reliable? Is it biased?

7. Bring all facts together and organize them.

8. Draw conclusions: oral stories, chart stories, bulletin board exhibits, construction displays.

The seed of the unit was planted five weeks after school started when I talked to them as follows:

"You all live at home; can you tell me in your words what a home is?" Some of the answers were:

A home is a place where you can go if you are afraid.
It's a place where you can run around without any clothes on, and no one will see you.
It's a place you live in.
A home is where you can play.
It's a place where you live with your father and mother because you love them and they love you.
It's a place where your father and mother work for you.
You can stay there if you are sick.
It's a nice quiet place.
You can have parties there.

We listened to all the ideas about home and then discussed them. The final definition as decided by the group was:

A home is a house where you live, work and play with the people you love and who love you.

They drew pictures of their homes and families and after the drawings were put on the bulletin board, a discussion about "our families" followed. The group wanted to know about mine first, so I told the story of my family. Each child was then most anxious to tell about his family. The pictures when completed were framed and put on the bulletin board with the title "Our Homes—Our Families."

Wanting to introduce another family new to them and one they would be interested in most of the year, I asked this question, "Do you think the family in our reader is anything like your own family?" Here the readers were passed out and the children took careful notice of all the pictures. The consensus was: they are alike in some respects and different in others.

In our discussion of how they were alike, these similarities were given:

The children play with each other and their friends.
Father goes to work like my father does.
They go to the store to buy things.
The girls play with dolls and so do I.
The children go to school.
They have family picnics.
There is a father, a mother, and children.
Mother stays home and does the housework.
The family has people who help them—see the milkman and the cleaners.

The differences noted were:

They have different names.
They have different faces—features. (Here a child asked, "What does *features* mean?" The child who had used the term said, "You know—it's what makes you pretty or homely.")
Their house is bigger and prettier than mine.
There are more people in this family than in mine.
The children are always happy—they never cry.
They never look tired.
They are always clean.

After our observations and discussion, a child asked, "Why did the man who drew these pictures make them like that?"
Some of the answers to this question were:

He just wanted to do it that way.
Maybe it was the only way he could think of.
He couldn't think of making the children look dirty.
He wanted to draw a happy family.
He wanted the pictures to look pretty—you aren't pretty when you're sad or dirty.
He wanted the pictures and the stories, too, to be happy. Children don't like sad stories.

We had completed our discussion and had a good understanding of our home, our familly, and the family in our readers. Wishing to branch out into the community, I put this question to the group:
"Could you live in your home with your mother, father, and sisters and brothers, with no one else at all around you, and be able to get along?"
The answer came quickly and unanimously, "No." This was an assumption subject to testing.
The question *Why?* now had to be answered. Again a few of the answers:

We'd have no friends to play with.
I couldn't go to school and learn to read.
If you needed food, you couldn't get any.
You wouldn't have any money 'cause your daddy couldn't work.
If you got sick, who could help you?
You might have a fire and couldn't get help.
It would hurt the Army because my daddy couldn't make guided missiles.
If you had lots of cavities, there wouldn't be anyone to fix them.
If you wanted to cross a busy street, there wouldn't be a policeman to help you.

You couldn't cook; you wouldn't have any electricity.
The electricity wouldn't do any good; you might not even have a stove.
When you wanted to drive your car, you wouldn't have any gas.
You would run out of food and clothes.

I then told the children we had a name for all the people they had mentioned who could help them. I said, "They are helpers—community helpers."
The question I had hoped for came:
"What is a community?"
Hands went up in answer. Some conceptions of the community were really amusing. This was anticipated since the meaning of the word was either a guess or learning from inference.
Some answers were:

A place where lots of people live together, but in different houses.
A community is a place where people play together.
It's a lot of buildings people work in.
It's a lot of houses and stores built together. You might find a factory where men make wheels and cars.

I showed them many pictures of a community, followed this with discussion, and read them stories. Then our generalizing, organizing, and deciding came to this definition: *
A community is a lot of people living near each other, and other people who help them.

The suggestion then came, "Can't we make a community with all the helpers on the bulletin board?" I suggested that before we make the bulletin-board display we decide who the helpers are and how they help us. This was accepted and we prepared the bulletin board and titled it "Community Helpers."
Other questions arose. How were we to tell who were the helpers? Where could we get pictures?
Just before the children went home, I suggested that on the way home on the bus and in the morning on their way to school they look out the windows at the buildings and see what helpers these buildings might suggest.
The reports and discussion the next morning showed that they had really been observant and had an understanding of helpers.
Another assignment followed: Tonight talk to your mother and father about the helpers and then, with them or alone, if you can, see how many pictures you can find in magazines of helpers. Bring them to school. The

* Ed. Note: Showing the pictures followed by discussion of how their own community compares with those in the pictures would be another way to reach a consensus on the meaning of the word community.

following morning almost every youngster came in joyfully clutching his pictures. As the pictures were brought in, they were cut out, mounted, labeled, and put on the bulletin board. As an incentive for those not interested and for those who had not yet contributed, I put the name of the contributor on each picture he brought in. This worked well.

A few examples of critical thinking were brought out as we were in the process of deciding which picture on the bulletin board showed a helper. A picture of a man in a hat and topcoat carrying a brief case attracted the most attention. They asked, "Who is he?" The girl who brought the picture announced, "Why, he's a salesman." Consternation could be noted on a few faces. One child said, "He's not a helper—he's a pest." (Example of bias.) Someone asked, "Why is he a pest?" "He's always ringing your doorbell and trying to sell junk." Another child called out, "No, he's the Jewel Tea man." Another added, "He sells Christmas cards." My question: "What do the rest of you think a salesman is?"

He's a man or lady who comes to your door to sell lots of things.
Sometimes children sell things; then they're salesmen.

I then asked, "What do you think would happen if everyone turned the salesman away and never bought anything from him?"

A good example of critical thinking came in the answers to the above question.

His feelings would be hurt.
He'd never get any money.
He wouldn't be able to buy anything for himself.
If no one bought cars, the factory would close—lots of men would be out of work.
If the factory man didn't work, he'd have no money.
My daddy's a doctor; nobody could pay him.
Lots of things would stop.
We'd have trouble.

We concluded that the salesman came to help us and we should help him. He is a community helper, too.

The next helpers discussed—policeman, fireman, farmer, milkman—were understood by the children. It was not too difficult to label them helpers.

The discussion concerning teachers was interesting:

A teacher helps you to have a happy day.
A person you can talk to—even secrets.
She is someone who can teach you something you don't know.
A person who teaches you how to read and write.
She always helps you.
She takes you on trips.

She listens to you.

She is nice and does things for you.

Not all teachers are nice. My brother's teacher yells and he doesn't learn anything.

The above led me to ask, "If you could have any person you want to be your teacher, how would you like to have her look and act?"

These answers were revealing:

She should be nice and never yell. Yelling gives me headaches.

I would like her to like to help me and play with me.

She should dress pretty and have pretty clothes.

She should know how to teach.

She should be quiet.

She should wear a pony tail.

I would like her to teach me to read and lots of things.

Help me when I need help.

I'd like her to be like—(here I was mentioned).

She should teach us things we don't know.

She shouldn't help us too much. We can do things ourselves.

Let us say what we want.

She should protect us.

I'd like her to smile lots.

She should be funny.

These are a few samples of the discussions; more will follow, for our bulletin board is covered with pictures of helpers. The children brought them for discussion and evaluation as to whether they are helpers who touch our lives. Some helpers yet to be discussed are: surveyor, secretary, telephone man, scientist, druggist, librarian, rabbi, priest, minister, architect, builder.

To satisfy the interest for inquiry and discovery, I can see imaginary trips to the oil fields as an outgrowth of our discussion of the gasoline man. An example of this interest might be illustrated by the remarks at the time the gasoline man was discussed. "I know there are containers for the gasoline under the ground, but where does he get more gasoline?"

From oil wells, I know, because I saw some in Canada.

I saw some when I went to Texas.

Gasoline isn't oil—oil is black.

Don't you know there are places, I forget the name, where they make gasoline out of oil?

We decided to go into this more after finishing our discussion of helpers.

Other studies I can foresee are: the study of building materials and their use in conjunction with the name *builder;* scientific experiments (on first-grade level) because of their interest in the scientist and his work; a study of foods, marketing, money value because of the groceryman; a study of fire, its origin, use, and effect on our lives because of interest in the fireman; a deeper study of the telephone, its parts and value, because of the "telephone man."

Trips will be planned at the time of study to broaden the children's knowledge and enrich their experience.

23. Productive Reading-Thinking at the First Grade Level

Russell G. Stauffer

That there is not enough reading for meaning is a canon of contemporary criticism often wearisome in its repetition and often blind in its application. The implication that there can be reading without resultant meaning sets unreasonable limits to the function of reading. It is a half-truth that tends to confuse the unthinking as well as the uninformed.

Possibly the idea that productive reading is a process closely akin to productive thinking has always been held by good teachers. Probably it is a concept held by mature readers as a result of wide experience in reading for many purposes and in different materials. Certainly it is a concept that authorities in reading as well as psychology have always expressed and advocated.

But the thought that productive reading-thinking involving the setting of purposes, reasoning while reading, and evaluation can be done by six-year-olds, or children in first grade, puzzles some and confounds others. Generally, children become lost in the word learning maze of initial reading instruction. Unwarranted attention is often given to memorizing words, to drilling on phonetic skills in isolation, to oral reading and re-reading, and to a telling of the story. Then, too, some teachers are of the opinion that six-year-olds can not think critically and cannot be trained to do so. In fact, the story is told that during the late forties, when the National Council of Teachers of English were drafting the new English curriculum, one college professor of English recommended that nothing be done about critical thinking at the elementary and high-school levels. To think critically, he said, was a skill to be acquired in college.

"Productive Reading-Thinking at the First Grade Level," by Russell G. Stauffer, *The Reading Teacher,* XIII (February 1960), 183–187. Reprinted with permission of Russell G. Stauffer and the International Reading Association.

Although the above is an absurd proposal, it is almost equally as absurd to be of the opinion that six-year-olds cannot be taught to do productive reading. The following illustration of a first-grade group in action should help to dispel such opinions.

In this first-grade classroom the teacher used both a group approach and an individualized approach to differentiated reading instruction. For the group sessions she had identified four groups, with each member of each group at about the same instructional level.

The group in the action described here was the teacher's second group, or, as she put it, her "average readers." Group instruction was being directed in a first-grade basic reader. To be sure that each story was new or unknown to the children, the books were stored in a closet and brought out only during the teacher-directed reading session.

The story for the session was entitled "A Newspaper Helps" and was located in the fourth unit of the book on pages 119–124.* Six new words were introduced in the span of six pages. This made the ratio of new words to running words 1:72. In addition, each new word was introduced in a meaningful and appropriate way to fit the communication demands of the context. Because of these facts, plus the fact that this group had already been taught certain word-attack skills of phonetic and structural analysis, the teacher did not write the new words on the board to be studied before the reading of the story. She wanted the children to meet the six words in the rich content of the story and have them use, if necessary, their word-attack skills under her supervision.

FIRST PURPOSE-SETTING

The teacher directed the group to turn to the Table of Contents and read the name of the story located on page 119. Then she asked, "What do you think will happen in the story?" The results of immediate speculation seemed logically possible. Some of the ideas were: "Perhaps a newspaper is used to train a dog. Maybe a family finds a place to live by using a newspaper. The paper may be used to wrap some toys. Maybe the paper is folded and used as a fly swat." Already interest was running high.

Next, the group was directed to turn to page 119, to study the picture for possible clues, and then close their books. New speculation was adjusted quickly in keeping with the new information provided by the first picture. (The picture showed three boys looking in a puzzled way at a small black dog.) Ideas now given were: "The boys looked worried because this is a strange dog. The dog didn't listen to them and they will

* R. G. Stauffer, *et al. Away We Go* (Philadelphia: John C. Winston, 1960).

use a newspaper to train him. The boys are wondering whose dog this is. They want to play ball and the dog gets in their way."

The group was eager to get on with the story to find out whose ideas were right. So the teacher directed them to read only the first page and then to close their books.

The pupil-purpose setting was the first step on the reading-thinking road. They had sized up the picture situation and evaluated the title. Ability to look ahead—to anticipate next steps—is a skill possessed by almost all typical six-year-olds and is used by them constantly in their day-to-day living. What was done here was to provide training in looking ahead in a reading situation. To be able to select and weigh and balance available beginning clues, in terms of ultimate story outcome, represents an important reading-thinking skill.

It took but a minute or so for all to read the page. Now the teacher observed a key teacher responsibility—she honored the pupil purposes, not by asking questions about the details of the story but by asking "Who was right?" The boy who had proposed that the dog was strange and the boys were worried immediately raised his hand. Then he read orally the lines that proved his point. All agreed, and again a major reading-thinking skill was being refined: knowing whether or not the answer to a question has been found.

SECOND PURPOSE-SETTING

Another brief speculation session followed after a quick look at the two pictures on the next two facing pages. (One picture showed the boys talking to Mother. The other showed the boys scanning a newspaper.) Ideas now presented were: "Mother tells them to go find the dog's owner. The boys look in the morning paper to see if someone has lost a dog."

Again, reading was done and posture, facial expressions, and occasional audible responses readily showed that the children were reading for meaning.

Checking on their purposes was accomplished by the teacher's initiating question: "Which idea was right?" This time none of the speculations had been completely accurate. The boys, at the mother's suggestion, had run an ad in the paper about the finding of a little black dog.

THIRD PURPOSE-SETTING

This time the teacher suggested that purposes be set without looking ahead. So, in light of the evidence or information so far accumulated, the children set purposes. Ideas now presented were: that the owner would

show up and claim the dog and reward the boys, that the owner might
not show up, and that the dog would run away again.

The predictions showed that the pupils were half-way through the
story. As they reflected over events to date, reconstructed them, and re-
evaluated them, the pupils were putting to work an excellent thinking-
learning technique. They were learning the value of reflective judgment
as contrasted with naïve and blind plunging ahead. As they read on, it
was interesting to note how the pupils read the next two pages and how
they examined the pictures. They were searching all sources of information in an effort to find clues to the possible fate of the lost dog.

When all were finished reading, the teacher once more asked, "Which
ideas were right this time?" Now the children were a bit puzzled. The
two pages had not answered their questions but they had given new information about the dog. This little black dog apparently was a trained
dog. He could do tricks.

Fourth Purpose-Setting

Ideas about how the story might end again reflected the degree to which
these young minds grasped and evaluated the information so far presented. Because the dog could do tricks, some pupils felt very sure that
the owners would be looking for the dog. One boy felt that the dog had
learned the tricks on his own because he had always been a runaway dog.
Some thought the owners would not turn up because they would have
missed seeing the small-town newspaper and would not know that the
dog had been found.

"On with the story," said the teacher, "and see who is right." The last
picture showed the boys, the mother, the dog, and two strangers. The
man seemed to be giving the boys some paper, but not money. The reading was done rapidly.

A check quickly revealed that the pupils who had predicted the owners
would show up were right. What they had not anticipated—and this is
what held their interest to the end in this well-conceived plot—was that
the dog was a circus dog, especially trained to do tricks. Again, lines were
read orally to prove points. A short discussion followed on how wisely
the boys had acted, and on the use of newspaper ads. All the reading and
discussion so far had taken twenty minutes.

The end of the story was a good time to check on concepts and story
understandings. Because the story was well written, the pupils could understand and enjoy its development and outcome. Now, at the end, was
the time for refinement.

A good story is likely to evoke many ideas and questions which can
send the reader beyond the story. When the reading of a story is directed

as a reading-thinking process, the readers will invariably be stimulated to seize upon every opportunity to learn more. All this means that going beyond a basic reader story should be a natural and almost an integral part of all group-directed reading.

IN CONCLUSION

Thus, here have been considered some of the steps to productive reading and thinking. This rather detailed description of one directed reading-thinking session should have shown that it is wrong to think that enthusiasm and clear thinking cannot go hand in hand. To the contrary, enthusiasm is indispensable for achieving clear thinking—be the resulting decisions great or small, immediate or remote.

Also shown was the age-old concept that effective skill-training is best accomplished under the watchful eye of an experienced teacher—one who has the skill to direct training as occasion or need demands. A person with such ability must be both resolute and informed.

Shown too was the fact that it is not enough to say that an answer has been found in a story. Proof must be produced. Pupils must learn to support constantly their statements of fact with specific proof. This directed reading activity required such performance.

Some boys and girls perform like some men and women. They are ready to present opinions unsupported by facts. They do this because they are constantly influenced by the beliefs and modes of behavior of the people around them. So, to establish in children the definite habits and emotional tendencies of sound thinking, training must be initiated early and must be vigorously continued.

It is especially important that those who concern themselves with the instruction of others be clear about what they are doing. As long as pupils can be helped in a firsthand, face-to-face situation, little difficulty should arise in promoting the habits of sound productive reading.

The roots of reading behavior must be very deep in the tradition of sound thinking, if boys and girls are to mature as rational individuals. A rational person is one who seeks answers, requires proof, and is aware that reasonable persons could have different beliefs. Persons so prepared can be deliberate and tolerant in their use of ideas. Rationality gives them, in turn, an authority and assurance that come only from knowing and doing.

Major types of thinking as declared by Guilford elsewhere in this issue of THE READING TEACHER are divergent production, convergent production, and evaluation. And, as he says, whether the reading material stimulates productive thinking by the reader will depend in part upon the nature of the material. It will also depend upon skillful questioning or directing of thinking on the part of the teacher. To this is added another thought: it will depend upon the degree to which pupils see clearly and declare openly purposes and problems.

The reading-thinking lesson described in this article and the supporting discussion should then, to a degree, provide answers for Guilford's four questions: Do the material and the teaching stir the imagination of the reader, and do they leave something for the reader to do? Do they open up alternative, inviting avenues that would suggest divergent thinking? Do they carry the reader logically forward step by step to an inevitable conclusion? And do they challenge beliefs and call for proof of facts and arguments?

24. Critical Reading in the Primary Grades

Walter Petty

Merely pronouncing the words on a printed page does not constitute reading. As Gray has said: "The concept of reading has expanded during recent decades from a simple activity of one dimension to a complex activity of four dimensions—perception, understanding, reaction, integration." [1] That is, before the act of reading is completed, words and phrases must be received by the visual apparatus, be understood and evaluated, and be used along with past experiences in the process of thinking and its improvement. Thus reading is a complex act of both physiological and psychological processes.

This concept implies that reading includes much that we commonly call thinking. Whether there is an actual distinction between the securing of ideas on the one hand and using these ideas in thinking on the other hand may not be of great importance, since efficient readers do think about what they read while they are reading whether this is a single complex act or several acts of lesser complexity. Actually "it is difficult, if not impossible, to determine the place where reading leaves off and only thought remains." [2] Even the relatively simple act of word recognition may be called thinking, since a word has its context in the past experiences of

[1] William S. Gray, "Growth in Understanding Reading and its Development Among Youth," *Supplementary Educational Monographs* (Proceedings of the Annual Conference on Reading, University of Chicago, 1950), Vol. 12, No. 72 (Oct. 1950), p. 10.

[2] Ernest Horn, *Methods of Instruction in the Social Studies* (New York: Charles Scribner's Sons, 1937), p. 153.

"Critical Reading in the Primary Grades," by Walter Petty, *Elementary English,* XXXIII (1956), 298–302. Reprinted with the permission of the National Council of Teachers of English and Walter Petty.

the individual and in other words that surround or are near it in the utterance and in other contemporaneous signs which affect it. Traxler points out, "Any conception of reading is inadequate that fails to include reflection, critical evaluation, and clarification of meanings." [3]

Types of reading, as well as types of thinking, may be classified, not only with respect to form and the reader's or thinker's general attitude, but also with respect to the specific purposes that lead to the reading or thinking on given occasions. For example, a child may read to find information relating to a problem or to follow detailed directions; an adult may read to understand a situation better or to determine the validity of arguments relating to a social or political issue. When the steps or processes involved in a variety of reading activities are analyzed, significant differences are noted. It is obvious, for example, that the mental processes involved in reading to answer a question which involves judgment are much more elaborate than in reading to answer a factual question. In the latter situation, one recognizes the various elements of meaning in a passage and identifies the particular word or phrase that answers that question. In reading to answer a question which involves judgment, a greater amount of analysis, reflection, and organization of ideas is essential.

Reading, thus, calls for a variety of skills which have to be adapted to fit the needs of different types of situations. Certain fundamental elements of word recognition, word meaning, and ability to deal with phrase and sentence units are involved in all reading situations. However, reading situations call for much more than ability to read words, phrases, and sentences. These situations involve many different kinds of higher-level skills, which vary according to the reader's purpose and the requirements set by the material to be read.

Of these higher-level skills one of the most important is the ability to do critical reading. Harris lists four types of critical reading that can be distinguished. These are: (1) "the ability to decide correctly whether a particular sentence or paragraph supplies information relevant to a question or topic . . . ," (2) the comparison of two or more sources of information, (3) the consideration of "new ideas or information in the light of one's previous knowledge and beliefs," and (4) "the ability to detect and resist the influences of undesirable propaganda." [4]

Critical reading, then, involves appraisal, evaluation, selection, judgment, or comparison of ideas during the total process as contrasted to mere reproduction of the substance as it actually appears. This is a distinction that is a subtle but important one. There are pupils of all ages whose

[3] A. E. Traxler, "Problems of Group Remedial Reading in the Secondary School," *High Points* (Vol. XX, 1938), pp. 5–18.
[4] Albert J. Harris, *How to Increase Reading Ability* (New York: Longmans, Green and Co., 1950), p. 387.

"reading" is largely literal. The reading may be selective in the sense that the pupils may not try to note and remember everything, but they are still engaged in direct recognition and faithful recall of something that is offered. Some of these children acquire considerable skill in reproducing, not merely all the details but also a summary or outline of the substance; yet they still do little thinking beyond the accumulation of the ideas as they understood them. To really think while reading, to evaluate, to judge what is important or unimportant, what is relevant or irrelevant, what is in harmony with an idea read in another book or acquired through experience, constitutes critical reading ability. That this aspect of reading is related to—or is a part of—thinking, and more specifically critical thinking, is clearly evident when one considers that critical thinking "involves (1) an attitude of being disposed to consider in a thoughtful way the problems and subjects that come within the range of one's experience, (2) knowledge of the methods of logical inquiry and reasoning, and (3) some skill in applying these methods." [5]

Ability to do critical reading as described here should and can begin to be developed even before actual reading is done because of its relationship to critical thinking. Critical thinking occurs in problem-solving situations. As Dewey and others have said, "Thinking of a problem-solving kind originates in a felt difficulty, state of doubt, or perplexity." [6]

Problems which have meaning for children afford excellent opportunities for critical thinking. Young children should learn to recognize problems that need solving and to state these in their own words. They can think about what the different aspects of a problem may be—that is, what things are involved, what actions must be taken, what must be found before the problem can be solved. They can make some judgments as to whether it will be possible to find the answers to some or all of their questions. They may even begin to decide whether a particular source of information is reliable. Problem-solving in the primary grades deals largely with community sources of information, with people to whom the students talk, places which they visit, pictures or objects they inspect, as well as with printed materials which they read or which are read to them. In collecting information from any source, children need to make judgments as to whether the material answers a specific question or adds important features to their understanding of the situation being studied. Thinking of a constructive and critical sort is involved in fitting together the parts of the study, as various committees or individuals report their information, and in drawing conclusions or in making generalizations. If the problem is of the sort which should result in decision and action on the

[5] Edward M. Glaser, *An Experiment in the Development of Critical Thinking* (New York: Teachers College, Columbia University, Contributions to Education, No. 843, 1941), p. 164.
[6] *Ibid.*, p. 25.

part of the class, critical thinking is also called into play in evaluating the results when such a decision is tested by action.

If the pupils in our schools are to develop reading ability of the type described here, the instructional program, from the readiness stage on, must be pointed in this direction. From their first contacts with children, teachers must be thinking not only of readiness for recognition of words and phrases and understanding of meanings, but also of readiness for critical or evaluative reading.

Too frequently, attempts have been made to develop critical reading and thinking abilities by the concentration of the teaching of certain skills in a few lessons, usually at one of the upper grade levels. A program of this type is built on an erroneous concept, for "critical thinking is not a simple gadget that can be taught and acquired on the spot in one lesson, unit, or even one single subject. It is something like a way of life. . . . It is necessary to see critical thinking as a developmental process." [7]

The role of the teacher in helping children develop the maturity necessary to carry on activities involving thought and understanding is that of a guide and clarifier rather than that of an imparter of information and ready-made concepts. As a first step a teacher can help a child to know what he is thinking. This may sometimes be done by merely repeating the child's words, objectifying them, letting him know how they sound, helping him decide if they mean what he really thinks they mean. Or the teacher may rephrase what the child has said and ask, "Is this what you mean?" Sometimes she may inquire about where a child acquired a certain idea. From such simple questions as, "Did the person who told you this know that it was true?" and "What makes you think he knew?" may arise the beginnings of critical evaluation of sources of information.

Needless to say, all processes designed to clarify the thinking of young children should deal in so far as possible, with simple, real problems, with definite and concrete thoughts, with understandable feelings. This does not mean, however, that children should not be given teacher help in order to understand as much as possible; they should be given serious attention and enough clues to help their thinking so that their natural curiosity will not be thwarted.

Important in the primary grades in teaching critical thinking is the fostering of an atmosphere in which problems arise and their solution is vital. For example, suppose that in a first grade classroom this question arises out of the discussion—whether the raising of the question was specifically planned for by the teacher or not—"What can we do now to get ready for a garden when it gets warm?" The first thing that would probably happen would be the giving of suggestions by various members

7 Hilda Taba, "Problems in Developing Critical Thinking," *Progressive Education* (Vol. 28, No., 1950), p. 614.

of the class. If the teacher keeps a record with the children of these suggestions, an opportunity is present for fostering critical thinking.

The teacher might say, "We've said all these things that are on the board. Now, what was the question we had in the beginning? How many of our statements answer the question? Do we know that we can do all these things? Should we read what others might think we can do?" By bringing the class back to the original question as a framework for their thinking, the teacher is teaching a lesson in critical thinking. The children will thus be aware that the evaluation of materials read, heard, and observed must be in terms of the problem.

Through such a recorded treatment of the class conversation and discussion, a fundamental ability in critical reading and thinking can be developed functionally. Here children learn the necessity for developing ability to differentiate between statements which are only generally related to the topic and those which actually help to solve the problem or answer the question.

Further development of the general problem topic of the garden might lead to such questions as: "Do we need a rake?" "Where can we get a watering can?" Such questions will lead to chances to differentiate between personal observations and generalizations incorrectly drawn from personal experiences, and thus, to differences between statements of fact and opinion.

As this type of pursuit of a problem continues, many other opportunities will arise for developing ability for critical reading. Various sources of information will need to be consulted. Ideas from books, interviews, pictures, radio and television programs, field trips, and other sources may be weighed and considered. The teacher can do much to set precedents for reading to solve problems as these sources are consulted.

Such techniques as those suggested here can set the stage for, and further the development of, the necessary maturity for more specifically defined critical reading and thinking. These things possibly relate to only a few of the components of what is called critical reading and thinking ability, but they are first steps in the sequential development of this ability. It must be remembered that any advance in reading ability is built upon steps that a child has already taken. Without these steps, we are in effect, trying to build a building without a foundation.

BIBLIOGRAPHY

HOWARD R. ANDERSON (ed.). *Teaching Critical Thinking in the Social Studies.* Washington, D.C.: The National Council for the Social Studies, 1942.

ROMA GANS, *A Study of Critical Reading Comprehension in the Interme-diate Grades.* (Contributions to Education, No. 811.) New York: Bureau of Publications, Teachers College, Columbia University, 1940.

EDWARD M. GLASER, *An Experiment in the Development of Critical Think-ing.* (Contributions to Education, No. 843.) New York: Bureau of Pub-lications, Teachers College, Columbia University, 1941.

WILLIAM S. GRAY, "Growth in Understanding Reading and its Develop-ment Among Youth," *Supplementary Educational Monographs* (Pro-ceedings of the Annual Conference on Reading, University of Chicago, 1950), Vol. 12, No. 72, Oct. 1950.

——, "The Nature and Types of Reading," *The Teaching of Reading: A Second Report.* (Thirty-Sixth Yearbook, The National Society for the Study of Education, 1937), Chapter II.

ALBERT J. HARRIS, *How to Increase Reading Ability.* New York: Long-mans, Green and Company, 1950.

ERNEST HORN, *Methods of Instruction in the Social Studies.* (Part XV, "Re-port of the Commission on the Social Studies," American Historical Association.) New York: Charles Scribners Sons, 1937.

Reading. ("Iowa Elementary Teachers Handbook," Volume II.) Des Moines, Iowa: Department of Public Instruction, 1943.

I. A. RICHARDS, *Interpretation in Teaching.* New York: Harcourt, Brace and Company, 1938.

HILDA TABA, "Problems in Developing Critical Thinking," *Progressive Education,* Vol. 28, Nov. 1950.

A. E. TRAXLER, "Problems of Group Remedial Reading in the Secondary School," *High Points,* Vol. XX, pp. 5–18, 1938.

25. Readiness for Critical Reading

Marjorie Seddon Johnson

Mere pronouncing of words from the printed page does not constitute reading. Dr. Gray (2, p. 10) has said: "The concept of reading has ex-panded during recent decades from a simple activity of one dimension to a complex activity of four dimensions—perception, understanding, reac-tion, integration." Before the reading act is complete the words and phrases must be taken in by the visual apparatus, be understood and

"Readiness for Critical Reading," by Marjorie Seddon Johnson. Reprinted from the February 1953 issue of *Education.* Copyright 1953 by the Bobbs-Merrill Company, Inc., Indianapolis, Indiana.

evaluated, and finally be used in conjunction with the past experiences to improve thinking and behavior.

SETTING THE STAGE

If the pupils in our schools are to develop reading ability of a four dimensional type, the instructional program, from the readiness stage on, must be pointed in this direction. From their first contacts with children, teachers must be thinking of not only readiness for any reading, but also readiness for critical or evaluative reading which leads to improved action on the part of the reader. Nila Banton Smith (3, pp. 556–51) discussed certain changes in our instructional program which will be necessary. The same wide experience, carefully linked with language; the use of field trips and visual aids, planned to give meaning to the language children meet; the attention of contextual setting, the determinate of meaning—all these must be included in the systematic readiness program designed to lead to achievement in reading as it is now seen.

A WAY OF LIFE

Many problems confront the teacher who attempts to help his pupils develop into thinking individuals, evaluating as they read, using what they read. He may find that they do not do this kind of critical reading and thinking without special suggestion from him. He may find that they do not know how to organize details or that the relationship among them can be seen. The pupils may never have been stimulated to consider critically the things which they hear and read in their every day experiences. Perhaps, in some ways, schools have created such problems in this area. When attempts have been made to develop critical reading and thinking abilities, they have frequently been concentrated in certain lessons and usually placed in the higher grades. The program seems to have been built on this erroneous concept: "Having learned to think, the pupils can now learn to think critically. Having learned to read, the pupils can now learn to read critically." No systematic program, starting when and before reading achievement started, has led to the aim of a thinking reader. "Critical thinking is not a simple gadget that can be taught and acquired on the spot in one lesson, unit, or even in one single subject. It is something like a way of life . . . It is necessary to see critical thinking as a developmental process, also, in which there is a psychological learning sequence that students need to follow." (4, p. 614).

In the well planned program this developmental process is recognized and receives attention in schools from the pupil's earliest experiences.

Readiness for critical reading should and can be developed even before actual reading is being done. The proper classroom setting for the development of this readiness is one in which children are facing problems which are important to them. Critical thinking occurs in problem solving situations. When a child has a question which he wants answered, he will seek various sources of information and attempt to arrive at an answer which satisfies him. Here is the opportunity for him to learn to evaluate sources of information, apply his thinking powers to deciding on the best solution to his problem. The first step, therefore, in teaching which develops readiness for critical thinking, is the growth of an atmosphere in which problems arise and their solution is vital.

In the Classroom

How can the teacher so guide his students as to make critical thinking and reading a part of their normal, everyday performance? Suppose that in a first grade classroom, in the daily exchange of ideas and experiences among the pupils, this question arises out of the discussion: "What can we do now to get ready for a garden when it gets warm?"

A PROBLEM ARISES

Certainly the first thing that would happen would be the giving of suggestions by various members of the class. If the teacher keeps a record with the children of these suggestions, he has his first opportunity of fostering some critical thinking. As comments, suggestions, and questions come from the group, the teacher may put these contributions on the board. Assume for the moment that this is done with a minimum of teacher direction. He allows a free flow of ideas from the children and accepts whatever they have to offer. He feels that at this stage his contributions should be to inject some rather nondirective questions which may keep the group thinking going, but in its own way—not his way. For example, if the first class were all relative to getting seeds and plants, the teacher would certainly realize that there were other problems to be solved before the group would be ready for seeds and plants. However, he would rather have them discover this than direct their thinking by asking, "Where are we going to have the garden?" "How will we get the ground ready?" "Should we have a flower garden or a vegetable garden?"

These problems will arise as the children go over their ideas and organize them. How much better to have the children see them, recognize their own problems, than to have the teacher point them out! The first step in doing real critical thinking is the recognition or identification of a problem.

Hence, the teacher proceeds as a member of the group, serving as re-corder at the same time that he participates as one contributor among many. Soon the board is filled with ideas given by various members of the group. Before the problem arose, this exchange of conversation had taken place in the circle:

"My mother got these seeds yesterday. She said I could have them."

"Let's plant them."

"We can't do that. It's too cold."

"I put some in a pot at home. Dad said our cellar was a good place to grow seeds."

"Why can't we plant Bill's seeds in our room?"

"Let's save them for a garden when it gets warm."

"Could we have a garden?"

"My brother had one last year in third grade."

"Would we have to wait 'till it's hot? Let's start now."

"It's too cold. Nothing will grow."

"We could do some things to get ready."

"What can we do now to get ready for a garden when it gets warm?"

TENTATIVE SOLUTIONS

Unfortunately, the teacher had no way of knowing that Bill's packet of seeds was going to develop into a real class project. Consequently, he had kept no record of the ideas contributed before the problem arose. Once the genuine interest of the group had been revealed, he started to keep account of all the comments which were contributed. The question was first placed on the board. Then each point was added as it came from a member of the group.

"We have my seeds to start with."

"I could plant them in my cellar with mine."

"Why does your father say that's such a good place for seeds?"

"Don't seeds need sun to grow?"

"I have some seeds I can bring, too."

"My mother and I saved seeds last year. We had great big flowers. She'll give us some."

"Can we put these plants in the garden?"

"They're inside plants."

"No, they're not. That's where I got them for the room, out of our garden."

"I have a shovel we could use."

"Can I dig?"

"It's too hard out there."

"Can we really make a garden in the yard?"

"I told you my brother and some kids had one last year."

And so on with spontaneous exchange of questions, answers, guesses, and observations from various members of the group.

APPROACHES TO ORGANIZATION

Two very different approaches could be used from this point on. The fastest one would no doubt be for the teacher to say, "We've been talking about so many things! We've heard about seeds that people can bring. We've heard about plants we could use. We know some tools we can use. We want to find out if we can have a garden and where we can have it. I'll make a list of the people who can bring things. Another list can have the questions we want to answer. When I get those ready, we'll see what we can do next." .

Everything is all nicely organized. Who profited from the process of the organization? The teacher had some fine practice in doing something he could already do. The children? It was not their organization; they had nothing to do with it. They learned little or nothing from it. In other words, fine opportunities to develop critical thinking ability had been missed.

Instead of imposing the organization of the material and the next steps, the teacher, alert to his responsibilities and opportunities to develop evaluative abilities, will guide the pupils in seeing the need for and accomplishing this task. "We've said all these things that are on the board. What was the question we had in the beginning?" He may have to read for the group. Some contributions may be read by members of the class. In either case, the children will be having a real experience in the fact that word symbols merely represent their ideas, record their spoken contributions.

By bringing the group back to the original question as a framework for their thinking the teacher is, by example, teaching a lesson in critical thinking. The problem must be kept in mind. All the evaluation of materials read, heard, observed must be in terms of the problem. Having gotten the attention of the group centered on the original question, the teacher might ask, "What help did we get on our problem?"

"Some of the children can bring things we'll need."

EVALUATING RELEVANCY

Here is the opportunity to do some work on evaluating the relevancy of statements. "What things can we bring to help with the garden? Let's find the statements that say people can bring things." From all the contributions recorded, the group picks out the ones which tell of things that can be brought to school to help with the garden. As these are put together, one child realizes that all the things were either seeds, plants, or tools. The teacher helps them to arrange these things in an elementary outline, using correct format so that they again have a chance to learn by participation and example. As truly relevant statements are selected from those on the board, they can be incorporated in the outline. Sooner or later some things related to the general topic, but not actually helpful in the solution of the problem will be picked. Perhaps Jim's statement that he had a little spade he could bring to school brought forth a comment from Fred that they had a big spade at home. Doris added that they had gotten a new rake last summer. These may be picked out as being related to the topic because they discuss tools. Here the direction must again be to the question, "What things can we bring to help with the garden?" Merely asking, "Did Fred say he could bring the spade?" will turn thinking in the direction of deciding the relevancy to the question. It demands some critical reading of his contribution. Does "We have a big spade at home" mean that he can bring a big spade to school? Does it belong with statements which answer the question?

Through such treatment of the recorded class conversation, a fundamental ability in critical reading and thinking can be developed functionally. Here children can see the necessity to and develop ability to differentiate between statements which are, in general, related to the topic and those which actually help to solve the problem or answer the question. This was the type discrimination that Roma Gans (1) found intermediate grade children unable to make with any degree of accuracy. Could it be because teachers have not directed activities toward the development of such abilities?

Varied Frameworks for Classifying

In addition to the classification of the type above, relationships according to topics, many other classifications might arise out of the organization of the materials. Perhaps in addition to the statements that certain tools could be brought to school, there might be some questions about tools. "Do we need a rake?" "Where can we get a watering can?" "How much would a little trowel cost?" These, like the statement about Fred's spade, might be selected as relevant to the question because they ask about tools. Here is an opportunity to build the ability to classify according to the purpose for which the contribution was made. Was it to tell about something that could be brought to school? Was it to get some information? Was it to tell about a personal experience or possession? The organization may be one, then, which takes into account the purpose or intent of the statement as well as one which shows relationships by topics.

In going over the materials there will be chances to differentiate between personal observations and generalizations incorrectly drawn from personal experiences. The personal observations cannot be disputed. The generalizations may be opinions taking the form of statements which purport to be facts and, therefore, need investigation. For instance, Joan had mentioned that she could bring sweet pea seeds from home. Her offering these seeds for the garden provided various comments from other members of the group. Bob said, "Sweet peas don't grow here." Edna added, "That's right. I planted some last year and they didn't grow." The rest of the pupils need to see the differences between these statements. Edna's statement that she planted some that didn't grow cannot be disputed. Bob's, however, may or may not be so.

Thus, the organization and consideration of the statements should help to make pupils aware of the differences between statements of "fact" and opinion. It should help them to see that we need more evidence than Edna's before we can accept or reject Bob's statement. It is his opinion. On what is it based? What sources will we have to use to check up on his statement? Is Arthur's suggestion that he'll ask the gardener on Mr. Flair's place a good one? Why might he be a better person to ask than Jane's sister? The older sister is Jane's living encyclopedia, but she knows nothing about gardening. How does Bob's statement about sweet peas compare with your own experiences in the past? Have you ever had sweet peas in your garden?

EVALUATING REFERENCES

As the pursuit of the class problem continues, many other opportunities will arise for developing readiness for critical reading. Various sources of information will be consulted. Ideas from these books, interviews, pictures, "green thumb" programs on the radio, field trips, etc., will need to be weighed and considered. The teacher can do much to set precedents for reading to solve problems as these sources are consulted. Even before the pupils can read for themselves, he can use references with them. Seed catalogues, price lists from a garden supply house, encyclopedias, the dictionary, science books, children's periodicals, the daily newspaper— all these, and many others should be available and their use made clear to the pupils. Here then, are further opportunities for development of the attitude of critical thinking and reading.

In Summary

A certain amount of maturity is necessary for critical thinking. Such techniques as those suggested here can set the stage for, and further the development of, that necessary maturity. Children, in solving their problems, will come to see the necessity for carrying on thoughtful investigation of varied sources of ideas and information. Finally these pupils, be-

cause they *use* the ideas they get from their language activities, will come
to recognize the worth of their study.

What is involved in critical reading? How much ability in this area can
be built in the early stages of school experience? The ideas presented in
this article have touched on only a few of the components of what we call
critical reading ability. Some suggestions have been made about ways
these basic abilities can be developed. Within a problem solving situation,
identification of problems, organization of materials, evaluation of ideas
and sources of information can develop. These are first steps in the sequence of development in critical reading. As pupils come, through experience and meaningful practice, to do these things naturally and without urging, the more complex tasks involved in critical reading will be
within their grasp. The alert teacher will continue to build readiness for,
and provide guidance in, accomplishing these tasks. Critical reading
ability will be taught functionally, in real life situations, not in isolated
practice lessons.

BIBLIOGRAPHY

1. ROMA GANS, *A Study of Critical Reading Comprehension in the Intermediate Grades.* Teachers College, Columbia University, Contributions
   to Education, No. 811. New York: Bureau of Publications, Teachers
   College, Columbia University, 1940.
2. WILLIAM S. GRAY, "Growth in Understanding of Reading and its Development Among Youth." *Supplementary Educational Monographs*
   (Proceedings of the Annual Conference on Reading, University of Chicago, 1950), Vol. 12, No. 72 (October 1950).
3. NILA B. SMITH, "How Will Semantic Emphasis Affect Reading Instruction?" *Education*, 69 (May 1949), 556–61.
4. HILDA TABA, "Problems in Developing Critical Thinking," *Progressive
   Education*, 28 (November 1950), 45–8.

26. Teaching Critical Reading through Logic

Willavene Wolf

"There is an eerie possibility that a long-dead Russian astronaut is today
hurtling silently through space at thousands of miles an hour—the victim

Acknowledgment is given to Mary Hevener, research assistant, for her many helpful suggestions in the writing of this article.

of a Soviet space shot that went wrong. His body perfectly preserved by intense cold, he may be a lonely wanderer in space for centuries to come." [1]

These statements about an amateur space-tracking station in Italy appear in the *Reader's Digest*. The implication of the article was that the Russians have spent freely of human life to achieve their space successes. Although this implication may or may not be true, it would be enlightening to know how many persons reading this article even stopped to consider the accuracy of the statements made.

THE NEED FOR TEACHING CRITICAL READING

A prevalent belief in our nation today is that the young child believes almost everything he reads, that the high school student displays more judgment, while the adult can adequately *judge the accuracy, validity and worth of what is read based upon sound criteria*, i.e., he can read critically. Research has shown that this is not an accurate account of what happens. When Rogers studied the reactions of high school students in an undirected reading situation as compared to a directed situation requiring critical reading, she concluded that students focused on remembering facts to the exclusion of evaluative thinking about what they had read. Rogers found that subjects attempted evaluations of the selection only when questions demanded that response.[2]

In 1956, Gray and Rogers surveyed the reading habits of a number of adults in various occupations and reported that these adults did not recognize implied meanings or draw the conclusions which the materials justified. According to them, many adults read on a mechanical level and either did not react to the printed ideas or did so at an unreflective level or in terms of their prejudices. An even more startling finding was that the high school graduates interviewed in the study did not display any more ability in interpreting meaning and reacting with sound judgment to the ideas read than did elementary school graduates.[3] The findings of these studies indicate that critical reading does not develop naturally as a concomitant of age.

If teachers are to assist students in critically evaluating articles similar to the one from the *Reader's Digest* they should acquire a knowledge of the skills of critical reading and develop some techniques for teaching

[1] J. D. Ratcliff, "Italy's Amazing Amateur Space Watchers," *Reader's Digest*, LXXXVI (April, 1965), p. 110.

[2] Bernice Rogers, "Directed and Undirected Critical Reading Responses of High School Students," (Unpublished Doctoral Dissertation, Department of Education, University of Chicago, 1960), p. 209.

[3] William S. Gray and Bernice Rogers, *Maturity in Reading* (Chicago: The University of Chicago Press, 1956), p. 273.

them. Skills in logic are needed to evaluate informative, argumentative, and persuasive-type materials. An individual who has studied logic would probably not read a biased article without questioning to some degree what he has read. Thoughts which might occur to him in such an instance might be as follows:

This author is obviously expecting me to accept an idea which is implied but not actually stated.

The conclusion to this paragraph does not follow from the premises upon which it is based.

The ideas are an incoherent jumble. One thought does not necessarily follow from the others.

The author is implying that something is true of *all* of a group when he actually means some.

These thoughts show that this reader has some knowledge of the nature of deductive logic or the structure of valid reasoning. Deductive logic can be defined as reasoning from a known principle to an unknown, or from a premise to a conclusion. The reasoning is valid if the conclusion necessarily follows from the premises. The validity of a deduction is established by checking the *form* of the argument.

Another type of logical thinking about the same passage is illustrated by these questions:

1. Can this generalization be tested, or is it an opinion or emotive type of statement which could never be empirically verified?

2. How was this generalization formed? Were there enough cases to justify the conclusion? Was there a representative dispersion of cases?

3. What fallacious reasoning, if any, does the author employ?

In these cases the reader is checking the reliability of the passage in an attempt to determine the probability that the information is accurate.

Establishing the Validity of Deductive Logic

Not all thinking is reasoning; not all writing contains reasoning. It is only in those instances where reasoning is present that an application of logic is fruitful.

When the type of reasoning or argumentation that is employed in printed material involves going from a supposed truth (the reason) to obtain another truth (the conclusion) by thinking alone, an inference has been made. In order to justify the inference, there must be some connection between the reasons and the conclusion. An inference that purports to be conclusive in and of itself without appeal to any information except that given in the reasons is said to be deductive. Since there are many cases of this in print, it becomes necessary for the critical reader to develop a knowledge of deductive logic so that he can adequately evaluate such reasoning.

In order to evaluate deductive logic, it is necessary for the reader to (1) recognize when such reasoning has occurred in printed material and (2) determine when the reasoning is valid.

HOW TO RECOGNIZE WHEN AN AUTHOR IS EMPLOYING DEDUCTIVE REASONING

Deductive reasoning is found most frequently in materials setting forth a particular point of view, such as when an individual is testing the soundness of his own conviction or attempting to change the reader's opinions. Common examples are editorials, political speeches, and similar passages. Although deductive argumentation may also occur in news reports and other articles where straight informative and factual writing is required, in most instances it is inappropriate. Clues that logical reasoning has occurred may be found in such words or phrases as *therefore, it then follows,* and *from this we know.* Also, when deductive reason has been applied, the conclusion must have been based on two previous statements. These are signals to the reader to stop and determine whether the reasoning is valid.

DETERMINING WHEN DEDUCTIVE REASONING IS VALID

A simple valid argument which could have been extracted from a written passage is as follows: All cities in South Viet Nam are under Communist control. Saigon is a city in South Viet Nam. Therefore, Saigon is under Communist control. In order to check the validity of this argument, the reader must assume that the premises are true. He then proceeds to determine if the conclusion follows necessarily from the premises, that is, if no other conclusion is possible on the basis of the given premises. In the example given, the conclusion does follow necessarily from the premises and therefore is valid even though the first major premise is not true.

There are several rules governing the form of a valid argument. One way of checking validity of an argument without learning the rules as such, is the use of circles. Various games can be created by the teacher using these circles to make the process interesting. For a complete explanation of the use of circles, the reader is referred to Irving Adler's *Logic for Beginners* (1) and Huppe and Kaminsky's *Logic and Language* (5).

It may be necessary for children to practice with many examples of simple arguments before they can evaluate the ones found in printed material. After the students understand the basic form of deductive reasoning and can check the validity of the conclusion, they can move on to finding a conclusion from two premises. For example: All fifth graders study geography. John is a fifth grader. Therefore, (John studies geography). A harder one: Some people are dishonest. Dishonest people will cheat whenever they get the chance. Therefore, (Some people will cheat whenever they get the chance).

There are a few steps which teachers may use to assist students in testing the validity of arguments found in printed materials. First, since the premises of the argument are often imbedded in voluminous amounts of material, the student may be asked to strip the argument of any excess words or sentences and pull out the basic premises.

Second, the student must be sure that he has access to all the premises. This involves the recognition of assumed premises. Although some premises are not explicitly stated in the reading material, they must be identified in order that the argument may be properly evaluated. The statement "Khrushchev is a Communist; therefore, he is dangerous" has an assumed but unstated premise that anyone who is a Communist is dangerous. Similarly, the statement "She is a teacher so you know she must be intelligent" contains the assumption that all teachers are intelligent. Although some assumptions may be perfectly legitimate premises, the student must understand that such premises are as important to the argument as those which are explicitly stated. The danger lies in the fact that many arguments may be based on *false* assumptions, but since they are not stated, the argument appears more credible.

Another step for students is to determine if an author is asserting that something is always the case, sometimes the case, or never the case or whether in a given situation the author is referring to all of a group, some of a group or none of a group. For example, it may be argued that socialists are dangerous people, that Professor X is a socialist and is, therefore, dangerous. The argument is valid. However, the first premise must mean *all* socialists are dangerous. If there is a case of one socialist who is not dangerous, then the premise from which we argue would have to be "*Some* socialists are dangerous," and the conclusion about Professor X then becomes invalid. Many arguments may prove to be indefensible if the statement is interpreted to mean all of a given class. When students are attempting the logical analysis of a passage, they should be cautioned to transform sentences so that they begin with *all, some* or *no*. Unfortunately, most arguments found in the typical passage are not in this form.

After a student has stripped the argument to its basic framework, identified all of the premises, both stated and assumed, and transformed the premises, he is then in a better position to determine if the conclusion logically follows from the premises.

Checking the Reliability of a Passage

It is possible for an argument to be valid and still not true. For example, the following argument is valid. All poisonous things are bitter. Potassium cyanide is not bitter. Therefore, potassium cyanide is not poison. The argument is valid, but anyone acting on the truth of the conclusion is likely to regret it. Reliability deals with establishing the truth or trustworthiness of the premises.

Whereas the validity of an argument involves the relationship between parts of the argument and can be established by thought alone, reliability deals with the truth of the premises and must be established empirically. Thus, reliability applies to the truth of the premises and conclusion of a deductive argument or to an inductive conclusion.

Reliable statements are verifiable. The first question that a student must ask, therefore, when checking the reliability of a statement is whether it can be tested. For example, the statement "Football is the best game there is" is not testable because it is a value judgment or an opinion. No amount of research can establish the truth or falsity of the statement. However, a statement such as "Americans have the lowest birth rate in the world" is testable. It is only when statements are capable of being verified that the reader can apply skills in this type of logic.

A student attempting a logical analysis must also recognize when a sentence is a specific statement about one object or event and when it is a generalization. The trustworthiness of a specific statement such as "John is six feet tall." is easy to establish. Verifying a generalization, however, presents more difficulties.

It is quite impossible, of course, to test every generalization in print. A few guidelines, however, will help students in judging the probability of something's being true. These guides may be phrased as questions which should be asked of every statement which one may wish to verify.

WHAT IS THE SOURCE OF THE PASSAGE?

(1) Who has control over the source? and (2) What is his connection with the subject matter under consideration?

Some publications have established reputations for honest, unbiased reporting. Others are known for exaggerating the facts. For example, if the item under suspicion is an article published in the *Proletarian News*, its slant can be established easily since the following information is given on the masthead:

PROLETARIAN NEWS
A Journal for the Working Class
Devoted to the Education of Workers and Their
Struggle for Power
Published by the Proletarian Party of America

Similarly, everyone is forewarned of bias by signed advertisements. Unfortunately, most propaganda is not distributed in this form but instead masquerades. Students should be informed of appropriate sources and together establish criteria for judging them. Establishment of some knowledge about sources and their importance is a crucial step in critical reading.

WHAT ARE THE QUALIFICATIONS OF THE AUTHOR?

A person who is qualified to give testimony should display special competence on the topic being discussed, should be a fairly well-established authority in his field, and should limit his writing to the topic for which he is qualified. Every person with a military title is not an expert on nuclear weapons. Casual travelers in Europe are probably not authorities on complex European problems. If the author is a well established authority on the subject being discussed, students can be more certain about the reliability of the article.

IS THE MATERIAL A PRIMARY OR SECONDARY REPORT?

In order to determine the reliability of a passage, students should learn to distinguish between primary and secondary reports. Statements found in primary reports, i.e., reports of direct observations or experience, personal testimony, records, etc., are often more reliable than inferences made from them or reports based on them. Typical secondary reports are found in newspapers, textbooks, and objective analyses of various kinds.

CAN THE STATEMENTS BE CONFIRMED THROUGH OTHER SOURCES?

A statement supported by several sources tends to be more reliable. The critical reader often looks in several types of material for corroboration of statements which he feels may be of questionable reliability. Social Studies materials are excellent to use in developing lessons on corroborating information. For example, children might read in *About Our Flag* how Betsy Ross made the first American flag in one day. Further reading in other sources may lend less credence to this statement. Since there is no general agreement that Betsy Ross did indeed make the first American flag. This will show children how important it is to check several sources before accepting a statement as true.

ARE THERE ANY LOGICAL FALLACIES IN THE STATEMENTS THEMSELVES?

When checking the reliability of a statement, the reader must be aware of the many fallacies which may appear in the formulation of generalizations and inductive conclusions. The term fallacy is used to refer to the use of faulty reasoning in an argument. Common fallacies include hasty generalizations, false analogies, assuming the cause "post hoc, *ergo propter hoc*," which means assuming one event causes another because it happens before it. Attributing a stomach ache to the last meal eaten infers a causal relationship which may or may not exist. Or consider the student who walks under a ladder, then fails an exam, and assumes that walking under the ladder was the cause of the failure. "Post hoc" reasoning is commonly found in conversation and in printed material.

Another example of the use of false premises is the faulty analogy, which occurs as a result of assuming that because two things may resemble each other in one respect they will resemble each other in some other respect. For example, some people argue: "Conditions today are like conditions prior to World War II. Therefore, since war followed then, war will follow now." Analogies of this kind can be satisfactory only if they compare two elements that have few differences. When differences are ignored and analogies are based on few similarities, the fallacy of imperfect analogy is committed.

Teaching a class to recognize the various fallacies might begin with the presentation of numerous examples of one type of fallacy. Students may then try to identify the mistake which is common to all examples mentioned. For example, the teacher might present several cases such as: (1) Our team lost the game because Bob wasn't there. (2) John got a bad grade in arithmetic because the teachers didn't like him. (3) Children don't get enough exercise because they are always watching television. If students have difficulty identifying the mistakes in reasoning here, the following questions may stimulate thought and discussion. Do you think this is really the cause? Is it the only possible cause? What other causes could there have been to account for each event? Students may be cautioned that the word *because* is another signal that an exercise in logic is about to take place. It is a signal to stop and consider whether the cause given is the real cause, or whether there is a probability of a causal relationship existing at all. As fallacies of this kind are quite prevalent in all types of writing, students can compile lists of fallacies met in their daily reading.

The reader may check the bibliography for good references which contain complete explanations and examples of logical fallacies. These are good sources to use in teaching logic. Older students may enjoy reading Max Shulman's *Love is a Fallacy*,[4] in which various fallacies are presented in an entertaining manner.

HOW DOES THE AUTHOR USE WORDS TO ACCOMPLISH HIS PURPOSE?

The critical readers will carefully examine the way in which an author may have chosen words to accomplish his purpose.

Even writers of highly-regarded publications will use words occasionally that color the facts and influence the reader. Some writers purposely strive to confound an issue with the use of appealing and emotion-laden language. They throw their readers off guard by shifting the focus of discussion from ideas to an emphasis on colorful or disturbing words.

Several techniques designed to influence thought and action by appealing to emotions or prejudices have been reported by the Institute of Propaganda Analysis and have since been popularized as "propaganda techniques." These techniques such as "bad names," "glad names," "testimonials," and others have become well-known.

Many people have been stirred to action through such words as Communist, racist, and un-American. The approach is to arouse an unfavorable reaction to a person by associating him with an unpopular group. This device appeals to the biases and prejudices of the reader by using words that can evoke a reaction that the writer desires. For various reasons, insurance agents sell life insurance instead of death insurance, depressions have become recessions, slow learners become exceptional children and the poor are disadvantaged. Words may also be ambiguous if a faulty grammatical construction is used and this may lead to misinterpretations by the reader. For example, the advertisement of a certain roadhouse which reads "Clean and Decent Dancing Every Night Except Sunday" makes you wonder what kind of dancing they have on Sunday.

Many errors in reasoning result from an inattention to language, i.e., they result from misused words and ambiguous statements. Words employed by propagandists in all occupations are means of persuasion and suggestion and modify and direct man's attitudes and decisions through their emotional appeal, often to his own detriment. The use and misuse of words is often a hindrance to critical reading. A first step in avoiding various mistakes in reasoning and in protecting students against some of the tricks of unscrupulous propagandists is, therefore, to teach them to pay special attention to words and their meanings. The student must learn to separate words which have the power to produce feelings from words which merely serve to identify referents. He must learn that he is subject

---

[4] Max Shulman, "Love is a Fallacy," in *Teen-age Treasury of Good Humor*. New York: Funk and Wagnalls Co., Inc., 1960.

to being influenced through the printed page and must determine how various authors are attempting to influence him.

When submitting an idea, a statement, or an entire passage to logical analysis, word meanings must be made explicit. Whereas emotion, attitude, and values are important in literature, they should not be a part of factual reporting. Therefore, when logically analyzing a passage, students can be asked to identify all words which carry emotionally-laden connotations and then neutralize the passage to obtain the exact meaning of the ideas involved.

APPLICATION OF CRITERIA FOR CHECKING RELIABILITY

The article from the *Reader's Digest* on Russians lost in space, mentioned at the beginning of this article, should be read with extreme caution when these criteria for determining reliability are applied. It is a secondary report by an unknown author of some experiences of two space amateurs and it appears in a magazine covering miscellaneous subjects and written for the public in general. It is likely that (1) some misinterpretations may have been made by the author of the experiences of these men, (2) that the author is not an authority in the area since this fact was omitted, (3) that it was made dramatic in order to hold the attention of the readers, and (4) that it would not be corroborated by a more scientific journal such as *Scientific American.*

The class members who investigate the source of the article, the authority of the writer and who check the statements with other references are in a better position to determine if the statements are dependable and trustworthy, that is, reliable.

SUMMARY

The logical dimension of critical reading has often been neglected in our schools. A better understanding of two aspects of logic, namely, validity and reliability, is a prerequisite to growth in critical reading. In analyzing the validity of a given passage, it is necessary to determine if the argument is internally consistent, i.e., if the conclusion follows necessarily from the premises. To accomplish this task, students must learn to strip the argument of any excess words, to make sure they have access to all the premises, and to determine the implied universality of the author's statements. However, it is not enough to determine if an argument is internally consistent or valid. The student must also establish whether the statements have any reliability i.e. whether they are trustworthy. Criteria for checking the reliability of a passage should include adequacy of the source, authority of the writer and corroboration of the statements. The passage should be neutralized by checking all biased words and obtaining the exact meaning of the statements. The truth of the premises or any inductive conclusions may be checked by looking for fallacies which may be present. When questions on logic pertaining to the reliability and validity of reading material are asked by students in schools throughout the country, teachers can be more confident of developing a nation of critical readers.

ANNOTATED BIBLIOGRAPHY

IRVING ADLER, *Logic for Beginners.* New York: John Day Company, 1964, pp. 158.
This book is appropriate for students in the upper elementary and junior high school grades. It contains several games that can be used in teaching the basic elements of logic.

MAX BLACK, *Critical Thinking.* Englewood Cliffs, New Jersey: Prentice-Hall, Inc., 1952.
This is a good book for those who would like a deeper understanding of logic. The first part deals with validity or deductive logic and gives an explanation of syllogisms and the components of valid argument. Each chapter is followed by a comprehension test.

W. WARD FEARNSIDE and WILLIAM B. HOLTHER, *Fallacy: The Counterfeit of Argument.* Englewood Cliffs, New Jersey: Prentice-Hall, Inc., 1959, p. 218.
This book examines all the common fallacies, giving explanations and examples of each. Helpful exercises, some of which can be used in high school, are given on pages 173–215.

HAROLD F. GRAVES and BERNARD S. OLDSEY, *From Fact to Judgment.* New York: The Macmillan Company, 1963, p. 422.
This book contains information on the selection of sources, the judgment of the connotation and denotation of words, and the development of some criteria for evaluating books and other materials.

BERNARD F. HUPPÉ and JACK KAMINSKY, *Logic and Language.* New York: Alfred A. Knopf, 1957, p. 216.
This book is excellent. It contains a very readable, clear explanation of the relationship of logic to language. Chapters 4, 5, and 6 deal specifically with validity and reliability and include many examples and questions to guide the reader.

WALTER LOBAN, MARGARET RYAN, and JAMES R. SQUIRE, *Teaching Language and Literature.* New York: Harcourt, Brace and World, Inc., 1961.
Chapter Two on "Logical Thinking" stresses the importance of objective reasoning in the reading process. The authors suggest a number of learning experiences to illustrate the principles discussed in the chapter.

Analyzing propaganda techniques, improving deductive and inductive reasoning, recognizing fallacious reasoning and discovering how bias influences interpretation are only a few of the skills which are represented in the suggested learning experiences.

GEORGE D. SPACHE and PAUL C. BERG, *The Art of Efficient Reading*. New York: The Macmillan Company, 1955.

Chapters V and VI of this book deal directly with the problems of critical reading. In these chapters the identification and evaluation of printed ideas are discussed. A number of practice exercises are also given to help the student gain skill in identifying and evaluating ideas in a variety of printed passages.

W. N. WERKMEISTER, *An Introduction to Critical Thinking*. New York: American Book-Stratford Press, Inc., 1957, pp. 663.

Part I deals with the use of language, errors in reasoning, and propaganda. Each chapter contains suggested activities for students and lists many sample passages which may be used as examples or exercises.

27. Reading and Semantics

William Eller

GENERAL NEED FOR SEMANTIC UNDERSTANDING
IN READING COMPREHENSION

The objectives of the long-range reading program in grades one to sixteen can be rather crudely summarized into the following three goals:

1. The teaching of the mechanics of reading—word recognition, word attack, study skills, efficient eye-movements, etc.

2. The development of maximum comprehension in terms of each student's ability and experience, and including critical analysis of reading matter.

3. The development of genuine interest in reading for a variety of purposes.

During the year 1955, most of the words written and spoken on the general subject of reading instruction were concerned with the first of these three goals. Consideration of the mechanics of reading probably dom-

"Reading and Semantics," by William Eller, is reprinted by permission from *Exploring the Goals of the College Reading Program*. Oscar Causey (ed.). *Fifth Yearbook Southwest Reading Conference*. Fort Worth, Tex.: Texas Christian University Press, 1955, pp. 18–22.

inates the literature even in a normal year, but in 1955, Rudolph Flesch's book *Why Johnny Can't Read* resulted in unusual emphasis on mechanics and corresponding neglect of the aspects of comprehension and interest. In spite of this emphasis in the popular and professional literature, reading teachers know that developing comprehension is at least as important as teaching mechanics, and anyone who has given even cursory attention to the nature of the reading process realizes that without "comprehension" —however it may be defined—no reading has really occurred.

Since reading comprehension is not an all-or-none proposition, the educational system must strive to develop comprehension to the highest possible degree for each student. The development of the finer components of reading comprehension very definitely requires a command of the fundamentals of semantics, although the word "semantics" may not be used by either the teacher or the students.

Because semanticists have applied their art and/or science to a great variety of subjects, it may be desirable to establish a definition of semantics before further consideration of the relationship with reading. S. I. Hayakawa is one of the pioneer semanticists in the United States, so one of his definitions should be useful. In *Etc., A Review of General Semantics* he has stated: "By semantics, we mean the interpretive habits that people have within them by means of which they apprehend and react to the signs and symbols of the world around them." Over-simplifying slightly, we might say that semantics is the study of the interactions between language and personality. To the teacher of reading comprehension, semantics seems to be some mixture of communications and the psychology of adjustment.

The previously mentioned book *Why Johnny Can't Read* illustrates, in both specific and general ways, the importance of semantic skill to reading comprehension. Specifically, when Dr. Flesch refers to "phonics" in primary reading instruction, he intends a very limited, archaic concept of phonics; furthermore, only those methodologists who employ out-of-date phonics systems similar to his own are really teaching phonics, according to Flesch. Thus, elementary teachers who perceive the twentieth-century meaning of the word "phonics" are bitterly resentful of Flesch's assertion that today's schools are not teaching any phonics. A semantic impasse has resulted from the author's use of a nineteenth-century meaning for a word to which the readers apply a modern interpretation.

Flesch's recent book also requires a *general* awareness of the fundamentals of semantics if it is to be read intelligently, because the author writes in a very unscientific style and uses a number of the techniques of propaganda. Some of these propaganda tools which would be detected by the student of semantics are: (1) misrepresentation of sources by quotation out of context, (2) implication that the author is the only one whose judgment can be trusted, (3) implication that those who are in opposition have dishonorable motives, (4) use of the "straw man" technique—assumptions which are not true—followed by the proposed remedies for these erroneous assumptions, (5) deduction which is not supported by the premises, (6) misinterpretation of research, and (7) insinuation.

The writings and speeches of Senator Joseph R. McCarthy provide similar illustrations of the need for semantic sophistication in reading comprehension, and they have reached a much larger audience. The specific semantic problem is illustrated in McCarthy's case by his distorted use of the term "communist sympathizer" to include nearly all persons who oppose him for any reason. In a more general sense, his book *McCarthyism, the Fight for America* could almost serve as textual material in the teaching of critical reading since it includes samples of all the propaganda techniques mentioned in the preceding paragraph about Dr. Flesch.

Perhaps the most obvious and frequent need for a semantic awareness on the part of the reader is associated with the reading of advertising, especially now that we are living in what has been called the "Era of Public Relations." Professor H. R. Huse of the University of North Carolina has stated this in a left-handed way: "No literature is tested as rigorously as advertising. To be successful, advertising copy must reflect accurately the critical sense or gullibility of those to whom it is addressed. To say that these advertisements display hypocrisy, lying, insincerity, and stupidity is to say only what every one with critical sense or a faint notion of honesty and candor already knows. After a look at the ads in some of the popular women's magazines, one can question seriously whether it is worth while to teach women how to read. The same can be said of some magazines for men. Our schools turn out their products equipped with a deceptive literacy like lambs ready for the slaughter."

Advertising copy-writers are not the only propagandists who are sensitive to the public's general lack of semantic judgment. Consider the following paragraphs by one of this century's masters of persuasion:

One can divide the readers as a whole into three groups: First, those who believe everything they read; secondly, those who no longer believe anything; thirdly, those who critically examine what they have read and judge accordingly.

The first group is numerically by far the greatest. It consists of the great masses of the people and therefore represents the mentally simple part of the nation . . . To it belong all those to whom independent thinking is neither inborn nor instilled by education, and who, partly through inability and partly through incompetence, believe everything that is put before them printed in black on white . . .

The second group is much smaller even in number. It is composed of the greater part of the elements which first belonged to the first group, and who, after long and bitter disappointments, changed over to the contrary and believe no longer in anything at all that comes in the form of print before their eyes.

The third group finally is by far the smallest; it consists of the mentally truly fine heads whom natural gifts and education have taught to think independently, who try to form a judgment of their own about everything, and who submit most thoroughly everything they have read to an examination and further development of their own . . .

No one doubts that the writer of these lines knew the art of propaganda; they are taken from Adolf Hitler's *Mein Kampf*.

Two Major Types of Semantic Problems in Reading Comprehension

Type A. The reader fails to get the author's meaning adequately, even though he glides over the words and may be convinced that he has understood what he has read. This sort of comprehension failure often results from erroneous interpretation of words and phrases. Professors Ernest Horn and Paul W. McKee have investigated this problem quite extensively among elementary school children, and McKee's reading methodology text contains several specific illustrations of pupil failure to accurately understand such phrases as "our great Northwest." For some reason, no one has investigated corresponding meaning difficulties at the college level, so much more study of the problem is needed at the higher educational levels.

Figurative language provides another major source of semantic difficulty in reading comprehension and seems to affect readers of all ages. By the time our students reach college, they should be so familiar with the language that they are no longer confused by similes, although college teachers report that they have some difficulties with metaphors. It would seem as though hyperbole should not mislead adolescents, considering their own liberal use of exaggeration; but euphemisms, or the substitution of inoffensive words for potentially annoying ones, can be deceptive to almost all readers at all levels of intellectual sophistication.

Type B. The reader interprets the context in the manner desired by the author, and thus the reader is deluded to some degree. As indicated in the quotation from Professor Huse, if the reader is equipped with an unguarded literacy, he can misinform himself, and might be better off if he couldn't read at all. In fairness to some authors, it is necessary to acknowledge that they have not deliberately sought to oversell their readers but have been carried away by their own sincere enthusiasm for the views being delineated; such writers are nonetheless biasing their readers, even though their motives are in contrast with those of the advertising copywriter, who has no genuine interest in the product described. Of course, some propaganda serves useful purposes, as, for example, the advertisements for UNESCO and UNICEF, but the reader should know that he is being propagandized, even when the cause is worthy.

Some of the more common propaganda techniques to which the semantically oriented reader would be alert are:

1. Use of emotive language to excess
2. Artificial dichotomization of an issue that has more than two sides (as in "those who are not with us are against us")
3. Conclusions drawn from false assumptions—the "straw man" technique
4. False or indefensible conclusions drawn from acceptable premises
5. Misinterpretation (deliberate or ignorant) of experimental data
6. Ridicule of the opposition
7. Exaggeration
8. Distortion by quotation out of context
9. Innuendo
10. Use of "loaded" words and phrases—rebels, scabs, Mother, etc.

SEMANTIC EQUIPMENT NEEDED FOR MAXIMUM COMPREHENSION IN READING

A. An awareness that a given set of words or phrases does not have a single, rigid meaning, but that it means different things to different people. The college student has probably been taught that reading is "getting meaning from the printed page." If he believes that teaching, he is satisfied that a printed phrase has a very exact, inflexible meaning, and that all people who really understand it will get exactly the same meaning from it. It is necessary to replace this notion with the realization that, in the reading act, most of the meaning is within the reader and that without his experience background, the printed phrase would have no meaning, even if he could somehow pronounce the words. The point can be made rather obvious to a group of students if they are asked to describe the mental pictures provoked by a phrase such as "a hard-fought ball game." As one student after another tells of his imagery, the class will be amused to find that different "readers" visualized different kinds of ball games. Training along this line makes the student realize further that there is less than perfect communication between the author and the reader; thus the importance of semantic alertness is emphasized.

B. An awareness that authors write for a variety of purposes. Some students have simply never bothered to ask themselves—or anyone else—why a book or an article was written. This lack of intellectual suspicion probably stems from the unquestioning respect accorded to books during grades one to twelve. Whatever the source, the student who becomes a discerning reader is going to learn to ask whether the author wrote for pleasure, for the money, to propagandise, or for a combination of reasons. The instruction can take the direction of some of the exercises in the Stroud-Ammons-Bamman manual *Improving Reading Ability*, exercises which ask "Who Would Have You Believe This?", "To Which of Your Needs is This Appeal Made?", and "What is the Author's Purpose?"

C. Knowledge of the propaganda techniques; also understanding of some of the antidotes for biased writing. Instruction in the rudiments of logic will help students crack the spell of propaganda, as will almost any approach to the scientific method. They should also become sensitive to the uses of emotive and informative language and particularly to the abuses of the former. College students should realize that human opinions on most subjects do not fall into two distinct categories but into continua, ranging from progressive to reactionary or from liberal to conservative. It is, of course, necessary to provide exercises which require the students to detect faulty logic, emotive language, and artificial dichotomization.

D. Understanding of the characteristics of the reader himself which make him a victim of his own prejudicial experience. This fourth essential is the least likely to be adequately developed, partly because the great majority of reading teachers at all levels do not appreciate its importance, and because it would take a considerable amount of training and guidance before the average college student could understand, to a useful degree, the nature and sources of his own interpretative biases. This understanding requires a lot more knowledge of the dynamics of personality than most people ever possess. However Ralph H. Ojemann's experiments in teaching personality adjustment to students in the seventh and twelfth grades suggest—but do not prove—that a few hours of instruction would enable the typical college student to detect and understand some of his biases, and to read with less prejudice in the future.

It would obviously take a generous allowance of instructional time to equip students with this semantic machinery, even if steps A through D were developed rather sketchily, and some reading instructors might insist that the program outlined is too ambitious to be feasible. Nevertheless, any reader who does not have this semantic sophistication can be deceived by a moderately skillful writer. Such a reader is just as well prepared to be deluded as he is to be enlightened.

28. Appeals to Selected Emotions: A Semantic Study of Advertising Techniques

William M. Rasschaert

Adolescent behavior is charged largely by the dynamos of emotions. In and out of school the total complex of the day-to-day life of an adolescent boy or girl is strongly influenced by emotional reaction to things, to people, and to symbols. *Words* are among the most meaningful emotional symbols used *by* and used *on* young people. Any study which helps pupils acquire and develop more objective knowledge about the power of words, their semantic uses and implications, is necessary and desirable. Understanding how words are made to appeal to the emotions can be of lifelong value to adolescents.

The world of advertising is now thoroughly aware of the power of words and emotional symbolism and uses these with skillful and consistent intensity. The success of the application of the principle "appeal to the emotions" is demonstrated daily by the buying habits of consumers who buy thousands of products to which are tied symbols of physical glorification, gratification of material wants, and social status.

George E. Sokolsky wrote *The American Way of Life* a generation ago and did a good job of demonstrating the economic values intrinsic to good, ethical advertising practices. His general theme: "Advertising, by informing the public about new products, creates demand which, in turn, raises our standard of living." Sokolsky's book was a reaction to *100,000,000 Guinea Pigs*, a Consumers' Research attempt to disclose the frauds in advertising.

Our present concern, partly, is to bring closer together two extreme points of view on the nature and value of advertising techniques and to develop in children understandings, appreciations, and insights regarding the use of symbols in advertising. The deeper the understandings young people possess concerning a subject, the greater the potential good for the individual and for society. Approaching "advertising and emotional appeal" by the avenue of semantics can have multiple benefits.

Children in our classes are either direct consumers or "sharing members" of consuming families. Young adults see, hear, talk about, and generally participate in the acquisition and use of advertised consumer goods. A semantic study of advertising techniques on a level appropriate to their experience can achieve at least several outcomes:

"Appeals to Selected Emotions: A Semantic Study of Advertising Techniques," by William M. Rasschaert, *Monograph for English Teachers*. New York: Harper & Row, n.d. Reprinted by permission of the publisher.

1. Strengthen understandings of specific ways in which words are used to appeal to emotions and "wants"
2. Develop awareness of words and pictures as "symbols"—symbols of success, acceptance, conformity, social status, and pleasure
3. Encourage appreciation of the beauty and power of words; develop analytical approach to the true meanings and purposes of words as used in advertisements
4. Reveal the high-level skills necessary to production of good advertising
5. Achieve closer balance between the intellectual potential of teen-age pupils and their emotional drives and wants

Emotional appeals in advertising are our main concern here. *"Printers' Ink* Check Lists of Advertising Essentials" presents the following list of emotional "appeals":

1. Pride—personal, family, civic, etc.
2. Sympathy
3. Curiosity
4. Generosity
5. Fear
6. Impatience—"quick" appeal
7. Sex desire—direct, disguised, open, latent, frank, idealized, etc.
8. Shame
9. Envy
10. Patriotism
11. Love
12. Laziness—"easy" appeal
13. Bandwagon feeling

These emotional appeals come under the head of "response factors for the copywriter to watch," according to the editors, and these are only 13 of a total 87 related factors.

The Study of Semantics on an Appropriate Level

The materials needed to lead students into the study of semantics on their level can consist of magazines, newspapers, and radio and television commercials. In the excellent book *Teaching Secondary English,* by De-Boer, Kaulfers, and Miller, Chapter Nine is devoted completely to "Mass Media of Communication: Magazines." There are eighteen pages devoted to the various activities leading toward purposes to which magazines can be put in the classroom. Any teacher who thinks he needs stimulation for ideas in the use of magazines would do well to look at this particular book and at this chapter. The authors of this book also list thirty-five suggested discussion topics for magazine study.

Our purposes are related to many of the activities and topics listed in this reference work. However, our major purpose is focused on a *semantic* study of the words as they are used in advertising and words used in advertisements in relation to pictorial aspects. Magazines are the greatest single source of "consumer persuasion" material. The number, type, and variety of advertisements reaches an apex in American magazines. Magazines are basic; radio and television advertising is also invaluable for our unit study.

A teacher should first of all check with his librarian to determine which magazines are approved for classroom or school library use. A few of the most commonly read are such magazines as *The Reader's Digest, Life, Saturday Evening Post, Hot Rod, Popular Science, McCall's, Good Housekeeping, Time, Ladies Home Journal, Look, Redbook, Ebony,* and *This Week.* Of course, there are many others.

After determining which magazines are approved for classroom use, the teacher usually will find no difficulty in having students bring one or two copies of old issues of any of these magazines from home. It doesn't really matter whether every person in the classroom has an identical copy of each magazine of the same issue. Each student can be functioning with a different magazine or different issues of the same magazine.

Newspapers can also be used, especially metropolitan daily newspapers, but we recommend reserving newspapers for a separate study. Those interested in working with newspapers would do well to secure a quantity of a single issue for classroom use. The advantage of working with a single issue of a newspaper is obvious in that skills needed commonly by all students in the classroom can more easily be taught.

How Much Time Should Be Given to the Unit? What Are the Goals?

A mimimum of six class periods, but more ideally ten or twelve, of forty to sixty minutes each should be considered the time span for a semester unit on semantics. The total length of the unit will depend on grade placement and students' ages, but generally one to three weeks is sufficient. It would be well to set aside one specific time period during the semester for this study. Usually a period of ten to fifteen days can profitably be used for development, instruction, and evaluation of such a unit. Time limits can reasonably be set by the limitations of each situation. Time limits will be affected by (1) maturity and interest of class, (2) depth of investigation, and (3) amounts and types of writing done by pupils.

The specific goals of the study of semantics will vary from teacher to teacher, but in general these are the major goals that each teacher will have in mind:

A. The systematic presentation of elementary semantic principles through activities and materials of interest to adolescent students
B. The development of insights, appreciations, and understandings on the part of students to *their own emotional reactions* to the symbolism in advertising as it appears in magazines
C. The development of equally important skills of composition and oral English as well as perfection of writing mechanics; all language arts skills can be developed in varying degrees during the study of the unit.

The goals of this study as perceived by the *student* would probably include the following:

A. An opportunity to look at and discuss pictures and other media that are common to their daily "out of school" lives
B. Pleasurable activities related to examination of popular sales slogans familiar to most young people
C. An opportunity to examine, first hand, copies of popular magazines and/or newspapers, to learn how pictures and words try to make products appealing

Introducing this study rests with the teacher. Usually the introduction proceeds quite well without the actual use of magazines. Various kinds of selling points for the unit can be readily thought of by most teachers. The opportunity to bring magazines to class and to work with them for at least six or more class periods appeals to students. They are especially intrigued, in many instances, by the thought that advertisements can teach them something of value.

The teacher should stress the need for more complete understanding of the English language. Students should be encouraged to recognize that English can be better understood through familiarity with its uses.

The teacher might ask students to list titles of popular magazines. Another interesting and profitable function on the introductory level is to encourage class members to list and discuss popular sales slogans currently used in magazines and on television—such as the following:

1. "Get satisfying flavor . . . so friendly to your taste."
2. "No filter feedback."
3. "Betrayed by a fickle deodorant?"
4. "You'll wonder where the yellow went."
5. "For people who can't brush after every meal."
6. "Look, Mom! No cavities!"
7. "The new car gasoline."

8. "The pause that refreshes."
9. "They said it couldn't be done."
10. "Know the real joy of good living."
11. "Sunkist."
12. "Just a little bit better."
13. "America's Number One road car."
14. "Snap, crackle, pop!"

Students may wish to identify or match such slogans with their respective products. The teacher can lead into one aspect of advertising: the esthetic appreciation for the high caliber art and photographic work that goes into a magazine page layout.

The great variety of forms that advertisements take in magazines should be pointed out to students. There are the multicolored, double-page spreads usually paid for by large companies or corporations. These are usually examples of some of the finest art work, photographic treatment, and use of color available in American printed media. The differences among advertisements should be pointed out. Attention should be called to such differences as the use of five or six basic colors contrasted with the plain black and white, which can also be an effective advertisement.

As early as possible the idea should be brought in that the way words are used in the advertisement shows the skill of the copywriter—for example, "Just a little bit better." It should be stressed that copywriters prefer the simple approach—three or four words in a slogan; if more words are used, they are so applied that remembering them is easy and meaningful. It should also be pointed out that some advertisements use simple slogans and multi-colored pictorial representation in conjunction with an instructional or educational approach. Examples of such advertisements are those that show how to load a cartridge pen, how to change the tape in a tape recorder quickly, or how easily solder can be applied to an electric wire.

SIMPLIFY BY BREAKING IDEAS INTO CATEGORIES

The teacher can help students get started with advertisements by having them categorize into major divisions most of them that appear in magazines. Once they have the magazines in their possessions, students might be asked to list the advertisements under such categories as food, drink, household goods, medicines, or cosmetics.

It is up to the teacher to decide how far he wants to go in classifying and subclassifying all the many products available to the public. For example, under such items as cosmetics, it is possible to list more than one kind of cosmetic: perfume, face powder, lipstick, and certain shampoos.

A finer subdivision would include such things as tooth pastes, tooth powders, and certain kinds of soaps which make an appeal to the vanity.

Examples or breakdowns of classifications under such headings as "transportation" might be of special interest to students when they are starting out in this unit. Students could make a distinction between individually-owned transportation (means of transportation owned by individual families or family members) and the kinds of transportation owned by private firms. Under the latter category students could list railroads, airlines, steamship lines, and water-going freight lines; they might even observe that some of these categories overlap.

Another aspect of advertising which is of value in catching students' interest is the "packaging" technique. In many advertisements, the various forms of packaging of products are made to appeal to the preferences of the public. There are squeeze bottles, roll-on sticks, creams, pastes, and liquids. Products are packaged in glass, plastic, cardboard, and tin in a variety of forms. Students should be informed that packaging techniques themselves are used to make specific overtures to men and women and to appeal to notions of beauty, convenience, and utility.

Another simple activity to get students started in analysis of advertising is to count the magazine pages that include one or more advertisements and compare the number with the total pages in the magazine. Students may also be encouraged to notice the differences in sizes of advertisements. For instance, one advertisement may take up two full pages, whereas another may take up only one column inch or even less.

Again, on the basis of tailoring the activities to the interests and capabilities of the students, the teacher might wish to refine this kind of analysis at the introductory stage by asking which kinds of products are most often represented in large color displays and which kinds are presented in simplest form. This analysis emphasizes the great difference of impact that size alone has on the reader.

USE FRESH AND MEANINGFUL ILLUSTRATIONS AS YOU DEVELOP THE UNIT

After the introductory activities are on the way, it is time for the teacher to begin a pointed kind of instruction and encourage investigation of the semantic aspects of advertising copy. It is desirable to begin the semantic investigation by emphasizing the clean simplicity that most copywriters master. The economy of language and the careful selection of words should be pointed out.

Also to be stressed is the precision of language needed to achieve the kinds of appeals made to the consumer through advertising. The class should be encouraged to take an objective look at various approaches.

One of the first approaches is the appeal to become more physically attractive. Countless companies list ways of improving almost all external aspects of the human body. There are special products that make the appeal to improve the condition and appearance of the hair, the eyes, the complexion, the lips, teeth, breath, weight, and physique.

A second major area is the appeal made to improve the physical comfort of individuals through freedom from pain incurred by headaches, neuritis, neuralgia, sinus trouble, tired eyes, arthritis, rheumatism, acne, and other physical ailments.

A third large dimension in which appeal is made systematically and pointedly is that of prestige appeal. Many companies appeal to the desire to be as good as, or better than, the man next door. They inform us that successful people drive certain cars or wear certain kinds of suits, carry certain kinds of luggage, use particular kinds of typewriters and shaving creams, have particular kinds of fences put around their back yards, and use special kinds of fertilizers on their special kinds of lawns.

The semantic aspects of this study come in when it is considered *how words are used* both alone and in conjunction with "art." The pictures and photographs usually symbolize status and success in a material sense. Students must now be shown how to develop a sensitivity to the part that artwork plays in relation to the word context of advertisements. Students should look especially for "What is the appeal?" "How are the words used?" "What are the words getting at?" "How do the words and pictures relate to each other?"

It is at this point that the teacher leads students to ask themselves, "Do advertisements try to make us buy things we actually need?" "Are these things always good for us?" "How harmful can some of them be to us?" "Are they harmful in that they urge us to spend money which we might better save?" "Are they urging us to use products which do us no real good?" If he determines a product is of value, the student should be led to ask himself, "Can I afford this item?"

Don't Forget the Propaganda Techniques

From this point we move in to discuss a limited number of propaganda techniques. The first of these we identify as *generalization* or, as it is often termed, *overgeneralization*. What do we mean by generalization? Such expressions as "*Everyone* wants . . . ," "All athletes prefer . . . ," and "Most girls and boys love . . ." are examples of the use of generalization, which often misleads people into buying products which are not really what they themselves as consumers like or want. It is the technique of getting the individual to identify with this huge, presumably correct-acting mass-group.

Another technique which injects into products qualities which they do not necessarily have are the use of *color words* or *taste words* which have some kind of an emotional reaction inherent in them. Such words as "flaming color," "rich, spicy taste," "thick, creamy texture"; "man-sized," "really, softly feminine" hold out a lure which may encourage unwise buying.

A third technique is that of the use of *symbols* such as the American flag, the eagle, the white-pillared mansion, the new car in front of the broad-lawned new home in the suburbs or parked incongruously on a golden beach where the blue ocean boils whitely around gleaming black boulders. All of these images are intended to be symbolic of patriotism, comfortable living, or material success. There is always the intimation, "Certainly, if you buy this, you will be shown to be patriotic, you will be genteel and comfortable, you will be debonair, urbane and successful."

The *band-wagon* technique is common to most people who have done any reading at all in the last twenty-five years. This business of "Do this because everyone else who counts is doing it" is one of the most commonly used methods of getting the individual to identify the mass. It is also related to some of the techniques mentioned earlier.

Finally, the *endorsement* technique (which is well-known to most adults but can come with fresh clarity to students) should be explained. Vincent Wise endorses Honer's Pink Blades for an "exhilarating shave"; Roma Starre endorses Slimms for weight control. Buck Hicks and Babe Mantle use meats from Kruger.

The book mentioned earlier, *Teaching Secondary English*, devotes an entire chapter to "Semantics as a Common Learning." One of the suggestions for an activity in semantics is the rewriting of advertisements that make exaggerated use of euphemism where none is required. The book defines euphemism as "the use of more pleasing words for the same act, condition, or thing having a subtle but influential effect on human behavior." Mention is made of such words as "filet mignon" as being more appealing than "a tender piece of dead cow." Roast beef "Au Jus" instead of "roast beef with juice" and "pie a la mode" instead of "pie with ice cream" are given as examples of euphemism found on restaurant menus. There are many advertisements that use euphemism; they can be found by a casual leafing through almost any magazine.

YOUNGSTERS ENJOY DISCOVERING AND UNDERSTANDING SEMANTIC SHIFT

Another vitally important aspect of study is semantic shift. DeBoer points out that the fact that words change their meaning according to the context in which they are used is a common source of confusion in language, especially when the same term is used in different senses in the same sentence or paragraph. Probably one of the most exciting things youngsters discover is that words can mean different things, according to the way in which they are used. DeBoer points out that some insights into the range and magnitude of the problem can be obtained from the fact that the 570 most commonly used words in English have approximately 7,000 different uses. Thus, the little word "run" with its compounds has 800 meanings, from "homerun" to "run on a bank" or "run in a stocking." Dr. S. I. Hayakawa in a *Saturday Evening Post* article points out the same thing concerning the common word "frog." Surely there is no problem about what "frog" means! But here are some simple variant uses of the word given by Dr. Hayakawa:

"If we're going fishing, we'll have to catch some *frogs* first."

"I have a *frog* in my throat."

"She wore a loose silk jacket fastened with braided *frogs*."

"The blacksmith pared down the *frog* and the hoof before shoeing the horse."

"In Hamilton, Ohio, there is a firm by the name of American *Frog* and Switch Company."

In addition to these "frogs," there is the "frog" in which a sword is carried, the "frog" at the bottom of a bowl or vase that is used in flower arrangements, and the "frog" which is part of a violin bow. Dr. Hayakawa mentions also another word, "order." There is the *order* that the salesman tries to get, which is quite different from the *order* which a captain gives to his crew. Some people enter holy *orders*. There is the *order* in the house when mother has finished tidying up; there is the batting *order* of the home team; there is an *order* of ham and eggs. As Dr. Hayakawa says, "It is surprising that with so many meanings to the word, people don't misunderstand one another oftener than they do."

ORAL AND WRITTEN ENGLISH CAN BE IMPROVED THROUGHOUT THIS SEMANTIC STUDY

Developing in students a sensitivity to the changing meaning of words is valuable. There are various ways that semantics can be interrelated with language arts skills. What are some possible outlines students are trained to make, using the content of the semantic unit?

I. *Outlining*

    A. An outline of two to four major parts classifying advertisements

    B. An outline of themes related to advertising

    C. An outline of similarities among techniques used on radio and television, and in magazines

D. An outline paralleling the similarities between format of a metropolitan daily newspaper and the offerings on a day of television programs
E. An outline of themes related to advertising
   1. "Advertising—a Magnet"
   2. "Watch Words for Meaning"
   3. "What Ads Try to Do"
   4. "Our Parents Read This Too"
   5. "The Steady Stream of Words"
F. An outline of oral English
   1. Individual talks before the class
   2. Group discussion
   3. Panels
   4. Debates
   5. Tape recording activities
   6. Assembly talks
G. An outline of bulletin board displays
   1. Magazines and related media
   2. Showcase material
   3. Letters to advertisers
   4. Letters to editors of magazines and newspapers
   5. Letters to sponsors of television and radio shows
   6. Letters to local merchants who advertise in local media

II. *Composition Work.* Composition work naturally follows outlining, and we offer the following as a bare, suggestive outline:

A. Some possible subjects for themes or compositions on advertising and related topics
   1. Newspaper and magazine articles on advertising which stress the useful and beneficial aspect of this field
   2. Books and articles in periodicals on advertising, public opinion, mass persuasion, propaganda, such as Doob's *Propaganda Analysis,* Packard's *The Hidden Persuaders,* Clyde Miller's *The Process of Persuasion,* can be located in the *Reader's Guide to Periodical Literature.* (The use of the *Reader's Guide* in itself can be of great benefit to the pupils.)
B. Short compositions analyzing a single advertisement
   1. Techniques used
   2. Use of words and pictures
   3. Use of color
   4. Appeals made to the reader
C. Themes discussing radio and television commercials

III. *Transference of "good writing" techniques used in advertising to student-written compositions*

   A. Studying the care with which advertisements are planned and words selected

      1. For the purpose of clarity and precision in writing, careful creation of opening sentences, color words, truthful descriptions, accurate quotations, objective interpretations, and good transition sentences

      2. For paragraphing and parallelism; development of major thesis and supporting ideas

      3. For writing concise and artful summary paragraphs leading to solid, well-prepared conclusions

   B. Students' examination of their own writing for certain faults

      1. Overgeneralization

      2. Loose words

      3. Guilt by association

      4. The endorsement technique

      5. Snobbishness

      6. Inappropriate emotional appeals

      7. Other flaws often present in thinking and writing

There are so many topics that lend themselves to profitable exploration and development in the oral and written phases of a unit on semantics that those mentioned above are merely suggestive of others, possibly more original, that will occur to the teacher.

In all the written work and as much oral work as applies, emphasis should be given to correctness in spelling, grammar and usage, punctuation, and mechanics. The theme, whether long or short, should aim at effectiveness, diction, unity, emphasis and clearness.

The aim of the unit on semantics should be primarily to teach the symbolic attachment we give to words. Specifically, when considered in the context of magazine advertising, students should be made aware of how the symbols are used to make people want to buy things which they might not otherwise buy.

The negative aspects of advertising techniques must be stressed as well as the positive ones. It is imperative that teachers do stress both views, for it is only with this balanced knowledge that students will develop a rational and critical approach to one of the greatest sources of our American daily word use.

Advertisers and people who prepare advertising realize most emphatically that the youngsters of today are the large-scale consumers of tomorrow. Actually, more than in past years, youngsters today are consumers on no mean scale before they are out of the eighth grade. Some of our largest industries survive and flourish because of the young consumer. An outstanding industry is that which supplies juke boxes with records for popular consumption. It is a well-known fact that the overwhelming market for popular music is the teen-agers and young adults.

Students must be prepared as early as possible to know that they *are* the target of advertising appeals. Teachers should give careful and systematic attention to advertisements that are current, meaningful, and easily available. The motivational aspect of using popular magazines is in itself a great help in leading students toward a more sophisticated knowledge of advertising and all the ramifications of the advertising profession.

It should not be surprising if a student who is especially gifted in art or related fields (such as photography and oral and written English) is encouraged through a well-planned unit of this kind to carry his specialty further and is stimulated to go into some professional aspects of advertising. Even though such is not the goal of the unit, the possibilities cannot be overlooked. Samuel R. Laycock, in his book *Gifted Children*, states:

> ". . . it is particularly important that the gifted child have considerable practice in recognizing the difference between fact and opinion; distinguishing the language of fact from the language of feeling; being able to recognize the tricks of propaganda, judging the adequacy of his information, distinguishing between the relevant and irrelevant, the important and the unimportant . . . Certainly these skills do not develop automatically. The teacher must *specifically* provide practice for the pupils if they are to learn them."

This statement summarizes quite well the various goals a well-planned unit on semantics can achieve and points out how teachers must provide for young people with special talents. However, it is imperative to train *all* children (with special kinds of emphases for those referred to as "gifted" or "academically talented") in the skills and insights described by Laycock. If teachers have students whose interests and skills lead them to pursue advertising as a career, they must train these students as early as possible to go into it as they would any other profession—to contribute to it, to improve it, and to make it even more of a profession than when they entered it. Such cannot be done, however, by one or two exposures of five- or ten-day duration. Semantics and related topics are fields which must be covered systematically over a period of years and repeated at various levels of difficulty and with varying degrees of intensity.

29. Language and the Habit of Credulity

Russell G. Stauffer

It is commonly accepted that language is the instrument that, better than any other, enables persons both to develop and to participate in their culture. Granted that this is true, it follows that language is a symbol-system of vital importance to each individual and to his society.

When an infant discovers that a cry can produce certain desired results, he has made a start on the long road toward acquiring a language and being a part of a collective communication system. This is especially so when the child begins to realize that he can participate in the language community as both a producer and receiver of symbols (4, p. 24). The knowledge that this presages the difference between man and animal is indeed vivifying. As a producer and receiver the child differs sharply from the Pavlovian dog who is also responding to a symbol (the bell) with a response (salivating) when the chain of events is initiated by man. And this difference is strikingly apparent when one notes that there can be no reciprocal relation between the dog and the man.

This ability to learn and use language is different from the power among insects to perform feats of amazing skill. A Sphex wasp, for instance, has the ability to perform a delicate and exacting nerve operation on an Ephippiger grasshopper. The operation paralyzes the legs, leaving the grasshopper helpless and a ready supply of living food for the wasps to be hatched.

"Once the paralysis is accomplished the wasp drags the victim to its nest by an antenna. When, however, the antenna is cut off, the wasp is baffled, and can't conceive of any other way to move the grasshopper. It has been concluded then that while insects possessed highly specialized instinctive skills, which they didn't need to learn by teaching or example, they completely lacked the ability to reason" (16, p. 119).

Unlike the Sphex wasp but like the Pavlovian dog, the child makes associations between a symbol and an experience. But unlike the Pavlovian dog the language symbols are not artificial products of an experimental situation. Most of the first symbols a child learns to isolate and use are acquired in a first-hand experience situation. Usually these learnings are related to concrete things which are perceived directly through the senses—milk, mother, doll. Whether children first learn to use words at age one or at age two and a half the demands are the same. Each child must associate, select, use, and remember.

Sooner or later children discover that not all symbols refer to concepts

"Language and the Habit of Credulity," by Russell G. Stauffer, *Elementary English*, (April 1965), 362–369. Reprinted with the permission of the National Council of Teachers of English and Russell G. Stauffer.

on the object level. While it is thought that between the age of eighteen to twenty-four months children live predominantly in the present, some ability to project into the future is developing. Ames reports that "Words indicating the present come in first, then words indicating the future, and finally those indicating the past. Thus 'today' (24 months) precedes 'tomorrow' (30 months) which in turn precedes 'yesterday' (36 months)" (3, p. 122).

It is at about this point in the child's long, slow progress toward language maturity that he attains an awareness, even though vaguely, of two basic conditions. First, he begins to realize that all the things in his world have names and that folks about him know these names. The period is sometimes affectionately labeled as the "What's this?" age. Second, little by little he learns to deal with words that represent relative and indefinite ideas—the *little* dog, the *little* boy, the *little* car, the *little* house. Puzzling as it may be, he gradually learns to use *little* discriminately and in so doing takes a big step on the road toward understanding multiple meanings and figurative language.

As the child learns to deal with words like *little* he learns to deal with incongruities of meaning and use. At first he uses the word appropriately in different contexts under different communication demands almost as if by intuition. Somehow he learns to recognize a common element in the different situations in which the concept of *little* fits. Not being articulate, though, about the many specifics that enter into each use of *little* (*little* toy—*little* storm) he operates in part on knowledge and in large part on extrasensory intuition. Here his intuition rests in the degree of constancy associated with the variables of *little*.

Even so, when dealing with concepts of *little*, referents usually are a part of the sensory world and can be reexamined. Thus while there is present a certain amount of blindness and a certain demand to accept by intuition or faith, the degree and amount is not as great as when the child deals with a concept like *tomorrow* because *tomorrow* never comes. Yet as Ames and others (12) point out, children learn to deal with the concept *tomorrow* at an early age. Somehow they must recognize some of the attributes of the concept *tomorrow*. Certainly, though, there may be judged to be present a greater degree of blindness and a greater demand on intuition than when dealing with concepts such a *little*.

It seems then that the intuition demands required when dealing with concepts like *shoes*, *little*, and *tomorrow* can provide the readiness for dealing with concepts like *democracy*, *peace*, and *eternity*. Could it be said therefore that the beginning of faith and of credulity originates in the "word" or in a symbol?

Today, tomorrow, then yesterday. One might well auger here the hope that springs eternal and use this early learning pattern as a revelation of man's vision—to look ahead from today and with increased maturity to have that look ahead be tempered wisely by the past. As Ames (3) goes on to say, the age of three to five brings with it much greater projection into the future, until by age eight even extremes of time span can be handled adequately.

Gradually, though, the veil of an individual's and his culture's emotional, intellectual, and spiritual world creates gossamers that may lead to stereotypes, prejudices, and sentiments as well as to convictions and beliefs. Now he learns the special idioms of the teens, the slogans and stock phrases of the propagandist and the publicity agents, and the stories and puns of the adults. Shifts of meaning are subtle and varied and their acuteness may often go unrecognized. Fortunately, though, over all is the innateness of laughter and the range of things laughed at (11, p. 86). And as Stephen Leacock believes "humor in its highest meaning and furtherest reach . . . finds its basis in the incongruity of life itself . . . and becomes the contemplation and interpretation of our life." (8, p. 15) Then as a person deals with the verbal conventions of his time, he discovers that humor can be the wedge that amplifies the need to adjust concepts to the ever-shifting realities of experience.

Children love fun. They seem to be natural pranksters unless, as one author puts it, it's been spanked out of them. The care-free, spontaneous, enthusiastic laughter of children uninhibited by the sober conventions of adult society has through the ages been a favorite *genre* of the poets.

From games and jokes and pranks to fun with words seems an easy step and usually occurs early in the word-life of children. Here their imaginations are undiminished. From nursery rhymes and ditties to *Winnie the Pooh* to *Paul Bunyan* is easily accomplished as they disarmingly toy with the protective masks of phantasy and unreality. They catch shifts of meaning that occur in children's puns, in simple name calling like "you're a grandmother," or "you're a hamburger with onions." All this requires a sense of intuition and of credulity. Humor seems to represent the early development of a language thermostat that permits them to keep their language habits on a controlled level and thus avoid the emotional breakdowns that stem so frequently from communication misunderstandings. A good sense of humor has for a long time been referred to as an emotional stabilizing asset.

So as children mature and achieve a clearer grasp of the common and uncommon concepts in their world of culture, the sophistication will surely remove the innocence from their eyes. And it is our duty to see to it that this change not be marred by the cold brittleness of bitter disillusionment. Rather we must see to it that the maturing be activated by the subtle vibrations resulting from a love for the creative and the substantial resources of an outlook on life that is built on faith.

And so the individual learns that "the symbols of language are slippery things. They do not stay put: they carry multiple meanings, which shift from time to time and differ from place to place; their ostensible references overlaid with meanings of a non-rational character. It (language) is the result of man's collective quest for expression, and it therefore reflects the cultural value, the changing attitudes and intentions and preoccupations by which man lives." (4, p. 17)

And so, too, man learns to accept meanings of things not experienced or if experienced not examined, or if examined not generalized. He learns to project on language a credulity that ranges from the naive to the sophisticated. First, he accepts names without question. For a while he tends to apply them indiscriminately on a class basis calling all children "boy" or all animals "bow-wow." Even as an adult he tends to accept labels such as *salt, grain,* and *love* without a check on their derivation and history or the reasons why their many uses developed and how they tend to be related. He learns to associate many meanings with *tomorrow* without perhaps ever being quite ready to deal with, "Tomorrow and tomorrow and tomorrow, comes ever and anon after today." He thinks of certain words as representing definite concepts and uses them as if they did until one day perchance he is asked to elaborate on the meaning of "How far is a mile?" Then he discovers that saying 5,280 feet or 1,760 yards adds only limited clarity. It says nothing about the kind of mile, i.e., a mile high, a mile deep, a mile under water, a mile wide canyon; the time of a mile, i.e., a mile a minute, a four minute mile, or two week mile; or reactions to a mile, how tired is a runner after a mile, a mountain climber after ascending a mile, a golf player after playing six holes, and so on. He now sees this "definite" term *mile* being overlaid with various credulities and multiple ramifications. The many faceted world of connotations and the many faces of use make a difference.

Now he accepts with a new kind of credulity the fact that our sun is 93,000,000 miles away in outer space and that other suns are even farther away. Light years take on an almost incredulous dimension as the old stereotype for *mile* is stretched seemingly beyond the demands made by an ageless generic.

As a result other stereotypes may come under surveillance: *mother, cowboy, astronaut, spartan.* Biases need to be juggled again: rich and poor, master and slave, old and new, near and far.

Throughout this multiplicand of change bounded by finite and infinite limits, humor can represent the impedance ratio between the polysemantic function of language and rudimentary single equivalence. It is through humor that he grows alert to the multiplicity of intents and implications latent in a single word or idea or concept, even though at times in their placing and stress they are contradictory. Such extravagance of meaning allows for full use of overtones and undertones of connotations and denotations, subtleties and acuities, synonyms and analogies.

And so, as man serves his apprenticeship to communication, his language and his thinking may be packed with fabulous credulities, beneath which may be, as Hook says of the peasant, a kind of vulgar empiricism (6). Needed is much training in the critical examination of language; in family circles, in classroom discussions, in friendship groups, and in private meditation.

Finally, as the child learns to deal with ideas through written language, he is introduced to more remote persons, places, and times. Now he should be led to discover anew that meaning depends upon the total incidences of a concept in his experiences and upon the context in which it is being used by the author.

The use of the simple verb *to brush* cannot be understood even if a dictionary is consulted unless the reader can examine the situation in which the word is used and examine his own experiences. "To brush a picture," means one thing and "to brush up in arithmetic," means quite another. Or, if a sentence read, "The settlers had a brush with the Indians," it might be necessary to do as one third-grade boy did: say that he didn't understand what *brush* meant here. With teacher help the boy did understand how he could brush against someone on the sidewalk and have a brief contact, perhaps almost a skirmish; and so he discovered that his experiences, when restructured, did provide some meaning for this different use of *brush*. Certainly his meaning was not as precise and vivid as that of his father who had a *brush* with the enemy on Okinawa. Even so, father and son would need a certain amount of credulity when reading about the American settlers and their *brush* with the Indians. Furthermore, for either the father or the son the "experience" of a "brush with the Indians" could be completely verbal. In other words, it could be that both father and son might have adequate understanding without ever actually having had a *brush* with anyone.

Then, too, it may be that the author never had a brush with the Indians. This fact together with the fact that the experiences of all three were different—father, son, author—makes perfect communication impossible. The necessity for interpretation always creates the need for credulity to some degree. So an intelligent and integrated person with a minimum of credulities might be described as ". . . one who is capable of sorting out his experiences, making pertinent distinctions among them, and seeing them in relation to his system of values. He is capable of making comparisons between two sets of data, two experiences, two generalized ideas, all without confusion between them. He cannot do any of these things at all unless he can attach verbal symbols to them for purposes of labelling, keep those symbols distinct, and manipulate them without confusion." (4, p. 4)

A SECOND APPRENTICESHIP

The first language apprenticeship a person serves is to the spoken word. Not only do most people first learn to formulate concepts and communicate ideas as receivers and producers of oral language, but they do so with increasing frequency and effectiveness as they grow and mature. Many use oral language with a considerable degree of adequacy without knowing their language's grammar, either its morphology or syntax. The skill results from actual experience with audience reaction. The drama of face to face communication spotlights the need for studying audience effects, for restating, and for clarifying abstract ideas. It is this experience of speaker-listener interrelationships which emphasizes the differences between oral and written communication (5).

In written communication, a face to face interaction between the author and the reader is an uncommon experience. The demands on the writer are greater than those made on the speaker. The writer must carefully choose his words. His first obligation is to write with precision. Certainly he must keep his audience in mind but he need not avoid using words that may tax his reader's vocabulary. Certainly he must know the demands of the language of prose and the language of poetry.

The reader, in turn, must understand that writing usually involves a more disciplined and compact form of communication. He must, in the final analysis, know how to find out the "whole" truth by carefully examining and weighing the ideas recorded so as to grasp their full meaning and to identify the hidden implications and the motives of the author. To do all this he must learn to read and do productive thinking.

To train a reader so that he can deal with different interpretations and examine the assumptions and implications of each is to help him avert habits of credulity. Such training should be started when the child first learns to read. Then as he increases in ability to recognize printed words as conveyors of ideas he will become more effective in understanding what is being said and why it is said (13).

Children just learning to read can be taught to sort out their experiences, make pertinent distinctions among them, compare them with those of the author, generalize concerning the ideas presented, and do so in relation to their system of values. As they mature emotionally, intellectually, and spiritually they can be taught how man's collective quest for wisdom is an ongoing process that reflects changing attitudes and intentions and preoccupations. They can also learn how to see things as they are, without illusion or emotional bias, and how to make choices or decisions that are sane, prudent, fair, and reasonable.

Such training is best initiated in a group situation in which all the children participating are required to deal with the same material. Under these conditions each member of the group can act as an auditor for each other member and require a searching examination of events to determine the facts and to test their quality, validity, truth, and accuracy (14).

It becomes apparent immediately that such learning to read is a demanding task. It requires a command of thinking skills as well as reading skills. Obviously, too, reading of this high caliber needs to be taught. And the training should be started, as it could be, at the primary level, by using material that can be thoroughly intelligible to the reader or lies within his experience grasp. Story materials, if well structured, do lend themselves to such use because, as Adler (1) indicates, in general the ground plan for reading story material resembles the division of rules for reading scientific or expository works.

Gradually, though, as the reading materials provided through the intermediate and secondary schools cause the reader to go beyond his immediate experiences, the training must prepare the reader to deal with scientific or expository material as a thinking reader just as he learned to deal with the narrative variety (15). Then knowledge of grammar and logic becomes increasingly more valuable. This is especially so when a man reads something that at first he doesn't understand. And, as Horn (7) points out, this is usually the case in school.

A child learning to perform as a thinking reader must learn to do his own thinking. When he turns to a story he must learn to use the title to conjecture about the story. Certainly every reader does this to some degree but the trained reader does so deliberately and thoughtfully. Then as he reads the story he checks his speculations against the story to see whether or not he was right about what he thought would occur. As additional facts are given he may either confirm his assumptions and be more certain about the story outcome or he may reject his assumptions and declare new ones. And so on to the end.

As is evident when the reader is trained as described here, he is given much opportunity to deal in discoveries as he unravels the problems set up by the story plot. This approach to reading training might be described as a problem solving approach. By so doing, the opening remarks in the preface to G. Polya's *How to Solve It* seem to be appropriate:

> A great discovery solves a great problem but there is a grain of discovery in the solution of any problem. Your problem may be modest; but if it challenges your curiosity and brings into play your inventive faculties, and if you solve it by your own means, you may experience the tension and enjoy the triumph of discovery. Such experiences at a susceptible age may create a taste for mental work and leave their imprint on mind and character for a lifetime (9).

If there is one quality to which every able reader must be committed, it is the ability to find and test evidence. To accomplish this high objective, pupils must become skillful in identifying the relevant and the truthful in the light of thoughtfully declared objectives. It has been said by the sage that a good question is half an answer. Thus the predicting or declaring of assumptions provides a first step in the reading-thinking process. Examining evidence, noting relationships and discovering story trends provides a second step. If basic reading materials designed for use at the primary level consist of carefully structured story plots, the basic reading training can be directed as described and result in reading-thinking experiences at a susceptible age which may create a taste for mental work and leave their imprint on mind and character for a lifetime.

For purposes of clinical study and research, thinking may be classified into five main types; associative thinking, convergent thinking, problem solving, critical thinking, and creative thinking (11). To a considerable degree, though, all of these thinking types are closely interrelated and are used almost as one or may all be used by the able reader-thinker in dealing with a reading problem. Constantly as he reads and speculates and reads again the reader is doing associative type thinking; he's putting together the two and two of story events by making associations, and by recalling related personal experiences that fit the scene. As he progresses through the story the reader does convergent type thinking. From a broad divergent approach based on limited initial clues he narrows down the possibilities as he approaches the story end. Each purpose declared or each question asked or each purpose changed creates a demand for problem solving type thinking. And certainly as he proceeds the reader does critical reading. He weighs the evidence found against his experience and knowledge of acceptable standards and accepts or rejects, and this requires a critical attitude. Surely, too, as he proceeds he will have opportunities to be creative in his use of the information supplied. Or when a story is finished or expository material has been read he may be ready to declare two or three other acceptable and creative endings or next steps.

In all this the role of the teacher is of vital importance. Again as Polya says:

> 1. Helping the student. One of the most important tasks of the teacher is to help his students. This task is not quite easy; it demands time, practice, devotion and sound principles.
> The student should acquire as much experience of independent work as possible. But if he is left alone with his problem without any help or with insufficient help, he may make no progress at all. If the teacher helps too much, nothing is left to the student. The teacher should help, but not too much and not too little, so that the student shall have a reasonable share of the work (9, p. 1).

The teacher must avoid being the product of authoritarian indoctrination. She does this by saying frequently: What do you think will happen next? Why do you think so? Were you right in your thinking? Read the lines that prove you were right. She does not do the thinking for the children. She does not use the Pavlovian conditioned response approach. Rather she quickens the reading performance in an astute way so that essential concepts of time, space, people, humor, numbers, and morality are not overlooked.

The teacher can help pupils unobtrusively and naturally when she takes advantage of group thinking and challenging, especially in the problem solving atmosphere of a directed reading-thinking circumstance. She allows each pupil opportunity to learn to exercise self-control, to be systematic, to evolve ideas of his own to which he is committed by considered judgment, and to tolerate and respect different ideas of others. The amenities of social adjustment are required and acquired in a circumstance that is primarily concerned with children's mental development. It is in such an atmosphere that pupils can acquire the attitudes of honest thinking so that later in life they will always desire to be enlightened and informed rather than to be blind and unreasoning. The attitudes of a thinking reader affect not only what he reads and hears, what he accepts and rejects, but also the objectivity of his thinking.

Such training in reading will result in effective reading and thinking and help break the habits of credulity which unexamined concepts produce. It will help students clarify concepts on the "sense-data" (10) level and in turn those that cannot be subject to immediate sensation. As the pupils develop skill in using thinking techniques, they develop an appreciation for the value of reflective thought. Finding and using facts takes on functional significance as over and over again they look for relevant facts rather than trying to attain an idle, rote recital of "all" the facts. Gathering evidence, even story evidence, to support an assumption, requires an evaluation of the facts, organization of the facts, and the drawing of sound conclusions. In addition, pupils learn from repeated experience as they read through story after story and stop to reflect and conjecture at various points that assumptions based on insufficient evidence are tentative and that judgment must be suspended.

CONCLUSION

It has been stated that reading can be an obstacle to thinking and help extend the habit of language credulity initiated through the spoken word. Or, it can be a means of developing habits of clear thinking. Half-truths, superstitions, falsehoods, and prejudices can be detected and dealt with. It remains for the reader as well as the listener to be alert, seek out valid inferences, follow a careful chain of reasoning from fact to fact, and attempt to draw sound conclusions by testing his hypotheses. When this is done the practiced reader will, as Altick says, find ". . . abiding evidence that he is not so easily deceived as his neighbor" (2, p. 112).

REFERENCES

1. MORTIMER J. ADLER, *What Man Has Made of Man*. New York: Frederick Unger Publishing Co., 1937.

2. RICHARD D. ALTICK, *Preface to Critical Reading*. New York: Henry Holt & Co., 1946.

3. L. AMES, "The Development of the Sense of Time in the Young Child," *Journal of Genetic Psychology*, 68 (1946) 97–125.

4. COMMISSION ON SECONDARY SCHOOL CURRICULUM, V. T. Thayer, Chairman, *Language in General Education*. New York: D. Appleton-Century Co., 1940.

5. W. J. GRACE and J. C. GRACE, *The Art of Communicating Ideas*. New York: The Devin-Adair Co., 1952.

6. SIDNEY HOOK, "The Philosophy of Reading," *The Science and Philosophy of Reading*. Proceedings of the Forty-first Annual Education Conference, University of Delaware, Newark, Delaware, 1959, pp. 20–34.

7. ERNEST HORN, "Language and Meaning," *National Society for the Study of Education*. Forty-first Yearbook, Part II. The Psychology of Learning. Chicago: University of Chicago Press, 1942, pp. 377–413.

8. STEPHEN LEACOCK, *Humor, Its Theory and Technique*. New York: Dodd, Mead, Co., 1935.

9. G. POLYA, *How to Solve It*. Princeton, N.J.: Princeton University Press, 1948.

10. BERTRAND RUSSELL, *The Problems of Philosophy*. London: G. Allen, 1912.

11. DAVID H. RUSSELL, *Children's Thinking*. Boston: Ginn and Co., 1956.

12. D. E. SCHECHTER, M. SYMONDS, and D. BERNSTEIN, "Development of the Concept of Time in Children," *Journal of Nervous and Mental Disorders*, 121 (1955) 301–10.

13. RUSSELL G. STAUFFER, "Breaking the Basal-Reader Lock Step," *Elementary School Journal*, 61 (1961) 269–76.

14. ——, "The Role of Group Instruction in Reading," *Elementary English*, 41 (1964) 230–40.

15. ——, "Reading and the Educated Guess," *Changing Concepts of Reading Instruction*. IRA Conference Proceedings, 1961. New York: Scholastic Magazines.

16. JOHN H. STORER, *The Web of Life*. New York: The Devin-Adair Co., 1953.

30.   Reading, Research, and Reporting in the Social Studies

Alvina Treut Burrows

THE LEARNING PROCESS

BASIC SKILLS FOR LEARNING

Reading words, pictures, and numbers is an essential skill for learning in the social studies. Very early the world of symbols becomes part and parcel of the here-and-now physical world of little children. Seeing and hearing adults read, turning pages and looking at pictures, or identifying labels on home appliances, on cookies and candies, on packages and grocery-store shelves—these mark the initiation of the beginning reader.

Research is practically an instinctive pursuit of children living in reasonably resourceful environments. The yearling patting his cereal, the kindergartner dramatizing the jet plane's take-off, and the ten-year-old making a clay tablet are exploring facts of texture, velocity, consistency, pressure, and resistance. Perhaps in the last instance the investigation reaches also into ideas of personal-historical continuity.

Checking picture facts with life facts begets many questions long before kindergarten. "Why doesn't the lady take her pocketbook to the store?" was asked about a picture of a mother and children leaving home to go shopping. "Where is the light switch?" was asked about a picture of a brightly lighted room. Answering how-to-do-it questions also takes children into books at an early age, as when a kindergartner finds how to make a pinwheel from illustrated directions in a science book and an eight-year-old follows instructions for dipping candles. Besides this tangibly productive reading, children range into an ever growing universe, transported there in part by symbols, either graphic or written. New questions loom up, fragments of new information mesh into earlier organizations of knowledge and feeling, fresh insights light up old beliefs. Thus does the "seeking behavior" of children galvanize learnings from reading as surely as it gives structure to physically overt learning.[1]

Reporting in the social studies is the natural outcome of the child's compelling urge to communicate both with other children and with adults. Reporting to one another is an almost constant process when children live

---

[1] Willard C. Olson, "Seeking, Self-selection, and Pacing in the Use of Books by Children," *Packet*, VII (Spring, 1952), 1–10 (Boston: D. C. Heath & Co.).

"Reading, Research, and Reporting in the Social Studies," by Alvina Treut Burrows, is reprinted by permission from *Social Studies in the Elementary School*, the Fifty-sixth Yearbook of the National Society for the Study of Education, Part II, 1957, 187–213.

in a stimulating, informal atmosphere. Such reporting does not wait until the child has exhausted the data of his problem. It provides an almost immediate balance to the stimulus of making discoveries.

All three of these normal behaviors of children—*reading, research, reporting*—are essential to learning in the social studies.

SKILLS INTERRELATED IN THE CLASSROOM

"Let *me* do it," is heard wherever children work freely. The satisfaction of overcoming difficulties is jealously defended, and *doing* almost always involves *finding out*. A first-grader drawing a locomotive wants to know whether the sand dome or the steam dome is closer to the smokestack. He has played trains; he has seen trains; he has built a train out of blocks. From his trip to the trainyard and from the "story" he has heard, he remembers discussion of the mounds on top of the boiler. He knows that a familiar storybook contains a well-labeled picture of the parts of the locomotive. He takes the book to his teacher to re-read the names on the diagram. Thus do research and reading open new doors for exploration. Thus they build new curiosity and new satisfactions. Now, making the locomotive picture becomes a reporting activity, involving precise knowledge unifying firsthand research and reading. Thus do reading, research, and reporting weave a fabric of enlarged and dynamic experience.

An older boy who makes a clay tablet as part of a class study of the development of writing lives through learning activities of similar sequence but of greater complexity. He must read more of both text and diagram; he must carefully measure to make a proper mold for the clay; he must copy the Egyptian characters carefully. His project takes several days. Interest is strengthened by the questions and comments of his friends. He does not wait until the tablet is complete to show it and tell about his findings. Others in his group learn something from daily contacts with the clay tablet as it nears completion. Contributions of primitive writing to the evolution of literacy become a concern of the rest of the class. When the report on this subject is finally presented in organized form, it finds a receptive audience, with many concepts ready for the two-way interaction of speaker and listener.

DEFINITION OF TERMS

In this presentation, *reading* refers to the selection of meanings from printed or written symbols. *Reference reading* is used to designate teacher-assigned reading of texts, encyclopedias, biographies, travel stories, or some types of factually true but imaginatively treated materials related to a topic being studied. Much exploratory reading is of this sort.

Research refers to investigations carried on in a spirit of honest inquiry.

Sometimes the quest with which the learner is actively identified may involve use of texts and references. At times it employs primary data such as persons with pertinent experience or training; at other times the search leads to statistical records or "on the spot" records such as tapes, photographs, written records, or diaries. Primary sources for children may be any authentic, pertinent realia observed at firsthand. The unique quality of juvenile research is twofold: The learner seeks authentic data on a problem which has truly become his own, and he organizes his findings in a way peculiar to his own purposes.

Reporting includes all methods of communication and interpretation of data which may inform the learner, clarify meaning, or influence action. Representative methods of communication in such situations might include telling, making and showing illustrations; displaying ready-made illustrations; explaining diagrams, maps, models, charts, artifacts, and other objects; dramatizing, giving planned quiz programs, interviewing, and conducting panel discussions. Reporting involves preparation of the audience and awareness of listeners' responsiveness. Planning methods of baiting audience interest may involve activities such as giving tentative solutions to questions to be considered in the report; checking these solutions with information as it is presented; adding specific items to a diagram or illustrated map; giving a new title to the topic; or even singing the refrain of a song incorporated in the report. In short, reporting, as interpreted here, is purposeful and reciprocal.

SOCIAL MOTIVATION OF LEARNING SKILLS

From these instances it is premised that motivation for reporting in the social studies is deeply rooted in children's social behavior. Frequently this drive is channelled into committee activity. Not only do individuals explore and communicate; they also work as group members with clear-cut responsibilities. Interaction within a committee provides further social stimulus for an activity which reaches out to the whole class or to the school, to the local hospital, or to the world-wide Red Cross.

Social motivation for the intellectual performance of reading and research is observed also in the infectious curiosity communicated from child to child. One boy's enthusiasm about great astronomers starts others in the same direction, branching over perhaps to a study of several constellations, to solar energy, or to making telescopes. Intellectual curiosity engenders intellectual curiosity among eager children who have some of the means of discovery at their disposal.

Social motivation for co-ordinating research and reporting is observed in plans resulting from a committee's presentation of the data they have found. A third grade studied changes in air transportation. They found the world closely brought together as they reported on latest jet speed-records. Each child chose one inventor or one kind of plane to study. Inevitably many found information for other searchers. Three children announced that their pilot fathers could arrange a trip to the International Airport, somewhat more distant than the local airport which handles continental transportation. Travel to and from the airport necessitated a change in school-bus schedules, letters of permission to and from parents, and numerous other adjustments in social living. Nearness to foreign countries became even more vivid after seeing and talking one day to pilots on Long Island who would be in Europe or Africa the next day. In this enterprise the social motivation was inextricably related to the intellectual gains and to the emotional milieu.

PERSONAL MOTIVATION OF LEARNING SKILLS

The individual, too, is enhanced as he projects himself through activities which affect his companions. A child feels power as he holds a group's attention to each detail of how his Roman trireme works or to the illustrated map of how Indian trails crisscrossed the hills around his school. Finding one's way in an ever enlarging, ever contracting world; relating bits of known experience and previous satisfactions with new findings in biography, travel stories, or textbooks fortifies the growing child. Acculturation is one of the strongest drives of childhood, particularly rapid in the period before adolescence. Self-development through reading, studying maps, exhibits, museum collections, and objects of many kinds; through trips to factories, piers, farms, fisheries; through the interviewing of people who *know* and *do* the special things under study—these are some of the ways the individual senses his strength and feels adequate. Coming into equable relations with the culture helps the young person to maintain selfhood. Individual entity is re-enforced by group inter-action.

In social-studies learnings as thus sketched, communication is the key process. Everyone knows how hard it is for children to learn to keep a secret. This homely observation is one clue to the motivation of social-studies reporting and the series of learnings sparked by the communication process. Social-studies content concerns man as a social being. Ways of learning in this discipline must challenge children's social potential as well as their individual resources. Social-individual reciprocity is as essential for optimum academic growth as it is natural to children's behavior. In this chapter an effort will be made to present techniques of stimulus and guidance which seem productive of a high quality of reading, reporting, and research in social-studies programs.

Relation of Learning Skills to Communication in Society

The learning processes of reading, research, and reporting, as carried on in dynamic classrooms parallel the use of these processes in society generally. Frontier research, whether in the science laboratory or in social services, is constantly served by reading many kinds of related material, both primary and secondary, and by recording current phenomena. Reporting to society at large goes on in varied ways through the newspaper, magazines, books, movies, and other mass media. True, the careful investigator prefers to delay reporting to any large section of the public until his results are verified. Children, however, need to report to a small audience at almost every step of the way. It might also be observed that the adult investigator reports informally to family and close co-workers upon hunches and hopes, long before completion of his study. Archimedes' announcement of the law of displacement did not wait for a formally assembled audience, it may be remembered!

Satisfactions stemming from the approval of one's peers give powerful impetus to children's driving further into the unknown. Coupled with intuitive curiosity this group motivation can be used to fire considerable attainment. Some children particularly need the assurance which comes from holding a group attentive to every word and sketch of a well-illustrated "lecture." Others need the fortification or teamwork such as is found in a play or carefully prepared panel. The shy child who is able to bring a neighbor to school to show his slides on the Swiss Alps projects himself through this experience. He feels good as a contributor to class affairs. Both intellectual and personal growth can be enhanced through vigorous and productive communication in social-studies programs.

One of the significant developments of the twentieth century is the application of scientific method to social phenomena. This process poses particular difficulties for children. With their eagerness to find out for themselves and to tell their discoveries, children often do violence to scientific objectivity. An impression is given as fact, a single observation is reported as a general truth. This immature responsiveness needs tactful guidance. A reservoir of help lies in the wisdom of the group. Almost any single experience reported by a child has been experienced by another. Differences of interpretation should be prized rather than discarded as inconvenient. In addition to evaluating similar experiences, teachers draw upon other techniques in relating children's immature communications to scientific procedure. Teams of children work together to collect paper for a Red Cross drive, to get opinions as to the best place for a bicycle rack, to give a really accurate account from reading and from questioning adults as to how UNESCO operates in providing needed help for certain new schools in Asia. Team members challenge one another's opinions and observations often with such vigor that adult moderation must intrude. But differing talents on a team illustrate one of the techniques of arriving at clarity, sometimes at objectivity.

In studying the ice age and the results of glaciation, a fifth-grade group raised many questions which could not be conclusively answered with present knowledge. Will there ever be another glacier covering this town? If a glacier like the one in Greenland could be dynamited and dissolved would it form again? Did the animals who were trapped in ice know what was happening to them? Precise answers to these conjectural questions were seen to be impossible. "Maybe we'll know someday, but we don't now." "This is the best idea people have about it, but no one can prove he's right." These were statements which summed up a healthy state of suspended judgment. Waiting for further data in the case of these dramatic curiosities could be vividly sensed. Application of this scientific attitude to other problems will have at least some foundation in experience. Experiments in science, in plant growth, evaporation, conductors and nonconductors also help to strengthen respect for the steps of gathering all available data and of testing a conclusion before making pronouncements. Thus do related disciplines contribute to understanding and to effective use of scientific method. Thus do adult and juvenile worlds come into mutual understanding.

PROBLEMS OF SPECIAL IMPORTANCE TO READING

THE NATURE OF READING MATERIALS IN THE SOCIAL STUDIES

Reading in the social studies shares with other reading the problem of drawing upon a reservoir of concepts which illuminate the mere words. One of the reasons the modern elementary school finds science-reading, both factual and pseudo-science material, so highly popular with children is that reality behind the words is so often discerned by the children. The data are tangible, in many cases, or close enough to sight, touch, and sound as presented by pictures, radio, and television, that only a little extension of the vicarious experience is necessary to bring the words to life. In social studies many abstractions and generalizations are likely to be found in the reading material, particularly in textbooks and in general references. Eskridge found children quite unable to form accurate concepts for geographic terms from reading alone, even from the reading of several texts.[2] He found that meanings were adaptations which must emerge from firsthand experience and its clarification.

[2] Thomas J. Eskridge, Jr., "Growth in Understanding of Geographic Terms in Grades IV-VII," *Research Studies in Education*. Durham, North Carolina: Duke University Press, 1939.

The experience of sensitive teachers has long substantiated this conclusion. Except as meanings are developed through multiple sensory experiences and shaped into ideas through expression and use, they are not available when the individual faces visual symbols. Even though words may often be rendered orally, the appropriate meaning may be absent. Hence, the intellectual importance of a wealth of learning media for both the primary-school pupil and for the intermediate-grade pupil whose important reading task is the extension and refinement of meanings in reading.

DEVELOPING SELECTIVE, CRITICAL READING

A second task of importance to reading in the social-studies program is that of learning to read selectively and critically. Too often this goal is disposed of through the assignment of certain pages to find the answers to given questions. Gans discovered that children do not hold assigned questions in mind beyond the fifth paragraph of assigned reading.[3]

The most fruitful procedures used at present to avoid this dilemma are exemplified in the realistic preparation for reading which some teachers provide their pupils. One class, embarking upon a study of machines and their service to people, brought to school many toys which were machines in miniature. Steam engines, a machine gun, model tractors, jeeps, trucks, model cars, and planes threatened to overcrowd the shelves set aside for them. Books about machines and inventors were collected. Their teacher read to them from a number of books and pamphlets of the work these machines could do and also of their displacement of workers and the safety problems they brought in their wake. A science teacher came to talk about the basic machines found in many of the complex mechanical toys in the collection. This exploration of the subject was not merely an intellectual preparation; attitudes and feelings were stirred, and ethical notions of human welfare were shown to have some relationship to physics. The tremendous scope of the study began to become apparent. Individual choices of activity and committee responsibilities could be intelligently planned.

From such background of information and concern for people and change, many different leads emerged. Some children became excited over the importance of the wheel. Who first made a wheel? Is a big wheel stronger than a little one made of the same material? Who thought of cogwheels and of getting cogwheels of different sizes to work together as gears? Is there any special number of spokes in a wheel, or can you put in any number? Are inventors still figuring out new jobs for wheels? In

[3] Roma Gans, *A Study of Critical Reading Comprehension in the Intermediate Grades.* Teachers College Contributions to Education, No. 811. New York: Bureau of Publications, Teachers College, Columbia University, 1940.

this study, as is so often true, the teacher knew when the class was really gripped by interest in machines. Questions became specific, pointed, insistent. The child's natural quest for details showed through.

When these children began to comb their bookshelves and library for pertinent data, they were ready to read selectively. They really cared about what they were looking for. Each searcher was part of a big enterprise of which his contribution was a discrete part. Continuing to use pictures and objects, they built further meanings from non-book sources and checked their readings against them. Finding vague statements led to questioning as to whether the author knew what he was writing about, and from this stemmed an important lesson in questioning whether the authors of a particular book were authorities.

Settling the matter of authoritative sources is difficult for elementary-school children. Perhaps only a beginning can be made, but even that beginning is important. Pointing out obvious discrepancies between two textbook accounts can be merely confusing, or it can be done in such a way as to build appreciation for the difficulty of getting and giving data accurately. Children who have themselves tried to find and tell what really happened in some skirmish on the playground or in adults' selection of a near-by factory site may understand both the difficulty and the obligation to report as honestly as one can with the facts one can get. Opening up the problem and seeing how carefully certain authors work to get their material may be as far as the elementary-school teacher need go. Certainly debunking and devaluating everything in print is to be avoided. So, too, is reverence for everything in print, even in school textbooks.

Beyond the child's intellectual difficulty in reconciling differing accounts of the same facts or conditions lies the emotional challenge to his assurance about reality. Concern for a child's security is warranted, of course, in the social studies as in other learnings, but overprotection lies woefully close to such concern. For many children, zest for discovery finds its own reward in considering conflicting data. For some, there is evident glee in learning that adults do not know everything, and this extends to the adults who wrote books which reveal opposing evidence. Others soberly accept uncertainty when a mature, man-to-man approach characterizes the teacher's relationships with them. To live in a realm of on-going discovery and reappraisal may offer no particular hardships to many children who begin to sense that adults live always with uncertainty in many areas of their lives. For those children unable to make this step of growth, it is of first importance that they experience respectful patience and reliability in their elders.

USE OF A SINGLE REQUIRED TEXTBOOK

Procedures leading to selective critical reading in social studies are premised upon children's having a number of books at their disposal. Extensive reading from many sources is one of the key characteristics of the emerging program. Intensive reading and rereading of a single text-book continues in wide use, but there are few who defend it as good practice. Neither from the standpoint of getting various views of the same topic nor from the standpoint of individual differences of the learners can the use of a single text be championed.

The dangers of memoriter learning, when teaching and testing are based upon a single text, are too obvious to need exposition. The limited horizons of even the best of a single series are even more dangerous in a world society in which fluidity of population becomes ever more dramatic. More-over, the practical problem of readability imposes itself with aggravat-ing stubbornness in a one-textbook situation. Most social-studies books measure higher in readability than the average reading ability of the grades for which they are intended. There are overwhelming frustrations in using a textbook of fifth-grade readability in a fourth grade, whose range of reading capacity inevitably stretches from about second grade to eighth grade. Classes, even when supposedly homogeneous in reading ability, contain a wide range of reading power needing widely varied materials. A single social-studies textbook is usually too difficult for many and too easy for others in any classroom, thus limiting the number who can use it independently with real success.

Several uses of textbooks are illustrated in good current practice. Some teachers, in building readiness for a unit of study, try to select those ex-periences which will equip the children with concepts needed for the reading. The period of preparation already described as regards the his-tory of machines and their effect upon a man necessitated films, oral read-ing by the teacher, good stories, anecdotes, pictures, trips, maps, exhibits, and a suitable collection of books. Class use of portions of the textbook may involve scanning, listening to, or following the print while others read, examination of pictures, and raising questions. At this exploratory stage, the textbook should be only one source of information, aided by the teacher, by illustrative materials, and by related experiences.

A later use of the same textbook may be in the nature of a summary. Re-reading for a general round-up of ideas to see if the class had slighted any essentials may occupy the able readers. Some paragraphs of dubious meaning to the children may be read aloud, sentence by sentence, and analyzed in the light of pictures, stories, and other materials in the class-room. A hand-made movie on colonial settlement (sequential pictures on a roller curtain) may be edited as to sequence by reading or re-reading the textbook. A further re-reading may be necessary to cement certain ideas to be narrated with the viewing of the movie.

Organizing a study of the industrial revolution by making a timeline may well use textual scanning and careful re-reading. Reading to check the points the class understands and to list those on which they need further detail is still another use the wise teacher makes of required text-books. The slavish reciting of texts which once was the trademark of the "good" pupil has no place in a program of social studies devoted to goals of social sensitivity, responsibility, and the use of scientific methods of inquiry.

REFERENCE-READING AND NOTE-TAKING

Certain reference skills are an integral part of the social-studies curriculum. How to locate topics in an index, in reference books, or in picture or pamphlet files can be learned with considerable efficiency by elementary-school pupils. First- and second-graders are shown the tables of contents and indexes of some books. They play with and read picture dictionaries and are led to deduce how they are arranged. They make a spelling dictionary in which to locate some words they need. They are shown how books are arranged on a library shelf. Quite a few second-graders can go along a library shelf to find the "S" authors to locate their beloved Dr. Seuss. Third-graders see how an encyclopedia is arranged and shelved and can follow the teacher's explanation of how he finds the right volume for *electricity* and *Indians*. As able readers catch on, they, too, can explain how they find topics and often guide the finding process for those who have difficulty in deciding upon clue words.

The kinds of reference-reading already sketched in this chapter embrace two purposes: the exploration of general components of a new topic and the selection of specifics for some clearly focused purpose. Involved as these goals are with reporting to a group and with solving practical local problems, the skill of note-taking becomes immediately important. Note-taking, along with study-type reading, presents an integration of skills which needs careful diagnostic teaching. To proceed too rapidly or too slowly risks learning losses.

The sequence of skills which some good elementary-school teachers seek to develop in note-taking may be outlined as follows:

Kindergarten. Picture-drawing to show the facts or ideas to be presented. Block building, sand, clay, or other representation. Teacher is asked to label salient parts.

Grades I and II. Picture drawing; child dictates title or descriptive labels; teacher writes; child shows and reads. Child finds sentence or passage pertinent to class or individual question or interest; puts marker in books; reads at appropriate time to class; leads discussion. Child formulates appropriate labels for drawing or exhibit.

Individual dictates a sentence based upon observation and reading; teacher writes. As writing-skill warrants, the child copies in his own handwriting.

Grades III and IV. More complex representations: replica, model, picture, diagram, illustrated map. More complex labeling of parts, asking teacher for help with spelling. Individuals or group dictate phrase memoranda or sentences based upon observation or reading; pupil copies appropriate dictated memoranda for his report.

Child tells about reading or observation in conference with teacher who makes brief memoranda of sequence; child and teacher interpret memoranda; child uses them in report to class.

Child locates pertinent reading material, reads with no notation, re-reads until he is sure of ideas (two or more times); puts page marker in book for reference if needed; talks informally to small group.

Child copies phrase or sentence from reference, giving exact number, size, comparison, or other precise data; records book title and page.

Grades V and VI. All of the above techniques of note-taking with more complex materials and more elaborate labeling.

Children are urged to take no notes during the first reading, to read as many times as needed to get the ideas so as to minimize note-taking labor.

Copy exact sentences or phrases, giving author, title, pages.

Group or class exercises in note-taking. Locate pages using index. Cite goal—what to find out. Scan pages to see if passage is pertinent. Read pertinent passage for general sequence. Re-read two or more times to choose "remembering clues." Discuss different ways of phrasing clues; point out individual differences in choice of clues. Value individuality; use "broken" phrases. Recheck findings with goal. Emphasize crediting source: author, title, publisher, page. For children who write laboriously, accept abbreviations for bibliographical citations. Note that handwriting quality differs with purpose; notes must be readable by the writer, not necessarily by another.

Individual application of general techniques taught to class. Necessary to provide opportunity for child to tell clues often before writing them. Oral step needed to clarify and to select. Illustrate dangers of superficial reading and too lengthy note-writing. Emphasize economy of effort. Able sixth-graders learn to use *Reader's Guide,* card index, to take brief notes to recall whole passage.

THE LIBRARY IN RELATION TO THE SOCIAL-STUDIES PROGRAM

The reading aspect of the social-studies program can be carried on with richness herein assumed only if the school library is well stocked and readily available to children many hours a day. The growth of elementary-school libraries in the past two decades is most heartening. Both fact and fiction, in a great range of readability and covering a wide scope of classifications, are needed to reward the out-reach of even a moderate-sized pupil population. Just how large a library is needed by a school of five hundred or a thousand children is, of course, undetermined. Conservatively viewed, such a library should be at least as large as for an equal number of highly literate adults.

Reference skills are a part of library teaching in many schools. Both the librarian and the classroom teacher share responsibility for teaching the techniques of using card indexes, encyclopedias, and for finding books according to the shelving plan used. Periodicals and their storage and use are, likewise, the subject of library teaching though only a few children are found to be able to use the *Readers' Guide*, even in late sixth grade. Alphabetized picture files and film slides are housed in the library in many schools, and their use, too, is a reference skill of considerable import.

Special services are rendered by the library to classes embarking on a topic of study. Often a committee of children confer with the librarian about a forthcoming study of medieval castle-life, requesting that a shelf or table be set aside for their class to use in the library and that a selection of books for heavy-duty use in the classroom be charged to the class.

The community library is likewise used as a resource for class and individual visits and for special loans. Schools and communities having no local libraries can often borrow them from their state traveling libraries.[4]

So important is this matter of adequate resources for wide and selective reading that it might fairly be said that where there is no good library for children's use the social-studies program cannot reach its full potential.

FICTION READING IN THE SOCIAL-STUDIES PROGRAM

The conflict over values of the historical novel or fictionalized biography in adult education applies in some measure to children's reading. Accurate presentation is essential in the selection of fiction for children, but more than accuracy of facts is involved. The task of helping children to personalize the data of social studies is perhaps best assumed by good fiction either in books or on the screen. Identification is essential to the building of sympathy with a people, whether of another area or another era. In fiction reading this identification with a hero or heroine not only assists the reader's vicariously entering into the life and struggle and feeling of the character but this kinship with book *dramatis personae* also quickens the sense of social drama in which the identification takes place. Questions

---

[4] See Lucy Tomkins, "Where To Get Books for Fairs and Exhibits," *Junior Libraries*, I (September 15, 1954), 40–45.

about point of view, about how people live, about their values, and about their economic standards and problems are inevitable.

One of the functions which textbooks can assume only in part is to supply sufficient concrete detail for children to generalize adequately. It is here that trade books fill an important niche. Details of dress, of speech, of customs, details of family life and community interaction—these and other mores woven into narrative structure give the young imagination some of the sustenance needed for projective imagination and the eventual residue of general, organized concepts.

Never before—and this is no idle superlative—has there been such a wealth of literature for children and teachers to choose from in books related to social studies. Each year since the mid-century, publishers and authors have produced approximately a thousand new titles and a respectable list of reprintings. In almost every social-studies area children's literature offers some of its riches. In some communities little of this wealth is available; in others much is at hand from which to choose. The more limited the budget the more selective must the buyer become.

Probably the first criterion for selection of any book in social studies is the author's qualifications. Ann Petry studied minutely the background from which she wrote the story of the triumphant slave, *Harriet Tubman*, and ends each chapter with some of the supporting evidence. Marguerite De Angeli went to Scotland to reaffirm certain details before completing *The Door in the Wall*. A brief biographical statement about modern juvenile authors may serve as a beginning point in the search for authors' qualifications.[5]

A second criterion for selecting books is the clarity with which the book tells it story. Librarians' opinion can be sampled from *Junior Libraries* and from many magazines and newspapers. Juvenile opinion can be had from *Junior Reviewers*.[6] Even more desirable is the practice of seeking direct reactions from children locally. Committees can help make selections in several ways: by reading borrowed books from town libraries, by scanning books at book fairs and exhibits, by examining reviews and advertising material. Clearly, adult guidance is needed in any such co-operative scheme.

The extent to which illustration adds to the story in an aesthetic manner appropriate to the text is a third criterion. It is not to be assumed that the most copiously illustrated book is necessarily the best, nor that the most colorful one will add most to the children's understanding. Color undoubtedly appeals to children but so, too, does black and white illustra-

[5] *Junior Book of Authors*. Edited by S. J. Kunitz and H. Haycraft. New York: H. W. Wilson Co., 1951.

[6] *Junior Reviewers*. Edited by William E. Dennen, 11 Easton Court, Wellesley Hills 82, Massachusetts.

tion. When the appeal of vitality is also considered, the question of color falls into reasonable proportion.

Other criteria exist, of course. Both staff and pupils may share in the statement of standards for book purchase and selection for given purposes. This gradual development of book standards should become itself a goal of teaching social studies.

KINDS OF RESEARCH IN ELEMENTARY SCHOOLS

MATERIALS AND ACTIVITIES RECOMMENDED

A good modern classroom contains much more than textbooks and writing equipment. It also contains many other books, both of fact and fiction, and at least a few juvenile or adult periodicals, some of them copiously illustrated. Further, a schoolroom today contains still other materials not seen in classrooms in times past: clay, wood, paint, and crayons; a costume box; a science center; a puppet stage; bulletin boards listing plans for study, for trips, and for holidays as well as charts, maps, graphs, and other visual records of children's interests and of their work. Evidence abounds in some modern classes that the pupils are learning from the world beyond the school walls. Evidence abounds that children are relating their in-school learnings with community-wide learnings and that they use a host of learning sources both in and out of school. Many of these learning activities are truly research activities as previously defined. They are carried on in a true spirit of inquiry using firsthand sources or those deemed most authentic; evidence is weighed and checked in several ways. In best modern practice, both in primary and later grades, children are encouraged to check one book with another and to compare book accounts with known facts or with firsthand experience whenever possible.

RESEARCH IN PRIMARY GRADES

Beginning reading is presently taught in a fashion conducive to testing the truth of written symbols against the facts they symbolize. The experience chart, stemming as it does from firsthand and usually objective experience, provides every child some measure of participation in the reading process, broadly conceived. Even the child who cannot remember printed words can report that the bunny, subject of an interesting observation and written record, has five toes on each forepaw or that the young bunnies do not open their eyes until they are twelve days old. Rewarding curiosity tends to nurture interests for further pursuit. Physical proximity of the material or the experience to its printed representation may be said to characterize good beginning instruction. The nature of such reading instruction carries many implications for elementary research.

Further than this matter of reading method, research potentialities abound for primary children. A study of the school, its workers, and its operation, offers dozens of opportunities for firsthand research. How many rooms are in our hall? How many children come to school by bus? What does our principal do? What does our school nurse do? Who keeps our building clean and warm? How do they do it? Who cooks for our cafeteria? Where do they get the food they cook? Answering these juvenile queries necessitates interviewing the persons who know and do; counting real things, questioning, and many kinds of observation.

A study of travel, frequently a part of primary curriculum, calls upon the firsthand experiences of children as well as those of friends and family. Trips to local bus terminals, railroad yards, and airports offer research opportunities to beginners of varying levels of maturity. Questions are planned for such excursions; other questions arise spontaneously at the scene of study. What does the Diesel engine use to make it go? Is it hard to keep it on the track? How much does a Diesel cost? Where was this one built? This range of curiosity is typical of the questions asked by first- and second-graders. The engineer or other persons assigned to conduct a group on an inspection tour is usually the authority whose word is accepted. Sketches made of the unique shape of the wheel rim, of the smokestack, or of the front of the new locomotive suffice as records of particular observations. Later research might necessitate the careful study of photographs or diagrams of Diesels.

Watching the local policeman direct traffic may be a research activity of true significance to a committee helping with a class study of safety. How does the officer signal cars to stop? How does he signal them to go ahead? Who should be listed on the school "Safety Honors" list? What does the policeman do if the driver doesn't stop when he is told to? How many children did the officer help from the time he went out to watch until we came in? How long a time was this? Second- or third-graders, whether able to read or not, carry on research of genuine vitality in social-studies projects focused upon problem-solving activities.

Of special interest in home-school relations is the kind of research children are asked to carry on at home. How many things did we buy at the supermarket this week that were made in our town? How many people work in the supermarket or in the bakery? What kinds of work do our own fathers and mothers do? Who is the oldest person in our house or in our neighborhood who can remember the first electric lights or the first buses in our town? Such questions, which are only a sample of those growing from the curiosity of an average group of pupils, use the home and community as laboratory resources for young children. However, they have another merit here. They open to children three kinds of research:

firsthand observation in a real laboratory, inquiry of authorities in their field of special knowledge, and classification of data in order to arrive at tentative answers. These activities have intrinsic validity as research procedures. They also mesh with purposeful reading and give support to meanings imprisoned by the written symbols.

RESEARCH ACTIVITIES OF ABLE READERS IN INTERMEDIATE GRADES

Able readers in later primary grades and in the middle grades continue all three of these research activities as, indeed, does the adult research student. In addition, the reader extends his research into the realm of symbols. "It says here . . ." is often the introduction to printed proof of some disputed point. The gleam of discovery shines in the eyes of the investigator who tracks down a good account of how patiently the burro serves the prospector who owns him. Research reading for the elementary-school pupil is likely to begin with the location of pertinent material about the question in which he is genuinely interested. Specific purposes may vary widely, but the factor of curiosity is of prime and common importance. Without this *zeal to find out,* no true research is likely to occur. With this zest for discovery, which can be fanned by enthusiastic teaching, by vigorous and frequent class-sharing, and by the use of firsthand materials, the intermediate-grade pupil uses reading as a productive research tool. The element of search vitalizes the reading process as it vitalizes much of human endeavor.

Materials abound for the research reader. Texts and references may serve as general guides into a new territory for the able child. They may more often yield help as a summary of varied learnings by average readers and sometimes by a whole class. In addition, children also need diaries, records, and statistical data; they need almanacs, dictionaries, biographies, and historical fiction. But the motivation which carries the worker through his sometimes-arduous pursuits must be constantly re-fired through face-to-face contacts. The enthusiastic teacher and curious and appreciative peers seem, in most classes, to stir this renewal of energy.

Some primary sources offer considerable difficulty to all but the most gifted readers in intermediate grades. The journals of Sergeant Ordway fascinated many children in one sixth grade which was studying the Lewis and Clark expedition. Excerpts were read aloud; only a few were able to read independently from this important source. Here is a challenge for gifted readers whose skill can take them far and wide. Studying rainfall data from the appendix of a good atlas in order to compare certain jungle conditions with rainfall "at home" necessitated careful guidance for another class in order to avoid shallow verbalism. Recalling earlier trips to the weather bureau, visiting another class to study the rain gauge they had made, and making accurate recordings of local rainfall for a month were activities which gave substance to the facts of rainfall in the jungles of the Amazon.

Elementary-school children can make only a beginning in learning to draw conclusions from firsthand data, whether those data be statistics, photographs, tape recordings, on-the-spot annotations, sketches, movies, or diaries. This beginning, however, is not only an important research skill but it also adds immeasurably to children's appreciation and intellectual curiosity—requisite ingredients of sound social participation.

RESEARCH FOR THE RETARDED READER IN INTERMEDIATE GRADES

Research processes such as those already sketched offer challenge and opportunity to the intermediate-grade youngster who has difficulty in reading. Of these activities, the more concrete examples hold the greater potential. Seeing, asking, making some pieces of apparatus for gathering data, and compiling simple records are possible even to the limited reader. One group studying rubber and its place in present-day life found that many research activities were needed for their work. Some of these activities required complex reading skills. Others were of the simplest order: In how many ways does this school use rubber? How much do different sizes of rubber tires cost? Do the rubber trees that people grow in their house have real latex in them? Coupled with the activities illustrating various stages of the gathering of latex and the refining of rubber—making diagrams, setting up an exhibit of local uses of rubber, coloring maps to show rubber-producing regions—these research activities not only employed the poor readers happily but these very children made contributions to the work of the entire class. They gained in status because they, too, worked on some activities shared by all the class and on some which were their special responsibility.

TECHNIQUES OF REPORTING IN SOCIAL STUDIES

PLANNING REPORTING ACTIVITIES

Organizing class instruction for individual or committee reporting in the social studies has to a large extent supplanted the question-and-answer recitation. Values usually cited for the newer focus are those of richer social interaction, increased responsibility and satisfaction for the reporter, accommodation of individual differences, and a closer parallel to out-of-school procedures. When well planned and skillfully guided, many of these values undoubtedly emerge. However, hearing a mechanical reproduction of shallow information from a fellow classmate results in no richer learnings than from traditional lecturing or catechetical quizzing.

Thorough preparation of both reporter and audience are essential if pupil reporting is to rise to any greater heights than did the memorized recitation or any of the methods now rather generally derided. Another caution, besides that of detailed preparation and varied illustrative materials, is that of length of time allotted for reporting. Reporting beyond the listening durability of the class is obviously wasteful. Length of time alone is not the decisive factor, however. Occasionally a single reporter can hold a group profitably for twenty minutes or even longer, but this is rare. If reports are brief and similar in substance and supporting illustration, only a few should be scheduled for one day. Both teacher and pupils need to be on guard against long-winded, dull reporting.

There are many styles from which to choose when a class is planning social-studies reports. The kind of material to be shared as well as the special talents of the reporter and interests of the audience determine the choices. Some of these forms of juvenile communication have been referred to in the selection on notetaking.

Oral narration or description *using a picture* or series of pictures as a guide appears as a frequent kind of reporting in the social studies. Pictures made by the reporter for the purpose must be large enough for the audience to see at normal distances. Labels and titles are usually needed. Pictures may be shown from texts, references, or other books; from magazines and other ephemeral sources. They should be arranged in sequence if they can be seen while the narrator points out items of interest or asks questions. A small desk or table for the speaker is helpful. Often a partner is needed to hold and manipulate large illustrations. Slides, either professionally made or child-made, or pictures shown on an opaque projector, need the same safeguards as to timing, sequence, and visibility for all. The handmade box-and-roller "movie" offers the same necessities of oral preparation and manipulation by an assistant.

Dramatization, from the simple acting out of signals of the traffic officer to the carefully prepared play depicting the Olympic games, offers varied and purposeful forms of reporting. For informal plays in the classroom few properties are needed. An announcer, a listing of scenes on the blackboard, and only ordinary classroom appurtenances are needed. A play is sometimes prepared by a committee and shared with the class the same day. Others are carefully developed from original documents and worked out with considerable accuracy as to language forms, costumes, and scenery. An example of the latter type is the enactment of a portion of the Constitutional Convention by a sixth grade. Examples of the former sort are manifold: a "lesson" in a colonial school, loading bananas on a boat at a pier as the inspector watches, or Columbus' landing and taking possession of San Salvador.

Often a brief bit of dramatization may be part of a lengthier oral report. Sometimes a dramatized incident may introduce a report, either having an announcer take the lead in interpreting it or having the audience interpret and ask questions which are answered by the dramatizing committee. Considering children's natural propensities for dramatization and its efficacy in learning, there should be much more opportunity for reporting through many kinds of classroom plays.

Question-and-answer panels are a form of reporting now familiar to children through radio and television programs. They may be arranged in many ways. Usually the children should sit around a table with the moderator in a central position. For children in the primary grades it is often helpful for the chairman to have the questions printed on paper large enough for the audience to see. Panelists may answer the questions orally. In preparing for a presentation to another class or to parents, the teacher may write children's answers from their dictation, help them with corrections, and write the responses large enough for all to see. This kind of panel obviously shares newly gained reading skills which, for primary-grade pupils, are a source of genuine pride. Spontaneous discussion supplements the reading framework. For older children, oral discussion is, of course, preferable. In either case, panels need to prepare and rehearse their questions, the sequence of events, and their cues. Unless well prepared, though not memorized, a panel discussion or question-answer presentation is usually a total waste of audience time.

Demonstration procedures with models, exhibits, costumes, and the like offer interesting ways of reporting. Audience attention is usually easier to focus when material objects are present. A borrowed candle-mold, a Viking ship model, and a set of dolls and flags representing members of the United Nations are only three of thousands of possibilities. Preparation by the reporter involves the best ways of displaying the material as well as his sequence of explanatory details. Telling and showing a committee first is a good practice-procedure.

Narration from notes is one of the more mature kinds of reporting which some fourth-grade pupils and older children learn to handle effectively. After research and study, assembling the data in some kind of order usually requires "talking it out" with someone. In the beginning the teacher makes notes as the child tells, then helps him see the outline as a guide to what he has said. He then uses this guide in presenting his information to the class.

As children develop more power in writing they may make notes in simplified outline form. Usually a great deal of teacher assistance is needed in this step of generalizing. Telling the teacher what one wants to say and co-operatively deciding upon a "remembering word" or a topic to use in one's outline remains a necessary process for most elementary-school children. Group exercises in making simple outline guides are sometimes helpful, but many children will need additional help when they attempt to apply these techniques to materials they have collected individually.

Written reports can be shared with a group by display or by reading aloud, or both. In either case, illustrative material is needed both for clarity and for stimulating varied interests. Practice in reading a written report is sharpened in efficiency by working with a partner. Partners read their reports to each other, correct sentences which may not be clear, alternate in holding illustrations or demonstrating with models or other objects. Smooth, effective oral reading to the class is a requisite for holding class interest. Practice for this occasion should be as definitely planned as any other teaching activity.

Bulletin-board displays of written reports can follow oral reading or can, at times, substitute for reading a report. Along with illustrations, maps, charts, or three-dimensional exhibits, a bulletin board display in hall or classroom serves to unify fragmentary learnings and to bring personal satisfaction to individuals or group. Occasionally it is helpful for older children to mount a series of reports so as to show original "rough" notes, the writer's outline-plan made with his teacher, his first draft of the written report, and the final, carefully copied product. This serves to show the many steps necessary in gathering data, organizing them, writing, correcting, and presenting the final form. Learning these techniques is essential in other disciplines as well as in social studies. Seeing the steps in graphic form, after their completion, is not only personally gratifying to the reporter at the moment but also solidifies these learnings for future reporting in new areas.

Written reports themselves take many forms. They may be exposition, outline, question-and-answer, or narrative-cartoon style. They may be bound in booklets or collected in a large book for class display or in more conventional size for the library. Portfolios are excellent for the preservation of notes, clippings, pictures, and brief written statements. A written report can capture the inventiveness of many children in its format as well as in its challenging message.

INDIVIDUAL AND AUDIENCE INTERACTION

Preparing the audience for effective listening is an obligation of the reporter and of the teacher. Building a common background of interests should go on throughout any major study. When a class has reached the stage of a study in which everyone, or almost everyone, is preparing to report on his own special interest, the group needs some unifying experience which may also lead to eager listening later on. Almost everyday there should be a brief time for sharing highlights. Asking if others have found "anything good" on the earliest kind of oil lamps or latest uses of solar heat often brings direct help as well as increased interest in the report to which one has made a small contribution. Posting pictures with captions or questions before one's report is finished is another helpful technique. So, too, is a request for certain materials on a "Help Wanted" bulletin board, such as a recipe for making soap or an appointment with someone who has worked as a forest ranger. A sense of mutuality and the cultivation of informed interest both result from this day-to-day sharing of progress and difficulty. It is doubtful whether any genuine interest in a report, no matter who gives it, is likely unless the audience possesses considerable pertinent information and lively concern.

Before a particular report of any length, the audience should have earlier related experiences brought briefly into focus and should have time to get physically comfortable and within hearing and seeing distance. The reporter himself must learn to use some techniques to capture audience interest in the beginning. These may be a pungent quotation, an anecdote, a good picture, or a placard hinting at some surprise bit to look for in the report to come. The initial stimulus may consist of asking the audience to answer some question or to perform some activity involving the subject upon which the reporter is to expound, such as jotting down guesses for the number of people who work in the local power plant or naming three things in the classroom made of steel.

In addition to preparing and goading the audience to react, reporters need to learn to sense audience interest. This seems very difficult for children who want the ego-satisfaction of enjoying the limelight, even if they have lost their audience. Sometimes the teacher must step in, ask a question or point out some graphic detail, and suggest that the reporter skip over to the part of his report where action holds interest. However, getting and using varied materials and careful preparation for reporting should preclude many such failures, else real damage is done. In group teaching, analysis should be made of those factors which hold interest. In individual or committee planning, each report should be checked in advance for interesting components as well as variety and length. Indeed, at every step of the way in developing reports, the teacher needs to remember that the dual purpose of reporting embraces both reporter and the entire audience.

The number of forms of reporting available for children allow ample latitude for the shy child who needs to fortify himself with a planned progression of pictures, demonstrations, or specific contributions in a panel or "movie" serial. The verbose individual can be held in check by trying out his report with a partner, timing it, and cutting it as needed. The use of pictures or written notes can help further to hold the marathon talker to his subject. Occasionally the teacher will have to give a warning that only a few minutes more can be used and save face for the youngster by asking him to arrange his report and materials for visual display.

Of equal importance with building active audience interest is the follow-up discussion. In some classes the child immediately asks for comments and questions after his report. Where children have been schooled to look for constructive leads and to be positive in their reactions, this is most desirable. Sometimes questions open up new areas for study or give the reporter another chance to clarify a foggy point. Comments may bring in related ideas or experiences which help to tie up the new learnings to other centers of interest. In any case, both relatedness and clarity should be the goals of such follow-up discussion. Never should it degenerate to fault-finding. It takes no skill to say, "Johnny used too many 'ands.'" Careful assimilation and preparation often prevent repetitive "ands." In any case, public denunciation does not cure the ill. Because time pressures are always insistent, some teachers limit comments to two or three for each report. More can be accomplished at times by reserving discussion until several related reports have been completed.

VALUES OF ORGANIZING AND PRESENTING REPORTS

One does not know for sure whether a boat will float until it is put into water. A report has not achieved its destiny until it is communicated. Testing the clarity of a report can only be done by the audience. In this sense, reporting to an audience is an evaluating procedure. The quality of questions, the degree of interest, the comprehension of the listening group tell how the worker has succeeded. After a series of reports, outstanding techniques may be noted, clear illustrations pointed up, forceful statements of ideas recalled. In this way both individual satisfaction can be assured and a more impersonal evaluation of technique achieved.

Another learning which stems from organizing written or oral reports is the intellectual one of unifying the fragmentary learnings which are inevitable in the unevenness of normal growth. To be available for future use, learnings must be related, organized, evaluated. Academic as this seems, it is a natural part of children's constant urge to do and to tell. Teaching reporting with reference to both individual and social growth becomes part of an unbroken chain, using old learnings to plan new ventures. The cycle is continuous and dynamic.

31. Patterns of Writing in Different Subject Areas

Nila Banton Smith

PART I

The need for making adjustments when reading subject-matter in the different content fields is a fairly recent concept insofar as the history of reading is concerned. It was about 1940 when the first investigations began to come through in regard to reading in the content fields. Since that time such investigations have continued in ever-increasing volume. Still we are in the midst of a period of discovery.

The present article reports one additional attempt to obtain information concerning special reading needs in different subject areas. Part I in this issue of THE JOURNAL OF READING deals especially with literature and science. Part II, which will appear in the ensuing issue, deals with social studies and mathematics.

AN ANALYSIS OF TEXTBOOK CONTENT

The cue for an analysis of textbook content in science, social studies, and mathematics arose from an awareness of different patterns of writing in literature. It was hypothized that there might also be special patterns of writing in the content of other subject fields. It was thought that if this were true and these specialized patterns could be detected and labelled, this information would be helpful to teachers in aiding their students to read subject matter in their respective teaching areas.

As analysis of text proceeded, an analysis also was made of questions, directions, explanations, and the various types of exercises that the books contained. All these aids and exercises in which the students are asked to make a response appear to be significant because they are indicative of the ways in which the subject specialist wants students to think and work with material in his particular field.

The materials analyzed embraced widely-used textbooks covering Grades 7 through 12: 52 science texts, 60 social studies texts (social studies and history), and history texts, 49 mathematics texts (advanced or commercial arithmetic, algebra, and geometry) and 45 literature texts.

In the two parts of this article only two aspects of the analysis will be reported: briefly, the one having to do with common study skills; primarily, and in greater detail, the one having to do with patterns of writing.

"Patterns of Writing in Different Subject Areas," Parts I and II, by Nila Banton Smith, *Journal of Reading*, VIII (October 1964), 31–37 and VIII (November 1964), 97–102. Reprinted with permission of Nila Banton Smith and the International Reading Association.

COMMON READING SKILLS

It requires no special analysis to reveal that regardless of whether a student is reading in literature, science, social studies, or mathematics, he must be able to pronounce the words to get meaning from printed symbols, and to use appropriate reading rates. Breaking these general skills down somewhat we have (1) word recognition, utilizing sight words, picture clues, context clues, phonics, analysis of word structure and dictionary techniques; (2) understanding meanings involving literal comprehension, interpretation, critical reading, specific word meaning; and (3) rate—making use of different speeds according to intent for reading and nature of subject matter. These skill areas are drawn upon in all kinds of reading. Since these basic skills are used in all kinds of reading, they will be referred to throughout this article as the *common reading skills*.

COMMON STUDY SKILLS

The writer considers the study skills to be those specialized skills used in study situations over, above, and in addition to the *common reading skills* employed in non-study situations. She finds it helpful to think of the reading study skills as those skills used especially in situations in which it is desired to make applications of content covered. Thus conceived, the study skills in reading may be broadly defined as those skills used when we intend to do something with content while reading it or after finishing the reading.

In high school a boy may read a sports column to find who won the game; he may read a detective story to find who stole the black diamond; he may read an article on space travel because he is intrigued with this subject. He doesn't do anything with the content in any of these cases. He isn't using study skills.

But he is using study skills when he studies his textbooks for the purpose of gathering facts or generalizations to use in class discussion, in experimentation, in making a report, in preparing a summary, in solving a problem, in getting ready to take a test.

The analysis of questions, exercises, explanations, and directions stated in the various textbooks studied, revealed that there were multiple instances in which the student was confronted with specialized situations calling for the use of study skills. Space does not permit a report of these many specialized situations. There were certain study skills, however, which occurred with high frequency in all subject fields. Hence, these will be referred to as the *common study skills*.

These *common study skills* are (1) selections and evaluation—selecting an idea, paragraph, or section of text and evaluating it in terms of its relevance, importance, contribution, or relationship to other factors; (2) organization—putting items together in a list, outline, summary or report; (3) recall—fixing in mind certain items for recall purposes; (4) location of information in textbooks, reference books and periodicals; (5) following directions for doing something with text read. Because these study skills are used with such high frequency in all subject areas, it is particularly important that secondary school teachers provide special practice for students who are deficient in the use of any one of them.

PATTERNS OF WRITING IN LITERATURE

In opening the discussion of patterns of writing, it is probably obvious but perhaps advisable to state that no special analysis is necessary in discerning patterns of writing in literature. Patterns in this field have been established for years. There are the *story* (short story or novel); *essay; drama; biography; fable;* and *poetry* of many kinds (ballad, lyric, elegiac, epic, sonnet), some written in rhymed verse, some in free verse, some in blank verse and of many different meters.

Each of these patterns requires a different approach. A student should not read a story, an essay, and a drama in the same way. His purpose is different. He reads a story to enjoy plot, character, and setting, an essay to get the slant of the author as he discusses some aspect of life, a drama to interpret the conversations of the characters involved. Drama is further differentiated in reading in that it is cast in an entirely different format. Biography and autobiography should be read not merely to follow separate chronological facts but to get a conclusive impression of the person writing it or being written about. Sometimes within the essay or biography the detailed statement-of-facts pattern appears, but this is very light as compared with this pattern which is characteristically used in science. Cause-and-effect relationships appear sometimes within typical literature patterns, but these are not prominent and usually remain for the teacher or exercises in the book to reveal.

Poetry varies widely in the purposes for which it should be read and the form in which it is written. A student certainly should not read a ballad for the same purpose and in the same way that he reads a sonnet.

As the student reads different patterns in literature for different purposes and in different forms, he must adjust his reading skills, using different combinations of skills in different situations. In general, different combinations of the *common reading skills,* with heavy emphasis upon interpretations, serve a student well in reading literature itself. However, in answering questions and carrying out assignments stated in the textbook exercises, he will have to use the *common study skills.* Thus it is that the teacher of literature has a fourfold task in reading: (1) to teach his students to identify different patterns of writing; (2) to give them help in sensing the purpose for reading each pattern and adjusting their reading skills to this pattern; (3) to give practice on any of the *common reading skills* to students who need improvement in any one of these skill areas; (4) to give special practice on any of the *common study skills* in which some students may be deficient.

PATTERNS OF WRITING IN SCIENCE

An analysis of science textbooks reveals that they, too, contain specialized patterns of writing. The science text, like all other kinds of texts, calls for the use of the *common reading skills*, and the exercises call for the use of the *common study skills*. Sometimes science writers make use of cause-and-effect text. However, it is in the social studies that this kind of text is most highly characteristic. But science does have unique science patterns which call for different approaches and different combinations of skills.

THE CLASSIFICATION PATTERN

One type of science text falls into the *classification pattern* in which living things, objects, materials, elements, gases, liquids, forces, etc., are classified under a common heading which in turn deals with sub-divisions, each of which has an element or elements in common with the other sub-classes but which vary in certain respects from one another. For example, in a chapter on "Hormones—Chemical Messengers of the Body," there is an introduction telling in general what hormones are; then follow sections of text each of which discusses a particular hormone, giving its location, name of its secretion or secretions, and their functions in the body. Under the general class known as hormones the following sub-classes are discussed: the thyroid gland, the adrenal glands, the parathyroid glands, the pancreas, the gonads, and the pituitary gland.

In reading this pattern, the student who identifies it as a classification pattern will concentrate on grasping the subdivisions and the chief characteristics of each one. In other words he will gear his reading procedure to obtaining the kind of information which is important in this particular pattern of writing.

EXPLANATION OF A TECHNICAL PROCESS

Another pattern of writing which is particularly characteristic of science, and perhaps the most difficult one to read, is the explanation of a technical process, which usually is accompanied with diagrams necessitating very careful reading of text with continuous reference to diagrams. The diagrams in themselves require special reading skills in addition to grasping the text explanations. As an example of this pattern, consider a section of text describing "How the Telephone Works." The entire process is explained and accompanied with numerous diagrams. This kind of reading requires a doubling of techniques: reading the text and reading the diagram alternately as one feeds into the other.

INSTRUCTIONS FOR AN EXPERIMENT

A third unique pattern in science is the one in which instructions are given for carrying out an experiment. This pattern consists of explicit directions that must be carried out exactly and which call for careful observations of what happens, an explanation of what happens; and the drawing of a conclusion.

> a. Obtain several strips of different metals, b. Place several different liquid solutions in glasses or jars. These might include such things as salt water, soda water, sulfuric acid, vinegar, sugar water, or other chemical materials, c. Use the voltmeter to test your different electric cells. Try all the possible combinations of metals and liquid solutions. In the same way try other materials that are not metal, d. Make a list of the different electric cells which you have tested, and write down the voltage discovered for each cell, e. What kinds of materials do you think are most useful in making electric cells? What types of materials seem to be unsuited for making electric cells?

The common study skill of following directions is used in this science pattern, but this skill isn't enough in itself. Experiments call for the plus mental activities of discriminating observation, careful explanation, and considered conclusion.

DETAILED STATEMENT-OF-FACTS PATTERN

Another pattern frequently encountered in science textbooks but not entirely unique to science is the *detailed statement-of-facts pattern*. This pattern in science differs from fact-giving text in other subjects in these respects: the facts are more dense, and they frequently embody a definition or a statement of a principle.

> The atoms of some elements exist in different forms, called *isotopes*. The nuclei of isotopes of the same element all have the same number of protons. The nuclei differ, however, in the number of neutrons they contain. Ordinary hydrogen has one proton in the nucleus. *Heavy hydrogen, or deuterium, has a nucleus containing one proton and one neutron.* This nucleus is called a *deuteron*.

In reading this pattern the student can use the usual skill of finding, first of all, the most important thought or main idea in each section of content, then proceed to find details that reinforce this statement noting particularly any definitions or principles embodied in them.

THE DESCRIPTIVE PROBLEM-SOLVING PATTERN

A science pattern which is less difficult to read is the description of a problem-solving situation which has been met through a series of experiments usually conducted by several different people. For example, a chapter on "Releasing the Atom" discusses the successive steps in discovering atomic energy and in learning how to release it. In reading this pattern, the student should approach it with the idea of finding out what each successive problem was and how it was met.

ABBREVIATIONS AND EQUATIONS

Another science pattern which requires a special kind of reading is that in which abbreviations are liberally used.

> The temperature at which water freezes is called $0°C$ or $32°F$ and fixes the ice point on the thermometer scale. The boiling point of water under a pressure of 760 mm of mercury is called $100°C$ or $212°F$ and determines the steam-point on the thermometer scale.

Grasping the meaning of the symbol $°$, and the abbreviations C, F and mm as these are integrated with words in text calls for recognition skills in addition to the usual recognition of word symbols. This pattern is still further complicated when the abbreviations are involved in equations.

MATHEMATICAL PROBLEMS

There are of course many mathematical problems in chemistry and physics books. While such problems involve specialized vocabulary and often specialized abbreviations and formulas, the problem pattern itself is not different from that used in mathematics and so will be discussed under that mathematics section of this article.

COMBINATION OF PATTERNS

A single chapter in science at the higher levels may contain several of these patterns. For example: a chapter on the atmosphere and weather starts out with light introductory material which is similar to that in a popular magazine; then suddenly it proceeds in succession to *detailed statement-of-fact, explanation of technical process, classification pattern, instructions for an experiment.*

If a student who starts to study this chapter fails to identify these different patterns and continues to use the same approach in reading all of them as he used in reading the light introductory materials, his resulting understandings and concepts of the subject discussed will undoubtedly be extremely limited.

Part II

Part I of this article dealt with patterns of writing revealed in an analysis of secondary school textbooks in literature and science. Part II discusses patterns resulting from an analysis of secondary texts in social studies and mathematics.

PATTERNS IN SOCIAL STUDIES

Picture and Map Patterns   The text in social studies books at the junior high level usually contains narrative accounts which are easy to read, and which do not represent specialized patterns as a whole. There are, however, embodied in these narrative accounts, features which call for skills peculiar to social studies content at all levels.

For one thing, a student reading social studies material of any level often encounters a direction within a paragraph or text. This direction requires him to leave the text, refer elsewhere in the textbook to gather information, then to return to the point at which he was reading in the paragraph, and to integrate the information gathered from the reference into the content of the paragraph as a whole. This reference is usually made either to a picture or a map, each of which in turn calls for the use of special reading skills.

The ability to read pictures is a skill needed in this field. At the secondary level often the text of a paragraph may be interrupted by a direction such as "Look at the picture of the Aztec temple. How do you think it was made? What transportation was Cortes using?"

In the above example, students were guided in making an interpretation and in noting a detail. In many cases the picture is presented without calling attention to details and implications. A wealth of information can be obtained from reading pictures in this subject field. Teachers might well increase their efforts to sensitize their students to the usefulness of pictures and give them practice in *reading* pictures as a valuable supplemental aid in obtaining information from the printed pages of their textbooks.

The reading of maps is a highly specialized kind of reading in the social studies area. Maps, atlases and globes require the use of such skills as recognizing and interpreting symbols for rivers, mountains, lakes, towns and cities, boundary lines, scale of miles, color keys, meridians, and symbols needed in interpreting special maps of population, products, topography, etc. The efficient use of all these symbols requires *reading* activities, and if secondary school students are deficient in any of them, no time should be lost in teaching them these skills.

The Cause and Effect Pattern   While this pattern occurs to some extent in other subject fields, it occurs with the highest frequency in social studies and history. Every major event in history comes about as the result of some cause or set of causes, and when the event happens its effect or effects are felt. Sometimes the effect of one event becomes the cause of another event. Thus it is that history is made up of a chain of causes and effects. The student who is adept in identifying the cause-and-effect pattern and who gears his reading specifically to ascertaining causes and effects will find this to be one of his most valuable assets in studying social studies and history.

Sequential Events with Dates   Another pattern specialized in history is one that presents events in specific time sequence accompanied with dates. The student should read this pattern for two purposes: (1) to grasp the larger periods or whole blocks of events in their chronological order, and (2) to fix in mind the important dates of happenings within each period or block, stopping to associate events with dates, and thinking how each event led to the next one.

There are several kinds of pencil work that students find helpful in studying this pattern. They may make a brief summary of dates and events as they read; they may fill in an outline map of the locale, marking dates and events in their appropriate locations; they may make a chart of events and dates; or they may prepare a conventional "Time Line."

The Comparison Pattern   A pattern calling for comparison of likenesses and/or differences is a common one in history and in the social studies. This pattern is most frequently encountered in a discussion of such coordinate and similar topics as differences in the theories of government, policies of different leaders, platforms of different political parties, the past and present functions of certain government agencies, and so on.

If the student is aware that he is about to read a comparison chapter or section of text he can approach it with the foremost purpose of noting likenesses and differences. Undoubtedly, such an approach will cause comparisons and contrasts to stand out in such sharp relief that both interpretation and recall will be facilitated.

Detailed Statement-of-Fact Pattern   There are sections of text in social studies and history which contain detailed facts. These sections, however, are usually included within one of the more characteristic patterns discussed above. The facts in such sections are not as dense as in this pattern in science, nor are they as technical. Too, these facts in history are more easily grasped because of their association with sequential events or with causes and effects.

The Propaganda Pattern   This pattern is one with which every student should be acquainted and one he should know how to read. Propaganda has been in existence throughout history. The astute reader can detect it in quotations from and actions of men as reported in history books, and by signs and cartoons sometimes depicted in history or social studies texts.

It is not the propaganda of the past, however, which should be our major concern. Students and teachers of the present are living in the midst of a communication network which is teeming with propaganda, and there is evidence that it will increase in volume in the years ahead. Some of this propaganda is used for good causes. More often it is misused for personal motives.

Every medium containing printed sentences or even phrases is used as a tool by the propagandist: billboards, handbills, leaflets, pamphlets as well as newspapers, magazines, and books. All these may serve this purpose. The important thing for the reader to know is how to detect the propaganda pattern so he will be aware of the intent of reading materials in which someone is trying to influence his thinking or behavior.

One of the most important things that the history teacher can do is to teach his students to recognize the propaganda pattern. It is true that propaganda can be intricate and subtle and not always easily detectable. There are, however, seven techniques which are generally considered to be basic among the tricks used by the propagandist. These tricks make use of "Glad Words" or "Glittering Generalities," "Unpleasant Words," "Transfer," "Testimonials," "Plain Folks Implications," "Band Wagon Techniques" and "Stacking the Cards."

Students should be made aware of these basic tricks, and given opportunities to detect and discuss them in various types of printed materials, encouraged to search for motives, and then to make decisions as to whether or not they care to be influenced by them.

PATTERN IN MATHEMATICS

One of the special characteristics of mathematical text is compactness. Every word and every symbol is important. Skipping an unfamiliar word or filling it in from context has no place in reading mathematics.

Another characteristic of mathematics texts is that they are composed of two or sometimes three kinds of symbols all mixed together in the same paragraph. There are word symbols, number symbols, and in algebra and geometry there are letter symbols and various other kinds of symbols. The interpretation of so many different kinds of symbols makes for difficult reading.

The Problem Pattern   The most highly specialized pattern of text in mathematics is the short paragraph setting forth a problem situation. Regardless of whether the text is in arithmetic, algebra, or geometry, problems are usually stated in this format: at the beginning the situation is given, or the condition under which the problem took place is stated; then follows a series of numbers or other mathematical values, and finally the reader is asked or told what to find.

Example: When a piece of brass is weighed in water, it weighs 1.977 lb. If it is weighed in glycerin, its weight is 1.971 lb. The specific gravity of glycerin is 1.26. How much does the brass weigh in air?

In geometry and physics, problems sometimes consist of only a single direction or a single question. The characteristic problem pattern, however, is as indicated above.

The *reading* of such problems involves four different processes: (1) reading the entire problem to grasp the situation as a whole; (2) concentrating on the question or statement at the end that asks or tells what to find; (3) deciding what processes or formulas to use in finding the answer; (4) pulling out the number facts or symbols presented for use in working the problem. After these *reading* activities accompanied with a high degree of reasoning have been completed, then the student is ready to compute the problem mentally or on paper. If a student is having difficulty in mathematics, it would be helpful to explain to him the importance of the *reading* activities which precede computation, and to provide him with special practice in the reading procedures involved.

Another adjustment which the student has to make to the *reading* of problems is a change from the basic eye-movement habits to which he has been accustomed. In reading problems he often uses vertical or left-directed movements to reread portions for better understanding or to pick out certain numbers or symbols. While some students read problems more rapidly than others, the problem pattern is most certainly not one that is appropriate for speed reading.

The Explanatory Pattern   The explanatory pattern in mathematics texts constitutes difficult reading. This pattern is similar to the explanation-of-a-process pattern appearing in science textbooks except that in this case the explanations expound a mathematical process rather than a technical scientific process, they are comparatively short in length rather than spreading over long sections of text, and usually they are accompanied with an example of a problem "worked out."

Students should be urged to read this pattern with the greatest of care. It is advisable in some cases for them to check their comprehension of the explanation by trying to repeat it to themselves in their own words. If an example is given to apply the explanation, they should of course follow through this step by step, referring to the explanation if necessary to find out why the step was taken. The success with which they are able to solve the problems that follow often hinges upon the thoroughness with which the explanation has been *read* and *comprehended*.

Graph and Chart Patterns   Other distinctive patterns in mathematics are found in graphs and charts. While these visual aids are used in science, social studies and other subjects, they represent mathematical concepts.

Reading a graph or a table is a different kind of reading than reading a paragraph. In order to get the most of a graph or table, students should be taught to: (1) read the title to determine exactly what is being compared; (2) read the figures or labels to make sure they grasp what it is that they stand for; (3) study the graph or chart to make comparisons in regard to the different items illustrated, (4) and finally, they should interpret the significance of the chart or graph as a whole. Due to the prevalence of graphs and charts, many secondary students might well profit from some additional practice in *reading* these types of pictured relationships.

Special Symbols, Signs and Formulas   Mathematics text carries with it a unique terminology: signs of various kinds, abbreviations, exponents, subscripts, formulas, equations, geometrical figures, and so on. For students, learning to recognize these symbols and their meanings is like learning to *read* all over again. It is, indeed, an astute teacher of mathematics who recognizes these characteristic symbols as *reading* content and who makes a special effort to teach his students to *read* them.

32. Planning the Literature Program
for the Elementary School
Charlotte S. Huck

Elementary school teachers have all but forgotten that the most important reason for teaching boys and girls to read is to help them become *readers*. Controversies continue to be waged over methods of teaching reading, the most appropriate age for beginning instruction, and machines versus basic materials. Many primary teachers report that they spend over one half the total school day on reading instruction alone. Teachers proudly point to the results of reading achievement tests to prove the effectiveness of their teaching. As a nation we take pride in the 98% literacy rate of our population. Recent criticism to the contrary, the majority of the evidence points to the fact that our schools are teaching children the skills of reading. And yet our schools have failed miserably in helping boys and girls develop the habit of reading. In many instances we have developed an illiterate group of literates—adults who know *how* to read

"Planning in the Literature Program for the Elementary School," by Charlotte S. Huck, *Elementary English*, XXXIX (April 1962), 307–313. Reprinted with the permission of the National Council of Teachers of English and Charlotte S. Huck.

but do *not* read. In one study,[1] nearly one half (48%) of the adults in the United States had not read one book during the year. Another study [2] which contrasted American reading habits with that of adults in other countries revealed that only 17 per cent of the Americans had been reading from a book the previous day whereas 55 per cent of the English sample had been engaged in this activity. Despite the rising educational level and the high standard of living, a large proportion of the American public expresses little interest in reading.

Although there are many factors which are responsible for the small amount of book reading in the United States, one major factor may well be the overemphasis of the instructional or basic reading program to the neglect of the literature program in the elementary school. In fact, some elementary school teachers would maintain that literature was something one studied in high school, not the elementary school. Others would say that reading and literature are synonymous. Still others would claim that the literature program is cared for by the "free reading" period on Friday afternoon when teachers are free to complete their attendance records while the children are free to develop appreciation and discrimination for fine literature by reading a Nancy Drew mystery! We have no literature program in the elementary school when we compare it with our carefully planned developmental programs in reading, spelling and arithmetic. All our efforts are directed towards teaching children to read—no one seems to be concerned that they *do* read or *what* they read. The means have become the end. We have developed better and better basic readers, we have even cut some of them apart and boxed them! Yet few children ever developed a love of reading by reading a basic reader or by progressing from one colored reading card to another. It is almost as if we had put our children in link trainers for reading, and then focused our attention on producing bigger and better link trainers and methods of using them without ever giving the children a chance to use the skill they have developed by discovering the thrill of flying. Link trainers do play an important role in training pilots; basic readers play an important role in helping children to learn to read. However, the ultimate goal of both of them should be self-elimination.

Teachers and children must not prize the skill of reading as an end in itself; they must see it as a beginning of a life-time pleasure with books. There are no values in knowing how to read; only values which are derived *from* reading. As teachers recognize the values which result from wide and varied reading, they will see the need for a planned literature program in the elementary school.

[1] David H. Russell, "We All Need to Read," *Saturday Review* 39:36, February 18, 1956.
[2] Lester Asheim, "A Survey of Recent Research," *Reading for Life,* edited by Jacob M. Price. Ann Arbor: University of Michigan Press, 1959, pp. 3–4.

The first major value of literature is enjoyment. Personal enjoyment of reading is a respectable activity and should be encouraged. Adults read for pleasure and not to produce a book report. Children too should discover the joy of just reading for fun. They *may* want to share their enjoyment in many different ways but children should not feel that they always have to *do* something with a book to celebrate its completion. Reading books should be a natural part of children's lives and not such a momentous occasion that we must shoot off firecrackers in the form of book reports, mobiles, or dioramas each time a book is completed. This practice is a remnant of the past when books were scarce and precious and reading ability was limited to a few. A wide variety of experiences in interpreting children's literature may deepen children's appreciations, but they should never become the required penalty for reading a book. Alert teachers know when children's needs have been met through reading; they do not ask for tangible verification. One fourth grader, whose mother had just died, was introduced to Corbett's *The Lemonade Trick*. This book contains some delightful spoofing of boys' and dog's behavior. You may remember the part where Waldo, the dog, drinks some of the magic lemonade and immediately becomes so good that he goes out in the backyard to *fill in* the holes which he had dug the day before. For two days, this fourth grader was completely absorbed in this book. Once he was observed reading it while he walked to the coat closet. Escapism, yes, but he had found an acceptable way to contain his problem, and in the midst of sorrow, a book had been able to make him laugh.

Personal-social growth may also be influenced by *what* children read. Probably many of us first experienced death and its accompanying feelings of loss and separation as we read of Beth's death in *Little Women*. American children today may realize some of the personal horrors of war as they identify with Tien Pao in De Jong's starkly written book, *The House of Sixty Fathers*. Some of our over-protected white children may experience the hurts of prejudice for the first time as they read and identify with Mary Jane, the main character in Dorothy Sterling's fine story by the same name which tells of desegregation in our public schools in the South. Or books may help children with the developmental task of growing-up and fulfilling their adult roles. They discover as they read such books as *Nkwala* by Edith Lambert Sharp that this is a universal experience and they identify with the Salish Indian boy whose "childhood itched him like a goatskin robe." Books help children explore living, "to try on" various roles and accept or reject them as they search for their own identity.

Children may satisfy their desire for information and intellectual stimulation through wide reading. Willard Olson has identified what he calls the "seeking behavior" of boys and girls. Certainly this is revealed in children's response to the recent flood of factual books. Informational books are no longer disguised by the fictional trappings of a trip to the farm with a favorite uncle. Children are hungry for knowledge about the physical and social world in which they live. Many well-written informational books contribute to the thrill of helping children discover specific facts by presenting them clearly and in a meaningful way. These books satisfy but they do not satiate; they supplement and extend texts in science and social studies. Such fine books as the special edition of Rachel Carson's *The Sea Around Us* widen children's vision and open new vistas of beauty and mystery.

Only as children are exposed to much fine writing will they develop an appreciation for a well-chosen phrase, rich descriptive prose or convincing characterization. After a story has been finished, the teacher and children may take time to reread and relish particularly enjoyable words or paragraphs: The beautiful but quiet story of *Miracles on Maple Hill* by Virginia Sorensen contains many such descriptive phrases. In one lovely passage Marly ponders the multiplicity of feeling which can be associated with one sound, sight or word:

> How so many things could be in a few words was something else Marly didn't know. But it was the same way the whole feel of school can be in the sound of a bell ringing. Or the way the whole feeling of spring can be in one robin on a fence post.[3]

One of the most unique books published this year is *Hailstones and Halibut Bones* [4] by Mary O'Neil. In twelve different poems the author explores the various dimensions of sight, sound and feeling conveyed by different colors. She describes purple as "sort of a great Grandmother to pink" and suggests that "the sound of green is a water-trickle." Her richest contrasts are in her poem "What is Black." This delightful book will help children to appreciate fine writing which creates vivid word pictures and describes emotions. One first grade teacher [5] had read selections from *The Lonely Doll, A Friend Is Someone Who Likes You, Bears on Hemlock Mountain* and *Love Is a Special Way of Feeling* to initiate discussions about love, friendship, sorrow, hate, and fear. Following the discussion on loneliness, a group poem was composed from the children's various contributions. It shows the sensitivity of these mature first graders to the books they had heard and to the insights which they had concerning their own feelings.

A Lonely Feeling

When I am lonely there's no one to walk with me.
No one loves me.
I feel sad and want to cry.

[3] Virginia Sorensen, *Miracles on Maple Hill.* New York: Harcourt Brace and Company, 1956, p. 4.
[4] Mary O'Neil, *Hailstones and Halibut Bones.* Garden City, New York: Doubleday and Company, Inc., 1961, p. 11.
[5] Mrs. Jack Holloway, Lincolnwood School, Evanston, Illinois.

This feeling comes when:
  I move away and a friend doesn't come too.
  or I wake up and am alone in the dark.
It's there when:
  No one eats with me,
  No one greets me after school
  A friend calls me a hurt-name or I'm sick in bed.
When I am lonely I am so by myself, it makes the
      me, inside, afraid.

Books can provide the stimulus for children's writing about their own joys, fears, and problems. Constant exposure to fine writing will be reflected in children's increased skill in their own oral and written expression and in their deepened appreciation for truth and beauty.

Another major value of wide and varied reading is that it acquaints children with their literary heritage and provides a firm foundation for future literary experiences. Bruner, in his much discussed little book *The Process of Education*,[6] maintains that the basic principles and concepts of each discipline should be identified and taught to children. He suggests that children can grasp the idea of tragedy and basic human plights as they are represented in myth. Children may become acquainted with various forms of literature as they are read and discussed. They may begin to build appreciation for the well-written biography or for poetry, that most neglected area in children's literature today. Some of our children literally jump from Mother Goose to Tennyson, without ever hearing any of the fine poetry of David McCord, Walter de La Mare, or Eleanor Farjeon. Teachers need not be afraid to introduce such literary terms as anthology, autobiography, or allegory to our modern day child whose TV vocabulary includes such words as "ammoniated" and "supersonic." Then there is a whole body of children's literature which forms a common background in our culture. Think of the many modern day expressions which have been derived from the field of children's literature:

> He was as mad as a Hatter
> I won't be your man Friday
> He has a Midas touch
> She was filled with "insatiable curiosity"
> His life is a good Horatio Alger Story

The period of childhood is limited. If children miss reading or hearing a book at the appropriate age for them, it is missed forever. No adult catches up on his reading by beginning with *Peter Rabbit* or *Homer Price*. There is no one book which must be read by all children, but there are many fine books which we would hate to have children miss. These include some

---

[6] Jerome S. Bruner, *The Process of Education*. Cambridge, Mass.: The Harvard University Press, 1960, p. 13.

of the classics but also, many of our modern books which may become the classics of tomorrow. There is a body of children's literature which is worthy of a solid place in the curriculum.

Finally, the true value of the effects of the literature program for today's children will be seen in the reading habits of adults in 1985. The explosion of knowledge makes it essential that our children become readers. The natural obsolescence of materials has so increased that adults must become constant readers if they are to stay abreast of new developments. The mark of the informed man is no longer whether he can read, or what he *has* read, it may be based upon what he is currently reading. Our sociologists are predicting amazing increases in the amount of leisure time for the average person (not in our profession). The acid test of the reading program in our schools will be the use which children and adults will make of books in this increased leisure time.

Obviously, these six values of literature will not be fulfilled by an instructional reading program or by a Friday afternoon recreational reading period. As teachers, librarians, and administrators become committed to these values—to the worth of literature in children's lives, they will plan a comprehensive literature program for every elementary school. The planning must start with teachers who read themselves, who enjoy reading and recognize its values for them. Their first task will begin with making books, many books and fine books available for boys and girls. The recent recommendations in the *Standards for School Library Programs* [7] suggest that all schools having two hundred or more students need well-organized central libraries *and* a qualified librarian. In 1958-59 some two thirds of our elementary schools did not have central libraries and the ratio of qualified school librarians to pupils was one librarian to some 4,261 pupils! When may we look forward to the day that parents and educators will begin to view libraries as being as worthy of school funds as multi-purpose rooms and $40,000 cafeterias! Books are the tools for learning, the very bread of knowledge. Must our children continue to be like Alice at the Mad Hatter's party, prepared to feast at the table of reading with no room and no books?

We must do more than make books available for boys and girls, we will want to create a climate which will encourage wide reading. While visiting schools during Book Week this year, I observed several classrooms that had small displays of new books on the window sills. I watched and I waited for two whole mornings and I never saw a single child have time to look at or read any one of those books. Like the mathematician counting his stars in the *Little Prince*, they were too busy with "matters of consequence" to take time to enjoy reading. A planned literature program does take time. It provides time for children to read books of their own

[7] American Association of School Librarians, *Standards for School Library Programs.* Chicago: American Library Association, 1960.

choice every day. It allows time for children to share their experiences with literature in many ways. In the planned literature program time is provided for the daily story hour regardless of the age of the group. For we know that most children's reading ability does not equal their appreciation level until sometime in the junior high school. During this daily story hour, the teacher will introduce the various kinds of literature which children might miss otherwise. Certain books need to be savored together in order to heighten children's appreciation. This seems to be particularly true of such fantasy as *The Gammage Cup, The Borrowers* and even that most American of all fantasy, *Charlotte's Web.* Teachers will not want to read books which children themselves will ordinarily read. It is fun to read a chapter of *Henry Huggins,* but children will eagerly finish this book themselves once they have been introduced to it. A variety of books should be presented in order to at least expose boys and girls to different types of books. Children in the middle grades go on reading jags—they read series books with the same avidity with which they collect bottle tops. This is characteristic of their developmental patterns and should not be a cause for concern. If fifth grade girls only want to read horse stories, let them. Could you fill in a balanced wheel for your reading pattern this year? A life time of reading will show a certain balance, but even an adult follows particular reading interests, completely absorbed in biography for a while, or perhaps plunging into theology for the first time, or avidly reading everything which has been written by a newly discovered author. Can't we extend children the same freedom of selection which we allow ourselves?

In planning a literature program, teachers will not only provide for separate times for literature experiences but they will make wide use of certain trade books to enrich and vitalize learning experiences in *all* areas of study. Children should be encouraged to verify, extend, or contradict the presentation in their textbook by contrasting it with facts found in other books. Social studies is greatly enriched by the many excellent books about children in different lands, by biography, and by fine historical fiction, those books which clothe the factual bones of history and make it come alive. Children who read Fritz's *The Cabin Faced West* or *The Courage of Sarah Noble* by Dalgleish will have a better understanding of their historical heritage than the children who are limited to a single textbook approach. History, by its very nature, is interpretative. Children need to read books with many different viewpoints in order to become critical assayers of the contemporary scene. The flood of factual books in science has been gratefully received by children and teachers. Future space pilots can find the most recent information in trade books rather than texts. For example, Beeland and Wells' book *Space Satellite, the Story of the Man Made Moon* came out in a third edition, three years after its first printing! Very few texts can be that up-to-date. Arithmetic, art, and music may all be enriched through the use of exciting books in children's literature. The day of the single text for all is gone, as many fine books find their rightful place in the curriculum.

The planned literature program will only be as effective as the teachers who make it. This means teachers will have to know children's literature; it means they will want to keep informed of the new developments in the field. A continuing in-service study group might read and review some of the 1500 juvenile titles which come off the press yearly. Some faculty meetings might well be devoted to discussions of the place of children's literature in the curriculum and the development of life-time reading habits of boys and girls.

Vertical planning of teachers from kindergarten through grade six might result in a guide for a literature program either as an integral part of the total curriculum or as a separate program. Such a guide might include purposes, plans for selection of books, recommended books for reading to children and by children, suggested experiences with literature and evaluation procedures. Texts in children's literature and such journals as *Elementary English, The Horn Book* and the *School Library Journal* should be a part of every school's professional library. Teachers and librarians might prepare recommended buying lists for Christmas and birthday gifts. Lists of books for reading at home could also be prepared, for children who become enthusiastic about books at school will want to continue their reading at home.

Finally, we may agree as to the values of a planned literature program but unless we evaluate that program, it probably will not be included in our curriculum. Provision should be made for a staff evaluation of the total literature program, values of it, time devoted to it, and the success of the program. Children's reading habits should be evaluated as well as their reading skill. Interest in reading is not as intangible as it may sound, it can be measured; not in terms of how many books boys and girls have read, although that is a part of it, but in terms of the depth of understanding and new insights which they have gained from their reading. Reading achievement tests do not measure this, nor do city-wide comparisons of grade level standings. But teachers, librarians, and parents know if children are reading. Hopefully, we would wish that all children might echo the feelings of this child in the third grade who wrote about her world of books.

My Own World [8]

When I open up my book I go into a world all my own
Into a world of sorrow or joy,
    but wherever it is I don't hear the things about me.
I could be reading in a busy noisy factory,
    but my world keeps me away, My world of books.

[8] From Wickliffe School, Upper Arlington, Ohio. Mrs. Donna Waldeck, teacher.

This, then, is the acid test of our literature program—not do children know how to read, but *do* they read, *what* do they read, and more important, do they *love* to read.

This enthusiasm for books doesn't just happen. It results from an effective instructional program which is well-balanced by a literature program that has definite purposes and a definite place in the curriculum. It requires a teacher who is dedicated to the values of literature and it demands that we lift our sights from our basic reading programs in the elementary school to a planned literature program for all!

Bibliography of Children's Books

Joan Walsh Anglund (author-illustrator). *A Friend Is Someone Who Likes You.* New York: Harcourt, Brace and Company, 1958.

——, *Love Is a Special Way of Feeling.* New York: Harcourt, Brace and Company, 1960.

Lee Beeland and Robert Wells, *Space Satellite, the Story of the Man-Made Moon.* Illustrated by Jack Coggins. Third Edition. Englewood Cliffs, N.J.: Prentice-Hall, Inc., 1960.

Rachel Louise Carson, *The Sea Around Us.* Special edition for young readers adapted by Anne Terry White. New York: Simon and Schuster, 1958.

Beverly Cleary, *Henry Huggins.* Illustrated by Louis Darling. New York: William Morrow and Company, 1950.

Scott Corbett, *The Lemonade Trick.* Illustrated by Paul Galdone. Boston: Atlantic-Little, Brown and Company, 1960.

Alice Dalgliesh, *The Bears on Hemlock Mountain.* Illustrated by Helen Sewell. New York: Charles Scribner's Sons, 1952.

——, *The Courage of Sarah Noble.* Illustrated by Leonard Weisgard. New York: Charles Scribner's Sons, 1954.

Meindert De Jong, *The House of Sixty Fathers.* Illustrated by Maurice Sendak. New York: Harper and Brothers, 1956.

Jean Fritz, *The Cabin Faced West.* Illustrated by Feodor Rojankovsky. New York: Coward McCann, Inc., 1958.

Carol Kendall, *The Gammage Cup.* Illustrated by Erik Blevgad. New York: Harcourt, Brace and Company, 1959.

Mary O'Neil, *Hailstones and Halibut Bones.* Illustrated by Leonard Weisgard. Garden City, New York: Doubleday and Company, Inc., 1961.

Mary Norton, *The Borrowers.* Illustrated by Beth and Joe Krush, New York: Harcourt, Brace and Company, 1953.

Elizabeth Lambert Sharp, *Nkwala.* Illustrated by William Winter. New York: Harcourt, Brace and Company, 1956.

Dorothy Sterling, *Mary Jane.* Illustrated by Ernest Crichlow. New York: Doubleday and Company, Inc., 1959.

Elwyn Brooks White, *Charlotte's Web.* Illustrated by Garth Williams. New York: Harper and Brothers, 1952.

Dare Wright (author-illustrator). *The Lonely Doll.* New York: Doubleday and Company, Inc., 1957.

33. Reading Skills in Teaching Literature in the Elementary School

William A. Jenkins

Introduction

Perhaps you will permit a non-expert in reading the luxury of beginning with a definition of terms. I do this because I believe that reading is the most complex of all language skills. It involves and is dependent on all the others. I hasten to add, however, that from my very biased vantage point, literature—the other part of my concern here—is the most important of the humanities. I take a cue from Edgar Dale who wrote in his *Newsletter* some time ago that the way we define reading will determine how we teach it.

Early Reading

Perhaps it is significant that the first readers were called *spellers,* a nomenclature long ago discarded. We no longer view *reading* only as the act of translating visual symbol to sound. Unfortunately, vestiges of this narrow definition remain to haunt those who teach reading. But the ability to understand and ferret the structure of our language is one important element in reading, and this is what basal readers attempt to develop. Basal readers are built on the idea that during beginning reading oral language outstrips what children can elicit from the page. In a systematic fashion a child must be taught the act of translating. Criticisms of basal readers are based on the hunch that children can translate more than the systematic, restricted readers permit them to do at any given reading level. Not accepting the fact that a child can encounter *and then retain* only a

"Reading Skills in Teaching Literature in the Elementary School," by William A. Jenkins, *Elementary English,* XLI (November 1964), 778–782. Reprinted with the permission of the National Council of Teachers of English and William A. Jenkins.

limited number of new symbols, questioners ask why readers must be stripped of all literary content while emphasizing symbol translation. Some of the new readers and some of the new approaches to teaching reading assume that a child can elicit more from the page than we have hitherto believed.

INDIVIDUALIZED READING

One of the approaches is individualized reading, which as an organized, systematic instructional program goes back to the 1930's. In the last decade it has enjoyed a Renaissance. Currently it is being tested, employed, and written about profusely, and it is working. Its use is dramatic recognition of the fact that basic reading programs are of greatest worth in the initial phases of reading instruction, and that reading from basal textbooks is intended to carry only part of the reading load that children will do. But the thing which troubles me about individualized reading is teachers' assumption that it is one thing. Actually it is many things, for it is individual guidance in reading. As such, it varies from teacher to teacher, from pupil to pupil.

LINGUISTICS AND READING

I began by indicating that reading is the most complicated of the communicative arts. Let me add here that we think we know more about it than we do the other language arts. At least the quantity of research which has been done on it and the volumes of writing about it would so indicate. But there are signs indicating that a great reassessment may be imperative in the near future. Harbingers of the new look are the oral language studies now being completed by such people as Loban and Strickland. Our notions about language development in children may well be reinforced if not replaced by radically different considerations. The work of the linguists on the nature of our language will eventually have great influence, too. Recently Creswell, a linguist, sounded such an alarm when he wrote this:

> Every reading program should be based (also) upon what we know about how children learn, upon a clear understanding of what children already know about language when we begin reading instruction, and upon what children typically learn about language from other sources and through other experiences while they are learning to read. It is extremely important to remember that learning to read does not take place in a linguistic vacuum. Beginning readers have already gained

great control over spoken language and continue to develop skill in its use while they are learning to read.[1]

A DEFINITION OF READING

Now for a working definition. To me reading is the act of translating written symbols into oral units of expression and meaning. Reading is thinking. Reading is obtaining meaning from the structural elements of written language, finding meaning between the elements, and understanding at least part of what has been implied beyond the elements. The understanding between and beyond the lines comprises at least half of the meaning and so cannot be overlooked. Reading is getting meaning from the page by bringing meaning to the page. Reading is the mechanical act of translating symbol to sound, and symbol to meaning. Reading is experiencing based on experiencing; it changes one, enhances one, reconstructs one. Reading is using concepts to increase our background of concepts. Reading is recognizing, using, and appreciating esthetic elements of language: figures, rhythm, and imagery. At its highest level reading is feeling, while thinking. But this is also literature—written material which makes one *feel* while he *thinks*. Let us look at literature for a moment.

A DEFINITION OF LITERATURE

Like reading, literature is many things to many people. Most people are agreed that it epitomizes the expressive and receptive arts. Many would agree that it is writing which has been kept alive by beauty of style or thought. But there are serious questions about literature, even when one restricts himself to literature for children, questions which we will not attempt to answer here. Matters such as what literature, how much, and in what proportions the various types should be offered are vital and yet not definitively resolved. Perhaps Leland Jacobs' dictum that children should have some old and some new, some realistic and some fanciful, some prose and some poetry, is as good an answer to the questions as we can find. This, incidentally, is exactly what our NCTE committee has done with the area. Their report, which will comprise most of the May, 1964, issue of *Elementary English*, is titled simply, "Children's Literature—Old and New."

[1] Thomas J. Creswell, "Remarks on B. Robert Tabachnick's Paper," in *Reading and the Language Arts,* edited by H. Alan Robinson. Chicago: The University of Chicago Press, 1963, p. 109.

Perhaps a constructive approach here would be to look at what literature does for elementary school children—things which reading *may or may not do,* but which literature by definition *must* do.

WHAT LITERATURE DOES

First of all literature presents a standard for judging language and experience. The best, the worst, the in-between, are open for inspection. Literature presents human nature, that great range of diffuse, diverse, and divergent ways in which we human beings have acted and thought and are capable of acting and thinking. Literature provides background which gives words their meaning. What does *run,* r-u-n, mean out of context? What are the possible dozens of contexts which can give it meaning? Literature can encompass the full range.

Literature has vocabulary, figures of speech, and sentence structure produced with artistry to delight the mind and the ear. Through history and biography, literature preserves cultures and civilizations. Literature holds forth an ideal, a set of values through such types as hero tales and myths. Good literature, according to May Hill Arbuthnot, gives children insights, satisfies curiosities, provides them with a zest for living, and imbues them with a reverence for life. These are unassailable reasons for teaching literature in the elementary school.

Stephen Dunning, co-director of the Project English center at Northwestern, has also offered reasons why we teach literature. He says:

1) Literature is taught so students will enjoy it.
2) Literature is taught so students will improve their taste and increase their capabilities as readers.
3) Literature is taught so students will have access to their literary heritage.[2]

Let me add a final, personal thought. Literature is that reading which *touches* a person, as he thinks, where he lives, and as he is. It's important to remember that no one book, or types of literature, or a single author can do this. Dr. Nila B. Smith has written in a study published by *Elementary English* in December, 1948, that in a group of elementary school pupils who indicated that their thinking and attitudes were changed or influenced by literature, with only one exception no child in any room mentioned the same book as other children. The effects and influences of a literary experience are highly subjective and personal.

[2] Stephen Dunning, "Some Reasons for Teaching Literature," *Bulletin* of the National Association of Secondary School Principals, 48 (February, 1964) 121–128.

Reading and Literature Unequally Emphasized

From what has been said so far, one might readily assume that in the elementary school, reading and literature are coequal partners in the language arts curriculum, complementing each other in developing literacy and appreciations. Unfortunately, this is not the case. The first group of skills, the reading skills, are always undertaken in the elementary school. The second step, the application of these skills to literature, to broaden, refine, and reinforce reading, may or may not be taken. As my colleagues may attest, the reverse of this situation—emphasizing literature to the neglect of reading—is the usual situation in the high school, while the junior high school frequently assumes the characteristics of a no-man's land where neither literature nor reading is highlighted; where a stand has been taken, it is usually in favor of literature in the junior high school.

In my area of primary interest, the elementary school, reading and literature are not only viewed as separate entities, they are also unequal; literature is the lesser light. In their preparation, elementary teachers are greatly concerned that they know all they can about reading. Knowledge of literature frequently is a concern of secondary importance, if not neglected altogether. The natural relationship of the two concerns, the skill of reading and the content of literature, is lamentably ignored. Perhaps the current emphasis to capitalize on the interrelatedness of all of the language arts will change this situation. Unfortunately, literature for children is not considered one of the arts as are reading, spelling, and handwriting at the elementary level, or literature and composition at the senior high level.

Similar Skills Needed

Why should this be so? Reading ability depends heavily on interest. Literature can provide for all types and ranges of interest. Reading depends on interest in as well as facility with language. Books of a literary type provide the means for creating an interest in language, for they interpret experiences of all ranges and types. Reading and literature have common purposes, symbols, and structures, and they involve common thinking processes. Yet they are still separated in far too many elementary classrooms.

When the concept *language arts* was advanced several decades ago it was felt that a breakaway from departmentalization had been achieved for the elementary school. The language arts, the skills, that is, were partly integrated, but the art of literature was kept apart. The condition, I submit, should no longer endure. Reading is vital because it is a basic skill.

Reading is also an art. Literature, too, is an art. Even for young children it is, I postulate, a vital skill.

READING SKILLS IN LITERATURE

What are vital reading skills that must be entertained when teaching literature in the elementary school? I think the list is as comprehensive as our knowledge of reading. However, let me highlight some basic ones.

First of all, I believe that as he is learning to read and increasing his power in reading, a child must be taught to interpret life in varying degrees of seriousness, whether through skimming or through reflective reading. Just as the contexts of literature can be varied widely to teach him words and phrases, they can be varied widely for depicting man and his concerns.

A child should be taught that language has nuances, subtleties, and intricacies. He should learn to recognize these and to understand how they create differences in the author's intent and effect. Only wide and varied types of reading can fully accomplish this objective.

A child should be taught to interpret a wide range of vocabulary and discourse, even in dialect. Again, only a wide acquaintance with books, authors, themes, plots, and styles can accomplish this aim. Least effective are the readers set in middle-class or suburban environments with children who never cheat or steal, who do not have to fight for life, sustenance, and recognition; who are never frustrated, thwarted, or defeated; who never seemingly encounter parental tyranny, yellow, red, or black skins; who do not know poverty, squalor, hunger, or fatigue. They do know these—only they know them outside of their books. Out of school they frequently have experienced these and even more impressive facts of life—a younger sister dying of starvation, as recently happened in Kansas City to a child who was regularly given breakfast at school. When this happened, he could no longer eat. He lost his appetite! Or they know nothing but fathers who communicate only when in a drunken stupor, as Charlotte Brooks has vividly described in her pictures of the culturally disadvantaged in Washington, D.C.

A child needs to be taught to pursue a series of events in order of time. Stories should do this for him.

He must be taught to grasp the tone and mood of a reading selection. Again wide reading will provide the opportunities. This includes being read to, and reading aloud connected discourse.

and pertinent details. Practice in this is readily provided by stories which have a skeleton of plot that can be stripped away and to which details can be readily fastened and pegged.

A child must, of course, be taught comprehension of both the main idea

In reading in the elementary school a child must be taught to use pictorial aids to meaning. Readers and trade books both afford opportunities for developing this skill, but in my experience teachers too seldom seize the chance or use it at its maximum.

A child must be taught to make generalizations from the specific instances he encounters in reading, and he must learn to become emotionally involved through characters and events which he encounters in his reading.

With limitations, a child must learn to recognize and understand the figures and other esthetic elements he encounters in his reading. I say with limitations, because here too our notions are being questioned. Many teachers at all levels have assumed that in his early reading of myths, folk tales, Bible stories, and so forth, a child builds a foundation of allusion upon which later literary experiences will rest. A study being conducted by Dr. James Squire, NCTE Executive Secretary, to be published some time this year, may change our position. Based on an analysis of fifty anthologies, Dr. Squire's study tentatively has found that upper grade children *do* need a background knowledge of the Greek myths (particularly the Trojan War); and of the Arthurian cycle. More allusions refer to Arthur and his Knights than to all other figures in British and American folklore combined. The study has found also that children need a knowledge of Bible stories of the Old Testament. Of less importance, according to this study, are the Norse myths, stories of the Far East, American folk tales, and English balladry.[3]

A final reading skill area in teaching literature in the elementary school must be vocabulary. In young children, vocabulary grows through finding the best word to share experience. Their language development evolves as they move from egocentric concerns to the group life of school and as their teacher takes them beyond themselves in both reading and nonreading activities. For older children, the quickest way to climb the reading vocabulary ladder is to read widely in books which are exciting or personally meaningful.

CONCLUSION

It has been said that whether a man writes with style and taste depends on the styles he has tasted. I think we can paraphrase that to say that how well and what a child reads depends on what he has read. No one honors a great poem until he has attempted to write one and then instead of a happy walk through field and meadow, writing a poem suddenly be-

[3] James R. Squire, "Reading and the Language Arts: A Probe into the Future," in *Reading and the Language Arts*, edited by H. Alan Robinson. Chicago: The University of Chicago Press, 1963, pp. 204–212.

comes a mountain to climb. I think we must teach children to climb mountains. Today, however, I only ask that we teach them to walk knowingly, appreciatingly, and confidently through field and meadow. Reading literature can do this for them.

34.   Reading Literature Critically

Bernice D. Ellinger and Sister Mary Julia MacDougall

INTRODUCTION

A child who reads one book a week during his entire elementary school career would even then only become familiar with 300 books. With the few outstanding books amid the 3,000 published for children each year, he could easily miss ever reading a really good book. Who could say that the primary grades are too soon to help children improve their ability to select good reading material? The child who recognizes the hallmarks of good writing will be much more likely to read some of the best books that have been written for him. Those who help a child to read literature critically are therefore guiding him to the selection of high quality books.

RATIONALE FOR TEACHING CRITICAL READING

Doubt has been expressed that direct instruction in critical reading skills is appropriate at the elementary school level. Some people fear that such instruction will contribute to the increasing number of youthful cynics and objectors. Critical reading as it is defined by today's educators implies a positive approach to the printed page, one in which the reader is open to a number of possible alternatives. It is only after careful examination of all the available options that a trustworthy decision can be made. The purpose of reading critically in literature is not to destroy or dissect the work, but to enhance one's appreciation of it. An understanding of the components of fine literature should contribute to a deeper appreciation of the totality of the work.

In this sense, critical reading involves an evaluation of the quality and significance of literature. For such thoughtful reading, certain skills are needed, skills that are different from those used in reading informational

"Reading Literature Critically," by Bernice D. Ellinger and Sister Mary Julia MacDougall, reports activities from The Critical Reading Project, The Ohio State University, June 1966.

material. Because critical reading is comprehensive in nature, effective utilization of it necessitates the ability to determine which skills are appropriate for use. For example, the reader would look for factual accuracy in a history book but not in a book of children's fantasy. Such ability to discriminate is constantly necessary. From the long list of critical reading skills which could be enumerated, only those related to the reading of literature will be discussed here. Even within this limitation, only a cursory explanation of the selected skills can be presented in this article. Illustrative situations are provided which were taken from actual incidents which occurred during the experimental phase of the Critical Reading Project entitled "The Critical Reading Ability of Elementary School Children." * Although the experimental treatment included analysis and evaluation of informational materials and literature, the discussion here is restricted to Literary Form, Components of Literature, and Literary Devices, the three major phases of the work with children's literature.

LITERARY FORM

Skills taught in the area of literary form are those which students use (1) to distinguish between types or forms of literature, (2) to recognize the characteristics of specific literary forms, and (3) to develop criteria for evaluating these forms. Ways of teaching some of these skills are illustrated below.

COMPARING FACT AND FICTION

A teacher who concentrated early efforts in critical reading on helping pupils to assess accuracy and authenticity in informational material made the transition to literature study by helping the second grade group to distinguish between informational books and books of fiction. The focus was thus placed on the form of the work. After *Ducks Don't Get Wet* by Goldin had been read in class during a science study, and McCloskey's *Make Way for Ducklings* had been read aloud for enjoyment, the children compared the two books. They noted that both books contained facts, but that the two authors used the facts in different ways. In comparing the reasons for the illustrations, the children decided that Mc-Closkey used his portrayal of the authentic Boston scenes and of the duck family to help him tell an amusing story, while Goldin used drawings to show the reader what she was explaining in the text. The children further discovered that, although McCloskey's ducks think, talk, and generally act

* "The Critical Reading Ability of Elementary School Children," supported by the U.S. Office of Education. The principal investigators are Willavene Wolf, Charlotte Huck and Martha King.

like people, there are no imaginary elements in Goldin's informational book.

The following questions helped to clarify the differences between the two literary forms for these second graders:

How are the two books different?
What did the author intend to do in each book?
How can you tell that a book is fiction?

DEVELOPING CRITERIA FOR FICTION

Certainly, knowing that a book is fiction is only the first step in learning to read literature critically. A much more important phase of the process is discerning whether the book is *good* fiction. This involves the complex skill of developing criteria. One fourth grade class, when faced with the problem of deciding what makes a book worthwhile, thought they needed a set of standards to use as a measuring stick. The set they developed served as a guide for some of their earliest literary judgments. They considered a book worthy of their time if:

It tells a good story.
The characters seem real.
There is meaning behind the story.
The story is told in an interesting way.

CATEGORIZING FICTION

Within the realm of fiction, children can be helped to see that there are two basic categories: fantasy and realistic fiction. Realistic fiction remains true to the nature of the characters involved; fantasy allows behavior which is not true or even possible in real life.

Children need the fanciful, but taste for it frequently has to be cultivated; likes and dislikes are strongly expressed in this area. The modern child may early come to believe that "the facts" are all important, that books of fantasy are a waste of time when there is so much to learn about the real world. Elementary school children may need help in wondering, questioning, venturing into unknown times and places. The wise teacher guides them to fill this need with imaginary literature.

It is easy for children in the primary grades to identify with Francisco and his desire for a pet dog in *Amigo*. Rather stark reality is displayed in the early text and pictures as the young boy learns some of the deprivations of poverty. About midway through the book, however, there is a subtle change to fantasy. By this time the young realist is so intent upon the budding friendship between Francisco and a prairie dog that he would not exchange this fantasy for all the informational books available.

According to the maturity and experiences of the class groups involved, children can be led to see further subdivisions in fantasy and realistic fiction. Within the first category are the folk tale, fairy tale, fable, myth, and modern fantasy; the second includes historical, biographical and modern fiction.

Fifth and sixth graders feel quite competent in the process of identifying forms of literature when they can separate historical fiction from biography by knowing, for example, how to correctly classify *Johnny Tremain* and *America's Paul Revere*, two of Esther Forbes' books for young people. Then there is autobiography that they can learn to keep separate from fiction written in the first person. A sixth grade boy was asked about the literary form of *Trace Through the Forest* after the class had enjoyed that book.

> Well, Lafe is telling the story, but since the author is Barbara Robinson, I know it's not an autobiography. It must be fiction then, but it's based on fact. Colonel Zane did cut a road through the wilderness. Since it took place in 1796, it must be historical fiction.

Such reasoning is indeed complicated, but children can work their way through such a process as they clarify ideas about books and stories. They learn to look for different qualities in the various types of literature. They learn to demand accuracy in historical background if the book rests in fact, but they will accept a character from the author's imagination if the hero is believable and true to the life of his times.

As children learn about literary form, poetry need not be slighted. Boys and girls in the primary grades can enjoy more than just the story line of *Amigo*. Since the book is written in verse, the children can have the added joy of listening for the sounds of the ending rhymes. They discover not only that poetry can be enjoyable, but that it can heighten the delight of an already enticing tale. After a happy experience with narrative poetry, lyrical forms may have more appeal. When the children know what to look for, they may find that poetry can be fun.

COMPONENTS OF LITERATURE

The major components of literature identified in the Critical Reading Study were (1) characterization, (2) plot structure, (3) theme and setting with careful analysis of these as an over-arching purpose. Materials were selected from children's literature to illustrate the use of each component.

APPRAISING CHARACTERIZATION

Since believable characters are a vital part of good literature, attention to characterization is necessary. The carefully delineated character in Stolz's *Dog on Barkham Street* and *Bully on Barkham Street* change during the story, but they meet the criteria of being both possible and believable changes. Fourth grade students found that they could understand why Martin Hastings acted as he did, once they had read the story told from his point of view. Characters who behaved the same at the end of the story as they did at the beginning were contrasted with ones who changed or developed during the story. First graders recognized that Madeline acted the same way at the end of the book *Madeline* as she did at the beginning, whereas Chibi had changed his behavior by the end of *Crow Boy*. The changes were made gradually and believably. Flat, stereotyped characters were compared in several books with well developed, believable ones in order to show the contribution the latter make to the quality of literature.

Sperry uses nine ways to reveal the character of Mafatu in the first chapter of *Call It Courage*. Fifth graders easily recognized the selections in which the author revealed Mafatu's thoughts, described him, his surroundings, and his actions, showed what others said to Mafatu and how they reacted to him. They used these ways of revealing character in their own writing as a way of becoming familiar with the techniques of characterization. The original stories were read aloud and the class members identified the approach used by each pupil. Books which had been read by the group were evaluated to determine how well the author had done in producing a believable character. Examining methods of developing characterization proved to be a useful approach to the study of this important component of literature.

IDENTIFYING PLOT STRUCTURE

Lessons on plot structure were developed to help students see why an author puts a story together as he does. Elements such as the introduction, build-up, climax, and ending of a story were identified by the children and viewed as a basic framework for a story. Children can see how each part of the story gets bigger and more fantastic as it progresses through the snowballing "tall tale" approach used by Dr. Seuss. In the Seuss selections of "Marco Come Late" and *To Think That I Saw It on Mulberry Street* there is a sudden drop in suspense at the end of the story when the main character comes back to reality with his tale.

Accumulative plot structures were found in Nic Leodhas's *All in the Morning Early*, and *Always Room for One More*, and Galdone's *House that Jack Built.* In these books, each event builds upon the preceding one until a peak is reached; then the action backtracks or ends with a dramatic climax. Books such as *Homer Price* and *Little House in the Big Woods* where the action begins and ends in each chapter were viewed as episodic. Some such books have a continuity in which one episode necessarily follows another, but each story stands independently in the chapters of *Homer Price.*

Parallel plot structure was illustrated in McCloskey's *Blueberries for Sal.* In this story, the author switches back and forth from Sal and her mother to Little Bear and his mother as both pairs go blueberry picking. The climaxes in the two plots appear one after the other and the stories end separately. The story of either Sal and her mother or of Little Bear and his mother going blueberry picking would not have been particularly interesting, but the crossing of the parallel plots made the tale an exciting one.

BECOMING ACQUAINTED WITH STORY THEME

Teachers who had allowed children to read at a literal level were not able to get them to identify the theme of a book easily. When a question such as "What is the main idea of this story?" was asked, these children would begin telling what happened in the plot. Only after illustrating with obvious themes in simple picture books could the teacher get the children to discover a message which goes beyond the plot of the story. The idea that we really ought to be ourselves is portrayed in *Dandelion, Little Rabbit Who Wanted Red Wings, Harry, the Dirty Dog,* and *The Unhappy Hippopotamus.* When first graders realized that the same basic idea came through in a number of different stories, they could make the distinction between theme and plot.

Comparing fairy tales proved to be a useful way to illustrate story themes. *The Emperor's New Clothes* and "Master Till Paints a Picture" both show that most people do not want to admit that they have anything but the highest virtues and qualities. In each story, a cruel hoax is exposed by one person's truthfulness.

RECOGNIZING STORY SETTING

A component of literature which is fairly easy for children to identify is story setting. The relevance of the setting to the plot can be illustrated by discussing the kinds of things that can happen in the story. If the time and place concern pioneer days in the west, one could not suddenly arrange an airplane flight. When the reader knows the time and place of a story he may to some extent predict what events will take place. He may even predict what a person will do, for he realizes that people are influenced by the circumstances in which they find themselves. The critical reader asks, "Why does the character think, act, and talk the way he does in the story?" and "Would the character have acted differently under different circumstances?" The fine work that is produced in some historical fiction is the result of meticulous planning of details. Jean Lee Latham studies reports of the period about which she writes. Treating the facts as a framework, she skillfully weaves her story among them. Many of the details do not appear overtly in the story, but they provide the backdrop of information as she writes. The critical reader evaluates how well the author stayed within the stricture of the time and place he has chosen and also determines how the setting affects the action and character development of the particular story.

LITERARY DEVICES

In the third section of the literary study an attempt was made to put the child in the place of the author and to help him think as an author thinks about writing. Some topics of study were: (1) devices for story development, (2) ways of achieving mood, and (3) characteristics of writing style. Children examined the techniques an author uses in the production of literature and began to evaluate his effectiveness. Examples of beginning classroom efforts at such evaluation follow.

LEARNING ABOUT STORY DEVICES

Some first graders learned about an author's use of foreshadowing in story development with Keats' *The Snowy Day*. After reading the page which tells that Peter put the snowball in his pocket, the teacher asked:

What will happen to Peter's snowball?
Will Peter be disappointed?

After the children's prediction had come true, the teacher questioned further:

Why was Peter sad?
Did he understand what happened to his snowball?
How did *you* know what was going to happen?

These children gained only the beginnings of an understanding of the foreshadowing technique from this story, but they showed that they understood a character's feelings better because they had gained some hint of them ahead of time.

Boys and girls who read widely discover that authors choose to present their stories from various points of view. Presenting the action from a definite perspective is a necessary element in story development and children can learn to grasp its importance. Some excellent books for fifth and sixth graders have been written in the first person; *Island of the Blue Dolphins* is but one example. Everything comes to the reader in this book through the words and thoughts of Karana. The reader gains an understanding of the character from this technique which could hardly be achieved in any other way. With guidance, children can critically consider the effectiveness of an author's choice of point of view.

A third grade teacher used *Where the Wild Things Are* to help a group learn about an author's use of symbolism. The pupils learned that ordinary things—such as the food that was still hot in the story discussed—can stand for complicated ideas. Here a mother's love and forgiveness were symbolized effectively by a warm supper for her son. This experience with symbolism in a picture book may open the door to richer experiences with literature. It is difficult for children to get the idea that one thing "represents" another, but numerous illustrations with stories in which this is done helps.

Only three of the many devices an author may use in developing his story have thus far been mentioned. A fourth is essential in a discussion of children's literature: an author's treatment of fantasy. This actually involves a number of techniques; one of the most intriguing is how the author makes fantasy believable. Of what good is a story which does not hold a reader's interest and, at least to some extent, his credibility?

Charlotte's Web was studied by a fifth grade at this level of analysis. Some of the key questions of the discussion were:

1. What type of literature does the book start out to be?
2. When and how does the fantasy begin?
3. How is Fern's appearance in the story treated after the fantasy is introduced?
4. Does Fern understand the talk of the animals?
5. Does Fern ever talk to the animals?

As children watch a story which begins in a realistic setting subtly turn into fantasy, they become aware of the skill of a master at work. Animals talk to each other and the story becomes quite involved, but people never talk to the animals, and for those who have not lost the wonder of childhood, the story remains believable to the end.

DETECTING MOOD

The mood of a book is a very subtle "feeling" that the reader gets as he reads or it may be considered the spell that is cast by a book. The pictures and the language in *The Moon Jumpers* combine to cast a spell of a warm summer moonlit night. Words such as "drowsy," "tired," "fall asleep," and "dream" contribute to the feeling of a late evening in the yard while the misty, dusk-like illustrations extend the eerie feeling of being outside late at night after others have gone to bed. The book has the effect of poetry; it creates a mood in a very few lines.

The language of a story generally carries the mood to the reader. From the first page of *Rabbit Hill* there is a feeling of excitement and suspense. Phrases such as "the hill was boiling with excitement," "new folks a' coming, new folks a' coming" quickly ensnare the reader in the mood of the story. Wojciehowska uses short snatches of conversation by unidentified townspeople to build up the feeling of expectation for Manola in *Shadow of a Bull*. "It's the eyes. He has exactly the same look in his eyes. The same sad eyes."

Books which describe a unique ethnic group or a particular period of history use authentic speech to help create a mood. The Amish in *Wonderful, Nice* use words such as "rootch over, Katy," and "Lost you are, maybe?" to create the mood in the story. *The Blind Colt* depicts life on the western plains and includes the words "critter," "yo'all," "little feller," and "young'un" to help the reader feel that he is really in the setting of the story.

APPRECIATING THE AUTHOR'S STYLE

Children can evaluate dialogue and authentic speech to see if they contribute to or detract from the story. Some of the spelling necessary to depict authentic speech makes reading difficult, but it is acceptable if it contributes to vivid characterization. Regional stories would not be authentic if their characters spoke standard English.

Metaphorical language contributes to writing style and can bring numerous mental pictures to the reader. The poet who wrote "The Moon's the North Wind's Cooky; He bites it day by day" certainly did not intend to be taken literally. Children are generally literal readers and act much like Amelia (in *Amelia Bedelia* by Peggy Parrish) as she follows her employer's list of housecleaning chores. To her, "Dusting the furniture" meant sprinkling dusting powder on the pieces.

Writing style is related to the point of view from which a story is told, the mood that it creates, and the content of the book. Children learn that an informational book should not try to couch facts in poetic, metaphorical terms, nor should a book of fantasy be written in terse declarative sentences. Books such as *May I Bring a Friend* and *Madeline*, which are written in rhyme, appeal to young children. Children frequently can supply the rhyming word or can join in a repetitive phrase such as "Hundreds of cats, Thousands of cats, Millions and billions and trillions of cats" from Gag's *Millions of Cats*. Children can also evaluate the writing style in relation to the type of book, the mood that it attempts to create, and the purpose for which it was written.

CONCLUSION

After a series of experiences in evaluation of literature, children were given reviews of children's books written by adults. The children read the book themselves, wrote their own reviews and then compared their reviews with those of adults. This technique of criticizing the critics provided an opportunity for the application of a number of the skills of literary analysis. Children were motivated to take a stand on a book and either recommend it or not recommend it and tell why they chose as they did. Critical reading involves taking a stand, making a judgment, and giving criteria for the stand taken. This kind of exercise was helpful in encouraging children to do these things.

Critical reading, then, involves skills which contribute to the development of criteria for evaluating literature. It requires that the reader go beyond the literal level of getting meaning from a printed page. It involves recognizing the hallmarks of good writing and gaining some understanding of the components of good literature. Primarily, the purpose of reading critically is to enhance or deepen the reader's appreciation of literature, and all activities that are directed toward critical reading must contribute to this over-arching purpose. Shallow teaching could distort these worthwhile goals and result in children's superficial ability to "label" components, devices, and forms of literature. At the elementary school level, the labels are not as important as the full enjoyment of literature. Inspired teaching can help children develop a love for good literature and can help them to recognize it in the morass of annual publications.

BIBLIOGRAPHY OF CHILDREN'S BOOKS

HANS CHRISTIAN ANDERSON, *The Emperor's New Clothes*. Illustrated and translated by Erik Blegvad. New York: Harcourt, Brace and World, 1959.

C. S. BAILEY, *Little Rabbit Who Wanted Red Wings*. New York: Platt and Munk, 1931.

LUDWIG BEMELMANS, *Madeline*. Illustrated by author. New York: Viking, 1939.

BEATRICE SCHENK DE REGNIERS, *May I Bring A Friend?* Illustrated by Beni Montresor. New York: Atheneum, 1964.

ESTHER FORBES, *Johnny Tremain*. Illustrated by Lynd Ward. Boston: Houghton Mifflin, 1943.

——, *America's Paul Revere*. Illustrated by Lynd Ward. Boston: Houghton Mifflin, 1946.

DON FREEMAN, *Dandelion*. New York: Macmillan, 1964.

GODFREY FREEMAN, "Master Till Paints a Picture," in *The Owl and the Mirror*. New York: Duell, Sloan and Pearce, 1960.

WANDA GAG, *Millions of Cats*. Illustrated by author. New York: Coward-McCann, 1928.

PAUL GALDONE, *House That Jack Built*. Whittlesey, 1961.

DR. THEODORE SEUSS GEISEL, "Marco Comes Late," in *Treat Shop*. Edited by Eleanor Johnson and Leland Jacobs. Columbus, Ohio: Charles E. Merrill, 1954.

——, *To Think That I Saw It on Mulberry Street*. New York: Vanguard, 1937.

AUGUSTA GOLDIN, *Ducks Don't Get Wet*. New York: Thomas Y. Crowell, 1965.

EZRA JACK KEATS, *The Snowy Day*. Illustrated by author. New York: Viking, 1962.

ROBERT LAWSON, *Rabbit Hill*. Illustrated by author. New York: Viking, 1944.

SORCHE NIC LEODHAS, *All In The Morning Early*. Illustrated by Evaline Ness. New York: Holt, Rinehart, and Winston, 1963.

——, *Always Room For One More*. New York: Holt, Rinehart, and Winston, 1965.

ROBERT McCLOSKEY, *Make Way For Ducklings*. Illustrated by author. New York: Viking, 1941.

——, *Homer Price*. Illustrated by author. New York: Viking, 1943.

——, *Blueberries For Sal*. New York: Viking, 1948.

NANCY MOORE, *The Unhappy Hippopotamus*. Illustrated by Edward Leight. New York: Vanguard Press, 1957.

SCOTT O'DELL, *Island of the Blue Dolphins*. New York: Houghton Mifflin, 1960.

PEGGY PARRISH, *Amelia Bedelia*. New York: Harper, 1963.

BARBARA ROBINSON, *Trace Through the Forest*. New York: Lothrop, Lee and Shepard, 1965.

GLEN ROUNDS, *The Blind Colt*. Illustrated by author. New York: Holiday House, 1941.

BYRD BAYLOR SCHWEITZER, *Amigo*. Illustrated by Garth Williams. New York: Macmillan, 1963.

IRMA SELZ, *Wonderful, Nice*. New York: Lothrop, Lee and Shepard, 1960.

MAURICE SENDAK, *Where The Wild Things Are*. Illustrated by author. New York: Harper, 1963.

ARMSTRONG SPERRY, *Call It Courage*. Illustrated by author. New York: Macmillan, 1940.

MARY STOLZ, A Dog on Barkham Street. New York: Harper, 1960.

——, The Bully of Barkham Street. Illustrated by Leonard Shortall. New York: Harper, 1963.

JANICE UDRY, The Moon Jumpers. Illustrated by Maurice Sendak. New York: Harper, 1959.

E. B. WHITE, Charlotte's Web. Illustrated by Garth Williams. New York: Harper, 1952.

LAURA INGALLS WILDER, Little House In The Big Woods. Illustrated by Garth Williams. New York: Harper, 1932; 1953.

MAIA WOJCIECHOWSKA, Shadow of a Bull. Illustrated by Alvin Smith. New York: Atheneum, 1964.

TARO YASHIMA, Crow Boy. Illustrated by author. New York: Viking, 1955.

GENE ZION, Harry, The Dirty Dog. New York: Harper and Row, 1956.

35. Teaching a Picture Book as Literature

Alexander Frazier and Esther E. Schatz

Once a decision has been made to attend more thoroughly to the literary analysis of some books read in common by young children, then the problem immediately arises of selecting discussable books that everybody can read. At the primary level, the search becomes particularly challenging. The slightness and indeed the very brevity of many of the books written to be read by young children would seem at first glance to be harder to deal with than the question of readability.

However, part of our first reaction may come from a lack of experience in thinking of books for the younger reader in this way. We have tended to provide experiences with literature for young children through reading to them good books that they cannot yet read for themselves. Certainly this kind of activity should be continued. But we need to review again the books we have been increasingly providing for children to read on their own. The review should be made from the standpoint of substance as well as readability. Perhaps many of us will have to conduct this review and test out our tentative selections with children if we intend to enlarge the base of literary experiences for younger readers to include their own direct encounters with books.

The present report describes one attempt to use a selected picture book toward this end.

"Teaching a Picture Book as Literature," by Alexander Frazier and Esther E. Schatz, Elementary English, XLIII (January 1966), 45–49, 59. Reprinted with the permission of the National Council of Teachers of English and Alexander Frazier and Esther E. Schatz.

THE NATURE OF THE BOOK

The book chosen to be read and discussed by a second-grade class at University School was Leo Lionni's *Swimmy* (Pantheon Books, 1963). The book is composed of 15 double-page pictures, each designed to be viewed as a unit, and a text of 298 words.

The pictures are multi-media (watercolor wash, ink, and stencil) with many colors and textures and have been planned by the writer-illustrator as integral to the story.

The text begins on the second two-page spread (the first includes the title page and sets the scene) and is composed altogether of 23 sentences. One of these has 6 direct objects, each of which sets the theme for a double spread; the sentence runs to 56 words or better than one-fourth of the text. The text as a whole contains 55 single-word modifiers, exclusive of articles; 27 word-cluster modifiers; and 5 subordinate clauses.

In terms of the figurative use of language, the text is equally rich. There are 12 easily identifiable "images," ranging in complexity from "corner of the sea" and "deep wet world" to "walked about like a water-moving machine" (of the lobster) and "whose tail was almost too far away to remember" (of the eel).

The story itself, as will be obvious from the following summary, has a strong storyline and also lends itself to treatment in terms of levels of meaning:

> One of a school of little fish, Swimmy differs in being black rather than red and in being a faster swimmer. He also becomes the sole survivor of a tuna's onslaught. Venturing out alone, Swimmy notes in passage a jellyfish, a lobster, an eel, and other items of interest. When he finds a new school, he urges his companions to leave the rocks and weeds and see the world. But they are afraid. Thinking it over, Swimmy proposes that they form themselves into the shape of giant fish. He trains the school and becomes its eye, after which they all swim out, scaring the big fish away, to enjoy the wider world.

GETTING READY FOR DISCUSSION

With one copy of the book and 25 children, the first problem in preparing for discussion was to find a way to get the book read by all. This was resolved by deciding that the book would remain in the classroom and that each child would sign his name on a sheet tacked to the display board when he had finished with the book. The sheet was headed: "I have read *Swimmy*." The class is organized for individualized reading for part of every morning. Under these circumstances, the little book made the rounds within a week.

The children were asked to make notes as they read the book of anything they felt they would like to discuss when the time came. The notes
consisted mostly of a few words that might serve to recall a particular
passage; not all the children brought notes to the discussion but many did.

In preparation for the discussion, the teacher had listed for herself a
series of questions that she thought might be drawn on in case the children found it difficult to get started. Actually, she did not need to call on
the list until the close of two sessions when it was decided to return to the
group for a general summary in relationship to the central theme of the
story.

The question of how many sessions of discussion might be required for
the book was left open in planning. As it happened, the book discussion
occupied three 20- to 25-minute periods over a span of four days.

What Discussion Covered: First Session

The session opened with an invitation to the half-circle gathered around
the teacher to react generally to the book. Mike remarked that the water
sometimes has pink under the blue. He left his seat and came to the
teacher to point out this fact on the pages to which she had opened
Swimmy as she held it up to invite reactions.

"Did you like the pictures all the way through?" the teacher asked.
There seemed to be agreement that they had.

Jeff then said, "I liked the rock candy under the sea." One of Swimmy's
sights, as he swam on alone after losing his first school, was "a forest of
seaweeds growing from sugar-candy rocks." The teacher opened the book
to these pages. In the ensuing discussion, question was raised about
whether there was actually rock candy under the sea. Jeff and Mike agreed
to try to find the answer and report on it later to the class.

Patty asked: "Why do they have schools of fish?" In response, the other
children and the teacher helped to clarify what the term means.

Julie said: "I liked the part where the little fish scared the big fish. They
went in order like marching."

William: "It was easy to get them to swim together because they swim
in schools except for a few stragglers. They already have good coordina-
tion."

Teacher: "They got themselves into a special shape or formation."

Jeff: "Like a basketball cheering section." What this meant was elab-
orated upon by Jeff and another child.

Then Matt proposed another tack: "Couldn't a whale eat up the whole
school? Would fish be that dumb, not to see all those little fish?" After
several others had responded to this latter question, Matt said he had his

own answer: "In the book it looks like a lot of little fish. But what would it look like to other fish?"

Teacher: "What else in the story do you want to talk about?"

Jeff: "I couldn't understand where it said the big fish were pulled by an invisible thread." Another of Swimmy's sights had been, as the text puts it, "strange fish, pulled by an invisible thread."

Billy: "It just seemed like they were being pulled by the way they moved."

Teacher: "Could it mean anything else?"

Kim: "Maybe it is a lure made of fish to catch other fish."

Pete: "This is a crazy idea . . . but maybe it's a sea spider's web."

William: "In the book it said it looked like they were being pulled by an invisible thread."

CONTENT OF THE SECOND SESSION

A question by Dale opened this session: "I don't see why Swimmy can swim faster than his brothers and sisters."

Christine: "Maybe he's a different kind of fish."

Dale: "I think that's it. They are different colors."

William: "Maybe it's just his lucky day."

In further discussion, the children refer to the book. William points out that Swimmy is the same color as the tuna fish.

As to why Swimmy could swim faster, Billy said: "It might be that he was at the head of all the other fish and heard his brothers yelling for help when the tuna attacked and then started swimming down and the tuna couldn't catch him."

Teacher (referring to the text): "The book does say he swam faster than his brothers and sisters."

Mark: "He couldn't be a different kind or the others wouldn't be his brothers and sisters."

Larry: "Maybe he was just born a different color."

Ainslie: "Maybe they are not really brothers and sisters but because they were in school, the author just says this. They are together."

Teacher: "We haven't really answered Dale's question, but we have given a lot of good ideas. Now [to Jeff and Mike] are you boys ready to report on rock candy?"

They report that they had asked the librarian to help them find books that would help them try to identify the picture but they couldn't find anything like it. They had A Guide to Minerals, Gems, and Rocks which had a picture something like the one in Swimmy. Jeff concluded their report: "We used the wrong term. The book says sugar-candy rock. We said rock candy." Mark takes the book and reads the correct wording.

Then he turns to another page which shows "a medusa of rainbow jelly" and reads these words aloud. "That's it," he says. "It's just a way of telling how it looks."

The discussion moves to another facet. Referring to her notes, Julie says: "I don't know what they mean by 'deep wet world.'"

Nicky: "It's like a world of water. It's just so big. And you know it's wet because it's water."

Rush: "I think he means, well, it's kind of lonely."

Teacher: "It kind of looks like it." She holds the book open to the gray-green double page picture that shows Swimmy as a small black form in the lower right hand corner.

Neal: "It looks like a cloud with one black dot in it."

Mary Lee: "It is somewhere where there were not many schools of fish."

Billy: "I think the author means it's a new world. Instead of air around, it's water."

Larry: "It looks like a map with one of those black spots on it."

William: "I got a book from the library and it showed that water is darker deeper down."

Teacher: "Do you think the water is deeper here?"

Mike: "It isn't darker."

Teacher: "Well, let's read what it says in the book: 'He swam away in the deep wet world. He was scared, lonely, and very sad.'"

Then the teacher asked specifically about the pages showing and telling about the lobster and the eel. She asked what was meant by describing the lobster as walking about "like a water-moving machine." Nancy said: "It picks up things with those claws like one of those bulldozers." "What do you remember about the eel?" the teacher asked. Several children tried but could not remember. But Billy did: "He had a tail that was almost too far away to remember."

William: "That's what happened to the dinosaurs."

Now the teacher asked for summary reactions: "What did you think about the book as a whole?"

Nicky: "It was good." To this statement there seemed to be general assent. Kim had her hand up.

Kim: "Almost every picture was beautiful and had some sentences I couldn't understand."

Teacher: "Did you have trouble reading it?"

Kim: "No, but there were things like 'pulled by an invisible thread' that I didn't understand."

Peter (shaking his hand vigorously): "I just wanted to say: it's good!"

Teacher: "Can you think of another book we might want to read this way?"

Suggestions included *Is This You?*, *Christopher Columbus* ("No, no, no" was the chorus of responses to this title), *Charlotte's Web*, and *The*

Wizard of Menlo Park. The first and third of these had been read by children seeking information for a group study on early days and how things began.

THIRD SESSION: ATTENTION TO THE THEME

This session came as an afterthought and was opened with a specific question by the teacher: "What do you think is the most important idea in *Swimmy?*"

Micky: "That he could swim so fast?"

Christine: "If this were made into a TV program, Swimmy would be the star."

Ainslie: "When he found the other fish, they made a big fish."

Nancy: "So he could be the eye."

Patty: "They would be eaten if they did not get together."

Larry: "I wonder why the first time he didn't get the school together."

Billy: "Maybe he didn't have much time to think before. He had to think this time so he could have fun."

Teacher: "Do you think he wanted it so he could have fun?"

Nancy: "He liked them a lot and if they were eaten up, he'd be alone."

Billy: "He wanted it partly to have fun and partly to be safe."

Teacher (referring to the text): "Swimmy does say, 'Let's go and play and see the things.'" She reads the rest of the relevant passage to the children.

Mike: "The main idea is they don't get eaten like the other school."

Teacher: "They found a way to protect themselves."

Mike: "There were so many of them, they could be as big as a whale."

William: "He got his idea from the other bad experience."

Kim: "They could still get into trouble. If they saw a worm on a hook and some went to get it, the big fish might notice. It would be important to stay together."

There ensued some discussion of the need to keep in formation. Then Mike came up to the teacher to point out that in the picture of the fish in formation, there were many gaps between the fish.

Billy (pointing to the blue behind the formation of red fish): "The author wanted to make this book kind of pretty."

Nancy: "I think there were two reasons for staying together: one, for the big fish to see and two, to keep from getting caught by a fishing rod."

William (reiterating what several boys had been trying to get said): "You don't put a worm on a deep sea hook. You put something bigger like shrimp."

Neal: "The big idea was when the fish were all together."

Nancy: "He was sad when he was alone."

Mark: "But he saw a lot of things."

Larry: "He wasn't alone very long. He soon found another school."

Nancy: "It seemed like a long time in the book but it was probably only a little while."

Teacher: "Well, we seem to agree on the main idea of *Swimmy*. Can you remember when you read the next book to ask yourself what the big idea is as you read? Take notes, too, on the things you think we ought to talk about."

She then reminds them that the book is *Once a Mouse* (by Marcia Brown; Scribner, 1961) and that the sheet on the bulletin board has already been signed by Billy and Jeff.

REFLECTIONS ON THE EXPERIENCE

Our first conclusion, in thinking through this experience of teaching a picture book as literature, is that *Swimmy* certainly does have sufficient substance to warrant teaching. It is a book that yields to close reading with some second graders.*

We are struck, as we review the record of the three sessions, by the primary concern for literal meaning. How can Swimmy be a different color from his brothers and sisters?

This concern merges into the accompanying problem of deciphering figurative language and images. "Sugar-candy rocks" becomes the more familiar and literal "rock candy." "Pulled by an invisible thread" can be held read but is hard to understand.

Then the third level of concern, that of thematic meanings, we find to be one that needs to be stimulated by the teacher. But when these children do begin to share their thoughts at this level, their depth of awareness surprises us . . . the role of the leader, the loneliness of being by oneself ("But he did see lots of things"), the need to stay together "partly to have fun and partly to be safe." No effort was made to ask whether these meanings could be applied more broadly. We recognize this question as nonliterary and also, perhaps more importantly, as inappropriate to the experience of second graders. Older readers, we are sure, would verbalize at once on still another set of meanings that could be read in these times from this little story.

In conclusion, we wish to return to an assumption that is basic to this report. That is, that experiences in reading literature for themselves and studying it together ought to have a larger place in the lives of young children. If we needed to defend this position, we could do so in terms of

* We recognize the value of having on hand several copies of any book used as *Swimmy* has been rather than only one. The additional two or three copies are needed most for reference to the text during group discussion.

the value of the experience as a social activity, of particular relevance in a program like ours that places priority on individualized reading for many purposes; as an opportunity to teach certain kinds of high-level reading skills; and, most excitingly to us in the current context of greater concern for the arts in education, as a neglected resource to be made better use of in full human development.

More specifically we have tried in planning and conducting the present experience to test out one example of such literature with one group of children. We think *Swimmy* meets our criteria for the selection of a readable and teachable piece of literature for our second graders.

The further need, as we see it, is for many of us to review the good books that children can read and to locate among them those that may be most worth teaching.

36. Critical Thinking Through Children's Literature

Mary Lou Usery

A means for putting purpose into practice is suggested in the following theory about one of the thinking processes. A model of the process is described and applied to an area of the elementary language arts curriculum. *Critical thinking*, one of the abilities commonly accepted as a part of the thinking act, is the focus of the study. *Children's literature* is the medium used for this application of the teaching of critical thinking. Certain underlying assumptions explain the somewhat unusual combination of activity and medium.

In order to view critical thinking as a workable and understandable process, its elements are defined, analyzed, and designated in terms of classroom behavior. By applying critical thinking to an area of the curriculum, emphasis is placed on the process goal of critical thinking, as well as on the content goal of the discipline. Shaver supported this view of process emphasis in a review of research that dealt with the teaching of critical thinking skills in the secondary school social studies. He drew conclusions that have relevance to application in other content areas:

. . . we should not expect that our students will learn to think critically as a by-product of the study of the usual social studies content. In-

"Critical Reading Through Children's Literature," by Mary Lou Usery, *Elementary English*, XLIII (February 1966), 115–118, 120. Reprinted with the permission of the National Council of Teachers of English and Mary Lou Usery.

stead, each teacher should determine what concepts are essential . . .
if his students are to perform the intellectual operations deemed necessary to critical thinking . . . Each of these should then be taught explicitly to the students.[1]

Children's literature was selected as one area in which the process of
critical thinking could be taught.

Children's literature belongs more to the arts than to the scientific disciplines; and, therefore, the purposes for including it in the curriculum are
unique. Instead of concerns for skill development and the acquisition of
knowledge, the goals of children's literature are usually defined by educators as being those of enjoying, appreciating, and developing taste.
These latter goals are intrinsic in nature and require behavior modifications within the person. Children's literature, then, is unique in that it
proposes the development of processes as its major goals. Other values can
be achieved by literature, as suggested by Phenix:

> The effects of literature, of course, usually extend beyond the es-
> thetic realm. . . . In fact, literature is one of the best sources of insight
> into personality and culture. . . . Literature may also be used for a
> variety of practical purposes, such as emotional therapy, moral in-
> struction, and ideological persuasion.[2]

Using children's literature for developing critical thinking skills is an application of literature that goes "beyond the esthetic realm." [3]

THE MODEL OF CRITICAL THINKING

Critical thinking may be defined as the act of searching for the clearest
ideas about a subject derived from the facts, points of view, observations,
and other elements. The searching continues until one reaches a point at
which he understands the intricacies of the problem so that he is able to
use logical and creative thinking to make judgments and act in the light
of those judgments.

The following model of the critical thinking process describes four related though not necessarily sequential types of behavior. These are: becoming aware of the situation (perceiving), analyzing the situation
(analyzing), projecting possible solutions (predicting), and drawing conclusions that lead to modified behavior (judging). These four areas of
behavior are analyzed, described in greater detail, and stated in terms of

---

[1] James P. Shaver, "Educational Research and Instruction for Critical Thinking,"
Social Education, 26 (January, 1962) 16.
[2] Philip H. Phenix, *Realms of Meaning*. New York: McGraw-Hill Book Company,
1964, p. 178.
[3] *Ibid.*

children's classroom behavior. A few examples from each of the four major areas suggest how these behaviors can be developed through children's literature. Examples of learning experiences are noted in relation to two children's books selected for differing grade levels, *The Biggest Bear* and *Call It Courage*.[4]

PERCEIVING

Becoming aware of a situation involves an alteration of the learner's perceptions about the situation. It is the stage of critical thinking in which the learner sees an overview of the situation before he moves on to more complex stages. Becoming aware is related to Schachtel's description of openness:

> [Openness] means . . . [that man] can try to be born more fully, . . . to become capable of interest in and love for the larger and richer world in which he lives, thus discovering its infinity and inexhaustible mystery. This discovery is possible only in the fully open encounter with the world when one does not cling to the protection of the familiar and the past.[5]

Foshay's comments about openness as a part of the creative process are related to this stage of the critical thinking process. He suggested that openness involves the suspension of judgments and described it as a time for "letting in all the data" and for taking "an unstructured look at things." [6]

The major behaviors that are involved in becoming aware of a situation are:

verbalizing a need
developing an open attitude
relying on more than one source of information
delegating elements of the situation to their positional relationships
evaluating the situation.

Learning experiences such as the following use the medium of children's literature for focusing attention on the kinds of critical thinking behavior that a child uses as he becomes aware of a situation:

To differentiate elements of the situation and thus delegate positional relationships, a child might act out how Johnny, the hero of *The Biggest Bear*, felt when he went into the woods to hunt a bear and how he felt when he walked out of the woods with a bear cub. When the scenes have

---

[4] Lynd Ward, *The Biggest Bear*. Boston: Houghton Mifflin Co. 1952; Armstrong Sperry, *Call It Courage*. New York: The Macmillan Co., 1940.

[5] Ernest G. Schachtel, *Metamorphosis*. New York: Basic Books, Inc., 1959, p. 83.

[6] Arthur W. Foshay, "The Creative Process Described," *Creativity and Teaching*, Alice Miel, editor. Belmont, California: Wadsworth Publishing Co., 1961, p. 24.

been dramatized, the pupil could explain to the class the inner feeling that he experienced as he played the role of Johnny.

To acquire skill in listening abilities and therefore develop a more open attitude, a student might listen to the sounds of Debussy's La Mer, selecting and replaying the sections that suggest the sea sounds that frightened Mafatu, the Polynesian boy hero of *Call It Courage.*

ANALYZING

Analyzing the situation involves separating the factors that make up the total situation so that the elements can be studied singularly. Whereas perceiving suggests a view of the whole, analyzing suggests a view of the parts. Bloom noted three levels of analysis in his educational taxonomy: identifying and classifying the elements, noting connections and interactions between the elements, and recognizing the arrangement and structure of the whole.[7] The learner draws from a broad comprehension of the situation in order to make his analysis. He also determines whether there are any existing criteria for evaluating the elements and decides in which direction the thinking should move.

The major behaviors that make up the process of analyzing are:

studying the elements of a situation
determining the relationships between the elements
studying the order in which elements are arranged if any order is apparent
evaluating the elements.

The following learning experiences might be used with certain children's literature selections in order to help develop the process of analyzing:

To evaluate the elements of the situation, a pupil could list the complaints that Johnny's neighbors made about the bear. From the complete list the child could pick out the items that did not seem to be fair complaints and support his reasoning in the light of the story situation.

To categorize the elements of the situation and thus determine the relationships between the elements, a youngster could group the things Mafatu learned about the uninhabited island to which he drifted. These items could be arranged according to such categories as "Food Sources" or "Safety Features." A child could develop his own categories and list the items to be included in those divisions.

---

[7] Benjamin S. Bloom (ed.), *Taxonomy of Educational Objectives, Handbook 1: Cognitive Domain.* New York: Longmans, Green and Co., 1956, pp. 144–45.

PREDICTING

Projecting possible solutions is the stage of critical thinking during which the learner moves from concrete to abstract processes. The activity of prediction may be logical or imaginative. Bartlett advocated that both ways of thinking would lead to prediction. He suggested that a learner might have a "special sensitivity" which would suggest leads that were "most likely to be fruitful." As a second means of prediction, Bartlett suggested that the learner could use logical, deductive, and experimental means when the general principles required for understanding an operation were known.[8]

Synthesis is involved during prediction since the learner must combine his perceptions about the situation in order to create new solutions.

Behaviors that make up the process of projecting possible solutions include:

visualizing ultimate outcomes

using a logical pattern or imaginative techniques for projecting possible solutions

evaluating the proposed solutions.

Learning experiences such as the following might be applied to other selections from children's literature to help children develop their abilities for predicting:

To invent new solutions and thus use an imaginative technique for predicting possible solutions, a small group of children could do some brainstorming in order to think of many other ways in which Johnny might have gotten rid of the bear.

To apply knowledge to the visualization of the outcomes of the situation, a pupil could recall other books, such as Robinson Crusoe and My Side of the Mountain, that deal with man's need to exist completely dependent upon his natural environment. The student could note what basic physical needs other fictional characters had to satisfy and compare the actions of those characters with Mafatu's activities. Illustrations from other reading could justify the pupil's comments about Mafatu's ingenuity.

JUDGING

Drawing conclusions that lead to modified behavior is the stage during which the learner completes the cognitive activity, converting his thoughts to action. Opinions are formed, and decisions are made. This phase of critical thinking is highly personal since the learner must use his own

[8] Sir Frederic Bartlett, Thinking. New York: Basic Books, Inc., 1958, pp. 156–57.

criteria for evaluating and judging. Action, which may be noted as modified behavior, is an ultimate outcome of critical thinking.

The decision making factor involved in this stage may also be related
to Foshay's work with the creative process. He wrote that "closure" or
"knowing when to stop" was essential to creativity and that the decision
to stop must be both "arbitrary [and] . . . personal." [9]

The placement of judgment in close relationship to action is a theory
supported by Freud:

> Judgement is the intellectual action which decides the choice of
> motor action, which puts an end to the procrastination of thinking, and
> which leads over from thinking to acting. [10]

The major steps of drawing conclusions that lead to modified behavior
are:

developing criteria for making evaluations
making judgments regarding the merits of various solutions
choosing the most appropriate solution
putting the solution into action
evaluating the action.

Classroom activities, such as the following, can be used to help children
develop their abilities for making judgments:

To evaluate the action that climaxed the story, a student could make
a list of the things Johnny actually did and another list of the things
Johnny might have done if he had not been honest in trying to get rid of
the bear. The pupil could share the list with the class, giving his personal
opinion of the outcome.

*To become aware of the influence of the affective nature in decision
making,* a pupil could make a chart of the various elements that entered
into the solution of the story. The pupil could then code these elements
according to whether they affected various feelings of Mafatu such as his
fears, his desire to be courageous, and his sense of personal victory.

EVALUATING THE TEACHING OF CRITICAL THINKING

The totality of the learning experience should involve a means for
determining whether the student is progressing in the development of his
critical thinking abilities. An instrument that both teacher and pupil could
use for evaluating pupil progress is a descriptive rating scale which is
supported by personal anecdotes. The descriptive rating statements are

[9] Foshay, *op. cit.,* pp. 38–39.
[10] Sigmund Freud, "Negation," *Organization and Pathology of Thought,* David
Rapaport, editor. New York: Columbia University Press, 1951, p. 346.

worded in simple terms for the pupil and with greater explication for the teacher. One item that might be evaluated is illustrated below:

SAMPLE EVALUATION

Directions: In the appropriate column, circle the evaluation that you think is the most accurate description of the pupil's most recent work. Briefly describe the pupil's actions that caused you to select this rating.

Pupil Evaluation	Teacher Evaluation
I can guess at "what might happen if . . ."	*Visualizes ultimate outcomes.*
1. Never can guess at "what might happen if . . ."	1. Works only in the present and the past. Cannot predict behavior.
2. Sometimes can guess at "what might happen if . . ."	2. Projects solutions cautiously but has difficulty in visualizing the outcomes of the solutions.
3. About half the time can guess at "what might happen if . . ."	3. Makes predictions but does not always rely on the facts of the total situation.
4. Usually can guess at "what might happen if . . ."	4. Predicts outcomes though this is sometimes done on too narrow a basis.
5. Always can guess at "what might happen if . . ."	5. Bases predictions of the future on foundations of knowledge, past experiences, and imaginative means.
Anecdote: "Everyone else's ideas were better than mine when we tried to find new ways to end the story."	*Anecdote:* "Tom had a number of ideas for solutions during the brainstorming session, but he found it difficult to bring any one proposal to a conclusion."

Conclusion

Three major ideas are combined in the preceding theory: the teachability of human processes, the development of critical thinking abilities, and the extended use of children's literature. These dimensions can be further studied, developed, and applied independent of each other. The fusion of the three ideas represents a refocused view of teaching. Thinking, a vital and dynamic process, can enliven children's literature.

37. Teaching Critical Reading in the Middle Grades

Jeraldine Hill

One of the purposes in teaching children to read is that they may ultimately be able to think for themselves. A good reader is not only one who can read, but one who does read, enjoys reading and knows how to use what he has read. A search through literature on teaching reading reveals much written on teaching children to read and to enjoy reading. However, there is very little practical material available on teaching a child how to use what he has read, or, put another way, to do critical reading. Most of the material found has been written on teaching critical reading through the content areas above the elementary school level.

Spache [1] lists six skills necessary for critical reading:

(1) Investigating sources
(2) Recognizing author's purposes
(3) Distinguishing opinion and fact
(4) Making inferences
(5) Forming judgments
(6) Detecting propaganda devices.

These are separate from comprehension skills that require a lower level of inferences and interpretations. These are skills that go beyond the comprehension skills needed. Although you would not expect younger children to think as maturely as those in high school, this does not prove that middle graders cannot be taught to think critically. In fact, middle grade children are at the point in their development when they are questioning. They ask, "Can you prove it?" of their peers, their teachers and their parents. They are skeptical when proof is not available. Content areas can be used to teach critical reading to these children. Beyond this, the very books read for recreation or as part of an individualized reading program can also be used to teach the skills necessary to do critical reading.

One of the types of books that is of interest to children is biography and biographical fiction. A way to help children grow in their ability to do critical thinking is to compare various biographies and fictionalized stories about one famous person. For example, the life of Benjamin Franklin might be used. The child could read *Ben and Me* [2] and the one the

[1] George Spache, *Toward Better Reading* (Champaign, Illinois; Garrard Press, 1961), Chapter 5.

[2] Robert Lawson, *Ben and Me* (Boston: Little Brown & Co., 1939).

"Teaching Critical Reading in the Middle Grades," by Jeraldine Hill, *Elementary English*, XXXIX (March 1962), 239–243. Reprinted with the permission of the National Council of Teachers of English and Jeraldine Hill. Mrs. Hill is an instructor at the P. K. Yonge Laboratory School, College of Education, University of Florida.

D'Aulaire's wrote on Benjamin Franklin [3] and use some reference book's account of the life of Benjamin Franklin. The three accounts could be compared as to what phases of the person's life are covered, any bias shown by the author, what is historically true, what is perhaps legend and what perhaps is pure fiction. For the more able readers, adult versions and the children's versions of the biography of a famous person written by the same author can be used. The four-volume biography of Abraham Lincoln by Sandburg [4] and the book he wrote for children, *Abe Lincoln*,[5] or Esther Forbes' factual account of Paul Revere [6] and *Johnny Tremain*,[7] the fictionalized account of Paul Revere, can be studied for the author's different purposes in each book, variations in style between adult and children's versions, as well as distinguishing fact, legend and fiction.

Books about families are another kind of book of interest to the middle grade child. These include books such as, *The Moffats*,[8] *The All-of-a-Kind Family*,[9] the *Little House* [10] books. Children can discuss the different types of families, their homes, their standards of living, their ideas of discipline, etc. This helps to build the understandings of how families differ and yet are basically alike. Books such as *Elder Brother*,[11] *Thirty One Brothers and Sisters*,[12] *Henner's Lydia* [13] and other De Angeli books give a picture of other cultures, ethnic and social groups and their type of family life. Books such as these also aid in developing more understandings of human interrelations.

Similar to the books about families are books about particular boys or girls. Such books as *Shen of the Sea*,[14] *The Courage of Sarah Noble*,[15] *Caddie Woodlawn*,[16] *Adam of the Road*,[17] *Isle of the Blue Dolphins*,[18]

[3] Ingri and Edgar P. D'Aulaire, *Benjamin Franklin* (Garden City, New York: Nelson, Doubleday, Inc., 1950).

[4] Carl Sandburg, *Abraham Lincoln* (4 Vols., New York: Harcourt, Brace and Co., 1928).

[5] Carl Sandburg, *Abe Lincoln, The Prairie Years* (New York: Harcourt, Brace & Co., 1928).

[6] Esther Forbes, *Paul Revere* (Boston: Houghton, Mifflin Co., 1942).

[7] Esther Forbes, *Johnny Tremain* (Boston: Houghton, Mifflin Co., 1943).

[8] Eleanor Estes, *The Moffats* (New York: Harcourt, Brace & Co., 1941).

[9] Sidney Taylor, *The All-of-a-Kind Family* (Chicago: Wilson & Follett Co., 1951).

[10] Laura Ingalls Wilder, *Little House* books (New Uniform Edition; New York: Harper & Bros., 1953).

[11] Evelyn S. Lampman, *Elder Brother* (Garden City, N.Y.: Doubleday, Inc., 1950).

[12] Reba P. Mirsky, *Thirty One Brothers and Sisters* (Chicago: Wilson & Follett, 1952).

[13] Marguerite De Angeli, *Henner's Lydia* (Garden City, N.Y.: Doubleday, Inc., 1936).

[14] Arthur Chrisman, *Shen of the Sea* (Garden City, N.Y.: E. P. Dutton, 1925).

[15] Alice Dalgliesh, *The Courage of Sarah Noble* (New York: Charles Scribner's Sons, 1954).

[16] Carol Brink, *Caddie Woodlawn* (New York: Macmillan Co., 1937).

[17] Elizabeth Janet Gray, *Adam of the Road* (New York: Viking Press, 1942).

[18] Scott O'Dell, *The Island of the Blue Dolphins* (Boston: Houghton, Mifflin Co., 1960).

can be used to discuss the problems of the main character, his fears, his dreams and how he shows courage beyond his fears. The personality of the main character can be studied as to his strengths and weaknesses shown in the story, his values and judgments, and whether he is shown to have strong biases or prejudices. Children can consider what they would do under similar circumstances and project what would have happened if the children's suggestions were followed.

Puzzles are a challenge to middle grade children that they find hard to resist. A way to use books to stimulate puzzles is to have children write their version of how a book came to be written, or write how they would have ended a particular book if they had written it. Then the children can go even further and write to publishers and authors and ask about the story behind the books. This would also give children an opportunity to learn more about the publication of books and give them more knowledge of authors as real people. There is, of course, already published, *The Story Behind Modern Books*,[19] but it is quite old. It might serve as a starting point to write about more current books.

Writing to publishers and authors can serve yet another purpose in teaching critical reading. A complete study can develop from writing to various publishers of books that are familiar and favorites of the children. This can take the form of a study of all the books of a particular author or illustrator. This can lead to a discussion of a particular style of one author, expressions he uses in more than one of his books, similarity of characters or locales. It can be a study of the new books for the year that will be published by one company, their variety, the subject most popular for that year. Sometimes publishers will loan a school original manuscripts, galley sheets or original illustrations. This can lead to an appraisal of the field of publishing, the cost, the way books are advertised, the format, and so forth. The impact that publishers have on what is available for children to read can be discovered from such a study. The people who write books are of much interest to young readers. They enjoy trying to find out as much as they can about the authors' lives and families. The *Junior Book of Authors*[20] and magazines such as *Horn Book* and *Elementary English* can be of much help to them in seeking information about authors. Of course, writing to the author is always a way to learn how he lives, how he chooses his plots, his philosophy of writing, his family and his interests.

The pictures in books fascinate young children. As they grow older they still enjoy pictures, but their books have fewer and fewer illustrations. Children's picture books can be used by older readers for a different pur-

[19] Elizabeth Montgomery, *The Story Behind Modern Books* (New York: Dodd, Mead & Co., 1949).

[20] *Junior Book of Authors*, ed. S. J. Kunitz & Howard Haycraft (2nd Revised Edition; New York: Wilson & Co., 1951).

pose. The different styles of various illustrators can be compared. The study of the style and media of one illustrator can be made by collecting as many books as possible and comparing the earlier books of an illustrator with his more recent books. One can never forget the change of style of Robert McCloskey from *Make Way for Ducklings* [21] to *Time of Wonder.*[22] It is very hard to believe that they were done by the same person. Another use of illustration is the comparison of media, color depth and the aesthetic aspects of illustrations. Older readers can appraise the part that the illustrations play in the stories in picture books. A more mature appraisal can be made by a consideration of how illustrators have affected the entire development of children's books.

Many of the basal reader series have a watered down version of famous children's books. Children can read the original books and compare the stories in the readers. They can evaluate the similarities and the differences of the two versions as to simplicity or difficulty, degrees of descriptive language, style and interest. Readers also have simplified versions of folk and fairy tales which can also be compared. Another comparison can be made between the original versions of classics, such as, *Little Women,*[23] *Tom Sawyer,*[24] *Treasure Island,*[25] and series of these that are published in simpler and more attractive form by some book publishers. Don't be surprised if some children do not prefer the original! Studies such as these may include possible reasons for making more than one version, the job of editing, the place of illustrations, differences in cost, and so on.

Children can examine the advantages of various kinds of book clubs in learning how to build up their own personal libraries. Such clubs as the Junior Literary Guild, the Arrow Book Club, the Weekly Reader Book Club, will be good for this. Some readers may move into the adult Book-of-the-Month Club, the Literary Guild Book Club, *American Heritage.* Then there are the scientific types of monthly books, such as *Around the World Program, Know Your America, Nature Program, National Aviation.* The good periodicals for children should be introduced to them, also, for lighter and shorter reading periods. We build discriminating adult readers by helping children to be discriminating in their reading tastes.

One of the many of the mass media that can be used in the classroom to help children develop the ability to read critically is the newspaper. The accounts of important events can be compared in several newspapers. The newspaper can also be used as a spring board into the study of how news

---

[21] Robert McCloskey, *Make Way for Ducklings* (New York: Viking Press, 1941).

[22] Robert McCloskey, *A Time of Wonder* (New York: Viking Press, 1957).

[23] Louisa M. Alcott, *Little Women* (Boston: Little Brown & Co., 1934). (1868)

[24] Mark Twain (Samuel Clemens), *Tom Sawyer* (New York: Harper & Bros., 1917). (1876)

[25] Robert L. Stevenson, *Treasure Island* (New York: Charles Scribner's Sons, 1924). (1882)

is gathered and reported, the effect that the printed word has on the children's lives. More advanced readers may be interested in the *New York Times,* the *Commercial Appeal.*

Poetry is one of the best ways to help children to read critically. For poetry is an abbreviated thought. The poet must leave so much to the reader's imagination. A keen interest in poetry is not developed in a short time. Poetry takes much tasting, much thinking, much time to assimilate the thoughts presented. But for these reasons it must not be neglected. Poetry, as all other reading, should be partly for enjoyment. It should never be presented to young children for analysis of structure, meter or rhyme. It should be presented for the beauty of the thought it brings, the release of emotion through verse. It can be used, without hindering any of these, to discuss and appraise the thought presented and its effect on the reader. Children should be encouraged to see that they, too, can write poetry. However, if we use poetry with children as we should, they will soon discover this for themselves.

There are many sources that a teacher can have in her classroom to help children develop an ability to use and learn more about books, authors and illustrators. Besides many and varied trade books, there are bibliographies put out by the American Library Association, listing books of various age levels and subjects. There are bibliographies of adult books that young people will enjoy. This association also publishes *Libraries Bulletin.* The University of Chicago Children's Book Center publishes an excellent book list about books, their authors and illustrators. The *New York Times* Book Review Section and Supplement has valuable articles, also. The *Saturday Review* and the *Atlantic Monthly* magazines will be of interest to more mature readers. There are many more, but one of the best is a teacher or librarian who tells children of new books, shows them or reads from them to children. This personal appraisal means more to most children than a printed account, no matter how well done the printed account may be. Children, too, can be instrumental in encouraging others to read favorites by preparing bibliographies that they feel other children may enjoy.

The role of a school librarian in helping children grow in interest and ability with books is very important. The public librarian is also important. One who reads and tells stories to children and discusses their reading with them is invaluable. She is the spirit of the library to children. How she helps and guides children with books is one indication of how they will continue their use of libraries in the future. A good librarian will encourage children to feel at home in the library, to enjoy it. She will help children learn the aids the library can give. It is possible for even young children to become acquainted with the card catalog. As they grow older, the librarian can introduce the indexes that are available, and help them to discover aids to their own book needs. If teacher and librarian work together, the ways they can help children keep growing and stretching their abilities to use books are unlimited.

Any one of these suggestions may be used as a starting point to get children to thinking for themselves and interacting with the science of linguistics has valid application to the classroom in ways that have not previously been practiced.

But those ways are not those of Mr. Dawkins. This writer feels he is as wrong as is Rudolf Flesch, the editors of the *Saturday Evening Post,* Hunter Diack, Leonard Bloomfield, and others. All of these individuals are also as wrong as those educators who advocate that letter sounds are never used in the teaching of reading and spelling. In fact, it is not a black or white situation. We cannot teach reading without the recognitions of whole words in a sight vocabulary or without the use of letter sounds. We need both. They are mutually inclusive rather than mutually exclusive. It is regrettable that space limitations forbid an adequate discussion of the way these two elements of language teaching fit together.

The fact that children have large measure of control over their language system by 4½ years of age makes the kind of repetitive "Look, look, look" type of reader at age 6 silly. The limitations of vocabulary control have forced a sterility of content that has aroused professional criticism as well as some hilarious stories for some time.[26] If Mr. Dawkins is suggesting that readers should be written that will "present minimally contrasting vowel patterns (mad-mid, hot-hut, and so on)" he is suggesting another restriction on content over and above vocabulary control. The result might make Alice and Jerry read like Perry Mason, which could be considered a kind of progress, I suppose.

It is to be hoped that those linguists that are trying to offer their contributions to professional education will exert some influence to prevent gross misinterpretations of the nature of language in the classroom. The exciting and important development in the teaching of grammar in the secondary school is a case in point. The need for educators to know more about linguistics is undeniable. Only three aspects have been discussed here; there are most certainly many more. But it is the educator who must make the application. This is a matter of cooperative effort, and, hopefully, debates like these will serve to increase progress towards the improvement of education.

[26] See Shel Silverstein, *"Uncle Shelby's ABZ Book."* Simon and Schuster, N.Y.C., 1961.

PART FOUR

Research in Critical Reading

The limited amount of research that has been done in critical reading focuses mainly on three topics: (1) critical reading as an ability distinct from general reading ability, (2) factors affecting critical reading or critical thinking, and (3) the influence of instruction on the ability to read or think critically.

Research in these areas has been beset by methodological problems, making it difficult for the reader to interpret the findings. For example, different meanings have been attached to the concept of critical reading by various investigators. In Sochor's article, critical reading is defined as "a level of interpretation higher than that needed for literal interpretation." She includes such skills as ability to identify the most important idea in the story and to distinguish the central topic from subordinate ones. These skills are considered by many other educators to be general comprehension skills of a different type than critical reading. In contrast, Wolf and Ellinger define critical responses of the reader as inferring, going beyond literal meanings, using data to make an evaluation, or detecting logical fallacies in the material. These and other differences in the various authors' interpretations of critical reading make evaluative comparisons difficult.

A major deterrent to research in critical reading has been the absence of adequate measuring instruments. Of necessity, most investigators have developed their own tests and although fairly high reliability has often been established for these tests, construct validity has been neglected. Since this type of validation requires gradual accumulation of information from a variety of sources, it is not surprising that it would be missing for measuring instruments in a field as little researched as critical reading.

Other problems are prevalent in the studies on critical reading: there is an absence of randomization that may seriously affect the validity of the results—some investigators attempt to match subjects rather than utilize the more preferable technique of pre-experimental equation of groups through randomization. Experimenter bias is frequently introduced by investigators who teach the experimental classes themselves; the teacher variable is often left uncontrolled; statistical treatment of the results is frequently inadequate; and the reporting is often incomplete or goes beyond the findings. All of these factors detract from the quality of the research in the field.

The studies selected for this section have some of the methodological errors mentioned above, but the selections are representative of the best in the field. For example, Livingston controls the teacher variable by assigning each teacher in his study to teach both an experimental and a control group. Suppes and Binford's study should also be noted for the interesting design comparing experimental classes in a fifth grade with control groups from university logic classes.

Some of the selected research studies in this section are on the topic presented in Section I, i.e., the nature of critical reading. Findings of these studies indicate that critical reading is an ability distinct from general reading ability. Although many educators assume that reading is a general ability and that there are no separate comprehension skills, the notion has been disputed by several investigators. (Maney,* McCullough,* Betts; * Sochor; Shores and Saupe) In the reports presented in this section, Sochor, and Shores and Saupe have demonstrated that there is a positive but low correlation between the various comprehension skills. Their findings are representative of those of other investigators. The correlations reported suggest that a common factor does pervade reading skills, but that the ability to read well literally does not necessarily ensure the ability to read well critically.

* All studies with an asterisk are annotated in the bibliography but do not appear in this section.

Research on factors affecting children's ability to read critically has not been extensive except in the area of the reader's attitudes. (Groff, McKillop,* Thayer and Pronko,* and Crossen) The investigations reported here by Groff and Crossen show that a person's biases at a given point in time may influence his ability to read a pasage critically. Other studies have shown similarly that the attitudes which subjects from fifth grade through college bring to a passage affect their comprehension of it. Open-mindedness has been found by Kemp to be one factor positively affecting critical thinking. Another factor, intelligence, has been shown by Sochor, and Suppes and Binford to be substantially related to critical reading or critical thinking ability.

Several investigators have studied the influence of instruction on the ability to read critically (the subject of Section III of this book). A major impediment to the development of critical readers has been the assumption by many teachers that critical thinking or reading will develop naturally as a result of maturation and that specific instruction is unnecessary. The accuracy of this assumption can be seriously questioned in light of the studies done in the 1950's by Gray and Rogers,* and Rogers,* who found that high school students and adults could not make judgments or evaluate printed materials without instruction. In this section, the articles of several investigators show the effects of specific instruction upon critical reading or thinking abilities. Livingston, Lundsteen, Nardelli, and Wolf and Ellinger's results indicate that direct instruction can influence children's ability to read or respond critically while studies by Hyram, and Suppes and Binford show that critical thinking can also be developed through instruction. Although the research in critical reading has been sparse and scattered, the findings from the studies do provide some basis for believing that instruction in critical reading should be included in the reading program.

Two overviews are presented at the beginning of this section in order to clarify further the state of the research in critical reading. The one by Durrell and Chambers was chosen for the authors' critique of the research in critical reading and their analysis of research needs in the field. Eller and Wolf take a somewhat different direction in their review. Since research in critical reading has been sparse, they review studies in the field of social psychology of communication that they consider relevant to critical reading. Factors are reviewed that influence the effectiveness of a communication such as (1) the communicator's trustworthiness and prestige, (2) the sidedness, order of presentation, specificness and emotional quality of a communication, and (3) the recipient's beliefs. Although the studies reported deal with communication in general, Eller and Wolf assume that the results can be applied to the reading process. Their final point—that research workers who are specialists in reading should conduct experiments which parallel many of the studies they cite—is well taken.

W. W.

38. Research in Thinking Abilities Related to Reading

Donald D. Durrell and J. Richard Chambers

Almost every school subject claims thinking as its special province or as one of its major objectives. Social studies, science, mathematics, literature, languages, fine arts, and vocational subjects claim improvement in thinking abilities as an outcome. Thinking abilities have been courted by educational methods throughout history: the Socratic method, the Montessori methods, case methods, problem methods, discussion methods, apprenticeships, and even "brain storming" are proposed as ways of inducing thinking. The art of questioning, formerly a staple in normal school training, was intended to improve thinking; remnants of this approach are found in the study guides at the ends of chapters in school textbooks. Since thinking is so widely and consistently approved as an objective of education in all subjects and at all levels of education, it is strange that it does not have a more established research background.

Various types of thinking are essential to later use of reading. Simple comprehension, when no relationships or analyses are made, is likely to result in rapid forgetting. Even the reading of fiction, if not associated with known situations in the child's life, may be little more than controlled daydreaming. If reading is to be useful in later behavior, some type of mental reaction must accompany or follow reading.

There is no single definition of thinking satisfactory for research or teaching purposes. Thinking seems to embrace many types of mental tasks, and since most definitions are ambiguous or elusive, it appears necessary to give illustrations and examples in order to make clear the type of thinking task being taught or measured. Russell (9) describes the following types of children's thinking: associative thinking and fantasy, concept formation, problem solving, critical thinking, and creative thinking. There is no clear agreement upon the definitions or numbers of types of thinking; a number of writers such as Dewey (3) equate thinking with problem solving, while others follow Symonds (11) in finding many different types of thinking. The fact that there are discrete functions in thinking is shown by low correlations between various measures of thinking. In a recent study Chambers (2) found correlations of .33 to .71 among several measures of thinking abilities, but these were reduced to .14 to .55 when mental ability was held constant, and were further reduced to .03 to .33 when reading achievement was controlled statistically.

The ability to think appears to rest upon training rather than upon in-

"Research in Thinking Abilities Related to Reading," by Donald D. Durrell and J. Richard Chambers, The Reading Teacher, XII, 89–91. Reprinted with permission of Donald D. Durrell and J. Richard Chambers and the International Reading Association.

telligence. Glaser (5) demonstrated marked gains in critical thinking among twelfth-grade pupils; Kay (7) showed that critical reading could be improved among pupils in high school; Salisbury (10) produced marked gains in the ability of high school students to organize and subordinate ideas; Jenkins (6) improved the elaborative thinking of sixth graders; and Arnold (1) showed that critical thinking can be taught in the fifth and sixth grades.

Several studies reported low relationships between intelligence and either initial or final scores in the thinking abilities taught; a high score in reading comprehension does not assure achievement in any of the thinking abilities measured thus far. Apparently, thinking abilities rest upon specific instruction, incidental instruction, or fortunate environment, or heredity. The important thing is that all types of thinking thus far taught respond well to specific instruction.

The first essential to research in thinking is definition; the second is measurement. Any person proposing research in children's thinking will do well to read the descriptions of thinking proposed by Russell (9), and follow by examining measures of various forms of thinking, such as those of Wrightstone (13), Raths (8), Gans (4), Tyler (12), and Jenkins (6). Any investigation of teaching higher mental processes will include a measure which may be adapted to new levels, subjects, or situations. Research in the construction of tests of thinking abilities of various types and in various subjects is to be encouraged.

There are numerous status studies to follow the construction of measures of thinking abilities, especially as they relate to reading and study. We need measures of ability to interpret ideas, to make inferences and applications, to generalize, to organize and subordinate ideas, and to do many forms of critical and creative thinking. When these measures are available, we may discover common and different factors among them and define better approaches to instruction and measurement. Probably we will find that certain types of thinking, such as elaborative or associational thinking, have a high transfer value, that the techniques of stimulating a "flow of ideas" in one subject transfer to other subjects with little effort. Salisbury (10) suggests that a high transfer results from lessons in organizing ideas. Critical thinking, which requires the evaluation of a product or performance against some standard, may be so dependent upon specialized knowledge that there is little transfer.

Further status studies are to be found in the examination of textbooks, workbooks, and study guides. It is sometimes difficult to discover any pattern among the suggested thinking activities for pupils; certainly, there appears to be no developmental sequence among them. If there is merit to the "art of questioning" as a stimulus to thought, there should be some examination of the types of questions presented in instructional materials. When we know more about thinking processes, the design of study guides for readers and textbooks will improve. The examination and classification of questions and study activities in textbooks should be accompanied by a similar examination of reading comprehension tests. Our measures of the outcomes of reading may be too largely the retention of facts or simple interpretation.

The most profitable research ventures will be those of design and evaluation of materials and methods of teaching thinking. From the miscellany of exercises found in current textbooks we will need to select types of questions and exercises, find possible sequences and levels among them, provide intensive practice, and evaluate outcomes. Probably the most important to the use of reading is elaborative thinking in its various forms: relating the content of reading to previous knowledge, illustrations and applications, opportunities for use, relationships to other fields, and various associations which integrate reading into knowledge or action. It will probably be found that well-designed exercises in elaborative thinking in reading will produce higher permanent retention and greater availability of knowledge to new situations. We may discover that elaborative thinking is better done in discussion groups of various sizes than in either individual or whole-class activities, that specific planning or applications are better than remote or academic tasks, that intensive sequential instruction is more effective than occasional or incidental instruction.

REFERENCES

1. DWIGHT L. ARNOLD, "Testing Ability to Use Data in the 5th and 6th Grade." *Educational Research Bulletin,* 17 (Dec., 1938), 255–59.
2. J. RICHARD CHAMBERS, "Relationships Among Measurable Mental Tasks Related to Reading." Doctor's Dissertation, Boston Univ., 1956. University Microfilms, Ann Arbor, Mich.
3. JOHN DEWEY, *How We Think.* Boston: D. C. Heath and Co., 1910.
4. ROMA GANS, *A Study of Critical Reading Comprehension in the Intermediate Grades.* New York: Bureau of Publications, Teachers College, Columbia Univ., 1940.
5. EDWARD M. GLASER, *An Experiment in the Development of Critical Thinking.* New York: Bureau of Publications, Teachers College, Columbia Univ., 1941.
6. ETHEL M. JENKINS, "An Evaluation of Directed Teaching of Associational Reading in Social Studies with Sixth Grade Children." Doctor's dissertation, Boston Univ., 1953. University Microfilms, Ann Arbor, Mich.
7. SYLVIA KAY, "Critical Reading: Its Importance and Development." *English Journal,* 35 (Sept., 1946), 380–85.

8. Louis Raths, "A Thinking Test." *Educational Research Bulletin*, 23 (March, 1944), 72–75.

9. David H. Russell, *Children's Thinking*. Boston: Ginn and Co., 1956.

10. Rachael Salisbury, "A Study of the Transfer Effects of Training in Logical Organization." *Journal of Educational Research*, 28 (Dec., 1934), 241–54.

11. Percival M. Symonds, *Education and the Psychology of Thinking*. New York: McGraw-Hill, 1936.

12. Ralph W. Tyler, "Measuring the Ability to Infer." *Educational Research Bulletin*, Ohio State Univ., Nov., 1930.

13. J. Wayne Wrightstone, *Test of Critical Thinking in the Social Studies*. New York: Bureau of Publications, Teachers College, Columbia Univ., 1938.

39. Factors in Critical Reading

William Eller and Judith G. Wolf

Improvement of critical reading ability is an acknowledged goal of many of the college reading programs in America, and of many courses in freshman English, rhetoric, or communications skills. A number of college reading handbooks—Stroud, Ammons, and Bauman (17), Glock (3), and Hill and Eller (4), for example—include assorted exercises for the extension of the critical skills, and a few complete textbooks are devoted to critical thinking and reading, usually with considerable emphasis upon logic. Altick's *Preface to Critical Reading* (1) is typical of these texts employed in teaching evaluative skill to college freshmen and sophomores.

Because college-level instruction in reading is usually provided by departments of English and education, the teaching methodologies commonly employed have been developed mainly by specialists from these two academic areas, and the bulk of the published materials have been created by authors who are either English instructors or professional educators or both. Inasmuch as reading teachers with English and education backgrounds tend to be skills-oriented rather than personality-oriented, the programs and materials which they have developed are directed toward the improvement of specific academic reading skills and give very little attention to the psychological, social, and emotional aspects of reading comprehension. Instruction in critical reading when planned by

William Eller and Judith Wolf, "Factors in Critical Reading," *The Philosophical and Sociological Bases of Reading*, 14th Yearbook of the N.R.C., Eric L. Thurston and Lawrence E. Hafner, editors, 1965, pp. 64–72. Reprinted with permission of William Eller and Judith Wolf and the National Reading Conference, Inc.

English teachers tends to feature the fundamentals of logic and the numerous propaganda devices against which the reader must learn to defend himself. Reading teachers trained in education departments, on the other hand, are inclined to construct and use exercises which appear to develop skills such as (1) determining the author's probable purpose, (2) gauging the extent of the writer's expertise, (3) detecting inconsistencies between statements of different authors and even within the writings of a single author, and (4) compensating for the known biases of standard publications such as the *Chicago Tribune* and *The Reporter*. Probably no one would argue that it is useless to teach these and other skills commonly pursued in college reading centers and rhetoric classes; the question is: Are there some factors in the process of reading comprehension which are so personal that the mastery of the so-called reading skills does not assure the ability to read critically, at least in some types of printed matter?

The experimentation of social psychologists and communication theorists over the past two decades would seem to indicate that the foregoing question must be answered in the affirmative; that relationships between the reader's personality, the portion of society in which he functions, and various aspects of the communicative act have considerable bearing upon the whole comprehension process, including the evaluative acts known as critical reading. It is true that most of this experimentation was not performed with the purpose of checking on the factors which relate to critical reading ability, but the studies subsequently cited appear to have definite implications for reading comprehension in general and critical reading, per se. At the very least these experiments suggest numerous possibilities for research in the evaluative processes of reading comprehension.

Since there are numerous experiments in the psychology of communications which would seem to have implications for teachers of reading comprehension, some organizational scheme should prove helpful to a scrutiny of the research. Perhaps the simplest acceptable arrangement of evidence would be one employing four categories: (1) Who is trying to convey a message? (2) What is the message conveyed? (3) What is the nature of the mode of communication? (4) Who is the recipient of the message? Each of the several studies reported herein will be considered under one of the four questions. Of course, many other investigations could be reported; but the ones cited are representative, it is hoped. For certain of the experiments contradictory data could be found elsewhere. The discrepancies among studies and the incomparability of some research works are attributable in part to the fact that different experimenters have based their designs upon different theoretical frameworks. Inasmuch as every one of these frameworks is at this point very incomplete, it is not surprising that research workers disagree concerning the interpretation of the findings of others as well as their own.

Who is trying to convey the message? Characteristics of the communicator which could be expected to influence the effectiveness or force of the communication are his (1) credibility, (2) prestige, and (3) attractiveness. The first of these has repeatedly been demonstrated to be a factor in communicative efficacy. In 1951, in a frequently-cited study, Hovland and Weiss (7) presented subjects (college students) with four articles, each of which was attributed by the experimenters to a highly credible source for half the subjects. A low-credibility individual was credited with the authorship of each article for the other half of the subjects. Analysis of subject responses indicated that communications attributed to high credibility sources were more often adjudged "fair" or "unbiased" than were the same communications attributed to low credibility writers, and the conclusions were more often considered "justified" when the subjects viewed the authors as of high credibility. Immediately following the reading the indication of change in opinion in the direction favored by an article was three-and-one-half times as great among those who thought they were reading the argument of a highly credible author as among subjects who viewed their author as having low credibility. However, this differential in attitude change did not persist. One month after the experiment no significant differences between groups could be detected. Although Mandell and Hovland (14) in 1952 were unable to establish significantly different changes in attitude among two groups, when one set of subjects thought they were reading the opinions of an author who was "suspect" and the other group viewed its author as "non-suspect," the bulk of the Yale studies of this variable of credibility indicates that a communicator who is perceived as credible or trustworthy is more persuasive than one not so perceived.

Bettelheim and Janowitz (2) mailed anti-Semitic literature attributed to various authors to several dozen male Gentiles. Analysis of responses revealed that the propaganda was more affective if it was attributed to a known Jew. The investigators interpreted this trend as an indication that the readers had regarded the ostensible Jewish authorship as reasonably objective.

In the matter of prestige as a characteristic of the communicator, Kishler (12) reported that the esteem in which Catholic priests were held by his subjects was related to the amount they learned from the motion picture "The Keys of the Kingdom" and to the magnitude of opinion change in the direction of religious tolerance. Kishler added the interesting observation that in this situation the subjects were reacting differentially, not to a genuine priest, but to an actor.

What is the nature of the communication? A number of variables in the content of a communication may be related to its efficacy. One such variable concerns the "sidedness" of a presentation: Is a communication more persuasive if it presents only one side of an issue, or if it presents arguments on two sides? The research on this question is not entirely clear-cut, because the investigators have usually confounded the sidedness variable with some other factor such as the degree of overt commitment (of subjects) to a certain point of view. However, Hovland et. al. (6) has attempted to summarize the literature with a few basic generalizations: (1) In the long run two-sided presentation is more effective than one-sided when the audience is subsequently exposed to counter-propaganda, regardless of initial opinions; or when the audience initially disagrees with the communicator's point of view, regardless of subsequent exposure to counter-propaganda. (2) One-sided communication is more effective than two-sided if the audience initially is in agreement with the point of view of the communicator and is not exposed to subsequent counter-propaganda. Klapper (13) modifies these generalizations with the addition of summary statements concerning some interacting variables: One-sided presentations are more effective with persons of limited education; one-sided communications are efficient persuaders of audiences which are required to publicly defend the presented view; and one-sided presentations are more susceptible to "boomerang" effect if the audience suspects that the communicator is "pouring it on" too much.

Somewhat related to the sidedness issue is the factor of order of presentation. Much of Hovland's 1957 volume (3) in the Yale series is devoted to a consideration of the effects of order of presentation and its interaction with other factors. The basic question is: If two different points of view are expressed to an audience, which is more persuasive, the argument presented first or the latter one? At the conclusion of a series of experiments on this primacy-versus-recency problem, Hovland settled upon the following summary statements: (1) If two opposing statements are offered by different communicators, the position stated first doesn't necessarily have the advantage. (2) If communicators make a public endorsement of one side of an issue before exposure to the opposing side, subsequent presentation of the second side is less effective; hence, there is a primacy effect. However, the anonymous statements of opinion through the use of questionnaires after presentation of one side of a controversy does not significantly reduce the persuasiveness of the second (and opposing) presentation. (3) If both sides of a controversial issue are presented in a single session by a single communicator, there is a distinct tendency for the viewpoints presented first to prevail. However, this primacy effect can be reduced either by interpolating other activities between the two presentations of controversy, or by warning the subjects against the tendency to respond to first impressions. (4) If communications highly desirable to the communicatees are presented first, followed by less desirable messages, there is more persuasion than when the reverse order is followed. (5) Order of presentation interacts with personality type to some extent in that experimental subjects with high cognition need are influenced by communications without regard for the order, whereas those with low cognitive needs demonstrate the law of primacy.

Another continuum which relates to persuasibility is the degree of specificness—as contrasted with implicitness—in the communicator's directives. As a rule, the persuasive effect is greater if the communicator draws specific conclusions rather than permitting the recipients to draw their own, or as Katz and Lazarsfeld summarized in 1955, "the more specific the suggestion which a personal contact makes, the more likely it is that his or her advice will be followed." (11:17)

In at least a couple of respects the emotional quality of message content seems to relate to the effectiveness of the communication. One of them, the emotional-versus-rational appeal factor, obviously interacts with so many other elements in communicative process that present research only begins to describe its role. Weiss (18) presented three types of content information (one each) to his three experimental groups: group E read a highly inflammatory statement designed to arouse aggressive emotion concerning criminals; group R was confronted with a rational treatment containing factual data on the same subject; and group ER read a text which contained both emotional and rational approaches. The emotion content "induced a greater degree of expressed arousal" than the rational material. Because Weiss had administered a personality inventory to his subjects, he was also able to observe that the attitudes of the high authoritarian aggressives in the sample were significantly more punitive than the opinions of those who were low in this trait measurement, after exposure to the communications.

Another facet of the emotional quality of messages to be investigated by a number of workers is the level of fear induced, or the intensity of the threat. One of the oft-cited studies of this facet was done by Janis and Feshbach (9), who developed three forms of an illustrated lecture on dental hygiene with three different intensities of fear appeal, the most threatening of which included some rather disturbing views of pathological conditions. High school students who constituted the experimental samples revealed more conformity with the position of the communication when the fear level was lowest (of the three); that is, the actual dental practices of the teen-agers were modified least in the groups which had been exposed to the strongest—most fear-arousing appeal. Similar results have been derived from experiments which employed varying levels of fear in communications designed to induce subjects to provide themselves with bomb shelters.

What is the nature of the mode of communication? Of the four questions posed earlier, this is probably the least important to the teacher of critical reading skills, since he is concerned only with printed media, at least in his role as reading teacher. Then, too, the printed word is not a very forceful communicative agency in comparison with more personal

and lively media, and thus interactions with other factors in opinion formation may be of less importance in the reading setting. At least two major
generalizations, however, should be worthy of the reading teacher's notice:
(1) The use of multiple media in communication results in greater persuasive effect than the use of a single media; and (2) the more personal
means of communication are most effective in persuasion, so that for most
recipients of presentations, "in-person" delivery, television and radio
achieve more attitude change than reading matter.

What are the characteristics of the recipient of the communication?
Manis and Blake (16:225) introduced a recent article with the suggestion
that "distorted interpretations of persuasive messages may often result
from the recipient's attempts to maintain his existing beliefs in relatively
unchanged form. Thus, given the fact that most messages can be reasonably interpreted in a variety of ways, it is assumed that the recipient will
select that interpretation which is least challenging to his convictions."
The manner in which existing views affect—by resistance or distortion—
the acceptance of new opinions has attracted the attention of a number
of writers who have investigated it from their differing theoretical bases.
Several experimenters have dealt with this phenomena under the heading
of "selective exposure" and one of Manis' (15) 1961 studies illustrates this
factor in operation. Three groups of college students whose attitudes towards fraternities varied were confronted with a series of short messages
about fraternities, half of them attributed to authors of high prestige, and
half to writers of low prestige. After reading each passage the subjects
attempted to describe fraternities as the author described them, using six
evaluative rating scales. When the student readers reacted to the high
prestige articles they distorted their reports of the authors' statements in
the direction of their own original attitudes; for the low prestige articles
there was no relationship between the subjects' views and their judgments
of the authors' positions. Thus, if the students felt that the writer of a
selection was an important person they tended to displace his position
toward their own views of fraternities.

As might be expected, numerous psychologists have manifested curiosity concerning the relationships between certain personality characteristics of message recipients and their perception of persuasive presentations; however, the research on this relationship has not been as productive
of definitive statements as in some of the areas already considered. The
Yale Studies, particularly those directed by Janis, have led to a few findings worthy of mention. Janis himself (8) reported that low self-esteem
is related to high persuasibility, and vice versa; thus, persons who do not
value themselves highly tend to be susceptible to opinion change. Janis
and Field (10) found no significant relationship between aggressiveness
and persuasibility. Most other investigators have been unable to provide
convincing data regarding any such relationship. Richness of fantasy was

found to be positively related to persuasibility for males but not for fe-
males by Janis and Field. (10)

Group affiliations is another characteristic of the recipient of a communication which has bearing on his persuasibility and comprehension of
the message. For three decades social psychologists have known that communications which accord with the general climate of opinion in a group
are more likely to be accepted by persons who identify themselves with
that group than messages that are at variance with group opinion.

Assorted other characteristics of communicators, their messages, media,
and audiences have been explored in the search for factors which influence the moulding and changing of attitudes. The research and conclusions already cited are by no means exhaustive; they are included chiefly
to demonstrate that a great variety of factors influence the reaction which
an individual recipient may have for a given persuasive communication.

IMPLICATIONS FOR TEACHING CRITICAL READING

Most of the research which has explored factors and relationships in
opinion changes was not conducted specifically to aid the teacher of
critical reading. In fact, some of it was performed under the auspices of
advertising agencies with goals almost diametrically opposed to those of
the reading teacher. Further, much of this research in communication
psychology did not involve reading as a means of presentation; the subjects' reading was in some instances limited to responses to a pencil and
paper instrument after the presentation. Yet certain broad implications
seem justified on the basis of the research and theory in these avenues of
social psychology.

(1) The conventional academic skills approach to the development of
critical reading ability does not even touch upon some of the major
sources of "uncriticalness."

(2) Research workers who are also specialists in reading instruction
should conduct experiments which parallel many of the studies cited
herein. Thus they will learn which of the factors which influences persuasibility in general communication are also important—and to what
extent—in the critical reading processes.

(3) At least on an experimental basis some teachers of critical reading
should incorporate into their methodologies moderately extensive consideration of the social psychology of communication—the facets of communicator, message and communicatee which influence persuasion and
comprehension—in an attempt to improve critical reading skill by arming
students with an understanding of some factors which ordinarily cause
them to be uncritical. This type of instruction has been provided experi-

mentally for at least a decade by Dr. Ralph R. Ojemann and his colleagues at the University of Iowa, apparently with some success.

(4) Reading comprehension is evidently a much more complicated process than the teaching method textbooks indicate, and must be completely re-considered in terms of the evidence handed over by the social psychologists.

REFERENCES

1. RICHARD D. ALTICK, *Preface to Critical Reading*. New York: Holt, Rinehart & Winston, 1960.
2. BRUNO BETTLEHEIM and MORRIS JANOWITZ, "Reactions to Fascist Propaganda: A Pilot Study," *Public Opinion Quarterly*, XIV: 53–60, 1950.
3. MARVIN D. GLOCK, *Improving College Reading*. Boston: Houghton-Mifflin, 1954.
4. WALTER R. HILL and WILLIAM ELLER, *Power in Reading Skills*. Belmont, California: Wadsworth, 1964.
5. C. I. HOVLAND (ed.), *The Order of Presentation in Persuasion*. New Haven: Yale University Press, 1957.
6. C. I. HOVLAND, I. L. JANIS, and H. H. KELLY, *Communication and Persuasion*. New Haven: Yale University Press, 1953.
7. C. I. HOVLAND and W. WEISS, "The Influence of Source Credibility on Communication Effectiveness," *Public Opinion Quarterly*, 15:635–650, 1951.
8. I. L. JANIS, "Personality Correlates of Susceptibility to Persuasion," *Journal of Personality*, 22:504–518, 1954.
9. IRVING L. JANIS and S. FESHBACH, "Effects of Fear—Arousing Communications," *Journal of Abnormal and Social Psychology*, XLVIII: 78–92, 1953.
10. I. L. JANIS and PETER B. FIELD, "A Behavioral Assessment of Persuasibility: Consistency of Individual Differences," *Sociometry*, 19:241–59, 1956.
11. ELIHU KATZ and PAUL F. LAZARSFELD, "Personal Influence: The Part Played by People in the Flow of Mass Communications," in J. T. Klapper, *The Effects of Mass Communication*. Glencoe, Ill.: Free Press, 1960, 117.
12. JOHN KISHLER, "Prediction of Differential Learning from a Motion Picture by Means of Indices of Identification Potentials Derived from Attitudes Toward the Main Character," *American Psychologist*, V: 298–99, 1950.
13. J. T. KLAPPER, *The Effects of Mass Communication*. Glencoe, Illinois: Free Press, 1960.

14. WALLACE MANDELL and CARL I. HOVLAND, "Is There a Law Of Primacy In Persuasion?" *American Psychologist*, VII: 538, 1952.
15. M. MANIS, "The Interpretation of Persuasive Messages as a Function of Recipient Attitude and Source Prestige," *Journal of Abnormal and Social Psychology*, 63: 82–86, 1961.
16. M. MANIS and J. B. BLAKE, "Interpretation of Persuasive Messages as a Function of Prior Immunization," *Journal of Abnormal and Social Psychology*, 66: 225–230, 1963.
17. JAMES B. STROUD, ROBERT B. AMMONS, and HARRY A. BAUMAN, *Improving Reading Ability*. New York: Appleton-Century-Crofts, Inc., 1956.
18. W. WEISS, Emotional Arousal and Attitude Change, *Psychological Reports*, 6: 267–280, 1960.

40.   Literal and Critical Reading in Social Studies

E. Elona Sochor

THE PROBLEM AND ITS SCOPE

The purpose of this study was to investigate certain aspects of reading comprehension among fifth-grade pupils. In order to explore the problem, it was necessary to construct and validate an intermediate-grade reading test in social studies. The specific problems considered were:

1. What is the relationship between verbal intelligence and
   a. "General" reading ability?
   b. Achievement in literal reading comprehension in social studies?
   c. Achievement in critical reading comprehension in social studies?
2. What is the relationship between "general" reading ability and
   a. The ability to comprehend literally in social studies?
   b. The ability to comprehend critically in social studies?
3. What is the relationship between proficiency in literal and critical interpretation of social studies?
4. What is the relationship between proficiency in each selected critical reading skill and the ability to comprehend literally in social studies?

"Literal and Critical Reading in Social Studies," by E. Elona Sochor, is reprinted by permission from *Journal of Experimental Education*, XXVII (September 1958), 49–56.

To date, the concepts of the measurement and development of reading comprehension as held in the 1920's are still widely evident at all educational levels. Reading tests, largely limited to the appraisal of "sense-meaning" and weighted with materials from the field of literature, are used commonly to determine all reading needs. Little attention is being given to critical reading skills in study situations. In practice, reading tends to remain a "unitary ability."

Such a concept of reading ability is no longer tenable. Conclusive data from studies by Dewey (11), Tyler (32), Thorndike (30), and Davis (10) indicate that adequate reading comprehension necessitates not one but several levels of mental functioning. Although this premise is well established, much research still needs to be conducted on the more specific aspects of reading comprehension.

Moreover, the skills and abilities characteristic of effective reading interpretation are not the same in all content areas. The specificity of skills within subject-matter areas at the secondary and college levels has been substantiated by Shores (27) and Humber (18). Further data are needed on the nature of these skills in each content area, particularly at the elementary school level.

Another major reading problem in education today is verbalism. Too much emphasis has been placed upon a low-level type of interpretation. Retardation in reading has been determined too frequently in terms of word perception alone. As early as 1921, investigators reported deficiencies in the reading comprehension of some school children. Although these children could reproduce what they had read with a "parrot-like precision," they had little real understanding. Since then, many educators and research workers have stressed the importance of this problem (4, 17, 25). Nevertheless, verbalism in reading still appears to be rampant in every phase of school activity. To help resolve this situation, measures of appraising and techniques for developing the various aspects of literal and critical interpretation in reading need to be investigated. The major solution, however, rests with the schools. Effective reading comprehension must be emphasized in all reading activities.

The importance of reading comprehension is not limited to school life. The ability to interpret what is read on current events is vital to the preservation of democracy. In such a social order, comprehending what is stated directly is a prerequisite. Mere literal interpretation, however, is not sufficient. The citizen must be skilled in evaluating critically the wealth of available printed materials.

LIMITATIONS OF THE STUDY

Experimental Design—The purpose of this investigation was to study the relationships between intelligence and three types of reading ability: "general" reading, literal interpretation, and critical interpretation. Final data were obtained on a representative sample of five hundred thirteen fifth-grade pupils. To obtain these data on reading skills in social studies, it was necessary to *construct and validate* the experimental edition of a reading test in that content area. A group test of verbal intelligence and a standardized reading test were used to help in estimating the normality of the distribution.

Statistical Design—The results were analyzed with large sample techniques which included the Chi-square test for presence or absence of relationship, and the product-moment and point-biserial methods of correlation. The reading test in social studies was evaluated by means of one technique estimating test reliability and three techniques estimating item validity.

The Population—A total of six hundred eleven pupils were tested. Complete results obtained on five hundred thirteen subjects were used in the study.

1. Source: Eighteen fifth-grade classes were tested in June 1949. Nine of these were from four suburban Philadelphia schools, and nine from four urban Philadelphia schools.

2. Age: The chronological age range was from 10–0 through 14–6.

3. Sex: Boys and girls were tested.

4. Race: White and Negro children were included.

5. Intelligence: Verbal intelligence quotients ranged from 57 through 158.

6. Reading Grade: The reading grade ranged from minus 2.5 through 10.3.

7. Final Population Criterion: Two hundred sixty-nine cases of the final population fell within plus or minus one standard deviation from the mean on the two criterion measures—intelligence and reading grade.

TESTS

The Gates Reading Survey, Form I, Level of Comprehension (Published by Teachers College, Columbia University), was administered as a power test in "general" reading comprehension. The Experimental Edition of the Intermediate Reading Test, Social Studies, was used to appraise literal and critical interpretation in social studies. The Pintner General Ability Test, Form A (published by World Book Company), was used as a measure of verbal intelligence.

The following terminology is basic to this study. For purposes of clarity, literal reading comprehension and the selected critical reading comprehension skills will be illustrated as well as defined. In each example, the correct response for the test item will be the first, and one of the distractors will be the second.

"Literal Reading" represents the ability to obtain a low-level type of interpretation by using only the information explicitly stated. For example, the selection states, "Millions of workers dragged stone blocks for the outside walls and packed basket after basket of earth between them." The test item appraising literal interpretation of this sentence is: "The outside walls were made of (1) stone, (2) earth . . ."

"Critical Reading" represents the ability to obtain a level of interpretation higher than that needed for literal interpretation. In this study the following critical reading comprehension skills were set up:

1. Functional Vocabulary tests the reader's background of experience in reference to a concept used in the selection.

2. Semantic Variation of Vocabulary tests the reader's ability to identify a similar usage of a given word from the selection. For example, the word "beat" is employed in this manner in a story: "Every day cruel slave drivers beat these workers. . . ." The test item is: "The sentence which uses the word *beat* just as it is used in line 26 of the story is (1) Mother said, 'Beat the rug until it is clean.' (2) The policeman's beat was several miles long. . . ."

3. Central Theme tests the ability to distinguish the central topic of the selection from subordinate ones. An example is: "This story as a whole is about (1) the largest wall in the world, (2) the early emperor of China. . . ."

4. Key Idea tests the ability to identify the key, or most important, idea in the story. One test item is: "The most important idea in the story is that the Great Wall was (1) acting like an army, (2) used as a highway. . . ."

5. Inference tests the ability to draw a specific conclusion indirectly from the material given. For example, the first selection discusses the need for the Great Wall and then states, "It was longer than 1500 miles, more than half the distance across our own country." The test item is: "The Emperor of China needed the Great Wall because China (1) was too large to protect with soldiers, (2) had only a few soldiers who rode on horseback. . . ."

6. Generalization tests the ability to identify a general conclusion or principle indirectly from information implicitly stated. An example is: "From the story we should believe that ALL (1) buildings that last have

been built carefully, (2) workers of China are better than the workers in our country. . . ."

7. Problem Solving tests the ability to apply information from the selection to a problematic situation. One test item is: "Mrs. Brown paid twenty-five cents for a can of peaches. She said, 'This is how the farmer gets rich.' She was wrong because (1) the farmer gets only a part of the twenty-five cents, (2) farmers get rich from dairy products. . . ."

8. Association of Ideas tests the ability to see the relationship among ideas in a series. For example, "The row with ideas from the story that belong together is (1) fierce, cruel, savage; (2) enemy, builders, horses. . . ."

9. Analogy tests the ability to perceive relationship between two pairs of ideas. The idea which completes an established relationship is identified: "*Stones* are to *building* as *people* are to (1) nation, (2) houses. . . ."

10. Antecedent tests the ability to recognize the word or words to which a selected pronoun refers. For example, "The word *them* in *line* 25 of the story refers to (1) outside walls, (2) people of China. . . ."

11. Sequence tests the ability to determine a time sequence. One test item: "Below is a story about how certain vegetables reach the store. The first idea out of order is (1) The vegetables are canned, (2) the vegetables are processed. . . ."

12. Extraneous Idea tests the ability to determine relevancy of ideas to a particular selection. For example, "The idea NOT found in the story is that many (1) people were buried in the Great Wall, (2) emperors used the wall for protection. . . ."

13. Author Purpose tests the ability to identify the author's primary motive in writing a given selection. One test item is: "The author wrote this story because he thinks we should know (1) about great things in other countries, (2) about the enemies of China. . . ."

"Survey Reading Comprehension" is a measure of understanding based on the results of a reading test which uses content largely from the field of literature. The comprehension section of the Gates Reading Survey was used in this study. "General" Reading Comprehension is used synonymously with "survey" reading comprehension.

"Verbal Intelligence" is a measure of capacity which is obtained from a test that usually requires a high degree of language facility both in understanding directions and in the subject's responses.

A Review of Kindred Literature

Although most of the research on reading comprehension and test construction has been conducted at the secondary or college levels, investigations at the elementary level tend to confirm the conclusions indicated in the research at the higher levels. Accordingly, the pertinent conclusions from all the studies are summarized in terms of two major areas: critical reading comprehension and test construction.

CRITICAL READING COMPREHENSION

In 1917 Thorndike published three articles emphasizing the premise that reading is a thinking process (29, 30, 31). Since that time, educators have been concerned not only with the "sense-meaning," or literal comprehension of printed material (14, 34), but also with a more thorough interpretation, or critical comprehension. Critical reading comprehension has been defined as critical thinking in reading situations (4).

Critical Thinking—Since critical thinking is basic to critical reading comprehension, a summary of the conclusions in the research on critical thinking is pertinent to this investigation:

1. Critical thinking necessitates the functioning of higher level thought processes (3, 30).

2. Critical thinking appears to be a complex of component abilities, some of which seem to have been identified (3, 12, 13, 32).

3. The manifestation of intelligence does not guarantee the ability to think critically (3, 13).

4. The ability to think critically in one content area cannot be assumed to indicate that the same is true in another (25).

5. Aspects of critical thinking can be measured by paper-and-pencil tests (13, 32, 33).

6. Certain aspects of critical thinking can be improved by instruction (13, 26, 33).

7. Fifth-grade children can think critically. Moreover, the difference between their ability to reason and that of adults is merely a quantitative one (8, 16, 21).

Critical Thinking in Reading Situations—The research on critical reading comprehension reveals:

1. Critical reading comprehension has the same attributes as those stated above for critical thinking, but they apply when critical thinking is done in reading situations (4, 10, 11, 12, 13, 26, 30, 31).

2. Literal reading comprehension appears to necessitate mental functioning of a lower level than critical reading comprehension (3, 11, 14, 32, 34).

3. The ability to comprehend critically cannot be predicted from the ability to comprehend literally, or factually (3, 11, 12, 25, 32).

TEST CONSTRUCTION

The need for better test measures at the elementary level has been stressed repeatedly in the literature (4, 7, 19). The following list of characteristics includes the major suggestions from pertinent literature.

Readability—In constructing a test, the author should consider the two aspects of readability (4, 9, 22):

1. The reader—his experience, interests and language facility,
2. The material—the interest level, the language, the concepts, and the mechanical features.

Reading in the Content Areas—This aspect of reading has significant implications for test construction:

1. Since reading skills vary between content areas and success in reading the materials of one content area cannot be used as a criterion of success in another content area, test materials should be built from materials within a given content area (6, 7, 18, 27).
2. Since reading is a complex of many abilities and skills which vary within one content area, specific skills should be appraised (3, 10, 11, 12, 18, 27).
3. Since ability in critical reading comprehension cannot be predicted from ability in literal comprehension, a reading test should include both (2, 4, 15, 20, 24, 25).

Mechanical Features—The following criteria are suggested in the literature for test construction (1, 7, 28):

1. The test materials should be valid and reliable.
2. The number of items appraising each skill should be large enough to show the degree to which the subject possesses that skill.
3. The directions should be clear and consistent for each administration of the test.
4. Each multiple-choice item should have: (1) at least five alternate responses, (2) one best answer, (3) the correct answer randomized, and (4) plausible distractors of about equal length.

Summary of Procedure

The following procedure was used in this study:

1. A preliminary edition of The Intermediate Reading Test: Social Studies, designed to appraise both literal interpretation and specific critical reading comprehension skills, was constructed and validated.

2. A preliminary study was conducted in which the test was administered to one hundred and forty-three children in grades four, five, and six. The results were used to evaluate the preliminary edition in terms of readability and the discriminating power and internal consistency of each test item.

3. The measure was revised and called the experimental edition of The Intermediate Reading Test: Social Studies.

4. The experimental edition of the reading test was administered to five hundred and thirteen children not included in the preliminary study.

   a. The reliability of the experimental edition was computed by means of the Kuder-Richardson Estimate of Test Reliability.

   b. The validity of each test item was evaluated by using (1) the Standard Error of the Difference Between Proportions, (2) an estimate of the product-moment coefficient of correlation based on the upper and lower 27% of the distribution, and (3) inspection of the total number of choices for each distractor.

5. Two standardized tests were administered to the population used in the major study: The Gates Reading Survey (Level of Comprehension) to appraise "general" reading ability and The Pintner General Ability Test (Verbal Series) to obtain verbal intelligence quotients.

6. The product-moment method of correlation was used to estimate the degree of relationship between the four variables: intelligence, "general" reading ability, literal comprehension in social studies, and critical interpretation in social studies.

7. Partial correlation was used to estimate the degree of relationship between the three types of reading ability ("general" reading ability, literal comprehension in social studies, and critical interpretation in social studies) when intelligence was partialled out.

8. Chi-square was used to determine the presence or absence of relationship between literal reading and each critical reading skill in social studies.

9. The point-biserial method of correlation was utilized to estimate the degree of relationship between literal reading and each critical reading skill in social studies.

SUMMARY OF RESULTS

Problem I: The degree of relationship between intelligence and "general" reading ability, literal reading comprehension, and critical reading interpretation in social studies, as estimated by the product-moment method of correlation, was $.83 \pm .01$, $.72 \pm .02$, and $.69 \pm .02$ respectively.

Problem II: The degree of relationship between "general" reading ability and literal and critical reading comprehension of social studies, as estimated by the product-moment formula, was .76 ± .02 and .64 ± .03 respectively. When intelligence was partialled out, the correlation coefficients were .42 and .17 respectively.

Problem III: The degree of relationship between literal and critical reading interpretation in social studies, as estimated by the product-moment formula, was .61 ± .03. With intelligence controlled, the correlation was .23.

Problem IV: The degree of relationship between success on each critical reading skill and the total literal reading score was computed by two methods:

a. The twenty-three point-biserial coefficients of correlation ranged from .45 to −.17 with a "median" coefficient of .23 and the seven "combined" point-biserial coefficients ranged from .28 to .06 with a median of .26 after those test items which failed to be significant on the chi-square test of significance were excluded. The critical reading skill with the greatest degree of relationship was "functional vocabulary" (.28), the skill with the least was "extraneous idea" (.06).

b. The estimates of the product-moment coefficients of correlation ranged from .61 to −.27 with a "median" coefficient of .25.

c. Twenty-two of the critical reading test items appeared to be significant on the basis of three probability values.

Conclusions

Within the limitations of this study as stated in Chapter I (see original thesis on file at Temple University) the following conclusions appear to be valid:

Problem I

1. Verbal intelligence appears to be very highly related to "general" reading ability (.83 ± .01).

2. Verbal intelligence appears to be substantially related to the ability to comprehend literally in social studies (.72 ± .02).

3. Verbal intelligence appears to be substantially related to the ability to comprehend critically in social studies (.69 ± .02).

Problem II

4. "General" reading ability appears to be highly related to literal reading interpretation of social studies materials (.76 ± .02). When intel-

ligence is partialled out, the relationship appears to be substantial (.41 ± .04).

5. "General" reading ability appears to be substantially related to critical reading interpretation in social studies (.64 ± .03). When intelligence is held constant, the relationship appears to be low (.17 ± .04).

Problem III

6. Literal reading comprehension appears to be substantially related to critical reading comprehension in social studies (.61 ± .03). With intelligence held constant, the relationship appears to be negligible (.23 ± .04).

Problem IV

7. Each selected critical reading skill appears to show a negligible or low relationship to the ability to comprehend literally in social studies.

General Conclusions

1. Reading comprehension in social studies appears to be a composite of many skills and abilities which apparently function at various levels of mental activity.

2. Literal and critical reading comprehension in social studies appear to be relatively independent abilities when intelligence is held constant.

3. Individual critical reading comprehension skills appear to be relatively independent of the ability to comprehend literally in social studies.

4. When intelligence is held constant, critical reading comprehension in social studies appears to be virtually independent of "general" reading ability; literal reading comprehension, relatively independent of "general" reading ability.

5. Group tests of "general" reading ability and group tests of verbal intelligence tend to measure common factors.

Implications

Several school practices need to be considered thoughtfully if reading instruction in social studies is to be improved:

1. The use of a "general" reading test to identify all reading needs.

2. The practice of teaching reading as a "unitary" ability in materials taken from the field of literature.

3. The use of a group, verbal intelligence test to estimate the intelligence of all pupils.

A reading test appraising "general" reading ability does not identify all reading needs. By definition, it is "survey" in nature and lacking in specificity. Frequently it is limited to a low-level type of interpretation. Furthermore, the usual reading test is composed primarily of materials from the field of literature.

Such a test is inadequate, in the first place, because reading comprehension cannot be confined to the interpretation of the sense-meaning in literature materials. Reading is a complex process embracing many levels of interpretation and many different skills and abilities.

In the second place, the reading skills and abilities necessary to adequate interpretation vary considerably within and between the various subject-matter fields. Accordingly, specific needs in reading comprehension, particularly in critical reading comprehension, should be identified by means of informally constructed tests and daily appraisal during teaching sessions.

The identification of specific needs in literal and critical reading comprehension is merely the first step in improving the reading skills of any school population. Developmental instruction in reading skills and abilities needs to be provided systematically in all content areas. More emphasis should be placed upon higher levels of reading interpretation to avoid verbalism. The comparison of the literal and critical scores in this study indicates that the pupils tested lacked the ability to interpret social studies materials critically. It is the responsibility of each classroom teacher to provide for the systematic training required to develop such abilities.

To appraise a retarded reader's mental capacity by means of a group, verbal intelligence test is a highly questionable procedure. The amount of relationship between the group, verbal intelligence test and the group reading test in this study as well as in other studies implies that one can be predicted from another with considerable accuracy. Therefore, a child unable to read cannot perform at or near his mental capacity level on such an intelligence test. When reading retardation is apparent, it is advisable to use an individual measure of mental capacity.

Another major need in education is the construction of reliable and valid measures to appraise critical reading skills in all subject matter areas at the elementary school level. Critical reading skills are not included in content-area tests available now. Such a test should yield a score on each critical reading comprehension skill so that specific needs can be identified.

Suggestions for Further Research

Further inquiry into reading comprehension appears to be warranted. The following problems are in need of investigation:

1. The relationships between, and interrelationships among the critical reading comprehension skills in social studies.
2. The investigation of other skills necessitating a higher level of interpretation in social studies.
3. A factorial analysis of critical reading comprehension in social studies.
4. The investigation of literal and critical reading comprehension within other content areas and between content areas.
5. Investigations on the development of each critical reading comprehension skill.
6. Studies to evaluate effective methods for developing critical thinking in reading.
7. The construction of valid measures to appraise literal and critical reading comprehension skills in all content areas at the elementary school level.

Bibliography

1. Dorothy C. Adkins, et al., *Construction and Analysis of Achievement Tests* (Washington, D.C.: Superintendent of Documents, U.S. Government Printing Office, 1947).
2. Howard R. Anderson (editor), "Teaching Critical Thinking in the Social Studies," *Thirteenth Yearbook of the National Council for the Social Studies* (Washington, D.C.: National Education Association, 1942).
3. Ralph Clarion Bedell, *The Relationship Between the Ability to Recall and the Ability to Infer in Specific Learning Situations*, unpublished Ph.D. Dissertation, University of Missouri, 1934.
4. Emmett A. Betts, "Guidance in the Critical Interpretation of Language," *Elementary English*, XXVII (January 1950), pp. 9–18, 22.
5. ———, "Readability: Its Application to the Elementary School," *Journal of Educational Research*, XLII (February 1949), pp. 438–59.
6. Eva Bond, *Reading and Ninth Grade Achievement*, Contributions to Education, No. 756 (New York: Bureau of Publications, Teachers College, Columbia University, 1938).
7. Margaret M. Conant, *The Construction of a Diagnostic Reading Test*, Contributions to Education, No. 861 (New York: Bureau of Publications, Teachers College, Columbia University, 1942).

8. W. C. Croxton, "Pupils' Ability to Generalize," *School Science and Mathematics*, XXXVI (June 1936), pp. 627–34.

9. Edgar Dale and Jeanne S. Chall, "A Formula for Predicting Readability: Instructions," *Educational Research Bulletin*, XXVI (February 17, 1948), pp. 37–54.

10. Frederick B. Davis, *Fundamental Factors of Comprehension in Reading*, unpublished Ph.D. Dissertation, Harvard University, 1941.

11. Joseph C. Dewey, "The Acquisition of Facts as a Measure of Reading Comprehension," *Elementary School Journal*, XXXV (January 1935), pp. 346–48.

12. Roma Gans, *A Study of Critical Reading Comprehension in the Intermediate Grades*, Contributions to Education, No. 811 (New York: Bureau of Publications, Teachers College, Columbia University, 1940).

13. Edward M. Glaser, *An Experiment in the Development of Critical Thinking*, Contributions to Education, No. 843 (New York: Bureau of Publications, Teachers College, Columbia University, 1941).

14. William S. Gray, "Reading and Factors Influencing Reading Efficiency," in *Reading in General Education* (Washington, D.C.: American Council on Education, 1940), pp. 18–44.

15. —— (Chairman). *Report of the National Committee on Reading*, Twenty-Fourth Yearbook of the National Society for the Study of Education, Part I (Bloomington, Ill.: Public School Publishing Co., 1925).

16. Victoria Hazlitt, "Children's Thinking," *British Journal of Psychology*, XX, Part IV (April 1930), pp. 354–61.

17. Ernest Horn, *Methods of Instruction in the Social Studies* (New York: Charles Scribner's Sons, 1937).

18. W. J. Humber, *An Experimental Analysis of Selected Reading Skills as Related to Certain Content Fields at the University of Minnesota*, unpublished Ph.D. Dissertation, University of Minnesota, 1942.

19. K. L. Husband and J. Harlan Shores, "Measurement of Reading for Problem Solving—A Critical Review of the Literature," *Journal of Educational Research*, XLIII (February 1950), pp. 453–65.

20. Theodore W. H. Irion, *Comprehension Difficulties of Ninth Grade Students in the Study of Literature*, Contributions to Education, No. 189 (New York: Bureau of Publications, Teachers College, Columbia University, 1925).

21. Louis Long and Livingston Welch, "Reasoning Ability in Young Children," *Journal of Psychology*, XII (July 1941), pp. 21–44.

22. Irving Lorge, "Predicting Readability," *Teachers College Record*, XLV (March 1944), pp. 404–19.

23. Ethel S. Maney, *Literal and Critical Reading in Science*, unpublished Ed.D. Dissertation, Temple University, 1952.

24. James M. McCallister, "Reading Difficulties in Studying Content

Subjects," *Elementary School Journal*, XXXI (November 1930), pp. 191–201.

25. HORACE T. MORSE and GEORGE H. McCUNE, *Selected Items for the Testing of Social Studies*, National Council for the Social Studies, Bulletin No. 15 (Washington, D.C.: National Education Association, 1949).

26. RACHEL SALISBURY, *A Study of the Transfer Effects of the Training in Logical Organization*, unpublished Ph.D. Dissertation, University of Wisconsin, 1934.

27. J. HARLAN SHORES, *Reading and Study Skills as Related to Comprehension of Science and History in the Ninth Grade*, unpublished Ph.D. Dissertation, University of Minnesota, 1940.

28. PERCIVAL M. SYMONDS, "Factors Influencing Test Reliability," *Journal of Educational Psychology*, XIX (February 1928), pp. 73–87.

29. EDWARD L. THORNDIKE, "The Psychology of Thinking in the Case of Reading," *Psychological Review*, XXIV (May 1917), pp. 220–34.

30. ——, "Reading as Reasoning: A Study of Mistakes in Paragraph Reading," *Journal of Educational Psychology*, VIII (June 1917), pp. 323–32.

31. ——, "The Understanding of Sentences," *Elementary School Journal*, XVIII (October 1917), pp. 98–114.

32. RALPH W. TYLER, "Measuring the Ability to Infer," *Educational Research Bulletin*, IX (November 19, 1930), pp. 475–80.

33. J. WAYNE WRIGHTSTONE, *Appraisal of Newer Elementary School Practices* (New York: Bureau of Publications, Teachers College, Columbia University, 1938).

34. LOUIS C. ZAHNER, "Approach to Reading Through Analysis of Meanings," *Reading in General Education* (Washington, D.C.: American Council on Education, 1940).

41. Reading for Problem-Solving in Science [1]
J. Harlan Shores and J. L. Saupe

The measurement of reading rate and comprehension has been the subject of numerous researches since the development of objective measuring devices. Few areas have received as large a share of the interest and energies of test-makers. Many of these researches were attempts to discover the basic nature of the reading process and subsequently to improve the measurement of this process. The reading tests so constructed and now in use are evidently based on the existence of a general ability to read (5). In general they include such sections as vocabulary, ability to follow directions, ability to grasp the central thought of a passage, and general comprehension (word, phrase, sentence and paragraph). In grades four, five and six, typical items measuring comprehension require the ability to grasp and retain facts contained in a short paragraph.

Within recent years doubt has been cast concerning the existence or at least the value of the concept of a generalized ability to read beyond the primary grades (2,3,13,14,15,17). Rather it has been hypothesized that reading skills differentiate with many variable factors, each of which, when varied from one test situation to another, would affect a student's test score. One analysis lists fifteen such factors which should be recognized and either held constant or measured (14). Three factors mentioned as having received very little consideration in reading test construction in the past are content area of material being read, reader's purpose (what he intends to get from the reading) and reader's experience background for the specific content of the reading passage (14).

Recent investigations leave little doubt that reading rate and comprehension are affected by the kind of material being read. It seems reasonable to expect that the reading skills required for science material will differ from those required for materials of history, mathematics, or other content areas, each of which requires its peculiar combination of abilities. Certainly good readers in one content area can be expected to read well in other areas and poor readers in one area can be expected to read poorly in other areas, but there are differences within these groups which cannot be explained by the concept of a general ability. Tinker (19) and McCallister (9) support the contention that reading ability differentiates with the content field in which the reading is done.

[1] This study was made possible by a research grant from the College of Education, Bureau of Research and Service, University of Illinois. The research design and conclusions, however, are those of the authors.

"Reading for Problem-Solving in Science," by Harlan J. Shores and J. L. Saupe, is reprinted by permission from *Journal of Educational Psychology*, XLIV (March 1953), 149–158.

The results of these and other investigations which point to the denial of a general ability to read regardless of the kind of material being read, imply that for reading test scores to be of real value they should be reported in terms of ability to read in different content areas. There would need be separate tests of ability to read historical materials, scientific materials, and the like. Only in this manner would it be possible to determine an individual's variable proficiencies in the various content areas.

Experimental evidence and expert opinion each support the theory that the specific purpose in the reader's mind when he approaches a work-type reading task is a major determinant of both reading rate and comprehension. More than twenty years ago Gray pointed to the effect of this factor on reading rate and comprehension (7). Since that time the results of research and considered judgment of scholars in the field of reading have supported him by reporting a relationship between purpose and reading rate and comprehension (1,4,11,19). Reading comprehension includes the ability to adjust the rate of reading and the specific skills employed to the purpose for which the material is being read. For test-makers this fact implies that the factor of reader's purpose should receive attention in the construction of reading tests. At present this factor is neglected and neither the test-maker nor the interpreter of test scores can know how proficient the readers might have been if they had been reading for a well defined purpose. Test taking is a special instance of a learning situation. Since learning involves goal seeking and the reader's purpose sets his immediate goals, the test-maker cannot know what he has measured until he can make fairly valid assumptions with respect to the similarity of purpose among the testees. Shores (14) suggested that prior to the printed passage of the test the reader should be given a clear purpose for his reading. Similarly, Dolch (6) recommended that since modern textbooks are written with a purpose in mind, reading tests should also have a purpose. Ideally reading tests should be as similar as possible in purpose to the purposes for which reading is taught.

With respect to experience background of the reader the test-maker must assume that the readers have had equivalent experience with the specialized subject matter of the reading passage in order for the test to be valid in comparing individuals or groups. A child with a wealth of experience in aviation will comprehend a passage about airplanes better and more rapidly than one who has not had this experience. This requirement of equivalent experience is not easily met and has been violated frequently in reading test construction. Methods for meeting this requirement would be to select the subject of the reading passage in such a manner that it might be assumed that the testees have had little if any specific background for it or to use a great number of passages with the expectation that the effects of experience background would cancel out.

At the same time the test passage should be typical of the kind of content and purpose for which measurement is desired.

The failure of current reading tests to take these factors into consideration would prompt the construction of a reading test or battery of tests which account for them more adequately. This work would culminate with a standardized battery of tests containing at least one test employing the content of science, one using the social studies, one arithmetic, and so on. Each test should have a clearly defined purpose stated for the reader at the beginning of each reading passage. Every possible attempt should be made in selecting the subject of the written material to hold the factor of experiential background constant.

For at least the past three decades, theory of method in elementary schools has assumed problem-solving as a primary approach. Thus the growth in the training and use of reading to solve individual and group problems that is evidenced in schools today may be expected to continue. It follows that if the new reading tests are to be of maximum use in predicting success or in measuring the relative position of an individual or a class with respect to the kinds of skills needed for normal classroom activity, the individual tests should be measuring reading as a tool in problem-solving. In other words, what the individual tests would measure is the ability to do that kind of reading ordinarily done in elementary-school classrooms with the materials of science, the social studies, and the like.

As a beginning in the construction of such a test battery there is now in the process of refinement a test at the fourth-, fifth-, and sixth-grade levels employing the content of elementary-school science. It has been called a Test of Reading for Problem-solving in Science. When scores on this test are reported and analyzed the question naturally arises: What are the relationships between that which is measured by this test of reading for problem-solving in science and that measured by other reading tests and tests of general ability commonly used in the public schools?

Tests Employed

The Test of Reading for Problem-solving in Science consists of two written passages of approximately eight hundred words each. In selecting the content for each passage, material was chosen to be typical of elementary-school science classes and yet such that children probably would not have come into contact with this particular content. This was an attempt on the part of the test-makers to hold the factor of experience background somewhat constant.

The student is told in the test directions and again immediately prior to the reading of each passage, the purpose for which he is doing the reading, i.e., the problem he is trying to solve. The problem of the first selection is, "What is the Best Way for the Farmer to Keep Grub Worms from Harming His Crops?" The student is told that he is reading the second passage to find out, "Do Plants or Animals Like Those on the Earth Live on Mars?" Following each passage are twenty-four multiple-choice-type items based on the content of the passage. In general each of the first nineteen items following each passage requires the testee to make inferences from the facts in the passage. Each inference is considered to have some relationship to the desired solution of the problem. The stem of the final item of each part is a statement of the problem the student has been asked to solve. There were also four choices for these final items, and the responses to them were included in the total test score without weighting. The correct alternative to each of these items is the solution of the respective problem which follows most logically from the passage.

Although reading rate is important within broad limits in the classroom situation due to the limited length of the school day, an attempt was made to remove the rate factor by allowing sufficient time for each student to complete the entire test. For the purposes of this study the test scores of the very few students (fewer than three per cent) who did not finish the test were considered not representative of their ability and hence were not used.

All test items showed positive discrimination with the upper and lower fourths of the sample as judged by the total score. The reliability coefficient as computed by the Kuder-Richardson formula was $+.82$. The nature of the test makes an estimate of statistical validity impossible because it was designed to measure an ability not heretofore measured. Hence logical validity is the necessary approach. For a statement concerning the logical validity of the test see Husbands and Shores (8) who report a study in which this test was used.

Tests of achievement and mental ability were administered to provide data for the relationships to be described later. These are as follows:

1) New California Short-form Test of Mental Maturity, Primary or Elementary Battery (the appropriate form was administered at each grade level) '47 S-form.

2) Progressive Achievement Tests, Primary or Elementary (the appropriate form was administered at each grade level) Battery, Form A.

In addition, sociometric measures of acceptance and rejection were taken. However, the correlations of these measures with all of the other test scores were so low and generally inconclusive that they are not included in this report.

A complete list of the scores used for each of the 182 cases is:

1) Test score, Reading for Problem-solving in Science (referred to in the tables as Science Reading)

2) Mental Age, language

3) Mental Age, non-language
4) Reading Age
5) Arithmetic Age
6) Chronological Age

METHOD OF INVESTIGATION

This study was conducted in a city of approximately eight thousand population in central Illinois. Classes were chosen in schools located in the middle socio-economic categories. All the pupils in each classroom were tested.

The test of Reading for Problem-solving in Science was administered to 214 fourth-, fifth-, and sixth-grade children. Of the 214 cases for which scores were taken on the reading for problem-solving test there were 182 cases for which there was complete data on the California Tests of Mental Maturity and the Progressive Achievement Tests.[2]

TABLE 1.—INTERRELATIONSHIPS BETWEEN READING FOR
PROBLEM-SOLVING IN SCIENCE AND OTHER-
MEASURED ABILITIES *,**

	Science Reading	California Language M. A.	California Non-Language M. A.	Progressive Reading Age	Progressive Arithmetic Age	C. A.	Mean	S.D.
Science Reading	.82	.61	.49	.63	.59	.08	23.75	6.47
California Language M. A.	.61	.95	.53	.81	.73	.29	124.50	20.39
California Non-Language M. A.	.49	.53	.91	.60	.64	.33	128.29	23.63
Progressive Reading Age	.63	.81	.60	.90	.83	.35	129.11	16.71
Progressive Arithmetic Age	.59	.73	.64	.83	.93	.44	128.53	12.24
C. A.	.08	.29	.33	.35	.44	1.00	123.06	14.61

$N = 182$

* Product moment correlation coefficients uncorrected.
** Self-correlations are reliability estimates.

[2] This discrepancy is due largely to absences when the various tests were administered and children moving into and away from the school district during the period when data were collected.

It is important to note that the data from all the tests except the Test of Reading for Problem-solving in Science were collected from the same students one full year previous to this investigation in connection with another study.[3] Consequently, any marked irregularities in rate of growth of these attributes during the intervening year would disturb the results reported.

TABLE 2.—CORRECTED INTERRELATIONSHIPS BETWEEN READING
FOR PROBLEM-SOLVING IN SCIENCE AND OTHER MEASURED
ABILITIES *

	Science Reading	M. A. Language	M. A. Non-Language	Reading Age	Arithmetic Age	C. A.
Science Reading		.69	.57	.73	.68	.09
M. A. Language	.69		.58	.88	.78	.30
M. A. Non-Language	.57	.58		.66	.70	.34
Reading Age	.73	.88	.66		.91	.37
Arithmetic Age	.68	.78	.70	.91		.46
C. A.	.09	.30	.34	.37	.46	

* Product moment correlation coefficients corrected for attenuation.

The data reported in Table 1 are product moment correlation coefficients computed from the raw scores. These data do not account for differences possibly due to the relative reliability of the measuring instruments. The data in Table 2 are corrected for attenuation and provide a better estimate of the true relationships among these factors.[4,5]

RESULTS

Limitations of sampling and the fact that the Test of Reading for Problem-solving in Science is still being revised suggest that this type of study

[3] G. Orville Johnson. "A study of the social position of mentally handicapped children in the regular grades." *American Journal of Mental Deficiency*, 55, No. 1, July, 1950.

[4] The formula employed to correct for attenuation is $r_{\infty\infty} = \dfrac{r_{xy}}{\sqrt{r_{x1x2}}\sqrt{r_{y1y2}}}$, where $r_{\infty\infty}$ is the corrected correlation coefficient, r_{xy} is the uncorrected product moment correlation coefficient, and r_{x1x2} and r_{y1y2} are the respective reliability estimates of the two instruments whose scores are being correlated.

[5] Quinn McNemar. *Psychological Statistics*. New York: John Wiley and Sons, 1949, p. 134.

should be repeated at a later date when more adequate instruments are available. At this stage factor analysis would seem to be appropriate to discover what the relationships are among the Reading for Problem-solving in Science test, current reading tests, and other tests of various mental abilities. The generalizations from the present study should be regarded as tentative. While many of the correlation coefficients reported in Table 2 are not statistically different from one another and others are not significantly different from zero,[6] there may be value in pointing to some relationships which seem to exist between reading for problem-solving in science and the other measured factors.

1) Intercorrelations among the first five measures listed in Tables 1 and 2 (Reading for Problem-solving in Science, Mental Age–Language, Mental Age–Non-Language, Reading Age, and Arithmetic Age) are significantly positive in each instance. This indicates some general ability measured in common by these tests and which is also present in the Test of Reading for Problem-solving in Science.

2) Reading to solve problems in science correlates highest with reading age and higher with language mental age than with non-language mental age. A major factor in this type of reading is probably the reading-language factor.

3) Reading for problem-solving in science correlates lower with each of the other of the first five factors listed in Table 2 than does language mental age and reading age. The important implication here is that this test is measuring an ability which has less of the general factor causing high intercorrelations among all of them. The suggestion is that ability to do the type of work-type reading required by problems in science, a reading skill which involves both reading and thinking critically about that which is read, is more independent of mental age than is general reading ability and is different in some degree from whatever is measured in tests of general verbal intelligence and general ability to read.

4) Ability to read to solve problems in science correlates significantly lower with chronological age than do any of the other measures of mental ability or achievement. This suggests that this ability is nurtured less by maturation and incidental cultural impact than are the other measured abilities. It also suggests that significant development of this ability probably requires deliberately planned learning situations not uniformly provided in the schools employed in this experiment.

5) Ability to read in order to solve problems in science correlates lower with Reading Age and Language Mental Age than do these two abilities with one another. Again the indication is that this ability is somewhat dissimilar to that measured as verbal intelligence or general ability to read.

[6] Correlations within the range of $+.18$ to $-.18$ are not regarded as significantly different from zero at the one per cent level of probability.

SUMMARY

Considerable evidence is accumulating to support the hypothesis that reading ability differentiates beyond the primary grades into somewhat specific abilities to read different kinds of material for different purposes. Research along these lines continues to be hampered by the lack of adequate instruments for measuring whatever form these differentiated abilities assume. This investigation, using an instrument which after considerable development is still being revised, tends to support the hypothesis that reading of the kind employed in grades four, five and six to solve problems in science has a large factor in common with mental ability and general achievement as these are commonly measured and yet is somewhat unique in a manner which cannot be accounted for by these generalized factors. A reasonable prediction is that sharper measuring instruments will not only substantiate the hypothesis that general ability to read does differentiate into specific abilities, but will also describe the extent and nature of this differentiation and the amount and character of the remaining common general factors.

BIBLIOGRAPHY

1. P. J. BLOOMERS, "Rate of comprehension of reading: Its measurement and its relationship to comprehension." *Journal Educational Psychol.*, XXXV, November, 1944, pp. 449–472.
2. E. A. BOND, *Tenth-grade Abilities and Achievements*. New York: Bureau of Publications, Teachers College, Columbia University, 1938.
3. ——, *Reading and Ninth-grade Achievement*. New York: Bureau of Publications, Teachers College, Columbia University, 1938.
4. H. M. CARPENTER and M. A. YOUNG, "Reading to Learn History." In National Council for the Social Studies, Seventeenth Yearbook, *Study and Teaching of American History*. Washington, D.C.: The American Council on Education, 1949, pp. 285–304.
5. F. B. DAVIS, "What do reading tests really measure?" *English Journal*, XXXIII, April, 1944, pp. 180–187.
6. E. W. DOLCH, "Teaching reading." *Elementary School Journal*, XXXIV, September, 1933, pp. 36–43.
7. W. S. GRAY, "The relation between study and reading." *Addresses and Proceedings*. Washington, D.C.: National Education Association, 1919, pp. 580–586.
8. K. L. HUSBANDS and J. H. SHORES, "Are fast readers the best readers." *Elementary English*, XXVII, January, 1950, pp. 52–57.

9. J. M. McCallister, "Reading difficulties in studying content subjects." *Elementary School Journal,* XXXI, November, 1930, pp. 191–201.

10. C. M. McCullough and others, *Problems in the Improvement of Reading.* New York: McGraw-Hill Book Co., 1946.

11. A. McIntire, "Reading social studies materials in the middle grades." *Elementary English Review,* XXI, November, 1944, pp. 262–266.

12. Q. McNemar, *Psychol. Statistics.* New York: John Wiley and Sons, Inc., 1949.

13. J. H. Shores, *The Ability to Read Historical Materials as Related to Eighth-grade Achievement and General Reading Ability.* Unpublished master's thesis. University of Minnesota, 1938.

14. ———, "Some considerations of invalidities of general reading tests." *Journal of Educational Res.,* XL, February, 1947, pp. 448–457.

15. ———, "Skills related to the ability to read history and science." *Journal of Educational Res.,* XXXVI, April, 1943, pp. 584–593.

16. E. T. Sullivan, W. W. Clark, and E. W. Tiegs, *New California Short-form Test of Mental Maturity—'47 S-form,* Los Angeles: California Test Bureau, 1947.

17. E. J. Swenson, "A study of the relationships among various types of reading scores on general and science materials." *Journal of Educational Res.,* XXXVI, October, 1942, pp. 81–90.

18. E. W. Tiegs and W. W. Clark, *Progressive Achievement Tests.* Los Angeles: California Test Bureau, 1943.

19. M. A. Tinker, "Speed vs. comprehension in reading as affected by level of difficulty." *Journal of Educational Psychol.,* XXXVIII, April, 1947, pp. 389–396.

42. Children's Attitudes Toward Reading and Their Critical Reading Abilities in Four Content-Type Materials

Patrick J. Groff

The principal hypothesis of this study was that a positive relationship exists between fifth and sixth grade children's expressed attitudes toward four different content types of reading material and their scores on an experimental test of critical reading. In addition, relationships between these critical reading scores and (1) attitudes expressed toward reading

"Children's Attitudes toward Reading and Their Critical Reading Abilities in Four Content-Type Areas," by P. J. Groff, is reprinted by permission from *Journal of Educational Research,* LV (April 1962), 313–319.

as a school activity and (2) attitudes expressed toward school, classmates and teacher were explored. Also examined were the relationships between attitudes expressed toward the four different content types of reading materials and 1) attitudes expressed toward reading as a school activity and 2) attitudes expressed toward school, classmates and teacher. The relationships between personal factors—sex, socioeconomic status, chronological age, general reading ability and intelligence—and the above variables were also determined.

Subjects: The subjects of this study were 305 fifth and sixth grade children (163 girls and 142 boys). As a group they were nearly "average" as evidenced from data obtained as to their chronological age, their intelligence [*Kuhlmann-Anderson Intelligence Test* (2) and the *California Test of Mental Maturity* (4)], their general reading ability [*California Reading Test* (7) and *Durrell-Sullivan Reading Test* (1)], and their socioeconomic status [Warner's *Index of Status Characteristics* (8)].

PROCEDURES

Measurements: Each of the subjects completed three attitude questionnaires. Scores on a modification of Remmers' *Scale for Measuring Attitude toward Any School Subject* (3) were interpreted as attitudes toward reading as a school activity. Scores on Tenenbaum's *School Attitudes Questionnaire* (5) were interpreted as attitudes toward school, classmates and teacher. The combined scores from a modified form of Thorndike's *Fictitious Annotated Titles Questionnaire* (6) plus the number ranking, depending on like or dislike, given to four different content types of reading material actually read were interpreted as attitudes toward these types of stories. These were 1) boys' sports stories, 2) girls' mild adventure stories, 3) airplane or flying stories, and 4) manners or social relations stories.

After completing the three attitude questionnaires, each of the subjects read four original experimental reading passages, the content types of which were identified as closely as possible with the content type of stories toward which attitudes had been expressed. The reading difficulty and length of these passages were controlled to provide four passages of approximate reading difficulty and approximate length.

After reading each passage the subjects completed an experimental reading test consisting of reading for immediate recall and of critical reading. The reading test for each of the four passages consisted of eight multiple-choice questions on recall and twenty-four multiple-choice questions on critical reading. The critical reading questions consisted of eight on sensing the organization of the passage, eight on making inferences and eight on drawing conclusions. The validity of the items in these experimental reading tests was determined from other research on critical reading measurement, from analysis of reading abilities, from the criticisms of a jury of faculty and of graduate students enrolled at the time with the writer in a graduate education course on children's thinking, and from the results of a pilot study of the experimental reading tests. Evidence of the reliability of the experimental reading tests was obtained by calculating coefficients of correlation between the scores from two administrations of the test given approximately two months apart. These correlations ranged from .77 to .84 which closely approximated the accepted minimum standards for group prediction. The tests, therefore, were judged to be reliable.

Analysis of the data: The statistical procedures employed in analyzing the data gathered were, first, to observe for significant differences the mean scores of the top twenty-five percent, the middle fifty percent, and the bottom twenty-five percent of the total population and the sex groups on each of the variables measured. For example, the subjects were arranged into three groups according to their scores made on the measurement of attitude toward a particular content type of reading material. A comparison was then to determine if the differences between the mean

TABLE 1.

INTERCORRELATIONS OF THE EXPERIMENTAL AND RELATED FACTORS OF THE
TOTAL GROUP

	AG	AA	AM	IQ	CA	RA	SS	CB	CG	CA	CM
AB	.01	.47*	.26*	.01	.11**	.12**	.00	.39*	.18*	.28*	22*
AG		-.09	.63*	.11	.04	.10	-.06	.00	.33*	-.14**	.26*
AA			.11**	-.06	.08	.09	-.03	.05	-.25*	.32*	-.06
AM				.05	.12**	.02	-.11	.04	.26*	-.05	.37*
IQ					-.54*	.45*	.35*	.48*	.55*	.51	.51*
CA						.09	-.19*	.20*	.20*	.25	.27*
RA							.26*	.71*	.70*	.73*	.69*
SS								.13**	.13**	.13**	.12**
CB									.77*	.80*	.81*
CG										.69*	.85*
CA											.76*

* Significant at the .01 level of confidence.
** Significant at the .05 level of confidence; all others not significant.

Interpretation of symbols:
  AB – attitude toward boys' sports stories
  AG – attitude toward girls' mild adventure stories
  AA – attitude toward airplane stories
  AM – attitude toward manners stories
  IQ – intelligence
  CA – chronological age
  RA – general reading ability

SS – socioeconomic status
CB – critical reading scores in the boys' sports passage
CG – critical reading scores in the girls' mild adventure passage
CA – critical reading scores in the airplane passage
CM – critical reading scores in the manners passage

scores of the different groups were significant. A second procedure obtained the coefficients of correlation between all the experimental and personal variables in the study. The data from the sex groups were intercorrelated as well as the data from the total group. (See Tables 1, 2 and 3.)

RESULTS

The conclusions that seemed probable in the light of the evidence gathered were as follows:

1. The major hypothesis of the study seemed to have been borne out. The correlations between attitudes toward content types of materials and critical reading test scores on these types of reading materials ranged from .23 to .50 and were all significant. The recall reading scores were not so closely related to attitudes expressed toward the material read. The correlations here ranged from −.12 to .35, with most of the correlations below .15. Breaking the total group into sex groups seemed to heighten the

TABLE 2.

INTERCORRELATIONS OF THE EXPERIMENTAL AND RELATED FACTORS OF THE BOY GROUP

	AG	AA	AM	IQ	CA	RA	SS	CB	CG	CA	CM
AB	.11	.44*	.24*	.20**	.10	.31*	.14	.43*	.26*	.36*	.29*
AG		−.13	.64*	−.04	−.02	−.18**	−.15	−.15	.24	−.21**	.07
AA			.00	.21	−.05	.21	.12	.15	.01	.37*	.03
AM				−.03	.11	−.17**	−.19**	−.06	.13	−.12	.23
IQ					−.52	.38*	.36*	.48*	.43*	.50*	.41*
CA						.19**	−.19**	.17**	.22*	.26*	.31*
RA							.25*	.72*	.56*	.80*	.65*
SS								.14	.04	.17**	.05
CB									.78*	.87*	.85*
CG										.69*	.83*
CA											.77*

* Significant at the .01 level of confidence.
** Significant at the .05 level of confidence; all others are not significant.

Interpretation of symbols:
AB – attitude toward boys' sports stories
AG – attitude toward girls' mild adventure stories
AA – attitude toward airplane stories
AM – attitude toward manners stories
IQ – intelligence
CA – chronological age
RA – general reading ability

SS – socioeconomic status
CB – critical reading scores in the boys' sports passage
CG – critical reading scores in the girls' mild adventure passage
CA – critical reading scores in the airplane passage
CM – critical reading scores in the manners passage

relationships between the attitudes toward content types of materials and critical reading scores. For example, the girls' attitudes toward manners stories were more highly correlated to critical reading scores (.50) than were the boys' reading scores and attitudes toward this passage (.23). Further substantiation of this relationship was shown when forty-eight comparisons were made of the subjects whose scores on the measures of attitude toward content types of reading material were in the lower twenty-five per cent, in the middle fifty per cent, and in the upper twenty-five per cent. On thirty of these comparisons the differences in the mean critical reading scores of these groups was significant. All of these significant differences were in favor of the group with the higher attitude score.

2. It appeared likely that the relationships between attitudes toward reading as a school activity and the critical reading scores were much the same as the relationships between attitudes toward content types of reading materials and the critical reading scores.

3. The evidence suggested that the relationship between general reading ability and attitude toward reading as a school activity approached a substantial level, with correlations ranging from .34 to .45.

TABLE 3.

INTERCORRELATIONS OF THE EXPERIMENTAL AND RELATED FACTORS OF THE GIRL GROUP

	AG	AA	AM	IQ	CA	RA	SS	CB	CG	CA	CM
AB	.26	.42*	.32*	−.10	.12	.04	−.11	.39*	.08	.21*	.11
AG		.00	.56*	.13	.13	.28*	.03	.21**	.43*	.18**	.40*
AA			.24*	−.13	.12	−.18**	−.15	.00	−.35*	.26*	−.07
AM				.14	.15	.16**	.01	.21**	.34*	.22*	.50*
IQ					.48	.52*	.37*	.50*	.62*	.54*	.65*
CA						.08	−.18**	.25*	.22*	.25*	.27*
RA							.29*	.72*	.85*	.71*	.76*
SS								.13	.24*	.12	.23*
CB									.78*	.77*	.81*
CG										.77*	.87*
CA											.72*

* Significant at the .01 level of confidence.
** Significant at the .05 level of confidence; all others not significant.

Interpretation of symbols:

AB – attitude toward boys' sports stories

AG – attitude toward girls' mild adventure stories

AA – attitude toward airplane stories

AM – attitude toward manners stories

IQ – intelligence

CA – chronological age

RA – general reading ability

SS – socioeconomic status

CB – critical reading scores in the boys' sports passage

CG – critical reading scores in the girls' mild adventure passage

CA – critical reading scores in the airplane passage

CM – critical reading scores in the manners passage

4. The relationships between general reading ability and the attitudes toward the four content types of reading material was negligible for the total group. It became significant when the total group was divided into sex groups, however. (See Tables 1, 2 and 3.)

5. Substantial negative correlations were indicated between intelligence and chronological age: $-.48$ to $-.52$.

6. A substantial positive relationship was indicated between intelligence and general reading ability as shown by correlations ranging from .38 to .52.

7. A small relationship was indicated between intelligence and socio-economic status as shown by correlations ranging from .36 to .37.

8. Negligible relationships were indicated between (a) intelligence and the attitudes measured, (c) socioeconomic status and the attitudes measured, and (d) critical reading scores and attitudes toward school, classmates and teacher.

9. Differences between boys and girls were seen to be consistent throughout the study. (See Tables 1, 2 and 3.)

SUMMARY

This study suggested that the reading comprehension of an individual child as he reads is influenced to a degree by his attitude toward the content type of material being read. This seems more likely to be true if he is asked to reason, or to read beyond the material, rather than if he is just asked to repeat verbatim. The study pointed up the significant differences in attitudes toward reading due to sex characteristics. It indicated that attitude toward reading as a school activity has an important enough effect on the other variables of the study to warrant serious consideration.

REFERENCES

1. DONALD D. DURRELL and HELEN B. SULLIVAN, *Durrell-Sullivan Reading Achievement Test*. Yonkers, New York: World Book, 1945.

2. FREDRICK KUHLMANN and ROSE G. ANDERSON, *Kuhlmann-Anderson Intelligence Tests*. Princeton, New Jersey: Personnel Press, 1952.

3. H. H. REMMERS, *A Scale for Measuring Attitude Toward Any School Subject*. Lafayette, Indiana: Purdue Research Foundation, 1934.

4. ELIZABETH T. SULLIVAN, WILLIS W. CLARK, and ERNEST W. TIEGS, *California Short-Form Test of Mental Maturity*. Los Angeles: California Test Bureau, 1951.

5. SAMUEL TENENBAUM, A Test to Measure a Child's Attitude toward

School, Classmates and Teacher. *Educational Administration and Supervision.* 20: 176–188, 1940.
6. ROBERT L. THORNDIKE, *Children's Reading Interests.* New York: Teachers College, Columbia University, 1941.
7. ERNEST W. TIEGS and WILLIS W. CLARK, *California Reading Test.* Los Angeles: California Test Bureau, 1950.
8. W. LLOYD WARNER, MARCHIA MEEKER, and KENNETH EELS, *Social Class in America.* Chicago: Science Research Associated, 1949.

43. Effect of the Attitudes of the Reader Upon Critical Reading Ability

Helen J. Crossen

In the past few years considerable experimental evidence has developed concerning the effect of reading upon attitudes held by the reader. Very little evidence, however, has been obtained concerning the effect of the reader's attitude upon his reading. It was the purpose of this study to discover what relationship, if any, exists between a pupil's attitude toward a topic and his ability to read critically material written about that topic. Two questions were proposed for investigation: (1) Will pupils who have the most favorable attitudes toward a topic read materials about that topic with more accuracy and discrimination than do the other pupils in their group? And, (2) will pupils who have the least favorable attitude toward a topic read with less accuracy and discrimination materials about the topic than do other pupils in their group?

DEFINITION OF TERMS

For the purpose of this study "critical reading" denotes reading which involves: (1) Gaining a clear and correct grasp of the sense meaning of the selection read, (2) Gaining an accurate perception of relationships, both expressed and implied, in the selection read, (3) Evaluating precisely the content as to its validity, comprehensiveness, accuracy, and usefulness to the reader's purpose, and (4) Drawing correct conclusions, and making valid inferences about what is read.

"Effects of the Attitudes of the Reader Upon Critical Reading Ability," by Helen J. Crossen, is reprinted by permission from *Journal of Educational Research*, XLII (December 1948), 289–298.

"Attitude" is here defined as a disposition to react in a favorable way toward any topic, group, institution, idea, act, person, or event. The reaction may take the form of verbalized response or overt behavior.

STEPS ESSENTIAL TO SECURING THE DATA

In order to obtain valid evidence regarding the possible effect of the reader's attitudes upon ability to read critically, the following steps were taken.

Selection of subjects.—A fairly representative group of ninth-grade pupils was chosen for the experiment. The pupils attended the Thornton Township High School, Harvey, Illinois.

Selection of topics.—It appeared essential that the topics selected for the reading materials should be those receiving wide current attention, so the pupils might be expected to be familiar with them. In addition, it was necessary that these topics possess possibilities for arousing emotional responses.

The two topics chosen related to the Negro, and the German people. The presence of a Negro minority group in many communities presents persistent problems, and, at the time the tests were given, World War II was in progress. It was thought, therefore, that these two areas offered possibilities for emotionalized attitudes of varying strengths.

Selection of data-gathering instruments.—Since the ability to read with skill and penetration materials on a subject toward which strong feeling is held may be conditioned by the reader's mental age, and by his level of general reading achievement, a measure of these two variables was necessary. Two satisfactory instruments were already available, the *Cooperative Reading Test* and the *California Short Form Test of Mental Maturity*. The former was especially desirable, for the reason that it tests several, although not all, of the aspects of critical reading ability which were proposed for investigation in this study. *The Cooperative Test* was useful, therefore, in testing some aspects of critical reading ability in situations in which emotionalized attitudes had little or no effect.

The *California Short Form Test of Mental Maturity* provided a measure of Language Mental Age based on tests of verbal abilities. These abilities appeared to be most closely related to the mental abilities involved in critical reading, and a measure of them was therefore most useful in making desired comparisons.

Construction of data-gathering instruments.—A critical reading test was devised to measure the pupil's ability to read critically materials about the Germans and the Negroes, and a "Survey of Opinions" was also constructed for the purpose of measuring the attitudes of the pupils toward these same peoples.

The critical reading test consisted of multiple-choice items following each two- or three-paragraph prose selection or short poem to be read by the pupils. Items were constructed to offer the pupil opportunity to err in the direction of his bias, so that some alternatives would seem plausible to those favorable, and some to those unfavorable, to the topic. Care was taken also that the items included might test the entire range of abilities previously defined as those essential to critical reading.

Two test items from the Critical Reading Test will show the general nature of the questions used.

15. The theory of "blood and iron" refers to
    15–1. economic control of small countries having valuable resources
    15–2. the natural vigor and vitality of a nation's people
    15–3. strict insistence upon national purity of race
    15–4. using war as a means of getting more territory.

19. It is evident from this selection that
    19–1. the true picture of Germany includes much that is pleasant
    19–2. Hitler's plans were long kept a secret
    19–3. the theory of "blood and iron" has been important in German history
    19–4. the German mind is misunderstood.

The "Survey of Opinions" was composed of statements about the peoples in question, to which the pupils responded by making symbols to indicate strong agreement, agreement, uncertainty, disagreement, or strong disagreement. The following are representative propositions concerning the Germans and the Negro:

1. The German people as a whole are good people.
2. If the German nation is destroyed by the war the world will be better off.

14. I think the Negroes are as good as white people.
15. The Negro gets angry too fast.

The statements were carefully constructed and selected so that both the meaning and direction of the propositions given were clear to pupils at the junior high school level. Scoring was arranged in such a way that a high score on each section was characteristic of those pupils who agreed most strongly to statements favorable to the Germans and the Negro, and disagreed most strongly to statements which were unfavorable to these peoples.

Collection of the Data

The tests previously described were administered by the investigator to a total of 625 ninth- and tenth-grade pupils in the Thornton Township

High School in April and May, 1943. An exception was the *Cooperative Reading Test,* which was given by the school staff at the beginning of the semester. Complete data were secured for 375 pupils.

Mental ages of the pupils.—As obtained by scores on the *California Short Form of Mental Maturity,* the mental ages of this pupil group ranged from 129 to 229 months.

Reading ability of the pupils.—The reading ability of the group, as measured by the *Cooperative Reading Test,* was somewhat lower than the average for ninth grade. The total scores of the group varied from 14 to 65, with a mean score of 36.41. The published norm of the *Cooperative Test* at the end of Grade Eight is 39.2 at the 50th percentile.

It was felt wise to eliminate from the study all those cases for whom reading was manifestly a slow and painful process of deciphering the literal meaning of the passage. Accordingly, twenty-four cases at the lower end of the distribution were dropped from the study.

Attitudes held by the pupils.—When the scores of 250 pupils who completed the "Survey of Opinions" (Negro Section) were tabulated, a fairly wide range was apparent. The mean of the distribution was found to be 113.4, which suggests that the group in general held a favorable, rather than unfavorable, attitude toward the Negro, since an average response of "uncertain" to the propositions in the Survey would yield a mean score of 102.

The scores of the 329 pupils who completed the German section of the "Survey of Opinions" again demonstrated a rather wide range, with a mean slightly above the theoretical mean score of 78, which would have indicated an average response of "uncertain." It should be observed that the scores on the two sections of the "Survey of Opinions" are not directly comparable for the reason that the section about the Negro contains thirty-four items, whereas the section about the Germans includes twenty-six items.

Critical reading ability.—Two hundred fifty pupils completed the Critical Reading Test (Negro Section), receiving scores ranging from 6 to 29, with a possible score of 32. The mean score was found to be 17.02. Similarly, a wide range of scores was found in the responses to the German section of the test. Here the range was from 4 to 27, with a possible score of 28. The mean score in this group was found to be 15.57.

SELECTION OF PUPIL GROUPS

Pupil groups according to attitude toward the Negro.—Three pupil groups were somewhat arbitrarily formed on the basis of scores on the "Survey of Opinions" (Negro Section). The 172 pupils having scores between 93 and 135, who thus fall within approximately one standard deviation of the mean, were designated as the "indifferent" group. The "favorable" group was made up of the forty pupils whose scores varied from 136 to 150, at the upper end of the distribution. Pupils whose scores were 92 or below made up the "unfavorable" group.

Pupil groups according to attitude toward the Germans.—Three similar pupil groups were formed on the basis of responses to the German section of the Survey. The middle, or "indifferent," group in this distribution was again defined as including the scores lying approximately within one standard deviation on each side of the mean. The "unfavorable" group included those pupils at the lower extreme whose scores were 70 or below, and the "favorable" group included those with scores of 100 or above. Forty-nine pupils were included in the former group, and fifty-two pupils in the latter.

Comparison of Pupil Groups

It was assumed at the outset that an indifferent, or neutral, attitude toward a topic would have no significant effect upon critical reading performance. Therefore, the critical reading test scores of the group indifferent to, and of the group most favorable to, the Negro were compared, taking into account differences which may have been due to other factors, such as general reading ability, chronological age, and mental age.

In the same manner groups most unfavorable to the Negro were compared with the group indifferent to the Negro. Groups favorable, unfavorable, and indifferent to the Germans were compared in the same way.

Differences in groups (Negro Section).—Mean scores of pupils grouped according to attitude toward the Negro for the *Critical Reading Test*, the *Cooperative Reading Test*, and for Language Mental Age, as measured by the *California Short Form Test of Mental Maturity*, are shown in Table I.

TABLE I

MEAN SCORES ON THE CRITICAL READING TEST (NEGRO SECTION), THE COOPERATIVE READING TEST, AND LANGUAGE MENTAL AGE AS MEASURED BY THE CALIFORNIA SHORT FORM TEST OF MENTAL MATURITY, OF PUPILS GROUPED ACCORDING TO ATTITUDE TOWARD THE NEGRO

Tests	Means of Groups			
	Favorable $N = 40$	Unfavorable $N = 38$	Indifferent $N = 172$	Total $N = 250$
Critical reading test	17.02	14.89	17.49	17.02
Cooperative reading test	38.50	37.87	38.36	38.31
Language mental age	188.0	188.55	187.90	185.55

It will be noted that, while the mean score of the Critical Reading Test for the group favorable to the Negro differs very little from the mean of the group indifferent to the Negro, the unfavorable group has a mean score appreciably lower. This lower mean critical reading score is not associated with a significantly lower score on the *Cooperative Reading Test*, a fact which may indicate that some factor other than general reading ability was operating to cause this difference.

TABLE II

INTERCORRELATIONS OF SCORES ON THE CRITICAL READING TEST (NEGRO SECTION), COOPERATIVE READING TEST, AND LANGUAGE MENTAL AGE OF PUPILS GROUPED ACCORDING TO ATTITUDE TOWARD THE NEGRO

	Pupil Groups							
	Favorable N = 40		Indifferent N = 172		Unfavorable N = 38		Total N = 250	
	r	SE	r	SE	r	SE	r	SE
Critical Reading Test and Co-operative Reading Test	.752	.069	.622	.047	.643	.095	.642	.037
Critical Reading Test and Language Mental Age	.694	.082	.704	.039	.393	.137	.643	.037
Cooperative Reading Test and Language Mental Age	.766	.057	.692	.040	.716	.079	.712	.031

Intercorrelation of scores on pairs of test variables are shown in Table II. Again the unfavorable group is not in line with the others. Most apparent is the difference in the correlation of scores on the Critical Reading Test with Language Mental Age. The correlation for the indifferent group is .70, while the unfavorable group has a correlation of .39. This correlation appears particularly significant when compared with the correlation between the scores on the *Cooperative Reading Test* and Language Mental Age for the unfavorable group, which is .716. The inference was made that these differences in relationship might be due to the nature of the biased reactions to the critical reading test.

Such an inference, however, does not take into account other variables having a possible effect on the reading performance of these groups. Such variables as chronological age, Language Mental Age, and general reading achievement were, therefore, considered. Since a very slight relationship was found to exist between the chronological ages of the pupils and their scores on the tests, it was decided to omit further consideration of chronological age. Differences in mean scores on the *Cooperative Reading Test*, and in mean mental age of the various pupil groups, however, merited consideration. One way of taking these differences into account might be to match individual pupils on the basis of mental age and reading test scores. Such a procedure would occasion the loss of a great number of cases, since the matched pairs of pupils would need to differ in attitude. A technique was, therefore, chosen by means of which the significance of differences between groups might be tested, taking other variables into account. For this purpose a generalized formula for testing the significance of experimental treatments developed by Shen [1] was used. The formula is as follows:

$$t^2 = \frac{N_a + N_b - 2 - k}{1 - r^2} \left\{ \frac{(\overline{Y}_a - \overline{Y}_b)^2 \, (1 - R^2)}{\left(\dfrac{1}{N_a} + \dfrac{1}{N_b} \right) [N\sigma_{ya}^2 + N_b\sigma_a^2] - (R^2 - r^2)} \right\}$$

Here R represents the correlation for the two groups combined, and r the correlation for the two groups combined without taking into consideration the differences in means. The subscript "a" applies to the group indifferent to the Negro, and "b" to the group unfavorable to the Negro. Y_a and Y_b denote the respective means of these two groups on the test of critical reading. The result of solving the above for *t* gives a value of 3.45, a difference significant at the one per cent level. The observed differences in scores for the two groups were therefore not due to a chance variation.

Although differences in means and intercorrelations for the group indifferent to the Negro and the group unfavorable to the Negro were very slight, as shown in Tables 1 and 2, the test for significance of differences in scores was carried out for the favorable group in the same manner as for the unfavorable group. The value of *t* for these groups was found to be 1.00, indicating a difference which is not statistically significant.

Differences in groups (German Section).—The same method of comparing differences in means and intercorrelations was used for the group indifferent to and the group favorable to the Germans. In both instances observed differences were very slight, and tests for significance revealed that such differences were not statistically significant.

Summary and Conclusions

This study was undertaken to discover what relationship, if any, exists between a pupil's attitude toward a topic and his ability to read critically about that topic. Significant findings follow:

(1) As far as could be determined from the data secured in this study, the critical reading performance of pupils favorable to a topic was not significantly different from that of pupils indifferent to the topic.

(2) Comparisons of mean scores on the test of critical reading for pu-

[1] Eugene Shen, "A Generalized Formula for Testing the Significance of Experimental Treatments," *Harvard Educational Review*, X (January, 1940), 70–74.

pils unfavorable to the Negro with those indifferent to the Negro, disclosed significantly lower mean scores for the former group. These lower scores were demonstrated to be due neither to the inferiority of the group in general reading ability, nor to lower mental age. Neither was the difference due to chance, as evidenced by the fact that it was significant at the one per cent level.

(3) For the group unfavorable to the Germans no such clear-cut difference was revealed.

The findings presented imply the need for careful guidance of pupils in the selection, interpretation, and evaluation of materials for reading in an area in which prejudices may operate. Particularly is this true of materials dealing with topics toward which an unfavorable attitude is held. In order to assist the pupil in acquiring competence in drawing rational and accurate conclusions, and in achieving a broadened viewpoint, both teacher and pupil should be aware of present biases, and assistance should be given in learning to read critically materials which either reinforce or contradict previously established points of view.

INTERPRETATION OF FINDINGS

The foregoing conclusions give rise to two fundamental questions which will be considered in turn: (a) Why did an unfavorable attitude affect the pupils' reading about the Negro, but not about the Germans? (b) Why did pupils having unfavorable rather than favorable attitudes obtain lower scores on the critical reading test?

Two answers appear possible in considering the first question. First, the nature of the materials used in the two sections of the test may have occasioned lack of agreement in the results. The Negro section contained three poems, while the German section contained only prose selections. It is a fair assumption that the reading of poetry requires a more precise and sensitive detection of implied meanings than does the reading of prose. Emotional biases may, therefore, have had a greater chance to interfere with the pupils' ability to read critically in the Negro section of the test.

Second, the difference may be due to the nature of the attitudes held toward the two peoples. In the case of the Germans, the unfavorable attitudes were undoubtedly brought about by events comparatively recent, involving persons not connected with the daily life of the pupils. Such attitudes may, therefore, have lacked the intensity and sharpness more characteristic of unfavorable attitudes toward the Negro.

The second question has also two possible answers. First, pupils strongly prejudiced against the Negro may have felt some disinclination to read about the topic, whereas those indifferent, or favorable, felt no such disinclination. Second, the errors made by the group most unfavorable to the

Negro may have been due to the reading of emotionally-toned materials contrary in view to the prevaling attitude. Materials in the Critical Reading Test which appeared to be most likely to arouse emotional reactions were found in the Negro section of the test, and were, in general, pro-Negro. To the extent that this is true, the anti-Negro reader was confronted with materials having a strong emotional appeal contrary to his present convictions. Evidence is available from other sources [2] which indicates that the effect of propaganda contrary to the attitude of the reader leads to a mental state of confusion and irritation, rather than to a change of attitude.

SUGGESTIONS FOR FURTHER STUDY

Further questions may be proposed as the basis for further research regarding the relationships of attitudinal biases and reading.

(1) Would the findings of this study be confirmed if a similar investigation were carried out, using other groups, and other topics?

(2) How consistently does prejudice affect reading?

(3) What effect on reading might be observed if pupils read only materials reinforcing their attitude, or only materials contradictory to their attitude?

(4) What effect would the attitudes of the reader have upon reading that is done voluntarily? In the situation obtaining in this experiment the reader had no choice. The materials were placed before him with the expectation that he would read, whether he wished to or not. A situation in which different materials representing various points of view are readily accessible to pupils presents a further possibility for learning about the effects of attitude upon reading.

The collection of further data concerning the nature of the interactions that take place between the idea expressed by the writer and the ideas and feelings aroused in the reader assumes considerable importance in an age so signally marked by rapid increase in the use of print for the promotion of special interests.

[2] R. L. Schanch and Charles Goodman, "Reaction to Propaganda on Both Sides of a Controversial Issue," *Public Opinion Quarterly*, III (January, 1939), 107–12.

44. Improvement of Critical Thinking in Relation to Open-Closed Belief Systems

C. Gratton Kemp

The quality of our thinking will determine our existence as a free people. In the past this ability was required of the few, now it is recognized as a necessity for the many. So complex and rapidly changing is our society that each citizen must become adequate in the exercise of the higher processes of thought. Improvement in critical thinking is an urgent necessity.

This is apparent in all disciplines by the growing emphasis placed upon training in critical thinking. The need is focused by educators who emphasize that more assistance be given to students to "develop problem-solving methods which will yield more complete and adequate solutions in a wide range of problem situations." [1]* Progress has been made in at least three directions: a recognition of the need for improvement; a clarification of the meaning of the term, critical thinking; and analysis of the deterrents to better performance. In the definition of the concept of critical thinking reference has been made to five abilities:

1. The ability to define a problem.
2. The ability to select pertinent information for the solution of a problem.
3. The ability to recognize stated and unstated assumptions.
4. The ability to formulate and select relevant and promising hypotheses.
5. The ability to draw conclusions validly and to judge the validity of inference. [2]

In the analyses of the deterrents to better performance it has been concluded that:

1. They tend to avoid real problem solving.
2. They apply only a limited stock of techniques to solve them.
3. They are satisfied with a partial solution.
4. They change the problem completely.
5. They escape from it entirely. [3]

These behaviors suggest the influence of emotional factors on critical thinking. The research of Else Frenkel-Brunswik,[4] Postman,[5] Allport,[6] Maslow,[7] Rokeach,[8] and others provide confirmation of the influence of

* Footnotes will be found at the end of the article.

"Improvement of Critical Thinking in Relation to Open-Closed Belief Systems," by C. Gratton Kemp, is reprinted by permission from *The Journal of Experimental Education*, XXXI, 3 (March 1963), 321–323.

the emotions on the cognitive spheres (thinking, perception, and memory). In a study [9] of the influence of dogmatism on critical thinking, it was found that high dogmatism or closed-mindedness decreased efficiency. It was concluded that this less efficient performance of the high dogmatic was due to the following factors:

1. Difficulty in tolerating ambiguities which leads to a "closure" before full consideration is given to each piece of contributing evidence.
2. A perceptual distortion of facts resulting in a decision which does not encompass all elements of the problem.
3. Lack of recognition or rejection of significant parts or of the whole problem in order to accommodate it into the performed value pattern, resulting in a poor or incorrect solution.[10]

On the other hand, "the more open-minded perceptively examine all aspects of the experience, try to clarify the ambiguity, and strive to see the relationship among parts." [11]

The contrast in the performance of those with an open belief system when compared with those having a closed belief system led to the assumption that improvement in critical thinking might also be influenced by the factor of dogmatism.

Purpose and Hypothesis of the Study

The purpose of the study was to compare the improvement in critical thinking of those low in dogmatism with those who were high.

It was hypothesized that those low in dogmatism would show greater improvement in critical thinking than those who were high.

Procedures

A total of 80 freshman students, 40 in the control group and 40 in the experimental group, participated in the study. The two groups were matched in intelligence and in degree of open- and closed-mindedness.

The Dogmatism Scale Form E [12] and the Otis Test of Mental Ability Form A were administered to the total sample of 80 students. On the basis of these criteria two comparable groups of 40 each were established. Both groups also took the Watson-Glaser Critical Thinking Appraisal.

The Control Group and Experimental Group were taught by the same instructor. The Control Group received no special help in solving critical thinking problems.

The Experimental Group was divided into five subgroups, of eight each, with four high and four low in dogmatism in each subgroup. Each of these subgroups participated in 10 one-hour meetings. Each meeting was used in solving critical thinking problems. Reasons for correct and incorrect conclusions were discussed. These were recorded and those which were general to the five groups are listed below as factors which affected efficiency.

Factors Which Increased Efficiency

1. Synthesis and evaluation of process relationships.
2. Evaluation of conclusions for inclusiveness and basicity.
3. A flexible approach.
4. Adherence to the conditions given.
5. Analysis of data provided.

Factors Which Decreased Efficiency

1. Ignore, distort or omit some of the given data.
2. Include additional words and/or ideas.
3. A rigid, often nonadaptive approach.
4. Failure to synthesize or a poor quality of synthesis.
5. Failure to evaluate conclusion or incompleteness of evaluation.

For each problem the student stated what he considered to be the factor or factors which led to a correct or incorrect conclusion. These factors are stated above in the rank order established on the frequency of occurrence indicated by the student with reference to those which either increased or decreased efficiency.

The critical thinking problems were selected from the following forms: Taxonomy of Educational Objectives; A Test of Problem Solving (High School Edition); and A Test of Critical Thinking Form G.

At the end of the study both groups were again administered the Watson-Glaser Critical Thinking Appraisal, and the results compared.

Analysis of the Data

The use of the Wilcoxon Matched-Pairs Signed-Ranks Test [13] gave the following results:

At the Beginning of the Study:

1. There was no significant difference in critical thinking between the Control Group and the Experimental Group.

2. In each of the Control and Experimental Groups, the "Low" did significantly better than the "High" at the five percent level of significance.

At the Completion of the Study:

1. The Experimental Group did significantly better in critical thinking than the Control Group at the five percent level.
2. In the Control Group, there was no significant improvement in the performance of either the "Low" or "High."
3. In the Experimental Group, the "High" improved but the improvement was not significant; the "Low" performed significantly better at the one percent level.

CONCLUSIONS

1. Improvement in critical thinking (as measured by the Watson-Glaser Critical Thinking Appraisal), is unlikely in the usual classroom situation.
2. Under favorable conditions those with open minds (as measured by the Rokeach Dogmatism Scale Form E), show greater improvement in critical thinking than those with closed minds.
3. The favorable conditions are permissive (safe) small group situations in which the usual threats are minimized and in which intensive attention given to the factors in critical thinking is accompanied by extensive practice.

IMPLICATIONS

1. Since dogmatism is learned, attention in the early life of the child should be given to the provision of a learning environment which encourages open-mindedness. This environment will provide safety, and encourage self-awareness and self-evaluation of internal and external stimuli.
2. Throughout the school life of the individual more opportunity should be provided for engaging in critical thinking.
3. More efficiency in critical thinking could be expected in those classroom environments which reduce the degree of threat, affording as much permissiveness (safety) as the students demonstrate they can use.
4. Emphasis should be placed upon helping the indivdual to understand those inefficiencies which are a result of dogmatism on both his attack on the problem and his performance in solving it.

FOOTNOTES

1 Benjamin S. Bloom, Editor, *Taxonomy of Educational Objectives* (New York: Longmans, Green and Co., 1956), p. 43.
2 Paul L. Dressel and Lewis B. Mayhew, *General Education: Explorations in Evaluation* (Washington, D.C.: American Council on Education, 1954), pp. 179–181.
3 Bloom, *op. cit.,* pp. 42–43.
4 Else Frenkel-Brunswik, "Intolerance of Ambiguity as an Emotional Perceptual Personality Variable," *Journal of Personality* (1949), pp. 18, 108–143.
5 L. Postman, J. Bruner, and E. McGinis, "Personal Values as Selective Factors in Perception," *Journal of Abnormal and Social Psychology* (1948), pp. 43, 142–154.
6 Gordon W. Allport and L. Postman, *The Psychology of Rumor* (New York: Henry Holt and Co., 1947), chapter 6.
7 A. H. Maslow, *Motivation and Personality* (New York: Harper and Bros., 1954), p. 266.
8 Milton Rokeach, *The Open and Closed Mind* (New York: Basic Books, 1960), chapter 3.
9 C. Gratton Kemp, "Effect of Dogmatism on Critical Thinking," *Journal of School Science and Mathematics* (April 1960), p. 318.
10 *Ibid.*
11 *Ibid.,* p. 315.
12 Rokeach, *op. cit.,* p. 72 ff.
13 Sidney Siegel, *Nonparametric Statistics* (New York: McGraw-Hill Book Co.), pp. 75–83.

45.   An Investigation of the Effect of Instruction in General Semantics on Critical Reading Ability

Howard Livingston

This paper reports the results of an investigation of the effects of lessons in general semantics on the critical reading competence of secondary school students. While many experts in the field disagree as to the specific skills involved in critical reading, most agree that whatever these skills are, they add up to a predisposition on the part of the reader to evaluate the ideas presented by the author.

Current methods and techniques for teaching critical reading center upon analysis of content; this investigation concerned itself with the hypothesis that greater competence in critical reading might result from an approach that focuses upon the processes by which language operates; that is, by lessons in general semantics.

"An Investigation of the Effect of Instruction in General Semantics on Critical Reading Ability," by Howard Livington, is reprinted by permission from *California Journal of Educational Research*, XVI (March 1965), 93–96.

The Problem

The purpose of this investigation was to compare the changes in the critical reading of a group of students who received instruction in general semantics with a similar group of students who did not.

The Procedure

The investigation was conducted in three public secondary schools in New York State. All three schools are located in suburban areas, where the residents are of predominantly middle socio-economic status. Six 10th-grade English classes, two from each school, comprised the sample for this study. The selection of each class for a particular group was determined by chance. An experimental group which received instruction in general semantics was made up of one class from each school; a control group which did not receive instruction in general semantics was also made up of one class from each school. Three English teachers, one from each school, participated. Each of the teachers taught a class in the experimental group and a class in the control group. Thus, the experimental group consisted of three 10th-grade English classes from three different schools who were taught by three different English teachers. These English teachers also taught a similar 10th-grade English class in the control group.

All of the English teachers devoted two full periods a week for five weeks to instruction in selected principles and techniques of general semantics. The lessons in general semantics were confined to the English classroom; there was no homework assigned. This procedure was followed for two reasons: First, it maintained the balance of instructional time in language arts for both groups; in other words, the experimental group did not receive any more homework in English than the control group. Second, it minimized the possibility of parents, neighbors, friends, and others who might have helped with homework from influencing the outcome of this study.

The *Watson-Glaser Critical Thinking Appraisal* was the instrument used to measure critical reading ability. In *Education for Effective Thinking*, Burton, Kimball, and Wing state that it is of small importance whether we call the abilities "critical thinking" or "critical reading" when the testing is done by a printed instrument. Several investigations concerned with the factors involved in critical thinking and critical reading confirm this observation. The Watson-Glaser test is available in two equated forms called the Ym form and the Zm form. Ym form was used for the pre-test and the Zm form was used for the post-test. The pre-test which took one class period was administered by the English teacher in the English classroom before the lessons in general semantics began. Within one week after the last lesson had been taught, the post-test was given. The difference in the scores on the pre-test and the post-test provided the basis for comparing the changes in critical reading of the experimental group with the changes in the control group. A two-way analysis of variance was performed in order to determine whether there was a significant difference between the change scores (post-test minus pre-test) of the experimental group and the change scores of the control group.

Since it was not known whether the participating teachers were familiar with the linguistic insights of general semantics, and since it was desirable for them to obtain a common overview of the field of general semantics, they were required to read the following: *Language in Thought and Action* by S. I. Hayakawa, *Language Habits in Human Affairs* by Irving Lee, and *Words and What They Do to You* by Catherine Minteer. It was felt that the reading of these three basic texts and the nature of their educational background and training in the language arts would enable the teachers to teach competently selected principles and techniques of general semantics. Although there was no prescribed methodology for the teaching of general semantics, all teachers were required to use material based on exercises from these three books. These exercises illustrated the principle or technique of general semantics that was being taught.

The limitation of time imposed upon this study made it impossible to use all the accepted principles and techniques of general semantics. Therefore, those principles and techniques used (abstracting process, two-valued orientation, Is of identity, Is of projection, referential and emotive functions of language, inferences, reports, and judgments, indexing, dating, Etc., and quotation marks) were selected because the treatment afforded them in the corpus of general semantic literature attests to their relative importance.

RESULTS

The two-way analysis of variance (see Table I) showed that there was a significant difference between the change scores of the experimental group and the change scores of the control group at the .01 level. In addition, the analysis of variance showed there was no difference among teachers at the .05 level, and that there was no significant interaction among teachers and groups.

Although the analysis of variance showed that there was a significant difference between the change scores of the experimental group and the change scores of the control group, a determination had to be made as

TABLE I

Two Way Analysis of Variance

Source of Variation	S.S.	df	M.S.	F
Between Groups (G)	592.67	1	592.67	9.7765 (p > .01)
Between Teachers (T)	317.46	2	158.73	2.6210 (p < .05)
Interaction (GXT)	64.02	2	32.01	.5285 (n.s.)
Within Group (Error)	6177.17	102	60.56	
TOTAL	7151.32	107*		

* Computation of the analysis of variance required the random elimination of thirty-four scores.

TABLE II

Comparison of the Means of Differences Between Paired Observations

	N	$\overline{D}$	Sd	t
Experimental Group	54	4.50	9.48	3.460 (p > .01)
Control Group	54	−1.85	5.75	−.236 (n.s.)

TABLE III

Comparison of the Means of the Pre-test Scores

	N	Mean	S.D.	t
Experimental Group	79	60.50	5.61	1.65 (p < .05)
Control Group	63	62.85	13.14	

to what the nature and direction of the changes were for the two groups. This determination was made through the use of the t-test for significant difference between the means of paired observations (see Table II). This test showed that the control group did not change significantly while the change (gain) of the experimental group was significant at the .01 level.

Since there was no way to assess inter-school similarity of classes, it was deemed advisable to determine if any significant difference in abilities as reflected by the testing instrument existed between the two groups. If such a difference existed, it might account for the difference between groups revealed by the analysis of variance. In order to ascertain this, a t-test was performed on the pre-test scores. This test showed that there was no significant difference between the pre-test scores of the experimental group and the pre-test scores of the control group at the .05 level.

The results of this investigation show that the experimental group made a significantly greater gain than did the control group. In addition, the results show that it is highly improbable that this gain could be attributed to differences among teachers, differences arising out of the interaction among teachers and groups, or to differences between groups in abilities and skills measured by the Watson-Glaser test. Therefore, it seems reasonable to infer from these findings that the students' critical reading ability improved as a result of instruction in general semantics.

46. An Experiment in Developing Critical Thinking in Children

George H. Hyram

THE PROBLEM

Evidence of the need for improved habits of thinking in both adults and children may be found abundantly not only in the attempts of such individuals to solve the problems of daily living (1, 2, 3), but also in an analysis of the democratic way of life. Such an analysis makes it clear that inasmuch as the ultimate directive force is the will of the people, the answers to the problems of a democratic society have to be discovered by the people themselves. Thus it follows that the people in such a society must be trained to think accurately (4).

This study represents an attempt to meet the above need. In general, the problem of this experiment was to improve the ability of upper grade children in the elementary school to think logically and therefore critically. More specifically, this problem became a study of the effectiveness of a specially designed instructional procedure in accomplishing the above general purpose.

PRINCIPLES AND BASIC ASSUMPTIONS

Many psychologists have correctly concluded that the principles of logic provide only conceptual models of correct thinking rather than psychological characterizations of this basically mental process. At the same time, there is general agreement that research has presented little, if any, objective evidence as to what psychological processes are involved in the

"An Experiment in Developing Critical Thinking in Children," G. M. Hyram, is reprinted by permission from *Journal of Experimental Education*, XXVI (December 1957), 125–132.

act of thinking. The most satisfactory descriptions of this kind seem to be limited to conclusions that thinking is a very complex and very probably disorderly mental activity having little in common with logical rules and principles (5).

From this point of view, it is widely inferred that no matter what experiences one undergoes, his "psychology" of thinking remains essentially unaltered; it is still a tendency toward disorderly and random mental activity directed in a kind of trial-and-error approach to the solution of some problem of which the thinker is cognizant. Thus it would appear that the more meaningful and attainable educational goal with regard to thinking is that of developing attitudes that are conducive to thinking rather than increased understanding and mastery of the rules and principles of logic (5).

To the writer, the fact that thinking does not appear to be inherently logical is of little significance with regard to the possibility that it can be developed into characteristically logical patterns through experience and habit formation.

In the endeavor to set up criteria for both the selection of content material and the development of teaching methods, the following assumptions were posited as basic principles and served as guiding hypotheses:

1. That thinking is critical when it is essentially logical.

2. That logical thinking is no more than the application of the rules of logic to factual data in order to arrive at valid as well as true conclusions (6).

It follows from this assumption that an individual's growth in the ability to do logical thinking must depend upon his acquiring a working knowledge of the basic rules of logic (7).

3. That children in the upper grades of the elementary school are, in general, mentally capable of acquiring the necessary understanding of logic and a proficiency in the use of its rules (8, 9, 10, 11).

4. That the most effective way of helping children to acquire the necessary working knowledge of the principles of logic is through direct instruction (12, 13).

5. That this direct instruction should consist of:

a. Materials and learning content which embody the principles of logic.[1]

b. Teaching methods that provide full opportunity for the pupil to discover for himself these principles and to formulate them as generalizations (14).

---

[1] The science of logic is but an expression of the real or true relationship existing between things which in themselves are either real or hypothetical. Thus, when one's thinking conforms to logic, it expresses these real relationships and therefore conforms to reality.

In order that the writer's position with regard to the nature of logical reasoning might be made more clear, the following definition was postulated:

> Reasoning, whether logical or autistic thinking, consists essentially of those mental activities which: 1. seek to infer valid implications; 2. attempt to demonstrate; or 3. try to systematize knowledge both deductively and inductively (15). The degree to which it accomplishes these purposes is the extent to which it is logical and therefore critical (16).

LIMITATIONS

Several limitations of this investigation were necessary. These were: 1. the voluntary limiting of the experiment to testing the effectiveness of a special instructional procedure, and 2. the involuntary limitations imposed by: (a) the inherent difficulties in constructing an original test of reasoning ability; (b) the very small number of children in the upper grades of three public elementary schools with I.Q. ratings of 110 or better; (c) the factor of time which did not permit the repetition of the experimental phase of this study; and (d) the assumptions themselves on which this study is based.

RELATED LITERATURE

A striking characteristic of much of the research undertaken in the field of the improvement of reasoning ability and of the literature written on the subject is the almost complete absence of the postulates listed above. An equally recurring trait in this literature is the general tendency to identify reasoning with empirical problem-solving or scientific thinking (17, 18, 19).

While research in the field of reasoning is relatively meager in both the scope of its objectives and the number of investigations attempted, it is possible to infer several educationally important conclusions from a survey of the literature. Among the general conclusions that seem to flow from such a survey are the following:

1. That the four purposes which have motivated much of the research in this area have not resulted in widely accepted conclusions. This may be so because:

   a. Efforts to establish experimentally the psychological nature of thinking have yielded no conclusive results.

   b. With regard to the relationship between thinking and other activities, research has shown that thinking and learning are not identical activities (2). However, there is abundant evidence that the logicality of thought is often adversely affected by the emotional state of the thinker (21). Vividness of imagination has been found to be a deterrent rather than an aid to logical thinking (22).

c. Research into the most effective methods of instruction for promoting growth in reasoning ability has been almost unanimous in the reliance placed by most investigators on pupil activity in problem solving and scientific induction. Except for a very few studies, the teaching of the rules of logic to children as the basis for their mastery of the techniques of correct thinking has been avoided (23).

d. Efforts to construct valid tests which are suitable for measuring the reasoning abilities of children have not produced entirely satisfactory results (24, 25, 26). There is, then, a rather urgent need for such tests designed specifically for the elementary school.

2. That current instructional practices are *not* producing satisfactory levels of thinking in pupils (27, 28, 29, 30, 31).

3. That children in the upper grades of the elementary school are mentally capable of developing satisfactory levels of thinking (8).

4. That since the transfer of learning is a distinct possibility, efforts directed towards teaching pupils how to think critically have a lasting educational potential (32).

5. That the primary trait of instruction designed to develop a general reasoning ability in pupils is its provision for pupil growth in the ability to formulate generalizations of the principles of logic.

PROCEDURE

The approach used in the endeavor to realize the objectives of this study was the experimental method. However, inasmuch as the definition of logical reasoning as accepted for this investigation assumed that the *necessary cause* of growth in the logicality of thought is an either consciously or unconsciously acquired knowledge of the fundamental rules of logic, only the Method of Difference which determines *sufficient causes* rather than *necessary* ones was employed [2] (33).

[2] The reader might recall that there are two types of causes: *necessary* causes and *sufficient* causes. The former are factors which are absolutely necessary to the existence of a given phenomenon. The latter are causes which are enough in themselves to bring about a certain effect, but are not always necessary. The following example might clarify this distinction: The cause of a forest fire was a lighted cigarette thrown carelessly in the tall grass. Here the *cause* is the burning cigarette and the *effect* is the forest fire. But, there seems to be an added factor which enabled the cause to bring about the effect. This factor is the fact that the cigarette was "thrown into the tall dry grass." It is a quality of the lighted cigarette; thus, it too must be considered as a part of the cause.

Accordingly, efforts were made to secure and maintain as much control as possible over all pertinent factors, allowing only the instruction of the Experimental Group to serve as the variable. These efforts to establish control consisted of: 1. a program of testing in order to select two equally matched and paired groups, and 2. two programs of instruction in which the only known variable of relevance was the instruction given the Experimental Group in the development of eight broad understandings deemed basic to an adequate concept of logical thinking.

However, three preliminary procedures were necessary before the efforts of control listed above could be put into effect. First among these steps was the identification of several possible *sufficient causes* of growth in logical thinking. The *necessary* cause, it will be remembered, was posited according to the definition of logical thinking as an understanding of, and proficiency in the use of the rules of logic. The following six factors, then, were singled out for control purposes as the possible *sufficient causative agents:* 1. General Intelligence, because reasoning is a mental activity; 2. Mental Age, because immature mental activity is characterized by its autistic dominance rather than logical; 3. Sex, since physical and perhaps mental maturation occur at varying levels according to sex; 4. Language Ability, because language is the vehicle of thought; 5. Reading Ability, because the very nature of the experimental instructional procedures required that the pupil be able to understand much written material; and 6. Instruction, because the learning of any skill is acquired through some kind of instruction, and because it was through instruction that, hypothetically, the Experimental Pupils could be led to extensive growth in reasoning ability.

A second preliminary step was the development of the experimental instructional procedure. This procedure was envisioned as comprising both content material and teaching methods. The former acquired through an analysis of the understandings deemed necessary to an adequate concept of the nature of logical thinking; the development of the latter grew out of the theory that the most meaningful learnings as well as the most transferable ones are those acquired through self-discovery on the part of the learner and formulated by him into generalizations. Thus, the method employed in the experimental instruction was essentially the Socratic Method and consisted of carefully phrased questions based on simple problems. These questions were designed to lead the pupil to discover a pattern in a series of such problems. Once the pattern had been discerned,

---

Now, when the question is asked: Does every forest fire have to be caused by a lighted cigarette thrown carelessly into dry grass?—the answer is no. There can be many different causes. The only real necessity is that some combustible object in the forest be raised to its kindling temperature and that it in turn ignite other objects. It is apparent then, that the lighted cigarette or any other spark of fire is merely sufficient as constituent factors to cause the fire. Neither alone is enough to cause the fire. Thus, they are not necessary as causes.

the pupil was encouraged to express his insight in the form of a generalization. The method of teaching, then, was primarily inductive in nature.

A third preliminary step leading to control of the experimental procedures was the construction of an original test of general reasoning ability suitable for use with upper grade children of the elementary school.
The construction of such a test was considered necessary because available tests do not appear to be adequate for the purposes of this study.
The content and skill coverage of this original test were based on the
theory that proficiency in reasoning includes not only the ability to infer
both inductively and deductively, but also the ability to recognize eductive and analogous thinking as well as the common errors made in reasoning.[3]

In the testing phase of the control efforts, 200 children were measured
in five areas: 1. Intelligence, 2. Mental Age, 3. General Reading Ability,
4. General Language Proficiency, and 5. Initial Reasoning Ability. The
data secured from these tests made possible the selection of two paired
and equated groups of thirty-three children each. Table I shows the statistical significance of the differences between these two groups in the five
areas listed above.

The instruction phase of the control efforts was arranged as follows:

1. The writer instructed the Experimental Group in the development
of an understanding of the following seven concepts of logical thinking:
   a. The Nature of Thinking in General
   b. The Tools of Thinking
   c. The Nature of Definition
   d. The Nature of Eductive Inference
   e. The Nature of Deductive Inference
   f. The Nature of Experimentation
   g. Common Errors in Reasoning

2. The experimental instruction covered a period of four months of 250
minutes per week.

3. Nine teachers taught that portion of the Control Group which was
selected from their respective rooms. The instruction given this group
consisted of the regular classroom activities and subject matter content as
provided in current Courses of Study of the St. Louis Public Schools. No
exposure of the Control Group was permitted either to the content or to
the methods employed in the experimental instructional procedure.

[3] A copy of this Original Reasoning Test may be found in Appendix I of the writer's
doctoral dissertation, *An Experimental Study of Classroom Procedures for Improving
the General Reasoning Ability of Upper Grade Pupils*, Saint Louis University, St.
Louis, Missouri, 1956.

TABLE I

STATISTICAL SIGNIFICANCE OF THE DIFFERENCES BETWEEN THE EXPERIMENTAL
AND CONTROL GROUPS EQUATED AND PAIRED ACCORDING TO THEIR RATINGS
IN FIVE VARIABLES AND ACCORDING TO SEX

Area	Experimental Group	Control Group
Intelligence	Mean: 106.18 S. D. : 8.82 σ_m : 1.56 σ_{m_D}: 2.516 Standard Error of the Difference: 2.516 Significant Ratio: .036	Mean: 106.091 S. D. : 11.18 σ_m : 1.56
Mental Age	Mean: 168.91 months S. D. : 11.62 σ_m : 2.05 σ_{m_D}: 3.17 Standard Error of the Difference: 3.17 Significance Ratio: .344	Mean: 167.82 months S. D. : 13.70 σ_m : 2.42
General Reading Ability	Mean: 8.61 grade S. D. : .998 σ_m : .176 σ_{m_D}: .261 Standard Error of the Difference: .261 Significance Ratio: .615	Mean: 8.45 grade S. D. : 1.08 σ_m : .193
General Language Ability	Mean: 7.73 grade S. D. : 1.25 σ_m : .21 σ_{m_D}: .309 Standard Error of the Difference: .309 Significance Ratio: .96	Mean: 8.03 grade S. D. : 1.29 σ_m : .23
Initial Reasoning Ability	Mean: 41.27 percent S. D. : 8.39 σ_m : 1.47 σ_{m_D}: 2.11 Standard Error of the Difference: 2.11 Significance Ratio: .47	Mean: 40.27 percent S. D. : 8.55 σ_m : 1.51
General Interpretation	Clearly, from these statistics, it is reasonable to assume that the Experimental and Control Groups were indeed equal in the five areas listed above.	

Results and Interpretation

At the end of the time allotted, a final test in reasoning was given to both groups and the difference in their mean achievement was tested for significance. The obvious purpose was to determine the effect of the experimental instruction on general reasoning ability.

Through statistical treatment of the data, it was found that, whereas the two groups had been equal in reasoning ability at the beginning of the study, they were greatly different in achievement in this area on the same test at the end of the experiment. Table II shows the statistical significance of the difference in the mean achievement of these two groups in final reasoning ability.

Table II

Significance of the Difference in Final Reasoning Ability
of the Experimental and Control Groups

Final Reasoning	
Experimental Group	Control Group
Mean: 72.77	Mean: 45.18
S. D. : 7.78	S. D. : 7.40
σ_m : 1.38	σ_m : 1.31

σ_{m_D}: 1.893

Standard Error of the Difference: 1.893
Significance Ratio: 14.57

Interpretation: A significance ratio as large as 14.57 shows clearly that the difference between the two means is statistically significant. Thus, it is highly feasible to conclude that the Experimental Group was superior to the Control Group in final reasoning ability as measured by the original test.

It was concluded, therefore, that since the only known variable of importance in this sample was the method of instruction, this factor seemed to be a cause sufficient to produce the desired growth in pupil logicality. Additional support for this conclusion was found in the coefficients of correlation between each of the following factors and the final tested reasoning ability of the Experimental Group: 1. I.Q. Levels, 2. Mental Ages, 3. Language Levels, and 4. Reading Levels.

In each case the coefficient of correlation was not statistically significant. This fact seems to indicate that each of the factors initially suspected of being the sufficient cause of pupil growth in the ability to do logical thinking was not a cause at all.

However, an analysis of the correlational scatter diagram revealed that a seventh grade reading level does seem to be the only prerequisite ability for success in learning how to think logically from the type of instruction given in this experiment.

These results and interpretations seem to strengthen the hypotheses which guided the attempts to solve the problem of this investigation. It was concluded, therefore, that there is experimental support for the following assumptions:

1. Correct or logical thinking does depend upon a knowledge of the principles of logic.

2. According to this sample, upper grade pupils can be taught to think critically and therefore logically through the use of instructional procedures which emphasize the principles of logic as the *learning content*.

Certain implications of educational significance seem to flow from these results and their interpretation as presented above. These implications may be listed as follows:

1. Current teaching methods are insufficient as means of promoting satisfactory growth in the ability to think logically and critically.

2. There is need for the inclusion within the elementary school curriculum provisions for the direct training of pupils in the techniques of logical thinking.

3. Curricular content for the improvement of reasoning ability must include the principles of logic as the basic generalizations to be formulated by pupils.

4. Critical thinking, like the ability to read, spell, write and use numbers, is a tool skill. As such, it cannot be left to develop only through incidental learning experiences.

5. Since there is evidence that a significant growth in logical thinking is not dependent upon language and reading skills alone, it might be inferred that the mere acquisition of factual data through reading does not necessarily lead to increased reasoning power.

6. Greater mastery and insight into, and perhaps, integration of the various subject-matter areas might be attained through "rationalizing" of these subjects. Thus greater attention should be given to pupil application of previously learned techniques of reasoning to problem situations in these subject-matter areas.

7. The acquisition of an understanding of the abstract generalizations inherent in an adequate concept of critical thinking through pupil discovery suggests that perhaps more meaningful concepts of the factual

subjects might be developed through instructional procedures which stress the habit of pupil generalization and problem solving.

RECOMMENDATIONS

Although the findings of this study indicate clearly that a knowledge of the principles of logic is basic to proficiency in logical thinking, there is yet need for more conclusive proof of this fact. Such proof might be found in a subsequent experimental study in which the procedures of this investigation are duplicated. Only through such a repetition, constituting the Method of Agreement and Difference, will it be possible to identify experimentally the necessary cause of pupil growth in logical reasoning.

Similarly, it is desirable that the superiority of the teaching method employed in this study be more convincingly demonstrated. This might be accomplished through an entirely different experiment, the only variable of which would be the method of teaching while the learning content consisting of the principles of logic would remain constant. It is recommended, therefore, that:

1. This study in its entirety be duplicated to establish experimentally the assumption that a knowledge of the principles of logic constitutes the necessary cause of pupil growth in critical thinking.

2. An experiment be conducted allowing only the method of instruction to vary while the learning content in both the experimental and control instruction be the principles of logic.

In addition to these general recommendations, it is suggested that the original test of reasoning ability be analyzed statistically in order to determine the difficulty and discriminating power of its items. Following such an analysis, it will be possible to revise and standardize the test in question for ready and meaningful use in all elementary schools.

It is suggested that a grade placement for the teaching of critical thinking be set up similar to the following plan:

Grade   Learning Content

1. Generalizations leading to an understanding of the *nature of logical thinking*.

7–Low

2. Generalizations leading to an understanding of the *tools of thinking*.

1. Generalizations leading to an understanding of *immediate inference*.

7–High

    2. Generalizations leading to an understanding of the *nature of definition.*

    1. Generalizations leading to an understanding of *deductive inference.*

8–Low

    2. Generalizations leading to an understanding of *experimentation.*

    1. Generalizations leading to an understanding of the *common errors in thinking.*

8–High

    2. Critical analysis of the thinking of others and *creative thinking.*

Finally, it is suggested that if training in critical thinking is to become an objective of the school to be reached through direct teaching efforts, teachers themselves must become proficient in the knowledge and use of the fundamentals of logic. Such knowledge and proficiency might be acquired more easily through the introduction of basic courses in critical thinking at teacher-training institutions.

While these recommendations might appear sweeping and drastic, it is the considered opinion of the writer that objective evidence justifies at least a serious consideration of them. If steps similar to those outlined in the above recommendations are taken, it is believed that a major effort toward bridging the gap between educational theoretical aims and the actual results of teaching practices will have been made.

REFERENCES

1. F. L. WHITNEY, *The Elements of Research* (New York: Prentice-Hall, Inc., 1937), p. 619.
2. E. H. MILLER, "The Vanishing R in Education," *Phi Delta-Kappan,* XXXV (1954), p. 201.
3. G. ULMER, *Some Suggestions for Teaching Geometry to Develop Clear Thinking,* University of Kansas Publications, II, No. 7 (Lawrence, Kansas: University of Kansas, 1949), p. 2.
4. E. H. REEDER, *Supervision in the Elementary School* (New York: Houghton Mifflin Co., 1953), pp. 138–39.
5. W. D. COMMINS and B. FAGIN. *Principles of Educational Psychology* (New York: The Ronald Press, 1954), p. 740.
6. E. E. WHITE, "A Study of the Possibility of Improving Habits of Thought in School Children by Training in Logic," *British Journal of Educational Psychology,* VI (1936), pp. 267–73.

7. MAX BLACK, *Critical Thinking* (New York: Prentice-Hall, Inc., 1946), pp. 3–9.

8. JEAN PIAGET, et al., *Judgment and Reasoning in the Child* (New York: Harcourt, Brace and Co., 1928), p. 309.

9. D. BERGER, "Untershiede der Abstraktionsfähigkeit nach Alter, Geschlechtund Milieu der Schulkinder," Z. Kinderforsch, XLVI (1937), pp. 250–82.

10. A. MARZI, "L'atteggiomento Critico Nella eta Evolutiva ad i Reattivi di Frasi Assurde," *Riv. Psicol. Norm. Pat.*, XXXII (1936), pp. 77–90; also reported in *Psychological Abstracts*, XI (1937), p. 52.

11. H. KOEPPE, "Psyche des Sauglings un Kleinkinde," *Arch. Kinderheilk*, CXIII (1938), pp. 34–9.

12. M. R. GOODSON, "The Improvement of Pupil Thinking," *Educational Administration and Supervision*, XXV (1939), p. 615.

13. LAVONE HANNA, "Providing for Individual Differences," *15th Yearbook, National Council for the Social Studies* (1944), p. 87.

14. H. C. ANDERSON, F. G. MARCHAM, and S. B. DUNN, "An Experiment in Teaching Certain Skills of Critical Thinking," *Journal of Educational Research*, XXXVIII (1944), pp. 241–45.

15. ANDREW H. BACHHUBER, *Logic* (St. Louis: Saint Louis University Book Store, 1952), pp. 3–6.

16. W. H. WERKMEISTER, *An Introduction to Critical Thinking* (Lincoln, Neb.: Johnson Publishing Co., 1948).

17. H. HUFFMAN, "Teaching Pupils to Think," *American Businss Education Yearbook*, VIII (1951), pp. 51–2.

18. E. M. SELBERG, "Developing Problem Solving Abilities in Students," *Science Education*, XXIII (1939), pp. 126–30.

19. V. H. NOLL, "Measuring Scientific Thinking," *Teachers College Record*, XXXV (1934), pp. 684–93.

20. NORMAN R. F. MAIER, "Reasoning and Learning," *Psychological Review*, XXXVIII (1931), pp. 336–41.

21. J. R. PATRICK, "Studies in Rational Behavior and Emotional Excitement: II. Effect of Emotional Excitement on Rational Behavior in Human Subjects," *Journal of Comparative Psychology*, XVIII (1934), pp. 153–95.

22. H. BOWERS, "The Role of Visual Imagery in Reasoning," *British Journal of Psychology*, XXV (1935), pp. 435–46.

23. M. HILL, *Training to Reason*, Australian Council for Educational Research Series No. 44 (Melbourne, Australia: Melbourne University Press, 1936), p. 416.

24. G. WATSON and E. M. GLASER, *Watson-Glaser Tests of Critical Thinking* (Chicago: World Book Co., 1942).

25. B. R. ULLSVIK, "An Attempt to Measure Critical Judgment," *School Science and Mathematics*, XLIX (1949), pp. 445–52.

26. F. T. TYLER, et al., "A Cooperative Approach to Educational Evaluation," *School*, XXXIII (1944), pp. 280–85.

27. JACQUES BARZUN, *Teacher in America* (Garden City, N.Y.: Doubleday and Co., 1954), p. 34.

28. T. M. ABEL, "Unsynthetic Modes of Thinking Among Adults," *American Journal of Psychology*, XLIV (1932), pp. 123–32.

29. MORTIMER SMITH, *The Diminished Mind* (New York: Henry Regnery Co., 1954), p. 150.

30. A. E. BESTOR, *Educational Wastelands* (Urbana, Ill.: University of Illinois Press, 1953), p. 226.

31. ——, "Prescribed Mediocrity," *Time Magazine*, LXIX (1954), p. 42.

32. PEDRO T. ORATA, *The Theory of Identical Elements* (Columbus, Ohio: Ohio State University Press, 1928), p. 204.

33. R. W. HOLMES, *Exercises in Reasoning* (New York: D. Appleton Co., 1940), pp. 15–16.

47. Experimental Teaching of Mathematical Logic in the Elementary School

Patrick Suppes and Frederick Binford

THE PROBLEM

For many years, especially since the successful launching of Sputnik I, there has been a great concern to upgrade the mastery of mathematics by students before they reach the college level. Initial efforts were directed toward a revision of the high school mathematics curriculum.

One primary goal was to introduce the high school senior to the concepts and skills of the calculus and analytic geometry, and to prepare him to use the calculus in college freshman physics. This aim was suggested by the Commission on Mathematics of the College Entrance Examination Board in its 1958 *Mathematics for Today*. The Commission also recommended that the high school student be introduced to basic concepts of mathematics, such as the different kinds of numbers, inequalities, sets, variables, functions, and relations, and to the nature and role of deductive reasoning in algebra as well as in geometry.

In recent years no one has supposed that high school students are in-

"Experimental Teaching of Mathematical Logic in the Elementary School," by Patrick Suppes and Frederick Binford, is reprinted by permission from *The Arithmetic Teacher*, XII (March 1965), 187–195.

capable of grasping such concepts. According to early views of the problem, the task was simply to raise the level of student achievement during the high school years from the average achievement upon entrance.

Attempts to carry out this program involved, first, allotting more time for mathematics in the high school curriculum and, second, increasing the efficiency of mathematics instruction. The mathematics curriculum was improved by eliminating nonessential topics and by emphasizing concepts basic to the various branches of mathematics. With the introduction of these more fundamental notions, the traditional picture of mathematics as a collection of separate topics gave way to a treatment of mathematics as the study of sets of assumptions and their deductive consequences. Hopefully, this more unified approach will make each stage of study more successful, and also will prepare the student more adequately for future work. So far, it appears that the changes are helping to bring about these objectives.

In recent years a third approach to the problem has developed: Attempts are being made to raise the level of mathematical achievement before the student enters high school. This is done by introducing topics previously not taught before high school and by emphasizing the logical nature of mathematics.

The central task of the present project was to explore the possibility of teaching deductive techniques to gifted elementary school children. In particular the project investigated the difficulty and suitability of teaching the elements of mathematical logic to fifth- and sixth-grade students.

Objectives and Hypotheses

The encouragement of critical thinking is generally acknowledged as one of the legitimate objectives of our schools. Yet there has been little effort to translate this goal into behavioral terms. If this objective is to be realized, a clear notion of the relevant skills must guide the selection of classroom subject matter and teaching methods. Critical thought requires the ability to make logically correct inferences, to recognize fallacies, and to identify inconsistencies among statements. If the school is to encourage these skills significantly, instruction must deal specifically with the ability to derive logical conclusions from given sets of premises, evidence, or data.

Through the study of logic, the child can also be introduced to clear and precise language usage. Emphasis can be given to the dual goals of clear, rigorous thought and of precise and effective formulation of ideas. The student can be introduced to the concept of logical structure in language; thus, he learns to recognize and analyze the forms of sentences. He also can come to understand the connection between formal structure and logical validity. Although the present project was considered a supplement to the elementary school mathematics program, the application of the concepts and skills learned is not limited to this subject. The principles of logical inference are applied in every branch of systematic knowledge. A class in formal logic is an opportunity to pay more than incidental attention to the development of the student's reasoning powers.

Advances by modern logicians and mathematicians have led to a systematic treatment of the relations between logic and mathematics. A completely explicit theory of inference has been formulated to deal with all the standard examples of deductive reasoning in mathematics and the empirical sciences.

The teaching of mathematical logic can not only develop general reasoning ability, but also provide for a deeper and more penetrating study of mathematics and mathematical methods. The student can learn to approach mathematics as a study of axiom systems and the derivation of theorems from axiom systems. This project assumed that the study of deductive methodology and the theory of proof can enrich the mathematical experience of the elementary school child. The subject matter at this fundamental level of mathematics was introduced in a rigorous fashion; yet the presentation and context were simple enough to permit comprehension by at least the more able elementary school students.

Specifically, the objective of the project was to experiment with teaching mathematical logic to classes of academically talented fifth- and sixth-grade students. Thus, it was a program for the enrichment of the more gifted students. A question of particular interest involved the capacity of children at the fifth- and sixth-grade age levels to do deductive proofs. Other questions concerned specific factors of difficulty, and the possible transfer of skills in analysis and correct reasoning to other subject areas, such as arithmetic, reading, and English.

The implementation of these objectives immediately raised the problem of teacher preparation. Thus, a secondary goal was the organization of a teacher-training program. It was necessary to determine the amount of preparation a teacher needs to present adequate instruction in logic to fifth- and sixth-grade children.

RELATED RESEARCH

Research on the capacities of children of particular ages to reason logically is scarcely definitive. Inhelder and Piaget [3][1] have concluded that development of capacity for "hypothetical" reasoning or formal aspects of logic begins at about age eleven. However, a recent study by Hill [1]

[1] Numbers in brackets refer to the References at the end of the article.

indicates that children of ages six, seven, and eight have a considerable intuitive grasp of many principles of logical inference, and, further, they can demonstrate their understanding in reasoning from hypothetical premises. Her results also indicate that simple demonstrations of correct deductions improve children's performance in the recognition of valid inference. A study by Hyram [2] also has suggested that improvement in children's inferences may be brought about by direct instruction in the logical rules.

PROCEDURE

PILOT STUDY, 1960–62

In the autumn of 1960, a pilot study in the teaching of mathematical logic was begun at an elementary school near Stanford University. The experimental group consisted of 25 students selected from all the fifth-grade classes on the basis of arithmetic achievement scores. The children had been given the arithmetic test during the seventh month of their fourth-grade year. Only students who had scored at or above the sixth-grade level at that time were chosen for the logic program. The class comprised about 27 per cent of the fifth-grade students in the school.

The class met three days per week throughout the school year for sessions of 30 to 35 minutes. The class was taught in 1960–61 by Dr. Shirley Hill and in 1961–62 by Mr. Frederick Binford, both project staff members.

The class used textbook material prepared by the project staff and composed of explanatory material and practice exercises.

TEACHER PREPARATION

During the summer of 1961 ten teachers and three school principals participated in an intensive four-week training session. The materials planned for the elementary schools were used in this course. Another fourteen teachers took a night school course in the spring of 1962.

Seventeen teachers from the first course enrolled in a second class in the fall of 1962. At the same time they were teaching their own first- or second-year classes in logic to fifth- and sixth-grade children.

Again, in the spring of 1963 a teacher preparation class was offered, with twenty-six teachers enrolled. Sixteen of the participants were given a second course in the fall of 1963.

EXPERIMENTAL CLASSES, 1961–62

Twelve classes with a total of 350 fifth-grade students began their study of logic in the fall of 1961. These classes represented 11 different schools in six school districts of the San Francisco Bay area. In ten schools the school administration selected approximately 25 to 30 per cent of the fifth graders for the logic program on the basis of general ability and high achievement in mathematics. In the other two schools all of the fifth graders were given logic; in both schools, however, it was necessary within a few months to divide the classes into fast and slow sections.

Most of the classes met three times a week for about 30 minutes, although a few met more often or for longer sessions. Each of the classes was taught by a classroom teacher from the staff of the school, with one exception: one class was taught by Mr. Binford of the project staff.

The work in the experimental classes largely followed the sequence presented in the textbook. No effort was made to maintain a uniform rate of progress in all groups; rather, each teacher proceeded at a pace that seemed appropriate for that class. During the year these classes completed between 115 and 195 pages of the text, *Mathematical Logic for the Schools,* by Patrick Suppes and Shirley Hill.

EXPERIMENTAL CLASSES: 1962–63

A second year of logic was completed by 11 sixth-grade classes consisting of 215 students who had their first year of logic in fifth grade (1961–62). Most of the classes were reviewing throughout the autumn. By June, they had completed between 162 and 284 pages of the text.

In addition, 12 new classes of 269 fifth-grade students began their first year of logic and completed between 117 and 183 pages of the text. One class began late in February with 18 pupils and completed 60 pages of the text.

CONTROL GROUPS

The control groups were two Stanford University logic classes, one of which met in the spring and the other in the autumn quarter of 1962. These students were taking logic at the customary age and educational level; the mode was between the sophomore and junior year of college. The text prepared for the elementary school students was used and the autumn-quarter class was taught by Professor Suppes.

It is fair to assume that the native ability of the elementary school children selected for the program is comparable to that of the Stanford University students.

The achievement of each class, experimental or control, was measured by a series of tests administered to each group whenever it had reached the appropriate point in the text.

The 1961–62 series consisted of two tests, one administered when the class had completed the standard rules of derivation, the other when the class completed truth tables. These tests were scored for each class by the teacher, who followed carefully prepared instructions and consulted with the project staff.

The 1962–63 series consisted of three tests, the first two covering the same material as the tests for 1961–62 and the third covering the first two chapters of predicate logic. These tests were objectively scored.

CURRICULUM MATERIAL

During the summer of 1961, the materials developed by Professor Suppes and Dr. Hill for the pilot class of 1960–61 were extended and revised with suggestions from Mr. Binford. This text material, titled *Mathematical Logic for the Schools*, was used for the classes in 1961–62.[2]

On the basis of the experience of teachers and children, the text was revised again in the summer of 1962. Further exercises were added, some changes in rules and form were made, and some of the materials were arranged in different order.

In the summer of 1961, Mr. Binford and Dr. Hill prepared a manual of solutions for all of the exercises in *Mathematical Logic for the Schools*. In the summer of 1962, Mr. Binford revised this manual to accompany the revised text; also, comments, suggestions, and explanations were added for the teacher.[3]

SUPERVISION

The project staff gave the teachers regular supervision. In 1961–62, a member of the project staff visited each class about every six weeks, to observe, to confer with the teacher, and to do some of the teaching. Also, regular monthly meetings were held with the teachers.

During the autumn of 1962, the teachers were taking the second course and thus were meeting with the project staff every week. For the re-

[2] An outline of the text appeared in THE ARITHMETIC TEACHER, IX (November, 1962), 398–399.

[3] Still additional revisions in the text were made subsequent to the project, and the revised version was published in 1964 under the title, *First Course in Mathematical Logic*, Blaisdell Publishing Co. Mr. Binford's manual was also revised and published at the same time.

mainder of the year a member of the staff visited each class and conferred with the teacher about every three weeks.

A special follow-up class was offered to the most successful of the elementary school children who had studied logic in both the fifth and sixth grades. Twenty-six students were selected upon the recommendation of their teachers and by a special examination given the candidates. Joining the class was entirely voluntary for the children.

Mr. Binford taught the four-week course, which met five days a week for one-hour sessions. In addition the students did outside assignments. The class used new materials which continued the text prepared for the regular course. These materials presented the logic of equivalence and developed the theory of multiplication and division from standard axioms.

At the end of four weeks a voluntary two-week extension of the special class was announced. Ten of the students continued. During these two weeks they studied the algebra of sets and some elementary topology. From Huntington's axioms for Boolean algebra they proved a number of theorems. Then, with four additional axioms on topological closure, they proved a number of elementary theorems of topology.

ANALYSES OF TEST DATA AND OTHER FINDINGS

Our examinations of achievement in mathematical logic indicate that the level of accomplishment of elementary school students is comparable to that of a college class. However, the college students put in about ten times as many hours each week on logic as did the elementary school students. So, although the college students completed in four weeks the material that the elementary school students covered in an academic year, their achievements per hour were comparable. Comparisons were not made of the relative progress of college and elementary school students at specified times. Rather, each group was tested when it reached particular points in the text material. Thus, mastery of course content by experimental and control groups could be compared.

Two tests were given to the college group of 186 students in the spring of 1962. The first of these tests was also given to the 260 students in the fifth-grade classes. The examination dealt with the recognition of the logical structure of sentences and with early work in symbolic deduction.

The results of Test I are given in Table 1. A few very low scores pulled the mean well below the median. Both mean and median are given in the table.

TABLE 1

SUMMARY TEST RESULTS FOR 1961-62

	N	Mean	Median	Range
			(possible score, 100)	
Test I				
College students	186	91	97	8–100
Fifth-grade students	260	76	83	17–100
Test II				
College students	189	70	72	19–99
Fifth-grade students	164	67*	77	6–100

* The mean scores of the seven classes taking Test II were 92, 87, 79, 78, 76, 49, and 36.

The elementary school classes progressed through the material at various rates. Seven of the classes with a total of 164 children got at least far enough to take Test II. This test was concerned with the symbolic manipulations involved in derivations. Table 1 shows that their median was above that of the college group. Two of these classes had very low mean scores, but the other five were well above the college mean. (See footnote to Table 1.)

These test results suggest that the symbolic manipulations performed in formal proofs are relatively easier for elementary school children than are the problems of recognizing the logical form or structure of sentences in ordinary English.

The testing program continued in 1962–63. Tests were administered to another control group of college students, to the experimental classes of students who had advanced to the sixth grade, and to beginning classes of fifth-grade students.

The 1962–63 edition of the tests was made out in multiple-choice form with answers to be transferred to a standard answer sheet. This was done to allow rapid objective scoring.

Sections A, B, and C of Test I covered the translation of English sentences into logical symbols, the construction of negations, and the classification of different logical forms of sentences. These are largely language skills. Section D dealt with application of rules of inference to one-step derivations. Section E tested logical vocabulary, and Sections F and G called for construction of multiple-step derivations.

Tables 2 and 2A summarize the findings on Test I in 1962–63. They show that the elementary school children, as compared to the college control group, did relatively better on the pure, symbolic, logical deductions (Sections F and G) than on work requiring language skills (Sections A, B, and C). Similar results were obtained in 1961–62. Except for question 41, which none of the elementary group answered correctly, the ranges for

TABLE 2
MEANS AND RANGES FOR SCORES FOR TEST I, 1962–63

	By section of test				Total test
	A, B, C	D	E	F, G	
Possible score	26	21	12	26	85
Mean					
Control	22.96	20.25	11.05	24.75	79.0
Experimental	19.0	17.0	10.1	22.9	69.5
Range					
Control	26–15	21–7	12–2	26–0	85–24
Experimental	25–5	21–7	12–5	26–4	84–32

TABLE 2A
RATIOS OF MEAN SCORE, ELEMENTARY SCHOOL TO COLLEGE

	By section of test				Total test
	A, B, C	D	E	F, G	
All experimental students to control	.83	.83	.90	.94	.88
Best experimental class to control	.96	.89	1.09	1.04	.975

each section of Test I were nearly identical for the two groups. Perfect test results were obtained by some students in both groups, and the best experimental class was quite comparable to the college class.

Section A of Test II (see Table 3) covered deductions in multiple-step problems. Sections B, C, D, and E tested the ability to do proofs of invalidity, of consistency, and of inconsistency. Ten of the experimental classes, totaling 196 students, completed the test.

TABLE 3
RESULTS OF TEST II AND TEST III, 1962-63

	Test II			Test III	Total of Test II and Test III
	A	B–E	Total		
Possible score	28	33	61	41	102
Mean					
College	27.3	25.8	53.1	27.7	80.0
Elementary school	25.2	19.7	44.2	26.0*	70.2*
Range					
College	28–12	33–6	61–18	41–13	102–31
Elementary school	28–12	33–3	61–19	39–15*	100–34*
Ratio of means:					
Experimental to control	.92	.76	.83	.94*	.87*

* These figures are based on the three classes (60 students) that took both Test II and Test III.

Three of these classes with a total of 60 students also completed Test III, which covered translation of English sentences into the symbolism of predicate logic and the carrying out of derivations in this symbolism.

On Test II the mean of the best class of elementary school children almost exactly matched the college mean. The ranges for experimental and control groups were identical; several perfect test papers were obtained from both groups.

Three experimental classes completed Test III. One college student handed in a perfect paper, while one elementary school student missed only two points. Table 3 summarizes the results on Tests II and III.

Comparisons between the 1961–62 and the 1962–63 test results require interpretation. The results from Test II in 1961–62 and Tests II and III in 1962–63 are of particular interest. In 1961–62 the elementary school median was 7 per cent above the college median, while in 1962–63 it was 15 per cent below. The teachers administering the latter tests reported that the students had difficulty handling the mechanics of the objective tests and were often confused by the multiple choices. One teacher whose class had a median of five points out of 15 on the last section of Test III later gave the students the same problems to work without any right and wrong suggestions. She reported that the great majority wrote perfect original solutions, many of which were highly idiosyncratic. Without doubt the college students were a great deal more practiced in the mechanics and strategy of multiple-choice examinations and more readily accepted a given, fixed approach to a proof.

INTELLIGENCE QUOTIENTS

Scores on the California Test of Mental Maturity were available for 176 of the students who began logic in 1961. The lower quartile ranged from 98 to 122, the second quartile 123 to 130, the third quartile 130 to 142, and the fourth quartile 142 to 184.

SUBJECTIVE EVALUATIONS BY TEACHERS

In June, 1962, the teachers in the program were asked for their subjective evaluations about what general benefits to the students could be attributed to the logic program. They were asked to be frank in giving comments of their own and comments they had heard from others.

The following replies were received.

Reading growth: the class *median* growth showed a gain of more than two grade points as shown by Iowa tests. Confidence in meeting new symbolisms or new systems of notation was realized.

Enthusiasm of the students for the program and support of the parents showed that the subject matter is interesting to above-average students. It offered good experience in vocabulary building by a greater awareness of language and meanings. Students began to challenge careless statements by the teacher.

A more precise way of attacking problems was acquired by some of the students. A lively interest appeared in solving problems in an original, individual kind of way on the part of some students. The excitement of a new subject in the curriculum at this grade level stimulated the students.

I have thoroughly enjoyed teaching this first year of mathematical logic. It has been a challenge to me, and it has been a rewarding experience to see children of this age respond intelligently and enthusiastically to a whole new way of thinking.

This experience has not been, however, a carefree adventure. Aside from the fact that it was a new subject for me to present, the time-consuming job of reviewing each day's assignments was sometimes a great burden. This was particularly true when we reached long proofs where the individuality of approach to solving problems became apparent. Absences of two or more days often required coaching outside of class time. The suggestion that we use some of the abler students to assist the teacher was a good one and helped to some extent, but not greatly.

In spite of these reservations I am looking forward to going on next year.

I think it is interesting to note some of the results of this last test. Two of the outstanding students were sixth graders, but the low scorers were also sixth graders. The fifth graders generally did much better. I have tried to analyze this difference and have concluded that it may be attributed to a difference in attitude toward this subject and possibly to other subjects. I discussed some of these children, with their homeroom teacher and learned that, with one exception, the low, low scorers in math logic were not performing up to their ability in other subjects. Another thing that may be considered in evaluating this class is the richness of this last year's curriculum. In the field of math alone they were exposed to new concepts not usually encountered before the eighth grade and high school—and so in every other subject. Therefore, their interest was not centered in math logic.

On the other hand, in Room 12, composed of the more able students of the two fifth grades, math logic was the new subject introduced into the regular fifth-grade curriculum. They were very proud to be studying it, and most of them worked diligently. In this last test, their median was seven points less than the other class of higher ability and their average only 2.3 points lower.

The program develops creative and critical thinking, responsibility for homework, provides challenge and stimulation to the advanced child, gives prestige in home and school to children who are not always as socially accepted as others.

There were no adverse comments from parents. They appeared to be flattered and curious as to the outcome. I think it made the pupils aware of the fact that there are other areas of learning than routine arithmetic, spelling, and reading.

Parents are impressed and interested. I enjoy teaching the program also.

Not very much transfer seemed to occur. I particularly stressed transfer when discussing *errata,* and students brought examples all year long. There was greater language awareness.

I found enhanced self-confidence in achieving a mastery of a kind of discipline that some students originally thought could not be mastered by them. They acquired a more critical attitude toward statements they ran across; a recognition of the need of analysis in complex situations; and an awareness of sentence structure in written language. Students who at the beginning seemed to have difficulties came through with good work eventually.

Signs of transfer were more apparent among the children with exceptional ability. They were very apparent in arithmetic. One child remarked that a section of his Reading Achievement Test was made easier because of the methods of logical interpretation he had learned. There was also some frustration in their trying to apply their knowledge or methods in other fields.

There has been a transfer in arithmetic. One helps the other. There is also a growing awareness in English grammar as the two are compared.

Conclusions and Implications

Our summary conclusions are the following:

1. The upper quartile of elementary school students can achieve a significant conceptual and technical mastery of elementary mathematical logic. The level of mastery is 85 to 90 per cent of that achieved by comparable university students.

2. This mastery of the subject matter by elementary school students can be accomplished in an amount of study time comparable to that needed by college students if study is allocated over a longer period of time if the students receive considerably more direct teacher supervision.

3. The more dedicated and able elementary school teachers can be adequately trained in five or six semester hours to teach classes in elementary mathematical logic. It is probably essential that this teacher-training program be very closely geared to the actual program of instruction the teacher will follow in the classroom.

4. Anecdotal evidence from teachers suggests that there is some carryover in critical thinking and attitude into other fields, especially arith-

metic, reading, and English. More explicit behavioral data on carry-over in critical thinking would be desirable.

5. The work with the special summer class in 1963 indicates that able elementary school students who have received prior training in mathematical logic can make rapid progress in other parts of modern mathematics organized on a deductive basis. We hope to be able to continue this line of investigation in the future and to determine to what extent the deductive methodology and viewpoint of modern mathematics may be made a natural and intuitive part of the young student's mathematical knowledge.

REFERENCES

1. S. A. HILL, "A study of the logical abilities of children," unpublished Ph.D. dissertation, Stanford University, 1960.
2. G. H. HYRAM, An experiment in developing critical thinking in children, *J. Exp. Educ.*, XXVI (1957), 125–132.
3. B. INHELDER and J. PIAGET, *The Growth of Logical Thinking*, translated by A. PARSONS and S. MILGRAM (New York: Basic Books, Inc., 1958).

48. Critical Listening: An Experiment

Sara W. Lundsteen

There is growing recognition of the importance of listening ability in the lives of children and adults. A number of studies—including investigations by Duker, Russell, and Witty—offer evidence on the significant role that listening plays in our daily lives (1–3).

The authors of some studies suggest that listening ability and critical listening ability are identifiable factors, separate from general verbal in-

"Critical Listening: An Experiment," by Sara W. Lundsteen, *The Elementary School Journal* LXVI, 6 (March 1966), published by the University of Chicago Press with the Department of Education of the University of Chicago. Copyright 1966 by the University of Chicago. Reprinted by permission of the University of Chicago Press. A year later, the author did a follow-up study of this experiment. She found that the experimental group still maintained significantly higher scores than the control group on the critical listening post-test. Their superiority was due to maintaining gains already made with no significant additional gains made since the post-test of the first study. A ceiling effect inherent in the test was given as a possible reason for the lack of additional gains. The follow-up study was published as "Critical Listening: Permanency and Transfer of Gains made During an Experiment in the Fifth and Sixth Grades" in *California Journal of Educational Research*, XVI: 210–216, November, 1965.

telligence, vocabulary, and reading abilities (4–7). Correlational and factor analytic studies suggest that there may be a constellation of inter-related listening abilities and that critical listening may be included in the constellation (8).

The purpose of this study was to explore critical listening abilities as part of general listening ability, a part that could be tested and improved by well-planned instructional procedures and materials. In effect, the purpose was to identify, define, teach, and test certain abilities in critical listening. For the study the researcher used verbal materials especially prepared for upper grades of the elementary school. The abilities chosen for investigation were detection of the speaker's purpose, analysis and judgment of propaganda, and analysis and judgment of arguments.

Critical listening was defined as a fourfold process that included examining spoken materials in the light of related objective evidence, comparing the ideas under evaluation with some criteria, making a judgment on the ideas, and acting on the judgment made. The main hypothesis follows: There is an ability or a group of abilities in critical listening that can be taught and tested, and test results will show that an experimental group that was taught these abilities will make significantly greater gains in critical listening than a similar control group that had regular instruction in English but no instruction in critical listening.

Although the primary purpose of the investigation was to examine growth in certain critical listening abilities, the procedures used provided the opportunity to investigate differences in performance at the two grade levels under study and differences in the listening abilities of boys and girls. The procedures also provided an opportunity to investigate the relationships of three variables: interest, transfer to other in-school and out-of-school activities, and the suitability of the lessons on critical listening for the grade levels chosen.

Design

A repeated-measurements design was used. Teachers who had volunteered the use of their classes for the study were randomly assigned to experimental and control groups. The interval between pre- and posttesting for the experimental and the control groups was nine weeks.

The sample, which was made up of twelve classes in a Texas city, included six fifth-grade classes and six sixth-grade classes. The experimental group had three fifth-grade classes and three sixth-grade classes. The control group likewise had three fifth-grade classes and three sixth-grade classes. In all, 287 pupils and twelve teachers took part. The experimental group had 146 pupils and six teachers. The control group had six teachers and 141 pupils.

Scores from measures of reading, mental ability, critical thinking, and general and critical listening ability were collected. On none of these measures was there any significant difference between the control group and the experimental group. The mean score for the sample on the California Test of Mental Maturity, Form E, was 123, the reading grade average for the Stanford Achievement Test, Form N, was seventh grade. Some pupils were described by the teachers, who knew the parents' occupations, as coming from low socioeconomic homes. But in general the pupils came from families from middle to high socioeconomic level.

TEACHING MATERIALS

The control group followed the usual curriculum. The experimental group was given a series of eighteen lessons. These lessons were derived from a survey of related literature and two years' empirical observation of pilot classes. The lessons were collected in a 142-page teacher's guide.

Each week for nine weeks the teachers of the experimental group taught two lessons. Each lesson lasted forty minutes. The first lesson of the week developed concepts in critical listening; the second lesson enriched the learning and provided additional practice on the concepts.

The theoretical structure of the lessons used concepts of programmed learning. The content involved a framework of related concepts for critical listening, presented to the pupils in a carefully planned sequence. The program provided branching for the teacher in the form of extra examples to be used as needed. Ideas were also borrowed from the concept of discovery in learning.

The pupils were presented with many illustrations of a certain concept important to critical listening. The children were expected to develop concepts from these concrete instances. For example, after examining advertising propaganda where the technique of "glad words" was used to sell a product, pupils were asked to name the trick.

The teachers were instructed to analyze the examples with the class and to elicit other examples from the pupils to illustrate the concept further. Guided by prompts and questions in the lesson, the pupils made charts that listed standards for judging.

The content of the lessons included three major areas, or abilities: detection of the speaker's purpose, analysis and judgment of propaganda, and analysis and judgment of arguments. The first three weeks were spent on introducing the unit and on developing abilities in detecting the speaker's purpose. The speaker's purpose included being funny, giving facts, or persuading. The next three weeks were spent on the study of propaganda. The pupils analyzed it and judged it according to the standards they themselves had evolved. The last three weeks were devoted to the study of arguments, weak and strong. During the lessons the pupils discovered such fallacies as false cause, improper use of expert opinion, circular thinking, and appeal to ignorance.

Test of Critical Listening

Because no available test at the elementary-school level measured the abilities taught in the lessons, the experimenter constructed an instrument, which was taped. It was made up of seventy-nine items. The items were grouped to follow the three main divisions of the lessons: detection of the speaker's purpose, analysis and judgment of propaganda, and analysis and judgment of arguments. The pupils were required to analyze the test selections, to select a judgment according to a given standard, and to select a reason for the judgment. The test itself and examples from the test are given elsewhere (8, 9).

How effective were the lessons designed to improve critical listening? Measures of critical listening ability showed a difference between the experimental group and the control group significant at the .01 level in favor of the experimental group, the group that had special lessons on critical listening (calculated $F = 76.91$). The statistic chosen was a simple one-way analysis of variance.

Evaluation of the Lessons

Questions on the transfer of learning in critical listening to other activities and questions on the suitability of the lessons were answered from data collected on weekly check sheets. These check sheets were filled in and turned in anonymously by the six teachers and the 146 pupils in the experimental group. On the check sheets teachers and pupils consistently reported examples of transfer from the lessons on critical listening to other in-school and out-of-school activities such as reading and interpersonal relations. During the study more than a thousand check sheets were turned in. Ninety per cent of these indicated that the lessons were suitable, well paced, and properly sequenced.

The differences between fifth- and sixth-grade test-score averages on critical listening were significant at the .01 level, in favor of the sixth grade. Test norms generally indicate progressive increase from grade to grade. There was no significant difference between the performance of the boys and the performance of the girls on the pretest. But the scores of the girls in the experimental group showed a significant difference between the results of the pretest and the results of the posttest. The difference was significant at the .05 level.

Evaluation of the Listening Test

An evaluation was made of the reliability and the validity of the test used to measure critical listening. Since the distribution of scores on the test of critical listening was normal, item analysis and indices of discrimination and difficulty were used to evaluate the test. The test and re-test method produced a reliability coefficient of .72 based on the results for a hundred pupils.

To evaluate the validity of the content of the test, five judges, who included university professors and a curriculum consultant, were asked to read the test critically. The judges generally agreed to the validity of the content of the test and the scoring key. After their evaluation, any item that they found questionable was revised or discarded.

The experimenter then used a factor analysis based on intercorrelations of sixteen test variables. The instrument appeared to yield four components of critical listening ability. On the basis of logical analysis of the content of the test items, these factors were labeled *general analysis and inference, value judgment regarding propaganda, factual judgment of arguments,* and *reasons for selecting a certain judgment of arguments.* In effect, there appeared to be differences between the two types of judgment: value judgment of good and bad propaganda and factual judgment of arguments. The evidence appears to support the theory that a critical listening process and critical listening abilities do exist.

The relationships between the critical listening scores and the scores on other measures used to describe the sample are positive and substantial. The results, which ranged from .26 to .64, are close to those that other investigators have found at the high-school level and at the elementary-school level (7, 10). The coefficients of correlation between total pretest scores of critical listening and other test scores obtained in the present study follow:

Pratt's (11) test of general listening .... .64
Hendrickson's (12) test of critical thinking .... .52
The Stanford Achievement Test, Form N, total reading .... .47
The California Test of Mental Maturity, Form E,
Total: Verbal and Non-verbal .... .39
Verbal .... .43
Non-verbal .... .26

The results suggest the possibility of an independent ability or abilities of critical listening. This ability appears to be positively related to, but not congruent with, other verbal and thinking abilities, such as the variables just cited.

IMPLICATIONS

Several implications for theory and practice emerge from this study. The content, the concepts, the processes, and the abilities in critical listening appear to be amenable to empirical analysis and can be improved by practice as described in this study. The materials used in the study may make a contribution to curriculum procedures. Lessons and tests similar to those used in this study may yield other useful data on the improvement of critical listening abilities.

REFERENCES

1. SAM DUKER, "Listening and Reading," *Elementary School Journal*, LXV (March 1965), 321–29.
2. DAVID H. RUSSELL, "A Conspectus of Recent Research on Listening Abilities," *Elementary English*, XLI (March 1964), 262–67.
3. PAUL A. WITTY, "A 1964 Study of TV: Comparisons and Comments," *Elementary English*, XLII (February 1965), 134–41.
4. JOHN G. CAFFREY, "Auding Ability as a Function of Certain Psychometric Variables." Unpublished doctoral dissertation. Berkeley, California: University of California, 1953.
5. DONALD SPEARRITT, "A Factorial Analysis of Listening Comprehension." Unpublished doctoral dissertation. Cambridge, Massachusetts: Harvard University, 1961.
6. WILLIAM C. WILSON, "Some Inter-relationships of Verbal and Musical Listening Abilities in Elementary School Children." Unpublished doctoral dissertation. Berkeley, California: University of California, 1960.
7. THOMAS GERARD DEVINE, "The Development and Evaluation of a Series of Recordings for Teaching Certain Critical Listening Abilities." Unpublished doctoral dissertation. Boston, Massachusetts: Boston University, 1961.
8. SARA W. LUNDSTEEN, "Teaching Abilities in Critical Listening in the Fifth and Sixth Grades." Unpublished doctoral dissertation. Berkeley, California: University of California, 1963.
9. ——, "Teaching and Testing Critical Listening in the Fifth and Sixth Grades," *Elementary English*, XLI (November 1964), 743–47.
10. GUS P. PLESSAS, "Auding and Intelligence," *California Journal of Educational Research*, XIV (March 1963), 90–94.
11. LLOYD EDWARD PRATT, "The Experimental Evaluation of a Program for the Improvement of Listening in the Elementary School." Unpub-

lished doctoral dissertation. Iowa City, Iowa: State University of Iowa, 1953.

12. DALE HENDRICKSON, "Some Correlates in Critical Thinking of Fifth-Grade Children." Unpublished doctoral dissertation. Berkeley, California: University of California, 1960.

49. Some Aspects of Creative Reading

Robert R. Nardelli

This study was based on the assumption that the ability to do creative reading is important for citizens of a democracy. In this investigation, creative reading is defined as an attitude of suspended judgment with regard to reading materials, the ability to read beyond the superficial, factual statements of the printed page, the ability to see relationships in verbal materials, and the ability to recognize authors' intensions and propaganda devices.

There is a considerable body of research and opinion in the area of creative reading (9, 8, 10). Many educators are agreed that the ability to interpret and evaluate written materials is a worthwhile educational objective (2, 3, 7, 6, 11).

Wrightstone (12), McCullough (8), Husbands and Shores (4) and Davis (1) have pointed to the need for instruments capable of measuring adequately certain high levels of reading ability, such as those mentioned above.

This experiment is an attempt to determine the effect of a short period of instruction upon the ability of sixth-grade pupils to draw inferences and to recognize propaganda devices. It is also an attempt to determine the relationship between creative reading ability and such factors as chronological age, mental age, intelligence, and reading ability. Finally, it is an attempt to determine pupil and teacher reaction to a unit of instruction in creative reading activities.

THE PROCEDURES

First, an instrument designed to measure creative reading ability was prepared. The instrument included three tests, with the following titles:

"Some Aspects of Creative Reading," by Robert R. Nardelli, is reprinted by permission from *Journal of Educational Research*, L (March 1957), 495–508.

(1) Interpreting Authors' Suggestions
(2) Interpreting Feelings
(3) Recognizing Propaganda Devices *

Lesson units were designed with the purpose of helping pupils to improve their ability to do the type of reading demanded by the three parts of the measuring instrument. These lesson units were used with five experimental sixth-grade classes in two elementary schools in Albany, California. All instruction was conducted by the writer.

The experimental classes were matched with two sixth-grade classes from Lafayette, California, and one sixth-grade class from Orinda, California. The classes were matched on these factors: reading ability, chronological age, intelligence quotient, and initial creative reading ability. In no cases were differences in the means of the two groups for any of these factors significant at the one per cent level of confidence.

At the beginning of the study, the tests of creative reading were administered to the experimental and control groups. Following the initial testing, the experimental classes received ten hours of instruction spread over a period of six weeks. Meanwhile, the control classes continued with their customary reading lessons, which were devoid of instruction in creative reading. At the end of the six weeks period, the pupils in both groups again were tested and their performance evaluated. Speed was not a factor in the testing.

Pupils and teachers from the experimental classes submitted brief papers evaluating the experiment. The pupil evaluations were anonymous and were made at the end of the experiment while the teacher evaluations were submitted five months after the close of the experiment.

THE TESTS

Test I—Interpreting Authors' Suggestions

This test was designed to evaluate the ability of pupils to interpret suggestions made by an author in statements where the basis for a conclusion is implied, rather than stated specifically. The reader is forced to go beyond the stated facts to reach the proper solution. For example, Item 1 reads:

1. After ten days on the tiny raft, without seeing a sign of life, the men began to wonder.

The author suggests that

* The first two tests were of the form used in McCullough, C.M., and Russell, David H., Ginn Basic Reading Tests, Ginn and Co., 1951–1952.

——the men could catch no fish.

——the ocean is a wonderful place.

——the men had doubts about their safety.

——a raft is better than nothing when you are in the water.

The reliability coefficient for this test, found by means of a Kuder-Richardson estimate of reliabilty, and based upon 174 cases, is .95. The final form of the test included 30 items.

Test II—Interpreting Feelings

This test was designed to test the ability of pupils to interpret the feelings of a person or an animal where the basis for the interpretation is implied, rather than stated specifically. The reader must go beyond the stated facts to reach the proper solution. For example, Item 7 reads:

7. He groped his way along the trail, moving his foot only after he had felt the ground with his hand.

He was

——Brave

——Speechless

——Afraid

——Cautious

The reliability coefficient for this test, found by means of a Kuder-Richardson estimate of reliability (same as for Test 1), and based upon 174 cases, is .95. The final form of the test included 30 items.

Test III—Recognizing Propaganda Devices

This test was designed to determine whether pupils in the sixth grade would be able to recognize and identify propaganda. Twelve items simulating newspaper stories, editorials, and advertisements were constructed, each containing two kinds of propaganda. The seven kinds of propaganda, as described by the Institute for Propaganda Analysis (5), were included in the items. Pupils were asked to determine which two propaganda devices were strongest in the particular item. For example, No. 5 reads:

CHICAGO, Oct. 1—(UP)—Foreigners are responsible for a large percent of the crimes committed in the United States, according to a study made by the Tribune Staff.

The Tribune found that crimes involving people from foreign countries included murder, robbery, and assault and battery. For purposes of the study, people who have come to this country in the last fifty years were classed as foreigners.

It is a pity that this country does not kick out these doubtful characters.

What two propaganda devices are strongest in this news article?

——Testimonial
——Band Wagon
——Plain Folks
——Name Calling
——Glittering Generalities
——Card Stacking
——Transfer

In addition to the twelve items described above, Test III included six-teen matching items, in which the pupils were asked to match the name of a propaganda device with an example of that device.

The reliability coefficient for Test III, found by means of the Kuder-Richardson estimate of reliability mentioned previously, and based upon 127 cases, is .88.

The validity of Tests I and II is indicated by the fact that:

(a) A jury of ten graduate students in education unanimously agreed that each item in the test demands that the reader arrive at an interpretation which is new (creative) for him.

(b) The jury unanimously agreed that the only correct response to each item is the one which is given in the scoring key.

(c) The jury helped to remove any ambiguous phrases which might have proved misleading to the reader.

The validity of Test III is indicated by the fact that:

(a) A jury of ten members of a graduate seminar in journalism reached agreement regarding the scoring key.

(b) The jury helped to remove ambiguous phrases which might have proved misleading to the reader.

THE LESSON UNITS

Unit I: *We Learn to Know Propaganda*

Seven of the ten hours devoted to instruction in creative reading were devoted to the study of propaganda. This instruction included a study of the different parts of a newspaper, the meaning of propaganda in general and the various devices in particular. The pupils then were provided with copies of various newspapers and magazines and asked to find examples of the seven devices. The examples found were to be labeled properly and pasted on newsprint, to become posters for an exhibition in the classrooms.

Considerable enthusiasm was expressed by the pupils upon finding propaganda, particularly the more subtle types. They worked individually or in groups, according to their desire.

Unit II: *Good Citizens Read Carefully*

Six lessons were given in an effort to help the pupils to understand the importance of suspended judgment in the drawing of inferences and conclusions. A number of reading exercises were prepared, providing the pupils with practice in those skills mentioned above.

The exercises consisted of reading passages of approximately 250 words, together with items calling for judgments based upon the reading of those passages. For example Item No. 5 in the "Drawing Inferences" exercise on a passage about George Washington read as follows:

"5. Washington had the cannons mounted on the heights   T——
    above Boston because he knew the British would be-   DK——
    come frightened and leave without fighting."   F——

On the basis of what they had read, the pupils were supposed to mark the statement as "True," "False," or even "Don't Know," if the information was insufficient to merit either a true or false response.

After the pupils had marked their exercise sheets, the class participated in open discussion on the merit of each response.

The same reading passages were used for exercises in "Making Generalizations." These exercises included items of the following type:

All   Most   Some   Don't   No
                    Know
——   ——   ——   ——   —— 1. Green Mountain Boys were
                                  good runners.

The pupils were asked to mark their answers on the basis of the information available to them. As in the case of the exercises on drawing inferences, the pupils then discussed openly the merits of each response. With each item, an attempt was made to help the pupils realize that sweeping generalizations of the "all" variety are at least open to question.

The Results

Table I indicates that the instructional techniques employed in this study resulted in a statistically significant mean gain for the experimental group over the control group on the battery of tests of creative reading. The gain is in favor of the experimental group. However, this gain must be attributed mostly to the gain in Test III, Recognizing Propaganda Devices, where the pupils gained an average of 8.76 points between the initial and the final testing, as may be seen in Table IV.

Tables II and III indicate that on Test I, Interpreting Authors' Suggestions, and Test II, Interpreting Feelings, the experimental group made only minor gains.

The control group failed to achieve a significant mean gain on any of the three sub-tests in the battery, having gained an average of 1.29 and 1.14 points, respectively, on Tests I and II. On Test III, the control group suffered a mean loss of 1.70 points between the initial and final testing.

An item analysis of pupil performance on Test III indicated that all propaganda devices are not equally comprehensible to sixth-grade pupils. Various devices have certain peculiarities which cause them to be more readily identified, while others are more subtle in nature and pose difficult problems for pupils at this grade level. The easiest devices for the pupils to recognize were the Plain Folks and Testimonial devices; the most difficult were the Card Stacking, Glittering Generalities, and Transfer devices. Results of the item analysis are shown in Table V.

RELATIONSHIPS OF FACTORS IN THE EXPERIMENTAL GROUP

One of the purposes of this study was to determine the relationships of the various experimental factors. Table VI includes the Pearson Product-Moment coefficients of Correlation among the Experimental Tests of Creative Reading for the initial and the final testing, and between the experimental tests and such factors as mental age and intelligence (as measured by the California Short Form Test of Mental Maturity), reading ability (as measured by the California Achievement Test, Elementary), and chronological age.

PUPIL AND TEACHER REACTION TO THE EXPERIMENT

Generally, pupils in the experimental group expressed approval of the techniques employed in the study, although a few complained about the instruction. Favorable reaction was indicated by pupils who found the instruction "interesting," "useful," "fun," and "something that we didn't know about." Other pupils complained that they did not understand what propaganda is, and that the instruction and experiences were boring. As the study progressed, pupils expressed delight upon finding examples of propaganda, particularly examples most subtle in nature.

The regular teachers of the experimental classes approved the techniques employed in the experiment and reported considerable pupil interest. However, they stated or implied that the study of propaganda would be more suitable at a higher grade level.

TABLE I

MEAN SCORES OF THE EXPERIMENTAL AND CONTROL CLASSES
ON THE EXPERIMENTAL TESTS OF CREATIVE READING

Group N–217		Initial Test		Final Test		
		Mean	S. D.	Mean	S. D.	Change
E1	29	62.07	16.79	72.55	17.46	+10.48
E2	28	64.43	21.98	75.43	21.45	+11.00
E3	16	60.50	16.64	71.75	20.47	+11.25
E4	28	58.21	16.06	68.75	17.66	+10.54
E5	26	57.88	13.60	70.62	16.00	+12.74
Composite						
E–	127	60.69	17.26	71.85	18.41	+11.16
C1	32	63.44	14.21	63.75	12.33	+ .31
C2	29	64.07	14.21	63.83	15.13	− .24
C3	29	63.93	16.19	66.10	14.04	+ 2.17
Composite						
C–	90	63.80	14.70	64.53	13.71	+ .73

TABLE II

MEAN GAINS OF THE EXPERIMENTAL AND CONTROL CLASSES ON
TEST I—INTERPRETING AUTHORS' SUGGESTIONS

Group N–217		Initial Test		Final Test		
		Mean	S. D.	Mean	S. D.	Change
E1	29	20.86	5.13	23.66	4.42	+2.80
E2	28	21.61	5.96	23.75	5.84	+2.14
E3	16	20.75	5.17	22.25	5.79	+1.50
E4	28	21.68	5.06	22.00	5.74	+ .32
E5	26	21.65	4.12	23.04	4.47	+1.39
Composite						
E–	127	21.35	5.06	23.00	5.22	+1.65
C1	32	22.28	4.79	23.91	3.79	+1.63
C2	29	23.24	4.04	23.69	4.60	+ .45
C3	29	22.59	4.04	24.34	3.21	+1.75
Composite						
C–	90	22.69	4.29	23.98	3.87	1.29

TABLE III

MEAN GAINS OF THE EXPERIMENTAL AND CONTROL CLASSES ON
TEST II—INTERPRETING FEELINGS

Group N–217		Initial Test		Final Test		Change
		Mean	S. D.	Mean	S. D.	
E1	29	24.21	5.71	24.41	5.45	+ .20
E2	28	23.18	8.96	23.93	7.85	+ .75
E3	16	22.63	6.35	23.06	7.44	+ .43
E4	28	21.07	7.28	22.89	6.94	+1.82
E5	26	22.77	6.04	23.15	6.43	+ .38
Composite E–	127	22.80	7.00	23.54	6.73	+ .74
C1	32	23.72	5.02	24.88	5.04	+1.16
C2	29	24.00	5.67	24.69	6.51	+ .69
C3	29	23.88	6.78	24.97	5.60	+1.59
Composite C–	90	23.70	5.78	24.84	5.67	+1.14

TABLE IV

MEAN SCORES OF THE EXPERIMENTAL AND CONTROL CLASSES ON
TEST III—RECOGNIZING PROPAGANDA DEVICES

Group N–217		Initial Test		Final Test		Change
		Mean	S. D.	Mean	S. D.	
E1	29	17.00	8.44	24.48	9.25	+ 7.48
E2	28	19.64	9.21	27.75	9.02	+ 8.11
E3	16	17.13	7.28	26.44	8.65	+ 9.31
E4	28	15.46	6.06	23.86	7.33	+ 8.40
E5	26	13.46	5.29	24.42	7.04	+10.96
Composite E–	127	16.54	7.63	25.30	8.31	+ 8.76
C1	32	17.44	7.04	14.97	5.70	−2.47
C2	29	16.83	7.16	15.45	6.61	−1.38
C3	29	17.97	7.29	16.79	7.55	−1.18
Composite C–	90	17.41	7.09	15.71	6.60	−1.70

TABLE V

PERCENT OF CORRECT RESPONSES ON TEST III, RECOGNIZING PROPAGANDA DEVICES, FOR PUPILS IN THE TOP AND BOTTOM 27 PERCENT OF THE EXPERIMENTAL GROUP

Device	Top 27 Percent		Bottom 27 Percent		Average—Top and Bottom 27 Percent		Average Change, Top and Bottom 27 Percent
	Initial Test	Final Test	Initial Test	Final Test	Initial Test	Final Test	
Plain Folks	85.4	98.7	25.1	45.4	55.2	72.0	+16.8
Testimonial	85.0	95.5	26.1	47.5	55.1	71.0	+15.9
Name Calling	79.5	93.5	30.2	33.0	54.8	63.2	+8.4
Band Wagon	70.0	91.5	21.8	34.0	45.9	62.7	+16.8
Transfer	45.8	74.2	18.3	28.7	32.1	51.5	+19.4
Glittering Generalities	55.0	72.5	27.7	30.0	41.1	51.2	+10.1
Card Stacking	57.9	77.9	22.7	22.1	40.3	50.0	+9.7

The number of correct responses possible on each device for the top and bottom groups were as follows: Plain Folks, 240; Testimonial, 200; Name Calling, 200; Band Wagon, 200; Transfer, 240; Glittering Generalities, 200; and Card Stacking, 240.

Table VI

Correlation Coefficients for the Five Classes
in the Experimental Group

	1	2	3	4	5	6	7	8
1. Test I-A								
2. Test II-A	.81							
3. Test III-A	.56	.60						
4. Total -A	.87	.91	.85					
5. Test I-B	.85	.76	.53	.79				
6. Test II-B	.83	.93	.56	.87	.83			
7. Test III-B	.74	.69	.70	.81	.71	.70		
8. Total -B	.88	.87	.67	.91	.91	.91	.64	
9. Age	−.32	−.39	−.23	−.35	−.30	−.32	−.26	−.34
10. Vocabulary	.62	.66	.41	.66	.54	.66	.59	.66
11. Comprehension	.58	.54	.59	.66	.48	.53	.61	.60
12. Total Reading Score	.67	.67	.66	.76	.58	.67	.67	.71
13. Mental Age	.70	.65	.60	.74	.59	.63	.62	.68
14. IQ–Total	.70	.68	.59	.74	.60	.66	.63	.70
15. IQ–LF	.76	.79	.64	.81	.67	.74	.69	.77
16. IQ–NLF	.29	.25	.24	.29	.19	.22	.24	.24

Interpretation of Symbols:
        A = Original Testing
        B = Final Testing
        I = Interpreting Author's Suggestions
        II = Interpreting Feelings
        III = Recognizing Propaganda Devices
   IQ–LF = Intelligence Quotient, Language Factor
  IQ–NLF = Intelligence Quotient, Nonlanguage Factor

Conclusions

1. Because of the gain which the experimental group made over the control group, the conclusion may be made that the lesson units developed for this study can be used effectively with similar sixth-grade groups to improve the ability to do creative reading, but only in the phase which concerned the recognition of propaganda devices.

2. All propaganda devices are not equally comprehensible to sixth-grade pupils. Various devices have certain peculiarities which cause them to be more readily identified, while others are more subtle in nature and pose difficult problems for pupils at this grade level. The easiest devices for the pupils to recognize were the Plain Folks and Testimonial devices; the most difficult were the Card Stacking, Glittering Generalities, and Transfer devices.

3. While the fact has been established that sixth-grade pupils are able to recognize and identify propaganda, this study does not suggest that

these pupils are, because of their newly acquired skill, able to resist propaganda in its various forms.

4. There is a high degree of relationship between intelligence test scores, reading achievement, and mental age and the ability to do creative reading as here measured.

5. While there is a high positive relationship between creative reading ability and intelligence test scores which have been derived largely from verbal tests, there is a low relationship between creative reading ability and nonlanguage factors such as the nonlanguage factor of the California Short Form Test of Mental Maturity.

6. It seems probable that instruction in creative reading would be more effective were it spread over a longer period of time, possibly a school year, rather than concentrated into a short period such as that employed in this study.

References

1. Frederick B. Davis, "What Do Reading Tests Really Measure? *English Journal,* XXXIII, pp. 180–87, April, 1944.

2. William S. Gray, "The Nature and Types of Reading," *The Teaching of Reading: A Second Report.* Thirty-Sixth Yearbook of the National Society for the Study of Education, Part I, Public School Company, 1937.

3. Ralph B. Guinness, "Critical Literacy," *Social Education,* VII, pp. 165–66, April, 1943.

4. K. L. Husbands and J. Harlan Shores, "Measurement of Reading for Problem Solving," *Journal of Educational Research,* XLIII, pp. 453–65, February, 1950.

5. Institute for Propaganda Analysis, Inc. *Propaganda Analysis.* Columbia University Press, I, pp. 1–3, November, 1937.

6. Charles H. Judd, *Education as Cultivation of the Higher Mental Processes.* The Macmillan Company, 1936.

7. Sheila Kragness, "Critical Thinking Through Language," *Modern Language Journal,* XXIX, pp. 521–23, October, 1945.

8. Constance M. McCullough, et al. *Problems in the Improvement of Reading.* McGraw-Hill Book Company, 1946.

9. Helen Rand Miller and John J. DeBoer, *Creative Reading.* Graessle-Mercer Company, Seymour, Indiana, 1951.

10. David H. Russell, *Children Learn to Read.* Ginn and Co., 1949.

11. Ralph W. Tyler, "Measuring the Ability to Infer," *Educational Research Bulletin,* IX, pp. 475–80, November, 1930.

12. J. Wayne Wrightstone, "Frontiers in Educational Research in the Measurement of Aptitudes and Achievement," *Journal of Educational Research,* XL, pp. 389–96, April, 1947.

50. Teaching Critical Reading: An Observational Study

Willavene Wolf and Bernice D. Ellinger

INTRODUCTION

In the past teachers and researchers have given a great deal of attention to word perception and general reading comprehension skills. Critical reading skills, however, have generally been neglected. Critical reading is the analysis and evaluation of the content and structure of fictional and informational materials. The critical reader makes judgments about the trustworthiness of informational material and the quality of literary material based upon valid criteria.

Although interest in critical reading has been shown by the publication of nearly two hundred articles on the topic in the last decade, few educators have attempted to test the possibility of teaching it below the junior and senior high school levels. In fact, the theories of Piaget suggest that certain types of critical thinking or applying critical thinking to the printed page is impossible before the age of twelve. Piaget (9) divided the development of the thinking process into successive periods which he called stages in the construction of operations. It is only in the advanced stage of thinking, around age eleven or twelve, that Piaget states that the child is able to hypothesize, state various propositions, and combine variables in order to check out relationships.

There is evidence from studies by Heidbreder (7), Grener and Raths (6), Woodcock (13), Crossen (4), and others, that children can perform these higher thinking processes to some degree before age 12. Furthermore, research in the child development area indicates that very young children of three and above are capable of critical reasoning, and that children of five and six years of age can use all of their thinking abilities (1), (12). Also, certain items on intelligence scales are based on the assumption that young children have the ability to reason. Critical reading is one manifestation of the critical thinking process; it is using critical thinking in the act of reading. Therefore, it follows that if elementary school children can think critically at an early age they can also be taught to read critically. Yet elementary school teachers frequently neglect the

This pilot study was conducted as a part of a project (Critical Reading Ability of Elementary School Children) supported by the U.S. Office of Education. The principal investigators are Willavene Wolf, Charlotte Huck and Martha King. Bernice D. Ellinger is Assistant Study Director. Bruce Gansneder assisted in data analysis.

"Teaching Critical Reading: An Observational Study," by Willavene Wolf and Bernice D. Ellinger, is from a paper presented at the American Educational Research Association meeting in Chicago, Ill., in February 1966.

higher thinking skills when teaching reading, and instead, spend most of their time teaching the mechanics of reading. An observational study (8) of 20 third-grade reading lessons revealed that only 1.8 per cent of all questions teachers asked could be classified as requiring critical thinking that includes an evaluative or a judgmental dimension. Instead, an overwhelming majority of the questions dealt with the literal skills of reading. Because of the apparent discrepancy between the research supporting the theory that young children can think critically and evidence of the lack of instruction in critical reading, a study was undertaken at The Ohio State University to test the feasibility of teaching young children to read critically.

As a preliminary phase of that project, the pilot study, reported in this paper, was undertaken to ascertain the kinds of teacher behavior that elicit critical responses from children. Although there were indications that critical reading was seldom being taught in the public schools, reading supervisors in the area identified a few teachers who were teaching it to some degree. Thus, the purposes of the study were (1) to determine if selected teachers were teaching reading in such a manner as to elicit critical responses from children, (2) to see whether the project staff could influence the number of critical responses that teachers obtained from children by writing lesson plans incorporating techniques purported to be effective for teaching critical reading, and (3) to analyze the question types within and across the teacher-prepared and staff-prepared lessons in order to determine if specific differences existed in the number of critical responses produced.

PROCEDURES

OBSERVATION INSTRUMENT

An observation scale for collecting data on verbal interaction related to critical reading was needed for this study. Attempts were made to use or adapt existing scales such as Flanders Interaction Analysis (5), Aschner's Scale of Cognitive Behaviors (2), Bellack's Language of the Classroom (3), and an adaptation of the Wright Proctor Scale of Verbal Interaction (14). However, the observers found that the specific verbal behaviors of interest were not appearing on the observation protocols and that extraneous data were being gathered. Thus, after several observations with each scale it was decided that a specially-developed scale was needed. The unique requirement for this scale was that data needed to be collected on (1) the critical responses of children, and (2) the type of teacher questions that elicited such responses. A scale meeting these criteria was developed and tested. The teacher questions were recorded on the horizontal rows of the scale and the children's responses were categorized in the vertical columns. Responses were recorded in a numerical sequence in order to preserve the relationship between the specific teacher comment and the pupil response or chain of responses to that comment. This procedure enabled the observers to record the number and sequence of critical and non-critical responses elicited by teacher questions. Teacher statements did not elicit enough pupil responses to warrant analysis.

The teacher behaviors which were analyzed were divided into three categories: (1) *gathering information,* which included the teacher's asking the pupils for specific ideas and facts gleaned from their reading material, (2) *refining and clarifying information,* which included the teacher's asking pupils to explain, rephrase or give illustrations, and (3) *applying and evaluating information,* which included questions requiring the pupils to use or evaluate information from the reading material or apply it to another situation.

Pupil responses were classified as *critical* or *non-critical,* depending upon the type of thinking exhibited. A response was defined as non-critical if it were simple recall or literal comprehension. A response was recorded as critical if the student went beyond the literal meaning, used data to make an evaluation, interpreted or extrapolated from facts, or detected logical fallacies in the material.

The measurement of critical responses was based on the verbal reactions of pupils in class discussions of reading materials, and the analysis of verbal behavior in this study was limited to the questions asked by teachers and the students' verbal responses to these questions.

OBSERVATIONS

The observational sample was composed of thirty teachers who were identified by their supervisors and the Critical Reading Project Staff as being outstanding teachers of reading who were teaching critical reading skills to some degree.

Two observers were trained to use the observation scale by extensive use of tape recordings and made a total of sixty observations. On-the-spot categorization was done along with audio tape recordings of the lessons. The tape recordings served later as a source for checking the recorded protocols. Inter-rater reliability coefficients, using the coefficient of concordance, for the teacher categories were equal to or greater than .83 (sig. at the $< .50$ level) for all lessons.

The purpose of the first observation was to determine if teachers, in their discussion of reading materials with pupils, were eliciting critical responses and, if so, what types of questions were eliciting such responses. Teachers were given a brief general definition of critical reading and were asked to use techniques which they believed would be successful in teaching such skills. Thus, only a minimal attempt was made to structure teaching behavior on the first observation. For the second observation, each teacher was asked to use a lesson which had been previously developed by the project staff. These lessons varied in content for each grade level but were similar in the types of questions that were asked. Questions that required the students to apply and to evaluate ideas from printed materials were included in most of these lessons. Thus, there was a definite attempt to structure teaching behavior for the second observation.

RESULTS AND TENTATIVE CONCLUSIONS

Since the number of teacher questions and pupil responses differed in the lessons observed, data were analyzed in terms of proportions. A significance level of .01 was set as the rejection point for all data.

TABLE I

RESPONSES ELICITED BY STAFF-PREPARED AND
TEACHER-PREPARED LESSON PLANS

Responses	Critical	Non-Critical	X^2
Lesson Plans			
Teacher-Prepared	803	580	35.96*
Staff-Prepared	1433	333	685.16*

Critical Responses by Lesson Plan z = 13.53, p < .01.
* p < .01, two tailed test.

FEASIBILITY OF TEACHING CRITICAL READING

The data were analyzed to determine if teacher-prepared and staff-prepared lessons did elicit critical responses, and, if so, whether there were significantly more critical than non-critical responses in each instance. The results of the chi-square tests reported in Table I show that each lesson did elicit critical responses and in each instance the number of critical responses was significantly higher than the number of non-critical responses. Using a z test of proportions it was found that there was a significantly higher number of critical responses to questions in the staff-prepared lessons than in the teacher-prepared lessons.

Thus, selected teachers were shown to be teaching in such a manner as to produce the responses labeled as critical by the project staff. Also, when teachers used the lessons which were developed for the specific purpose of eliciting higher levels of thinking they obtained more critical responses than when they used their own lesson plans in which a more general approach was used.

DETERMINANTS OF CRITICAL RESPONSES

In order to determine how critical responses are induced, and why the staff-prepared lesson plans elicited more critical responses than the teacher-prepared lesson plans, further analysis focused upon the following: (1) What kinds of questions did the teachers ask? (2) What types of questions elicited the greatest number of critical responses? and (3) Were there any differences in number of critical responses to the types of questions between the two lesson plans?

KINDS OF QUESTIONS ASKED

Table II presents the number of questions of each type asked by teachers in the two lesson plans. There was no difference in the total number of questions asked when different lesson plans were used. Yet the overall chi-square indicates that there was a lesson plan by question-type association. This was due to the significantly higher number of refining-clarifying questions and the significantly lower number of questions to gather information asked by the teachers when they were using the staff-prepared lesson plans. There was no difference between the number of applying-evaluating questions asked between the two types of lesson plans.

TABLE II

TYPE OF TEACHERS' QUESTIONS
BY LESSON PLAN USED

	(1) Teacher Lesson Plan		(2) Staff Lesson Plan			z of diff.
Question Type	n	p	n	p	N	6.00*
(A) Gathering Information	371	.34	219	.22	590	6.00*
(B) Refining-Clarifying	128	.12	238	.24	366	7.06*
(C) Applying-Evaluating	597	.54	535	.54	1132	0.00 n.s.
Total	1096	1.00	992	1.00	2088	

Total Number of Questions by Lesson Type $X^2 = 5.29$ n.s.
Question Type by Lesson Type $X^2 = 69.39$, p $<$ .01.
* p $<$ .01, two tailed test.

TABLE III

DIFFERENCES IN THE NUMBER OF CRITICAL RESPONSES TO THE TYPE OF QUESTIONS BETWEEN THE TYPES OF LESSON PLANS

	Response Type												z of Difference of Responses to Question Types Between Lesson Plans 1 and 2
	(1) Teacher Lesson Plans						(2) Staff Lesson Plans						
	Critical		Non-Critical		Total		Critical		Non-Critical		Total		
Question Type	n	p	n	p	N	P	n	p	n	p	N	P	
(A) Gathering Information	110	.26	310	.74	420	1.00	117	.37	197	.63	314	1.00	3.33*
(B) Refining-Clarifying	17	.41	24	.59	41	1.00	287	.81	66	.19	353	1.00	5.71*
(C) Applying-Evaluating	676	.73	246	.27	922	1.00	1029	.93	70	.07	1099	1.00	12.50*
N	803	.58	580	.42	1383	1.00	1433	.81	333	.19	1766	1.00	

Z OF DIFFERENCE BETWEEN CRITICAL RESPONSES TO QUESTION TYPES

For Teacher Lessons	For Staff Lessons
A — B = 2.05 n.s.	A — B = 11.89*
A — C = 17.41*	A — C = 23.75*
B — C = 5.33*	B — C = 7.76*

* p < .01, two tailed test.

TYPES OF QUESTIONS THAT ELICITED THE GREATEST NUMBER OF CRITICAL RESPONSES

There was a question type by response-type association in the teacher-prepared lessons ($X^2 = 263.14$ p $< .01$) which was due to the high number of non-critical responses to gathering information questions and the high number of critical responses to applying-evaluating questions. In the staff-prepared lessons there was also a question type by response-type association ($X^2 = 509.18$, p $< .01$) which was due to the high number of critical responses to refining-clarifying and applying-evaluating questions.

The bottom portion of Table III presents the z test of difference between critical responses to various question types for both the teacher-prepared and staff-prepared lessons. It can be noted that in the teacher-prepared lessons there was no significant difference between the number of critical responses to questions to gather information (A) and questions to refine and clarify (B). In contrast, applying-evaluating questions (C) produced a significantly higher number of critical responses than either of the other question types. There were similar findings for the staff-prepared lessons with the exception that questions to refine and clarify received a significantly higher number of critical responses than did questions to gather information.

TABLE IV

CRITICAL RESPONSES ELICITED BY DIFFERENT TYPES OF QUESTIONS WHEN TEACHERS USED STAFF-PREPARED LESSON PLANS

	Critical		Non-Critical		Total		z of Difference
Response Type	n	p	n	p	N	P	Between Critical Responses to Question Types
(A) Convergent	117	.37	197	.63	314	1.00	A–B = 11.89*
(B) Refining-Clarifying	287	.81	66	.19	353	1.00	A–C = 23.75*
(C) Divergent	1029	.93	70	.07	1099	1.00	B–B = 7.76*
Total	1433		333		1766		

Question Type by Response Type $X^2 = 509.18$, p $< .01$.
* p $< .01$, two tailed test.

An analysis of the staff-prepared lessons (see Table IV) also indicated a question type by response-type association. The z tests of difference indicate that this was due to the high number of critical responses to refining-clarifying and divergent questions and the high number of non-critical responses to convergent questions. A significantly higher number of critical responses was elicited by refining-clarifying questions than convergent questions. Also, a significantly higher number of critical responses was elicited to divergent questions than convergent, and a signifi-

TABLE V

DIFFERENCES IN THE NUMBER OF CRITICAL RESPONSES TO THE TYPES OF QUESTIONS BETWEEN THE TYPES OF LESSON PLANS

	Response Type												
Question Type	(1) Teacher Lesson Plans						(2) Staff Lesson Plans						z of Difference of Responses to Question Types Between Lesson Plans 1 and 2
	Critical		Non-Critical		Total		Critical		Non-Critical		Total		
	n	p	n	p	N	P	n	p	n	p	N	P	
(A) Convergent	110	.26	310	.74	420	1.00	117	.37	197	.63	314	1.00	3.33*
(B) Refining-Clarifying	17	.41	24	.59	41	1.00	287	.81	66	.19	353	1.00	5.71*
(C) Divergent	676	.73	246	.27	922	1.00	1029	.93	70	.07	1099	1.00	12.50*
N	803	.58	580	.42	1383	1.00	1433	.81	333	.19	1766	1.00	

* p < .01, two tailed test.

442

CRITICAL READING

cantly higher number of critical responses was elicited by divergent questions than refining-clarifying.

DIFFERENCES BETWEEN TYPES OF LESSONS

An inspection of Table V reveals a higher percentage of critical responses to all question types in staff-prepared lessons. Through comparing Table II and Table V it may be seen that (1) there was no significant difference in the number of divergent questions asked in the two lesson plans, yet divergent questions in the staff-prepared lessons received a significantly higher number of critical responses and (2) there was a significantly lower number of convergent questions asked in the staff-prepared lessons, yet a significantly higher number of critical responses was elicited. Therefore, it appears that the high number of critical responses to convergent and divergent questions was not due to the number of questions asked but rather to some other factor. Refining-clarifying questions occurred more frequently and elicited a higher number of critical responses in staff-prepared lessons than in teacher-prepared lessons.

CONCLUSIONS

1. Selected teachers were teaching in such a manner as to elicit critical responses.
2. The number of critical responses elicited was increased through the use of special lesson plans.
3. Some types of questions are more effective than others in eliciting critical responses. Applying-evaluating questions elicited the highest number of critical responses, refining-clarifying the second highest number, and gathering-information the lowest number of critical responses.
4. It appears that the increase in the number of critical responses elicited in the second lesson was affected by a factor, or factors, in addition to type of question.

TRENDS AND INDICATIONS FROM THE STUDY

The main value of this pilot study was in its heuristic nature. In addition to the findings previously reported, there were several indications and trends noted in the observations which may be fruitful leads for future research.

Although there did not appear to be any *essential* order to the teachers' questions and statements, it did seem that teachers who obtained critical responses established a background of information early in the lesson.

When teachers moved directly to divergent questions without establishing the substantive knowledge on a topic, they obtained non-critical responses from the majority of the students. However, when the teacher established information and refined or clarified it before they asked divergent questions, critical responses were more likely to occur.

Teachers who were successful in obtaining a high number of critical responses seemed to have established a climate in their classrooms which encourages critical questioning. In these classes, children did not hesitate to question the authority of the textbook, each other, or the teacher. One child might say, "I don't agree with John," and then another child or the teacher would request evidence for his stand. These teachers seemed to expect students to make evaluative statements and to substantiate them with the criteria used in making the judgment. The demand for evidence seemed to prevent the hypercritical attitude children are prone to exhibit in the beginning stages of learning to evaluate materials.

During the observation period some questions occurred which repeatedly obtained critical responses. Some of these were as follows: (1) What is the author implying in that sentence? (2) How does this story compare with the first one? (3) Does that conclusion necessarily follow from the premises? (4) How would you use the information from this story in solving the problem? and (5) Why don't you believe the claim made in this advertisement?

It was difficult to record such questions under the teacher categories on the observation instrument used in the pilot study; therefore, a new scale was developed for the next phase of the critical reading research study. Categories such as inferring, analyzing, applying and evaluating were added.

SUMMARY

The researchers are currently conducting a study entitled, "Critical Reading Ability of Elementary School Children."

A pilot observational study was undertaken as a preliminary part of this project. The purposes of this phase were to see if critical reading was being taught in the public elementary schools, to see if the number of critical responses could be affected by specially-written lesson plans, and to see if any particular question type elicited more critical responses than another.

An observation instrument was developed with three question categories—convergent, refining-clarifying, and divergent. Pupil responses were categorized as critical or non-critical. Thirty teachers who had been identified as ones teaching critical reading were each observed twice. Teacher-prepared lessons were taught during the first observation and staff-prepared lessons were taught during the second observation. Records of pupil responses reveal that selected teachers were teaching in such a manner as to elicit critical responses and that the number of critical responses elicited was affected by specially-designed lesson plans. Question types were analyzed to determine the number of critical responses elicited by each type and the analysis shows that divergent questions were more effective for producing critical responses than the other two question types. Convergent questions were *least* effective for producing critical responses but they seemed to be necessary in lessons directed toward critical reading.

The main value of this pilot study has been the refinement and clarification of ideas for future research.

BIBLIOGRAPHY

1. MILLIE C. ALMY, "Are They Too Young for Problem Solving?" *Progressive Education,* Vol. 27 (1950), pp. 148–151.

2. MARY J. ASCHNER, "The Analysis of Classroom Discourse: A Method and Its Uses." Unpublished doctoral dissertation, University of Illinois, 1958.

3. ARNO BELLACK and JOEL DAVITZ, *The Language of the Classroom.* Institute of Psychological Research, Teachers College, Columbia University, 1963.

4. HELEN J. CROSSEN, "Effects of the Attitudes of the Reader Upon Critical Reading Ability," *Journal of Educational Research,* Vol. 42 (1948), pp. 289–298.

5. N. A. FLANDERS, *Teacher Influence, Pupil Attitudes and Achievement: Studies in Interaction Analysis.* Final Report, CRP No. 397, Minneapolis, University of Minnesota, 1960, (C).

6. NORMA GRENER and L. E. RATHS, "Thinking in Grade III," *Educational Research Bulletin,* Vol. 24 (1945), pp. 38–42.

7. EDNA F. HEIDBREDER, "Studying Human Thinking," T. G. Andrews (Ed.), *Methods of Psychology.* Wiley, 1948, pp. 96–123.

8. ELIZABETH A. HOSTETLER, "An Analysis of Questions Asked in Third Grade Reading Classes." M.A. Thesis, Ohio State University, 1965.

9. JEAN PIAGET, *The Psychology of Intelligence.* Translated by Malcolm Pierey and E. E. Berlyne. Harcourt, 1950.

10. L. E. RATHS, "Thinking Test," *Educational Research Bulletin,* Vol. 23 (1944), pp. 72–75, 84.

11. MADORAH E. SMITH, "The Preschool Child's Use of Criticism," *Child Development,* Vol. 3 (1932), pp. 137–141.

12. KENNETH WANN, *Fostering Intellectual Development in Young Children,* Teachers College, Columbia, 1963.

13. Louise Woodcock, *Life and Ways of the 2 Year Old: A Teacher's Study,* New York: Dutton, 1941.
14. Muriel Wright and Virginia Proctor, *Systematic Observation of Verbal Interaction.* CRP No. 816, Washington University, St. Louis, 1961.

Annotated Bibliography

THE IMPORTANCE AND NATURE OF CRITICAL READING

Artley, A. Sterl. "Critical Reading in the Content Areas," *Elementary English,* Vol. XXXVII (1959), pp. 122–130.
Critical reading is the process of judging with severity the ideas expressed by a writer. Factors that predispose a child to read critically in the content areas are intelligence, freedom from biases and prejudices, a background of experience in the area of reading, and a legitimate purpose for engaging in critical reading.

Dale, Edgar. "Teaching Critical Thinking," *The News Letter,* Vol. XXIV, No. 4 (January 1959), pp. 1–2.
Value placed on thinking is expanded to include the necessary element of critical thinking. The need for teaching children to think critically is stressed and illustrative means are suggested.

Eller, William. "Fundamentals of Critical Reading," *The Reading Teacher's Reader.* Oscar S. Causey (Editor). New York: The Ronald Press, 1958, pp. 30–34.
Critical reading, according to Eller, requires a wide background of information, average or better intelligence, appropriate skills for evaluative reading, and personal adjustment which will permit objective consideration.

Ennis, Robert. "A Concept of Critical Thinking," *Harvard Educational Review,* Vol. XXXII (Winter 1962).
Three dimensions of critical thinking are defined as (1) the logical dimension which includes judging the relationships between statements, (2) the criterial dimension which involves judging the ideas presented, and (3) the pragmatic dimension which includes judging whether the material is good enough for the purpose held.

Gainsburg, J. C. "Critical Reading is Creative Reading and Needs Creative Teaching," *Reading Teacher,* Vol. XV (December 1961), pp. 185–192.
Critical reading is reading with a thoughtful attitude which involves

reflecting and interpreting. The author calls it creative reading because the reader is creating more than the author put into the story.

GANS, ROMA. "Developing Critical Reading as a Basic Skill," *Reading in Action,* International Reading Association Conference Proceedings, New York. *Scholastic Magazine,* Vol. II (1957), pp. 124–127.

The mature critical reader is characterized as one who (1) draws upon his reading and relates it to topics in conversation, to problems, and to studies, (2) is aware of the need to evaluate the sources of material read, (3) assesses the ways in which words influence ideas, (4) selects wisely what he reads, and (5) is willing to take a stand about what he read.

GUILFORD, J. P. "Frontiers in Thinking that Teachers Should Know About," *The Reading Teacher,* Vol. XIII (February 1960), pp. 176–182.

A structure of the intellect presented in a three dimensional model suggests many facets of intelligence which have not been measured. Critical thinking can be classified as an evaluative operation.

HARRIS, A. J. "Three Kinds of Reading," *NEA Journal,* Vol. LII (January 1963), pp. 42–43.

Critical reading skills operate in *developmental reading, functional reading* and *recreational reading.* Some of the skills are establishing sequence, judging relevancy, and perceiving relationships.

MAW, ETHEL. "Teaching Critical Thinking Through Reading," *Dimensions of Critical Reading,* Vol. XI (1964), University of Delaware, Newark, Delaware, pp. 75–87.

Describes lessons used in an experiment in teaching critical thinking. The skills emphasized are selecting relevant facts, judging the reliability of data, making generalizations and inferences, recognizing insufficiency of data, determining cause and effect, and evaluating arguments.

RUSSELL, DAVID H. "Higher Mental Processes," *Encyclopedia of Educational Research,* Harris, C. W. (Editor). New York: Macmillan, 1960, pp. 645–661.

Thinking is described as associative, problem-solving, critical, and creative. Critical thinking is a process of evaluation or categorization in terms of some previously accepted standards. It is a logical examination of data which avoids fallacies and judgments on an emotional basis only. Critical thinking involves attitudes plus knowledge of facts plus some thinking skills.

RUSSELL, DAVID H. "Personal Values in Reading," "*Reading Teacher,* Vol. XV (December 1961), pp. 172–178.

Three levels of reading are described: recognizing the word, understanding the literal meaning of the word, and going below the surface to discover new and personal meanings. The deepest level of reading is affected by the reader's personal values.

SMITH, NILA B. "What is Critical Reading?" *Elementary English,* Vol. XL (April 1963), pp. 409–410.

The umbrella term "comprehension" is divided into three types of reading skills: literal, interpretive, and critical. Critical reading involves both of the preceding skills but requires an evaluation of the quality, the value, the accuracy and truthfulness of what is read.

SOCHOR, E. ELONA. "Critical Reading in the Content Areas," *Reading in Action,* International Reading Association Conference Proceedings, Vol. II (1957), New York: *Scholastic Magazine,* pp. 127–128.

Provides illustrations of the application of critical reading skills in all areas of the curriculum at several grade levels. Until critical reading skills can be used with any kind of material that must be read, educators have not finished the job.

SOCHOR, E. ELONA. "The Nature of Critical Reading," *Critical Reading,* National Council of Teachers of English, Champaign, Illinois (1959), pp. 3–14.

A reprint of an article first published in *Elementary English,* which defines critical reading in relation to the total reading and thinking processes. Reading is a complex process, of which background experiences and thinking are an essential part. Literal reading involves understanding what is stated, and critical reading includes dealing with the facts in some way.

STAUFFER, RUSSELL G. "Language and the Habit of Credulity," *Elementary English,* Vol. XLII (April 1965), pp. 362–369.

Reading can continue the habit of language credulity initiated through spoken language and thus be an obstacle to thinking, or it can be a means for developing clear thinking.

TABA, HILDA. "Problems in Developing Critical Thinking," *Progressive Education,* Vol. XXVIII (November 1950), pp. 45–48.

Taba holds that a precise definition of critical thinking and identification of a developmental sequence of skills are prerequisite to teaching children to think and read critically.

THELEN, HERBERT A. "Reading for Inquiry," *Controversial Issues in Reading and Promising Solutions,* Supplementary Education Monographs, No. 91, University of Chicago (1961), pp. 35–53.

The process of "inquiry" subsumes skills identified as critical reading skills. The reader uses printed material to solve problems and tests what he reads against reality.

TORRANCE, E. P. "Creativity in the Classroom, Developing Creative Readers," *Instructor,* Vol. LXXIV (February 1965), p. 23+.

Describes creative readers as those who anticipate outcomes, use what is read, and transform or rearrange what is read. Critical reading is given a restricting connotation.

Triggs, F. O. "Promoting Growth in Critical Reading," *The Reading Teacher,* Vol. XXV (February 1959), pp. 158–164.
Critical reading requires a contribution by both the author and the reader, and an interplay between the two usually results in a new understanding. Instruction in critical reading can be a part of instruction in all other basic reading skills.

Weir, Edward C. "Meaning of Learning and the Learning of Meaning," *Phi Delta Kappan,* Vol. XLVI (February 1965), pp. 280–284.
A description of the role of personal meaning as an individual learns. The more deeply personal the meaning acquired through a learning experience, the more effective and lasting the learning will be. If allowances are made for the "intuitive hypothesis," the processes of systematic thinking are probably productive of the most highly dependable and fruitful meanings.

TEACHING CRITICAL READING

Barbe, W. B., and Williams, T. E. "Developing Creative Thinking in Gifted Children Through the Reading Program," *Reading Teacher,* Vol. XV (December 1961), pp. 198–201.
The distinguishing characteristic of gifted children, according to Barbe and Williams, is their creativity, which should be cultivated through those reading experiences that cause the reader to question, analyze, interpret, and create something unique from the text.

Bland, Phyllis. "Helping Bright Students Who Read Poorly," *The Reading Teacher,* (April 1956), pp. 209–214.
Describes how bright students are lead to read with greater understanding through instruction in critical reading skills, word meanings, and study skills.

Burton, Dwight L. "Teaching Students to Read Literature," *Perspectives in Reading,* International Reading Association, Newark, Delaware, 1964, pp. 87–100.
Burton warns that students may be forced to judge literary works before they have become aware of the central purpose, meaning or effect of the work. He believes that students must progress toward "felt knowledge" and that surface level criticism impedes rather than helps them along the way. He believes that cumulative development of experience with literature from the elementary school through high school is necessary to develop the ability to perceive artistic unity and significance.

Carpenter, Helen M. "Study Skills: Learning To Be Truly Critical," *Instructor,* Vol. LXXIV, No. 6 (February 1965), pp. 23–24, 138.
Teaching critical evaluation of information and ideas in all forms of

communication should be the goal of the elementary school. Both obstacles to the goals and guidelines for reaching them are provided.

CHAPMAN, CARITA A. "Methods of Materials for Teaching Critical Reaction to What is Read in Grades Four Through Six," *Sequential Development of Reading Abilities.* Helen M. Robinson (Editor). Conference on Reading, University of Chicago, 1960, pp. 84–87.
This paper considers factors which condition critical reaction and proposes five levels of instruction appropriate for the middle grades.

CHARLES, C. M. "Teaching About Facts," *The Instructor,* Vol. LXXIV (February 1965), pp. 48, 54.
Proposes that we change our conception of "fact" and stop confusing "fact" with unchanging truth. Man's knowledge is changing; children should learn to see "facts" as best *present* knowledge.

CLEMENTS, H. M. "Inferences and Reading Instruction," *Claremont Reading Conference Yearbook,* Vol. XXVIII (1964), pp. 144–156.
A clarification of the distinction between factual statements and inferential statements. A list of questions to evaluate statements of fact and statements of inference is suggested. Facts can be seen, felt, observed. Inferences are thoughts, opinions, conjectures.

CRISCUOLO, NICHOLAS. "Enriching the Reading Program for Superior Readers," *Elementary School Journal,* Vol. LXIV (October 1963), pp. 26–30.
Author suggests that instruction in higher level comprehension skills are necessary for reading programs for superior students.

DALLMAN, MARTHA. "Critical Evaluation," *Grade Teacher,* Vol. LXXV (September 1957), pp. 46–47.
Critical evaluation is defined and guidelines for teaching critical evaluation (with specific illustrations) are presented.

ELLSWORTH, RUTH. "Critical Thinking, Its Encouragement," *National Elementary Principal,* Vol. XLII, No. 6 (May 1963).
The stated requisites for critical thinking and the suggested procedures for teaching children are applicable to critical reading.

FIGUREL, J. ALLEN. "Evaluating the Ability to Interpret Materials," *Corrective and Remedial Reading,* 16th Conference on Reading. Donald Cleland and Josephine Benson (Editors). University of Pittsburgh, 1960, pp. 205–213.
Realistic expectations for pupils' performance depend on teacher's knowing their experiential background; comprehensive evaluation depends upon pupils' opportunity to read widely and to react to reading through numerous media—writing, speaking, drama.

FINCH, HARDY R. "How To Teach Students to Read Mass Magazines Critically," *English Journal,* Vol. XXXVIII (1949), pp. 388–91.
Finch suggests ways to teach students to read mass magazines critically.

Huck, Charlotte, and Ellinger, Bernice. "Reading Critically," *Grade Teacher*, Vol. LXXXII, No. 7 (March 1965), pp. 101–105.

The authors identify certain critical reading skills and suggest ways that they can be taught in social studies, science, math, and literature.

Huus, Helen. "Reading and Thinking in the Social Studies," *Reading and Thinking:* A Report of the 17th Annual Conference and Course on Reading. Donald Cleland (Editor). Pittsburgh: University of Pittsburgh, (June 12–June 23, 1961), pp. 27–33.

Discusses four basic skills of reading and thinking—understanding vocabulary, understanding the organization, evaluating the material critically, and using the information—and applies them to middle grade social studies content.

Karlin, Robert. "Sequence in Thoughtful and Critical Reaction to What is Read," *Sequential Development of Reading Abilities*. Helen Robinson (Editor). Conference on Reading, University of Chicago, 1960, pp. 74–79.

A hierarchy of critical reading skills appropriate for development at primary, middle grades, and high school levels follows a definition and discussion of need for, problems in teaching, and factors that influence critical reading.

Kermoian, Samuel. "Catus Pete," *The NEA Journal*, Vol. L (September 1961), p. 29.

Provides a detailed description of first grade pupils comparing a statement in a book with other sources of information (experience, other books, experts in the field) in order to resolve discrepancies in information about the number of toes their pet turtle had.

Lackey, George H., Jr., and Rollins, Doris. "History and Current Events: A Time and Place for Critical Reading," *Journal of Reading*, Vol. VIII, No. 6 (May 1965), pp. 373–377.

A report of the methods, materials, and organization used to teach junior high school students critical reading skills through social studies content.

Langman, Muriel Potter. "Teaching Reading as Thinking," *Education*, Vol. LXXXII, No. 1 (September 1961), pp. 19–25.

In teaching reading as thinking, special attention should be given to sentence structure, concepts formation, evaluation of ideas, and the influence of biases of both author and reader.

Massey, Will J. "Critical Reading in the Content Areas," *Reading As An Intellectual Activity*, International Reading Association Conference Proceedings, New York. *Scholastic Magazine*, Vol. VIII (1963), pp. 104–107.

A definition of critical reading with illustrations of its applicability to literature and social studies is provided.

Mattila, Ruth H. "Accent on Thinking Through Reading at the Intermediate and Upper Grade Levels," *Science Education,* Vol. XLVI (March 1962), pp. 174–176.

Ways that critical reading can be taught through the use of current science topics are illustrated. Materials are drawn from advertisements, news articles, and television programs.

McCALLISTER, JAMES M. "Methods and Materials for Teaching Creative Reading in Grades Ten Through Fourteen," *Sequential Development of Reading Abilities.* Helen M. Robinson (Editor). Conference on Reading, University of Chicago, 1960, pp. 119–123.

Two sets of guiding principles for the selection of method and materials for developing creative readers are stated. Creative reading requires the reader to abstract meanings, classify and evaluate them, relate them to his own experience, and formulate conclusions or apply the meaning in some way.

McCULLOUGH, CONSTANCE M. "Conditions Favorable to Comprehension," *Education,* Vol. LXXIX (May 1959), pp. 533–536.

In a light readable style the author presents four conditions essential to reading for comprehension.

MUESSIG, R. H. "Can High School Students Read a Newspaper Critically?" *Social Studies,* Vol. LVI (January 1965), pp. 3–5.

Muessig stresses the need for teaching critical reading of newspapers and provides specific helpful teaching techniques and materials.

RAPPARLIE, EVALYN. "Election Year, A Time to Teach Critical Thinking," *Grade Teacher,* Vol. LXXXII (October 1964), pp. 100–103+, 143.

A report of a one-classroom study of the extent to which middle-primary students are able to apply skills of critical thinking in a unit concerned with the "responsibilities that accompany freedom to choose."

REINKE, RALPH L. "Methods and Materials for Teaching Creative Reading in Grades Four Through Six," *Sequential Development of Reading Abilities.* Helen Robinson (Editor). Conference on Reading, University of Chicago, 1960, pp. 12–115.

A presentation of four major behavioral goals of creative reading which the author believes are closely related to thinking. "Creative reading is a process by which a reader brings his appreciative mass, his attitudes, and emotions to the printed page," p. 115.

ROBINSON, HELEN M. (Editor). "Methods and Materials for Teaching Critical Reaction to What Is Read," *Sequential Development of Reading Abilities,* Chapter VII. Conference on Reading, University of Chicago, 1960, pp. 80–99.

This chapter contains papers by five authors, who consider materials and ways of teaching critical reading in kindergarten through grade twelve, as well as in remedial classes.

SMITH, NILA B. "The Good Reader Thinks Critically," *The Reading Teacher,* Vol. VII (February 1954), pp. 162–171.

Illustrates how teachers can question students about material they have read to push them toward use of higher mental processes. Mere repetition of literal information available in the reading material is not adequate. Critical reading involves getting the facts and interpreting deeper meanings as well as making use of the personal judgment of the reader in deciding upon the validity of the material. In critical reading the reader evaluates and passes judgment upon the purpose, the fairmindedness, the bias, the truthfulness of statements made in the text.

——. "Reading in Depth at Middle Grades," *The Instructor*, Vol. LXXIV (March 1965), pp. 73+, 101.

Critical reading is defined as the highest level of comprehension, which includes also literal comprehension and interpretation. Examples of both incidental and planned teaching of critical reading are provided.

SHOTKA, JOSEPHINE. "Creative Reading," *Education*, Vol. LXXXII (September 1961), pp. 26–28.

Suggested questions and follow-up activities are offered as ways of helping gifted pupils to read creatively.

STAUFFER, R. G. "Children Can Read and Think Critically," *Education*, Vol. LXXX (May 1960), pp. 522–525.

Children, even at first grade level, can read and think critically about matters that are within their experience, providing such experience is (1) examined, (2) pertinent facts indexed, (3) relationships noted, and (4) generalizations reached.

STAUFFER, RUSSELL G. "Critical Reading at Upper Levels," *The Instructor*, Vol. LXXIV (March 1965), pp. 74–75, 101.

Critical readers in upper grades must have strength of their convictions and courage to deal with ideas. In the process the reader moves from divergent to convergent thinking as he examines evidence, declares hypotheses, suspends judgments until proof is found, and makes decisions.

——. "Directed Reading–Thinking Plan," *Education*, Vol. LXXIX (May 1959), pp. 527–532.

Utilizing the work of Thorndike, Dewey, and Russell the author makes a plea for teaching children to read critically through fostering proper attitudes, establishing purpose, learning skills, making inferences, reflecting, and judging.

RESEARCH IN CRITICAL READING

ARNOLD, DWIGHT. "Testing Ability to Use Data in the 5th and 6th Grades," *Educational Research Bulletin*. Ohio State University, 1938, pp. 255–259.

A study in 5th and 6th grade classrooms supported the hypothesis that critical thinking can be taught in the elementary school. Intelligent use of data is defined as the ability to recognize relevance, dependability, bias in source, and adequacy of data.

BALOW, I. H. "Reading and Computation Ability as Determinants of Problem-Solving," *Arithmetic Teacher*, Vol. II (June 1964), pp. 18–22.
A study of the relationship between reading ability and problem-solving ability as evidenced in the performance of 1400 sixth grade children on standardized tests of arithmetic and reading. He found that general reading ability does have an effect on problem-solving when intelligence was controlled.

BETTS, EMMETT A. "Research on Reading as a Thinking Process," *Journal of Educational Research*, Vol. L (1956), pp. 1–15.
Betts describes the procedures, findings and implications of the doctoral studies of Sterl A. Artley, Ethel Maney, and Elona Sochor, which deal with critical reading. Author concludes that the studies support the contention that there is a substantial relationship between the abilities to do literal reading and critical reading.

BLOOMER, R. H. "Concepts of Meaning and the Reading and Spelling Difficulty of Words," *Journal of Educational Research*, Vol. LIV (January 1961), pp. 178–182.
Bloomer found that knowledge of a number of meanings for a word facilitated ability to spell and read that word. Frequency of occurrence correlated most highly to both spelling and reading difficulty. Concreteness of the word related to reading difficulty, but not to spelling difficulty.

BLOOMER, R. H. "Connotative Meaning and the Reading and Spelling Difficulty of Words," *Journal of Educational Research*, Vol. LV (November 1961), pp. 107–112.
In another study Bloomer found that the learning difficulty of reading and spelling words bore no relation to either the connotative emotional tone or emotional intensity of the word.

BROWNELL, JOHN ARNOLD. "The Influence of Training in Reading in the Social Studies on the Ability to Think Critically," *California Journal of Educational Research*, Vol. IV (January 1953), pp. 28–31.
A study of the effect of an instructional program in two ninth grade reading classes on the gain scores on the *Watson-Glaser Critical Thinking Appraisal*. The data provisionally support the hypothesis that a twenty-eight week program designed to improve reading skills in social studies will result in significant total score gains on the critical thinking test. The data do not provide conclusive evidence that the significant gains were caused by the training in reading alone.

CLYMER, THEODORE. "Implications of Research on Critical Reading and Thinking," *Reading and Thinking*. A Report of the 17th Annual Conference and Course on Reading. Donald Cleland (Editor). Pittsburgh: University of Pittsburgh (June 12–June 23, 1961), pp. 41–45.

An overview of some of the research studies in critical reading (with special attention to Sochor's review and Thorndike's early study of "Reading as Reasoning") followed by several useful techniques for evaluating critical reading skills.

FERRELL, FRANCES H. "An Experiment in the Development of Critical Thinking," *American Teacher,* Vol. XXX (January 1946), pp. 24–25.

The idea that growth in certain components assumed to be inherent in critical thinking can be affected by instruction was tested in a two year instructional program in a high school history class. No formal evaluation was made, but observed behavior showed increased critical thinking.

GANS, ROMA. *A Study of Critical Reading Comprehension in the Intermediate Grades.* New York: Bureau of Publications, Teachers College, Columbia University, 1940.

A study of the ability of fourth, fifth, and sixth graders to select relevant information for answering questions. Reference reading is a composite of three variables: reading ability, selection-rejection patterns, and a type of delayed recall.

GLASER, EDWARD M. *An Experiment in the Development of Critical Thinking.* Teachers College, Columbia University. No. 843, 1941.

Materials and techniques were developed to activate a spirit of inquiry and to stimulate growth in ability to think critically among twelfth grade students. After ten weeks, the experimental groups made a substantially greater average gain than comparable control groups.

GRAY, WILLIAM S., and ROGERS, BERNICE. *Maturity in Reading, Its Nature and Appraisal.* Chicago: The University of Chicago Press, 1956.

This was a study in which adults were interviewed in order to determine the characteristics of mature, competent readers and to determine the range of reading behavior within the adult population.

HARRIS, CHESTER W. "Measurement of Comprehension of Literature," *School Review,* Vol. LVI (May 1948), pp. 280–289, and (June 1948), pp. 332–342.

Pre-college men were subjects of a study to ascertain the "generality" of specific comprehension skills when applied to various forms of literature—drama, prose, poetry.

KAY, SYLVIA. "Critical Reading: Its Importance and Development," *The Journal,* Vol. XXXV (January–December 1946). The University of Chicago Press, Illinois, pp. 380–385.

Pre-tests and post-tests were used with 385 senior high school students to see how they could (a) form their own conclusion, (b) discern the author's purpose, (c) make comparisons of conflicting or correlating ideas by the same author or different authors, and (d) discover inaccuracies, inconsistencies, and omissions of essential information. Sizeable gains in the first three abilities and a minor increase in the fourth ability were produced after instruction in these areas.

MANEY, ETHEL. "Literal and Critical Reading in Science," *Journal of Experimental Education,* Vol. XXVII (1958), pp. 57–64.
General reading achievement, verbal I.Q., literal and critical reading in science tests were given to 513 fifth grade students. When intelligence was partialled out the correlation between general reading ability and critical reading ability in science was .11.

McCULLOUGH, CONSTANCE. "Responses of Elementary School Children to Common Types of Reading Comprehension Questions," *Journal of Educational Research,* Vol. LI (September 1957), pp. 65–70.
An analysis of test results of 258 first, second, and fourth grade children was made to see if testing for different types of comprehension is actually testing different reading abilities. Prediction for all types of comprehension is impossible on the basis of any single score; however, fact-getting ability appears to be a common factor in various types of comprehension.

McKILLOP, A. S. *The Relationships Between the Reader's Attitude and Certain Types of Reading Response.* New York: Bureau of Publications, Teachers College, Columbia University, 1952.
Five hundred and twelve students in the eleventh grade were involved in an investigation of the relationship between the reader's verbally expressed attitude and his responses to questions relative to reading material which was in agreement with, or in opposition to, his attitudes. Responses to questions which allowed judgments to be made were more strongly affected by attitudes than responses to purely factual questions.

OSBORNE, WAYLAND W. "An Experiment in Teaching Resistance to Propaganda," *Journal of Experimental Education,* Vol. VIII (1939), pp. 1–17.
Reports the results of a study in teaching high school social studies pupils to resist propaganda. He found negligible correlations between measures of knowledge concerning propaganda devices and measures of immediate and delayed shifts of attitude in response to propaganda. Attempts to teach resistance to propaganda with respect to social issues by emphasis only on the "form" in which propaganda commonly appears are unlikely to succeed. Neither achievement nor intelligence is a dependable index of ability to resist propaganda.

PIEKARZ, JOSEPHINE A. "Getting Meaning From Reading," *Elementary School Journal,* Vol. LVI (March 1956), pp. 303–309.
A report of a doctoral study at University of Chicago, in which the case study method was used to compare the reading abilities of one sixth grade boy and one sixth grade girl. Subjects were rated equal in intelligence and in general reading competency but varied greatly in their ability to do critical reading.

ROBINSON, H. ALAN. "Reading Skills Employed in Solving Social Studies Problems," *Reading Teacher*, Vol. XVIII, No. 4 (January 1965), pp. 263–269.

Introspective and observational methods were combined to study behavior of fourth graders as they read to solve problems in social studies content. Data regarding number of pupils using specific comprehension skills are given, e.g., 67 per cent "did not compare ideas found in various sources."

ROGERS, BERNICE. "Directed and Undirected Critical Reading Responses of High School Students." Unpublished Doctoral Dissertation, Department of Education, University of Chicago, 1960.

Students remember facts to the exclusion of evaluative thinking about what was read. The kinds of questions teachers ask will markedly influence the development of critical reading.

THAYER, LEE O. and PRONKO, N. H. "Factors Affecting Conceptual Perception in Reading," *Journal of General Psychology*, Vol. LXI (July 1959), pp. 51–59.

An investigation of the relationship between the reader's ethical and moral values and his conceptualization of a fictitious character and environment. The 112 college sophomores who were the subjects of the study ascribed characteristics they value to a fictitious character. Findings indicate that moral and ethical values color the reader's conceptualization and provide a stereotyped sociocultural frame of reference for structuring ambiguous reading situations.

WILLIAMS, GERTRUDE. "Provisions for Critical Reading in Basic Readers," *Elementary English*, Vol. XXXVI (May 1959), pp. 323–331.

Williams examined ten series of basic readers and found suggestions for teaching thirty-three different critical reading skills. However, only three skills were found in all ten basic readers.

WITT, MARY. "Developing Reading Skills and Critical Thinking," *Social Education*, Vol. XXV (May 1961), pp. 239–242.

Report of a study of ten post-seventh grade students who were given planned instruction in specific critical reading skills for a six weeks period. Measurable gains were shown on the *Iowa Silent Reading Test* but the author pointed out that objective tests are a poor way to measure the major outcomes of critical thinking.

GENERAL REFERENCES IN CRITICAL READING

ALTICK, RICHARD. *Preface to Critical Reading*. New York: Holt, Rinehart and Winston, 1960.

A text designed for college freshmen composition classes, which specifically defines the relationship between critical reading and effective writing, is a useful resource book for teachers of critical reading at the elementary and secondary school levels. Presents the major elements of critical reading and provides a generous amount of practices materials.

BOND, GUY L., and WAGNER, EVA BOND. *Teaching the Child to Read.* New York: The Macmillan Company, 1966, pp. 283–286.
Critical reading, which is applied to social studies content, is defined as "the process of evaluating the authenticity and validity of material and formulating opinion about it."

GRAY, LILLIAN. *Teaching Children to Read.* New York: The Ronald Press Co., 1963, pp. 27–31, 173.
Critical reading is viewed as critical thinking in the reading media and applications are made to different types of content. Specific attention is given to kinds of questions that promote critical reaction from pupils.

McKEE, PAUL. *Reading: A Program of Instruction for the Elementary School.* Boston: Houghton Mifflin Company, 1966, Chapter 10.
This book is unique among reading textbooks in that an entire chapter is devoted to critical reading. Provides excellent suggestions for teaching selected critical reading skills.

SMITH, HENRY P., and DECHANT, EMERALD V. *Psychology in Teaching Reading.* Englewood Cliffs, New Jersey: Prentice-Hall, Inc., 1961, pp. 357–60.
Defines critical reading by presenting definitions, which include lists of specific skills, of six reading authorities.

SMITH, NILA BANTON. *Reading Instruction for Today's Children.* Englewood Cliffs, New Jersey: Prentice-Hall, Inc., 1963, Chapter 9.
Critical Reading is defined as one level of reading within the comprehension skills. Discusses propaganda devices, semantics, and the role of concepts in critical reading. Selected research is included.

SPACHE, GEORGE D. *Reading in the Elementary School.* Boston: Allyn and Bacon, Inc., 1964, Chapter 9.
Critical reading is discussed within a general framework of skills for reading in the content fields and study skills. Specific attention in critical reading to critical reading is given on pp. 228–232.

Name Index

Subject Index